A
HISTORY OF
MODERN GERMANY

The Reformation

A
HISTORY OF
MODERN GERMANY

The Reformation

BY

HAJO HOLBORN

Princeton University Press
Princeton, New Jersey

Published by Princeton University Press, 41 William Street,
Princeton, New Jersey 08540
In the United Kingdom: Princeton University Press,
Oxford
Copyright © 1959 by Hajo Holborn
All rights reserved
First Princeton Paperback printing, 1982

9 8 7 6 5 4

LCC 82-0126
ISBN 0-691-05357-X
ISBN 0-691-00795-0 pbk.

Printed in the United States of America by
Princeton University Press, Princeton, New Jersey

Reprinted by arrangement with Alfred A. Knopf, Inc.

TO ANNEMARIE

Foreword

HISTORIANS WILL READILY AGREE that the unity of the West in
its social and cultural institutions as well as in its political
life has been so marked as to make it impossible to treat
the history of any of the European nations in isolation. But
the history of Germany in particular defies almost every attempt to
trace even a relatively autonomous national development over a longer
period of time. In the Middle Ages Germany identified herself so intimately with the ideas of Christian universalism that German history
seemingly merged with the general history of Europe. The dissolution
of all political authority which followed the defeat of the medieval
German emperors left only local or at best regional centers of political
power. Where these grew strong, either they extended their influence
into the non-German world, as for example in the case of the Hanseatic League in northern Europe, or, as in the case of Switzerland and
the Netherlands, they began to develop a distinct national character
of their own. Universalism and regionalism blurred the contours of a
national German history.

For a while the Protestant Reformation seemed destined to create
a German nation through the unity of faith. But whereas England,
France, and other European countries emerged from the age of the
religious wars strengthened in their national coherence by a common religion, Germany experienced a religious struggle of such a destructive intensity that it resulted in a lasting division. For a long time
thereafter practically two Germanies existed side by side, and new
political divisions followed the religious rift. The two major German
states, Austria and Prussia, conducted their policies in the eighteenth
century without giving heed to the common fate of Germany. In the
following century, when nationalism swept the Continent, Germany
achieved political unification only by the exclusion of Austria.

Germany, broken up internally through most of her history, felt the impact of general European history more directly and intensely than any of the other big European nations. Her outward geographical forms changed vastly through the ages, and the continuity of her cultural and political development was interrupted by repeated catastrophes. But in spite of this lack of unity and continuity in German history, there has never been any doubt among the German people, and for that matter among their neighbors, that a German nation existed even at times when this nation was completely incapable of common political action and its civilization was torn asunder or flooded by foreign influences. Tenuous and dependent on outside forces as the development of the German nation may appear, the largest people of Europe displayed its own distinctive traits and made contributions to the growth of European culture which sprang from its own resources.

The complexity of German history has, no doubt, been responsible for the fact that no complete histories of Germany are in existence which satisfy the reasonable demands of an educated reader. Modern historical research originated largely in Germany. But although the father of critical historiography, Leopold von Ranke, devoted many of his numerous writings to the history of Germany, he always selected individual periods of German history as subjects of his great works, beginning in 1839 with his *History of Germany in the Age of the Reformation.* The trend of more recent historical research toward ever greater specialization has interfered even with the production of comprehensive histories of certain periods.

During the last century the number of publications in the field of German history has been immense, but among them there has been no readable work that would introduce an interested public to the general course of German history and at the same time combine a sufficiently detailed narrative with an interpretation of the greatest possible objectivity. This task cannot be accomplished by simply tying together a string of histories of individual epochs, because events or movements may acquire a very different significance depending on whether they are viewed in the light of a single age or that of the whole history of a nation. Moreover, in the contemplation of the total course of the history of a nation, new problems come into view which deserve close and serious study by themselves. By refusing to write general history German professional historians have left these problems that are most intimately related to the ultimate interpretation of German history outside of their critical review. Unwittingly they have thus facilitated the spread of conceptions of German history which were either plainly amateurish or grossly political, a tendency we have seen at its worst in the falsification of German history by the Nazis. It is obvious that the development of a strong public spirit capable of sustaining the new democratic institutions of present-day Germany calls for a fresh study of the German past. This reappraisal ought to be absolutely frank and should not hesitate to criticize even cherished traditional ideals, although it is inevitable that in such a search historic sources of strength will be revealed which will encourage creative endeavor in the future. But the understanding of German history is essential also for Americans. The lack of a clear conception of German history proved a severe handicap in the formation of American war aims and postwar policy and should not be allowed to confuse our policies in the future. Equally important, however, is a knowledge of the origins of modern German culture, which has been a powerful ferment of modern Western civilization, and particularly of American civilization.

In this *History of Modern Germany*, I have undertaken a reassessment of the last five centuries of German history. Actually, the first volume, which attempts to show the transformation of medieval Germany under the impact of the Protestant and Catholic Reformations, has in places to reach even further back, in order to clarify some developments that came to a head in the sixteenth century. Since the age of the Reformation was the historic period in which Germany exercised her greatest influence on the rest of Europe, while at the same time she was deeply exposed to the political and cultural movements of other countries, the book had to present also many aspects of the general European history of this epoch. The present volume, entitled *The Reformation*, has been designed to be used by itself by all those readers who are chiefly interested in the Reformation. A considerably larger volume, *Germany Since 1648*, also usable by itself, will bring the history down to 1945.

At the moment of the publication of this work I remember with profound gratitude the men who instructed me in history, and particularly in German history. It was my good fortune to study under great teachers at the University of Berlin in the years after 1920. Friedrich Meinecke was my foremost teacher from the first day I entered the university. From him I received the major part of my professional training, and it should be recorded that in his lecture courses he gave his students a much broader and more many-sided historical education than might be judged on the strength of his published works, which reflect distinctly his own predilections. My relations with Friedrich Meinecke, which soon became close and intimate, lasted to his death in 1953. We managed to remain in contact even after I had left Germany following the Nazi revolution of 1933.

Friedrich Meinecke awakened my lasting interest in intellectual history, but he also prepared me for an understanding of the work of his eminent friend, Otto Hintze, in constitutional history. Simultaneously Adolf von Harnack and Karl Holl introduced me to the history of Christian religion and of the Church. The universal scope of historical learning and the liberal concept of religion that characterized Harnack, as well as Holl's deep Lutheran piety combined with his sharp analytical mind, remain unforgettable. The dynamic personality of Ernst Troeltsch aroused my early concern about the history of philosophy and philosophy in general. His philosophical criticism of civilization and society made me receptive to many of the ideas of Max Weber, whose spirit was still alive in the members of the sociological school whom I met as colleagues when I began my career as an academic lecturer at Heidelberg University in 1926. Here, too, I found in Hans von Schubert a revered friend, from whom I learned to view religion not only as a movement of ideas but also as a force in the life of the people.

While I remain conscious of these and many other formative influences on my historical thinking and still regard myself as standing in the tradition of Leopold von Ranke, my own reflections on history, past and present, have led me to new conceptions in many respects. My transformation into an American has given me a broader perspective on all things German. Many political or intellectual issues over which Germans like to feud lose their significance if looked at from a distance. Even more important was my growing inclination to evaluate historical phenomena on a comparative level. Seen in this light many events and ideas of German history assume, I believe, their proper proportions. This revision of my view of the history of Germany gained still another dimension through the contemplation of contemporary events in Germany. The rise of the Nazi empire raised profound doubts about any interpretation of German history that could not account for the disastrous forces dominating Germany in those years. Many explanations were offered to the public. The most facile one was the assertion that all Germans were congenitally wicked. Clearly this was no historical but rather a biological explanation, logically indistinguishable from the racialist doctrines of the Nazis themselves. On the other hand we heard the accusation that the German spiritual tradition had been contaminated at an early stage by the worship of power. From Luther to Hitler or at least from Hegel to Rosenberg, so it was argued, theories of power had been prevalent in German thought. But then it had to be admitted that there was another Germany representing a universalist and peaceful philosophy, and it remained entirely unexplained why one or the other Germany should have gained full control of the nation. Neither biological materialism nor an abstract idealism provide a safe basis for answering the historical questions posed by recent events.

Yet the Rankean preference for the history of states, or of states and Churches, cannot alone give us an adequate understanding of history either, nor does the simple addition of the history of ideas provide more than a partial insight into the process of history. To be sure, ideas, more than any other expressions of life, reveal human motives and aspirations. They also establish a connection over the ages and for that matter even between civilizations. But it would be erroneous to assume that man possesses the capacity of expressing the full range of his aims in clear ideas and, least of all, that he has the ability to direct the course of human affairs more than partially through ideas. If it is the ultimate intent of historical study to comprehend the potentialities of man in history, we must view him in all his struggles within the conditions of his existence, from the necessity of making a living and of adjusting to the social and political order that surrounds him to the actions through which he intervenes in the historical process, as well as to the thought through which he attempts to transcend his narrow station.

The belief that we can hope to understand history only if we try to visualize the totality of historical life has led me to extend the scope of this history of Germany beyond the political and constitutional history to social and economic as well as to religious and intellectual history. These branches of history cannot be separated, although literary exigencies impose some departmentalization. But I have deliberately avoided using the same divisionary pattern through all the periods of German history, because in various ages the forward movement of general history may appear with differing strength in one or the other field of human endeavor.

The present work was begun in 1951. I gratefully acknowledge the grant of a fellowship from the John Simon Guggenheim Memorial Foundation in 1954, which allowed me to devote a full year away from academic duties to research and writing. A visit to Austria as Fulbright professor at the University of Vienna in the spring of 1955 and a stay in Germany during the summer of 1957 gave me an opportunity for acquainting myself with present-day historical research in both countries.

It proved impossible to document and footnote this book with references to the sources and literature of German history, which are simply enormous. Without some discussion of this literature, for which the available space would not have sufficed, references would have been of little use to any student. Although good bibliographies of German history exist, all of them are probably too big for the beginner. I myself have put together for the graduate student a selective bibliography of the history of Germany, Austria, and Switzerland since 1495 which will appear in *A Guide to Historical Literature*, edited and shortly to be published by the American Historical Association.

I wish to express my thanks to Mrs. Genevieve Highland and Professor Charles M. Gray for their good counsel in improving the style of this volume. The assistance of the members of the College Department of Alfred A. Knopf, Inc. is deeply appreciated. Mr. Theodore R. Miller drew the maps using as starting point the drafts prepared by Mr. Anton Zell of Stuttgart and myself for the forthcoming German edition of this book.

The book is dedicated to my wife. Without her untiring co-operation it could not be published at this moment. Not only has she assumed many tedious burdens in the technical preparation of the manuscript; she also has contributed immensely to the improvement of the book itself. Her literary judgment discovered innumerable inaccuracies and obscurities of style, and her critical questioning led to many changes in details as well as in the general contents of my narrative.

I am aware of many shortcomings, even beyond those springing from the sheer size and complexity of the subject. Still, I hope that both the general reader and the student will find the book a reliable source of information and a guide toward an understanding of German history.

HAJO HOLBORN

New Haven, Connecticut

December 15, 1958

Contents

PART III

The Catholic Reformation and the Great War

Maps

BY THEODORE R. MILLER

PART

I

The Foundations of
Modern German
History

CHAPTER 1

The Setting of German History

Germany cannot be described in clear-cut geographical terms. During more than a thousand years the boundaries of Germany have continuously and drastically changed, as has the area settled by Germans. Usually Germany is simply said to be the country in the center of the European continent. But it is doubtful whether Germany can be called the heart of Europe. The expression overlooks the frontier character that was a determining factor through many centuries of German history. As a matter of fact, Germany came into being as an extension of the Roman-Western world to the east and northeast of Europe.

✎ Germany Joins the Western World

Germany became a partner of the Western world in three major stages. The first began when Germany's western and southernmost sections became provinces of the Roman Empire in the first centuries B.C. and A.D.; Emperor Hadrian undertook the construction of the long line of fortifications known as the Limes, which ran east of the lower and central Rhine, then followed the upper Neckar and swung over to the northern Danube. Although intended to prevent the inroads of barbaric tribes, like most fortifications in history the Roman Limes did not prove to be a definitive barrier. But for centuries the boundaries that they marked were held, and the enclosed parts of Germany formed an important region of the Roman Empire.

It was in Trier, the Roman *Augusta Treverorum,* that Constantine the Great was proclaimed emperor by his legions. More important for the future history of Germany was Germanic participation in the ripe Mediterranean civilization. Synagogues, temples of Mithras, and churches of Christ were found in Roman Germany. The vineyards of the Rhine and Moselle are a lasting monument to the material culture that the Romans brought to Germany. Mediterranean civilization was, however, largely a city civilization, and the first German cities were built under the Romans. Cologne, Bonn, Trier, Mainz, Strasbourg, Augsburg, Regensburg, Vienna—to name only a few—all rest on Roman foundations. It is probably not a mere accident of history that Roman Catholicism struck its firmest roots in "Roman Germany."

The second stage began when the German territories between the Rhine in the west and the Elbe and Saale rivers in the east were joined to the Western world more than five centuries after the time of Constantine. Charlemagne's subjugation and Christianization of the Saxons in the late eighth and early ninth centuries were the central event in bringing the Teutonic tribes under a common government. The division of Charlemagne's empire opened the way for a separate development of its eastern parts. For a while this seemed to lead to new fragmentation. But in A.D. 911 a German king was elected. This was the birth year of German history. After 962 the German king became also Roman emperor, following his imperial coronation by the pope.

Germany consisted in 911 of the five tribal, or, as the Germans call them, "stem" (*Stamm*), duchies of Saxony, Franconia, Bavaria, Swabia, and Lorraine. The Teutonic tribes or "stems" were by no means aboriginal races. The physical characteristics they displayed were the result of mixture with older races. In southern Germany the influence of the Dinaric race was apparent, whereas in the German northwest Nordic elements prevailed. The people of the various "stem" duchies showed characteristic traits also in culture and language. And though the tribal duchies had lost their political role in German history by the thirteenth century and had been replaced by other and usually smaller regional units, their tribal dialects and folklore have survived to the present day and even now act as strong forces toward cultural diversity. In this respect "Teutonic" Germany has had a thousand years of historical unity.

But beyond the "Roman" and "Teutonic" Germanies, a "colonial" Germany was brought into existence, marking the third stage during which parts of Germany joined the Western world. The Carolingian rulers had already attempted to extend their control east of the Elbe-Saale line and down the Danube river. This policy was renewed by the Saxon and Salian emperors in the tenth century. Once the Magyars were decisively beaten by Otto I on the Lechfeld near Augsburg in 955, progress in the Germanization of what later became the Austrian lands was relatively swift and steady. The Slav population of these territories had been decimated by the Magyar invasions, and with the

German frontier against the Magyars soon established at the Leitha river, where it has remained to our day, Bavarian and, later, Franconian settlers poured into this region and easily absorbed the weak Slav elements. After the twelfth century nothing more was heard of Slavs in the area, which had become an integral part of "Teutonic" Germany. A similar development occurred in the north, in Holstein.

German expansion to the northeast was not marked by uninterrupted progress. By the end of the tenth century German political influence seemed to have reached the Oder river and to have crossed it in certain places. But the Slav revolt of 982 undid most of these early German successes. It was only between 1150 and 1350 that the country that until 1945 formed a third of modern Germany was actually German-ized. German migration and settlement in the east is frequently thought to be the main phase of the historic struggle between Germans and Slavs. But national sentiment and national direction were lacking on both sides. The German emperors were totally engrossed in their Italian schemes, which led to their downfall and the "emperorless" period of the Interregnum between 1250 and 1273. Whatever planned political direction was found among the Germans was exercised by individual princes, both secular and ecclesiastical, by cities, and by the German nobility. Their policies would have been to no avail had they not had strong popular support. The dynamic force in the eastward German migration was the fast-growing population of Germany and its hunger for new land.

◇ *Forces Behind German Migration to Eastern Regions*

OVERPOPULATION IS A RELATIVE TERM. The number of people who can live in a square mile depends not only on the fertility of the soil but also on the technological skill of the people. Moreover, the industrial and commercial opportunities of any region and age have to be taken into consideration. Overpopulation in these terms occurred first in the oldest parts of Germany, namely in the Netherlands and Frisia; and the "Flemings" began the eastward drive. The Rhinelanders were next, but eventually people from every German "stem" contributed to the migration. The economic motive provided the common force behind it. This is not to deny that antagonism between Germans and Slavs existed. The name "Slavs," i.e., serfs, which the Germans gave their eastern neighbors, was indicative of the contempt they felt for them. The Church often enough fanned this sentiment into violent hatred of the

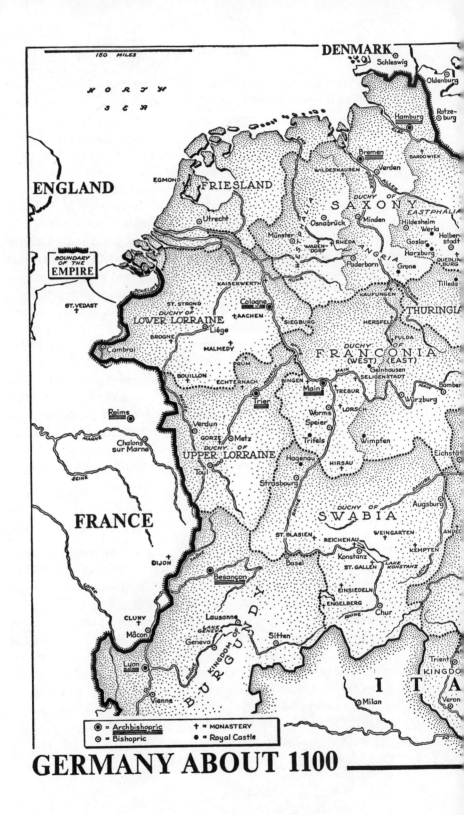

GERMANY ABOUT 1100

BALTIC SEA

RÜGEN

PRUSSIA

Kolberg
†BELGARD

Mecklenburg
BILLUNG
MARCH
Schwerin

POMERANIA

STETTIN
GARZ †
†PYRITZ

Plozk

LENZEN

Havelberg

NORTH MARCH

NETZE

WARTHE

ODER

VISTULA

NAREW

Gnesen

Brandenburg

Magdeburg

EAST
MARCH

+DOBRILUGK

POLAND

EV-
RG

Merseburg
Leisnig
Naumburg
Zeitz
Alten-
burg

Meissen

†BAUTZEN

Breslau

MARCH OF THURINGIA

ODER

VISTULA

Eger

Prague

BOHEMIA

Olmütz
MORAVIA
†TISCHNOWITZ

ORDGAU

MOLDAU

HUNGARY

Regensburg
ALTAICH

MARCH OF
AUSTRIA
MELK
KLOSTER-
NEUBURG

Passau
Freisung

WELS

†PRESSBURG

DUCHY OF
AVARIA
LAMBACH

DANUBE

Chiemsee
Salzburg
EGERNSEE †REICHENHALL
†BERCHTESGADEN

MARCH OF
STYRIA

RAAB

Raab

VORAU

THE
STEM
DUCHIES

150 MILES

CARINTHIA
Gurk

†ST. LAMBRECHT
†FRIESACH

DRAV

MOL

ELBE

FRIESLAND

DUCHY OF
SAXONY

POLAND

ixen

ben

MARCH OF
VERONA

Udine

MARCH OF
CARNIOLA

D. OF
LOWER
LORRAINE

THUR-
INGIA

MEISSEN

BOHEMIA

DUCHY OF
FRANCONIA

LY

Trieste

FRANCE

D. OF
UPPER
LORRAINE

DUCHY OF
SWABIA

DUCHY OF
BAVARIA

DANUBE

Venice

MARCH OF
ISTRIA

CROATIA

ADRIATIC
SEA

BURGUNDY

CARINTHIA

VERONA

ITALY

T.R.MILLER

heathens. The worst outbreak of this wild crusading spirit occurred in 1147, in the so-called Wendish crusade. But in the decisive period of the German eastward migration, from 1150 to 1400, no serious fighting took place except in Holstein and in the neighboring parts of Mecklenburg, as well as in Prussia, where the Teutonic Knights, a German military religious order, exterminated the Slav tribe of the Prussians. In most of Mecklenburg, in Pomerania, Brandenburg, and Silesia the settlement of the Germanic immigrants was a peaceful process.

The individual Slav tribes had no political unity among themselves. They were rather thinly scattered in the lands east of the Elbe, and had suffered heavy losses in fighting invasions from the east and from the west. The economy of the Slavs was primitive agrarianism. Their tools did not allow them intensive agriculture or extensive clearance of woods. The Germans brought with them higher techniques—notably, their heavy iron plow—and superior methods of husbandry. They were capable of clearing forests, and the Dutch and Frisians were particularly skillful in building dikes and draining swamps. Mining was an art in which the medieval Germans excelled and which they brought to the east, together with the older industrial crafts of the West. The Germans built the first towns and cities in the region east of the Elbe. The improvement of living conditions that followed the arrival of these newcomers made most Germans welcome residents in the Slav countries. Their freer political forms and laws were attractive, too. The Slavs between the Elbe and the Oder proved impervious to Polish attempts to win them over, because they preferred, as they expressed it, German freedom to Polish tyranny. Even in Prussia, where the Slav desire for independence led to tragic conflict, German political and social institutions were considered preferable to those of Poland. In contrast to the situation as it existed in later centuries, the medieval Germans east of the Elbe enjoyed greater individual rights than did those in the west, chiefly because the economic opportunities in the east were at that time still unlimited and there was a great demand for man power, particularly skilled man power from the Empire.

∽ Characteristics of Eastern Germany

THE "COLONIAL" GERMANY that was created as a result of the eastward migration of Germans between 1150 and 1350 was of uncertain frontiers and of a new complexion. In the country between the Elbe and the Oder, in Pomerania and most of Prussia, Germans and Slavs were mixed. In the Spreewald of Lusatia a small Serbo-Wend community held aloof and preserved its language and much of its old folklore into the twentieth century. Likewise in the southern part of Prussia, after the extermination of the Prussians by the Teutonic Knights, Polish tribes settled; they became the Masurians, who never showed a desire for political separation but continued to speak their Slav language and adhere to their own customs.

In the mixture of Germans and Slavs the Germanic elements were probably stronger in some districts than in others. Brandenburg received in all likelihood more German settlers than eastern Pomerania or Silesia. The various eastern regions showed to some extent the peculiarities of the old "stem" duchies. Mecklenburg speech came quite close to that of the old Lower Saxons, whereas the Upper Saxons, the inhabitants of the region north of the Erzgebirge, as well as the Silesians, followed central German and Franconian patterns more closely. But on the whole the Brandenburgers, Pomeranians, Silesians, Prussians, and Mecklenburgers differed among themselves much less than did the members of the old "stem" duchies. The east-Elbian Germans were the descendants of migrants from all the historic German duchies settling together in the Slavic country and blending rather rapidly with the Slav inhabitants into a new race. Only where the German immigrants came overwhelmingly from one or two old duchies, as in Holstein, Schleswig, Austria, and, though to a much lesser degree, in Upper Saxony, did the new territories show a close resemblance to the neighboring duchies.

But in the long run racial origins were not the important factors in the growth of a distinct east-Elbian character. The relative geographical separation of this region from the rest of Germany and the special natural and historical forces that the east-Elbian Germans had to meet set them apart from the Germans in the original empire. As resistance from the east stiffened, as the economy reached its limits of expansion and was shaken by great external and internal crises, east Elbia became the Germany in which discipline and subordination, both in civilian and military life, were considered the highest virtues and individual rights counted for little.

Political Factors in Later Migrations

AFTER 1350 the steady flow of German peasants and townsmen to the eastern regions subsided. It is true that some additional German groups went there in subsequent centuries. Frederick William I invited the Protestants, who were driven out by the archbishop of Salzburg, to settle in eastern Prussia, and Frederick the Great welcomed every colonist after the Seven Years' War. Yet the major movement of eastern German colonization, which has sometimes been called by German historians the greatest achievement of the German people in the Middle Ages, drew to a close after the middle of the fourteenth century. At the same time there were increasing signs that the new Slav kingdoms in the east would resist further German encroachments. The rise of Poland and her acquisition of Galicia and Lithuania enabled her to aspire to predominance in eastern Europe. Now the absence of a strong central power in Germany that could have protected the outlying German colonies became the weakness of the whole German position. The land between the Elbe and the Oder, and even the parts of Pomerania and Silesia on the eastern bank of the Oder, were not directly threatened, but the Order of the Teutonic Knights was isolated, and succumbed to the Polish army in the battle of Tannenberg in 1410. This defeat wrecked the strength of the Order forever. By 1466 it had to accept Polish overlordship and to cede to Poland the Vistula valley, known at that time as Pomerelia, in modern times as western Prussia, and more recently as the Polish Corridor. In this region the German settlements were not yet predominant and the amalgamation of German and Slav elements not far advanced. The new Polish regime once and for all hindered such amalgamation, and though Frederick the Great again placed this region under a German government for more than a century, the bitter conflict between the two nationalities did not abate.

With her victory over the Teutonic Order, Poland gained access to the Baltic Sea and cut Prussia off from the rest of Germany. Her overlordship over the Order, made even more effective by her full seizure of the Ermland, one of the districts in the heart of Prussia, seemed to spell the end of German colonization beyond the Vistula. Prussia was saved, however, by the early decline of the Polish state. But the advanced German outposts that had been established to the northeast of Prussia were much too weak to become effective centers for the Germanization of Courland, Livonia, and Estonia. The first wave of German immigration to these regions was led by German merchants and knights, who could establish themselves only as a thin upper layer of society. Although they became a great influence in the economic, social, and even political life of the Baltic provinces far into the nineteenth century, they remained a small minority and, in the absence of the immigration of German peasants, were incapable of turning them into German lands. The fate of these Baltic territories was to be decided by other powers.

While the rise of Poland brought German colonization in the northeast to a standstill, similar events occurred farther to the south. With the Germanization of upper Saxony, Silesia, and Austria, Bohemia was surrounded by German territories and German colonists began to penetrate within its borders, settling in the mountains that encircle it, turning the uncleared forests into farmholdings. The Bohemian kings looked with favor on these developments and, particularly in the thirteenth century, deliberately supported the German immigration. German noblemen seemed useful allies for royal resistance to the political ambitions of the Czech nobility. The German townbuilders strengthened not only the defenses of the kingdom but also its financial resources. As early as the eleventh century German merchants formed a special colony in Prague, and a century later they received far-reaching privileges. The Germans also opened and worked the Bohemian mines. Thus large German settlements sprang up inside the Bohemian mountain ranges, and some German towns and cities grew up in the center of Bohemia.

The stage seemed set for a merger of Czech and German elements and the general acceptance of German civilization, as was occurring at this time in neighboring Silesia. The Bohemian kings of the thirteenth century not only appeared willing to countenance the further spread of German influence but were also actively aiming to bring German territories under the Bohemian crown. These attempts were defeated by Rudolf of Habsburg in the battle on the Marchfeld in 1278, and a growing popular hostility between Czechs and Germans became noticeable almost immediately. In the fourteenth century, when Charles IV built his imperial power on his control of Bohemia, Moravia, Lusatia, Silesia, and Brandenburg, the brewing animosity between Germans and Czechs was kept within bounds. It needed a religious issue, which the Hussite revolution provided, to separate Germans and Czechs; in 1436 Bohemia became a Czech state, and Germans were excluded from political and ecclesiastical offices. The acquisition of Bohemia and Moravia by the Austrian Habsburgs in 1526, and even more the battle at White Mountain in 1620, changed the balance again, but in spite of more than three centuries of attempted Germanization by Vienna the German-Czech conflict was not resolved.

✍ *Geographical Features*

THIS SURVEY SHOWS the difficulties involved in defining the boundaries of Germany. The settlements of the German people fluctuated very considerably in a history of a thousand years. In the east there were no clear landmarks that might have served as national frontiers. One might ask why the Elbe, Oder, or Vistula rivers could not have formed natural lines of division. But nowhere in the world, except for delimited sections, have large navigable rivers constituted national frontiers. They are formidable barriers against a military conqueror, but once they have been crossed the unifying character of a river valley asserts itself. What had been a barrier turns into a link and a line of strong communication. This was the situation in western Germany, with the Rhine. In the High Middle Ages the Rhine was the center of the German Empire, and only around the middle of the seventeenth century did the French monarchy begin to threaten the unity of German political control over the upper Rhine valley.

Mountains are considered obvious "natural" divides. But in German history they did not prove to be absolute barriers. German settlements, as we have seen, straddled the Bohemian mountain ranges. German expansion bridged even the Alps. Their central passes did not generally become the dividing line between Germanic and Latin territories. The Germans moved beyond the Brenner pass and all the Alpine passes east of it practically down to the southern feet of the Alps. Historical Germany, consequently, cannot be defined in terms of physical geography. Naturally, any effort to do so would be even more difficult if one were to take into account territories of non-Germanic settlement which at one time or another were ruled by the German Empire or one of its princes. Even after 1500 countries of French civilization, such as Burgundy and Lorraine, parts of upper Italy, Bohemia, Hungary, and sections of Poland were under the control of German rulers at various times. Furthermore, Germanic territories seceded from the Empire. Switzerland and the Low Countries were practically lost to Germany by the beginning of the sixteenth century, although official recognition of the new states was deferred until 1648.

The setting of German history has shifted drastically through the ages, as has also the center or centers of gravity of German life. Germany did not grow as did the Roman Empire, or medieval and modern France, from a single point, the city of Rome or the Île de France, around which in ever widening circles the realms expanded. Nature did not endow Germany with such unity. Under primitive conditions, navigable rivers and coast-bound shipping provide important opportunities for intercommunication. In this respect England was in an ideal position; at no place in England is one far from the coast or from a river running to the sea. France's seacoast is broken by the Iberian peninsula, but the great French river systems all converge toward the Île de France; this goes far to explain the central role that Paris has played in French history.

In German history the geographical elements making for the integration of the country were weak. The coasts of the North and Baltic Seas constituted a strong link for the north German lands, in spite of the short interruption by Holstein and the Jutland peninsula, which at times gave Denmark a chance to intervene in north German affairs. The Weser, Elbe, and Oder rivers were important waterways connecting the German territories north of the central German mountain ranges with the sea, but southern Germany was separated by the mountains north of the Main river, loosely called in Germany the Main Line, consisting of the Fichtelgebirge, the Franconian and Thuringian forests, the Rhön and Spessart. These central mountain groups proved a serious obstacle to easy and direct interchange between south and north Germany. The only important German river that tied together substantial regions of south and north Germany and connected both of them with the North Sea, was the mighty Rhine. It, therefore, formed the strongest pivot of the German Empire in the High Middle Ages. Through its southern tributaries, the Main and Neckar, most of Franconia and northwestern Swabia had access to the Rhine valley. But southeastern Swabia, Bavaria, and even more so Austria, felt little of the Rhine's magnetic pull. They tended to look southeast down the Danube or south toward the Adriatic. In northern Germany the Rhine's three tributaries, the Wupper, Ruhr, and Lippe, brought the part of lower Saxony that became Westphalia into close contact with the Rhineland, but even in the days of the Salian and Hohenstaufen emperors the bulk of Saxony was somewhat removed from the rest of Germany. The great northeastern colonizing movement that took place from the twelfth to the fourteenth centuries strengthened the aloofness of the northwest and created a relatively separated region east of the Elbe. The Rhine could no longer hold Germany together. The river lost even more of its integrating force when its lower section and its estuaries came finally, in the sixteenth century, under the control of an independent political state. Within Germany the shift of political power from the Rhine toward the east began as far back as the thirteenth century. The two great German powers in modern history, Austria and Brandenburg-Prussia, originated in regions farthest removed from the Rhine.

The geographical compartmentalization of Germany made for division and operated against the formation of a strong national government. Moreover, the various sections were differentiated not only by their domestic but also by their foreign interests, and they were brought into conflict among themselves by their alliances with foreign powers.

CHAPTER 2

The German Empire and the German Territorial States Before 1500

I**N CONTEMPLATING THE HISTORY** of the medieval states that succeeded the empire of Charlemagne, it must always be a source
of wonder that the Teutonic parts should so suddenly have assumed the political leadership of Europe. The *regnum Teutoni-
cum* that was launched in 911—the official name occurred for the first
time as early as 920—not only was the most powerful state in European
affairs for the next two centuries, but also seemed the one that made
the greatest strides toward solution of its own internal problems. But
this assumption was proved illusory by the outbreak of the historic
conflict between popes and emperors, usually known as the Investiture
Contest, which led to grievous internecine struggle in the years 1076–
1122. This crisis was overcome, and a new period of rich political
development opened, only to be cut short by the death of Emperor
Frederick II in 1250; and in the disasters that befell the last members
of the Hohenstaufen dynasty, German royal and imperial might crashed
to the ground.

While in the subsequent centuries France, England, and finally Spain
succeeded in building strong national monarchies, Germany lapsed,
both on the national and regional level, into complete chaos, from
which she emerged only slowly. A strong national German government did not come into existence again for more than five centuries,
and such forces of order as grew up in Germany emerged against
tremendous odds and were regional powers, often closely related to
foreign states and therefore a continuous threat to German unity.

✍ Factors in the Collapse of the Medieval National State

SINCE THE TRAGIC HISTORY of medieval Germany casts its shadow over the larger part of her modern development, the chief reasons for the collapse of the medieval national state are significant for an understanding of modern German history. Of equal importance are the organizational forms taken by the institutions of German public life in the late Middle Ages. These events were exceedingly complex, and we shall have to beware of facile generalizations, not always avoided by former generations of historians.

German historians of the Bismarckian age found the principal error in the policy of the medieval kings to have been their acquisition of imperial dignity and their resulting involvement in Italian politics. This imperial policy, so it was argued, had alienated the German monarchs from their most immediate task: promoting the healthy growth of a German national kingdom north of the Alps. It was asserted that in reaching out for the stars the emperors had squandered the German patrimony and ultimately left the Empire in ruins. But this was an appraisal of medieval politics in terms of German nationalism and modern *Realpolitik*. A German national consciousness did not exist in the tenth century, nor for a long time thereafter; and political authority, being as much a moral as a physical force, can be acquired and maintained only if it participates in the spiritual aspirations of its own age.

The policy of the medieval German rulers was motivated by the high ideals of Western Christianity. In the struggle for their realization, the recently converted Germans became in the full sense members and guardians of a Christian civilization and inherited what the Roman Church had preserved of the ideas and institutions of classical antiquity. Otto I (936–73) went to Italy in 961. That country was then in turmoil, and the papacy, which had called for help, was in danger of becoming a mere adjunct of local forces. Otto's intervention and his coronation as Roman Emperor restored the papacy to a universal position, though for the next century it was the weaker of the two swords that were supposed to rule Christendom.

Otto's Italian policy also had its realistic side. If he had not intervened in Italy, others would have done so. Since there were close connections between southern Germany and upper Italy, this could not have failed to affect Germany profoundly, irrespective of whether the king of Provence or the dukes of Bavaria and Swabia had made the opening move. The second possibility, in particular, might have shaken the internal coherence of the German kingdom. It was in origin a union of the Teutonic "stem" duchies, but the quasi-royal power of the dukes proved the main obstacle to the growth of a strong central government in Germany. Otto I and his successors sought to subordinate the dukes by turning them into feudal vassals and by appointing members of their own families to ducal positions. These policies were of no avail. As dukes, even sons of emperors soon became champions of "stem" interests, and in this they had the backing of the indigenous nobility, whose rank and position, like those of the dukes themselves, antedated the feudal system. If these noblemen became royal vassals, they could still claim independent privileges on their alodial lands. The direct officers of the king, the counts, whom the Carolingian Empire had introduced as the representatives of the crown on the local district level, chiefly for the administration of popular law among the freemen, were easily absorbed by the old local nobility.

Feudalism is often considered the single villain that brought about the fatal weakness of the Empire and the wild growth of particular forces. But though one may call medieval states feudal states, since feudal organization prevailed, kingship and all forms of dominion had their roots in older Germanic and Roman ideas. This is one reason for the differences in form and effect which characterized feudalism in the various European countries.

✎ Feudal Law and Organization

THE BEGINNINGS OF FEUDALISM, to be found in the late period of the Roman Empire, were closely connected with the disintegration of the economy of the empire and its relapse into an agrarian economy. The rise of medieval feudalism also was conditioned by primitive agrarian production. It was the inevitable form of organization for a society that commanded only meager resources but was forced to make strong military exertions. The old Germanic military organization that made every freeman liable to be on call for military duty was superseded in the seventh and eighth centuries by a new system that was centered around a class of trained professional warriors fighting on horseback. For their services they demanded the means for an independent life; this was granted to them in the form of feuds or benefices. These consisted of land given for use and not as a possession, but soon benefices became hereditary and the original relationship between king and vassals was blurred.

The creation of a special caste of privileged soldiers led to a transformation of society which continued for centuries. The peasant lost his military value. The final agrarian settlement brought large-scale transition from cattle raising to grain culture and tied the peasant to the land. Without experience in arms, he needed the protection of a potent lord. The old clan and the village community did not disappear, but the peasants came under the tutelage of landlords, who were either the king or noblemen or ecclesiastical bodies. The old Germanic freedom vanished, and the peasants were burdened with a large variety of servitudes, which in many cases amounted to virtual serfdom.

The social and economic revolution that enabled the secular and ecclesiastical feudal lords to live on the work of the peasants also had its political consequences. The landlords began to acquire political rights in addition to their manorial ones. The feudal domain received "immunity" from royal intervention, making it possible for the landlord to set up a paternal government. But the process did not stop at the local level. Once the count's offices became hereditary, whole judicial districts came into private hands, and the grant of further governmental rights led finally to the formation of states within the state. Those who acquired the highest judicial rights, the rights dealing with life and death, rose to a new rank. These noblemen became princes.

Feudalism, as Otto Hintze has most clearly shown, had three historical functions: military, governmental, and social. It ran through three stages: an early period reaching into the twelfth century, in which the military aspect prevailed; a second age extending into the sixteenth and seventeenth centuries, in which the nobility gained its highest influence in politics; and a third period, in which the nobility chiefly defended its social and economic privileges. The feudal epoch drew to a close only with the French Revolution and the replacement of the agrarian economy by a free industrial system in the nineteenth century. The military exigencies that had given rise to the feudal system ceased to exist after 1500, but the nobility retained a significant role in the development of the officer corps of modern armies.

Feudal law and organization have had the profoundest effect on European history far into modern times. But they operated differently in different countries. The French kings found the way to the establishment of a modern state by strengthening the centralizing elements that were not lacking among feudal concepts. The salient point in the history of feudal institutions was the extent to which the king could assert his authority as feudal overlord not only over his great vassals but also over their rear-vassals. Since the vassals were bound to fidelity to the king, a breach of fealty on the part of the vassals ought to have freed the rear-vassals from their fealty to the vassals. In order to make explicit the rear-vassals' loyalty also to the king, a formula might have been included in any oath of fealty taken by any member of the feudal pyramid. Such a theory, which the French kings tried to enforce in bitter struggles, stressed the sense of public obligation in a system that tended to confuse public functions with private possessions. No doubt the French kings were helped in their national policy by the fact that the French people had been welded into greater unity by the Roman and Frankish empires than had been the case in Germany.

In Germany the existence of "tribal" dukes, who thought of themselves as small kings of "peoples," was from the beginning a serious handicap to the rise of a strong royal power. The dukes threatened the direct royal administration of the counts and under feudal law accepted the privileges but not the obligations of vassalage. The emperors of the tenth and early eleventh centuries first attempted to control and then to minimize the duchies. Franconia was early left without a duke and was considered an appurtenance of the German crown; other duchies, for example Saxony and Lorraine, were divided or, like Bavaria, lost substantial parts. But these policies met with only limited success. Therefore the Saxon and Salian emperors turned to the Church and made its dignitaries their trusted servants in the government of Germany. The archbishops and bishops of Mainz, Trier, Cologne, Bremen, Hildesheim, Magdeburg, Würzburg, Bamberg, Passau, Salzburg, and the abbots of Fulda, Hersfeld, Corvey, Reichenau —to name only some of the group—were given wide political authority and endowed with many benefices. The new ecclesiastical princes were without exception noblemen, but they could not well conceive of their office as a private possession. With the death of the incumbent, the benefices returned to the king and were lent again to men of his confidence.

The system of government that used bishoprics and monasteries to spread royal authority through the realm rested on the king's control of the German Church, and this logically called for a directing influence on the Roman Curia. One of the major reasons for Otto's intervention in Italy was his need for the spiritual authority of the universal Church and its German organs as a support of his policies. He did not aspire to dominate Western Christianity. The possession of the three kingdoms of Germany, Burgundy, and Lombardy was in itself an adequate ground for the acceptance of the Roman imperial crown. At no time was the claim made that the renovated Roman Empire was congruous with the totality of Western Christendom, the *respublica Christiana* of the Middle Ages. Beyond the three kingdoms the German medieval emperors only assumed some sort of protectorate over the Church states. Although at various times feudal bonds tied other countries loosely to Germany, it was pre-eminence among the European kings and princes, and not dominion over them, that was the political aim of the German emperors.

✍ *The Investiture Contest*

THE ARCHES OF THE PROUD EDIFICE that the Saxon and early Salian emperors had erected were broken when the papacy revolted against the dominant influence of the emperors on the Church, accusing them of corrupting the Church or, as the contemporary expression ran, of simony. The program of the new papal school, first publicly proclaimed by Pope Gregory VII in 1075, aimed at the absolute superiority of the pope over the emperor. Temporal power, it was said, could be justified only insofar as it aimed at the realization of justice. But Christ's vicar on earth alone knew the true meaning of Christian justice. The popes made themselves judges of the actions of princes, kings, and emperors and assumed the right to depose them.

The new ecclesiastical ideals were a challenge to the political constitution of Germany as it had been developed by the Saxon and Salian emperors. For more than a generation a bitter civil war, known as the Investiture Contest, raged; the princes fought against the emperor, class against class, and often enough brother against brother. The princes took full advantage of the weakness of the imperial authority which resulted from the papal attack. Everywhere they eliminated the counts, the agents of a direct royal administration, from their princely territories. Only in a few cases did the old counts manage to become princes. Feudalism showed its full force of disintegration by cutting the feudal overlord off from any direct power over rear-vassals. About sixteen secular and sixty ecclesiastical princes appeared as the *principes imperii*. They were the princes who recognized no other lord than the emperor, but in view of the elective character of the royal and imperial offices they themselves claimed to represent the Empire in some fashion and to be entitled to special privileges. As a group or an estate they pressed their demands upon the crown. The Concordat of Worms of 1122, which after almost fifty years created an uneasy compromise between the emperor and the pope, did not restore the emperor's power over the ecclesiastical princes. Although the emperors regained some influence on the elections of German bishops, the ecclesiastical princes were henceforth to receive their dignity from the pope and only their secular authority from the emperor. Their double loyalty made them weak allies of the emperor. Bishops and abbots gained a position practically identical with that of the secular princes, and they were certainly as eager as the latter to exclude all imperial intervention from the administration of their territories.

Simultaneously with this political shift the last act of the social revolution that feudalism had promoted took place. The Investiture Contest destroyed what was still left of the old free classes. Most of the free peasants, wanting a patron in these stormy days, lost their freedom to a feudal lord. But the protracted warfare also called for increasing numbers of fighting men, and the old nobility was no longer able to fill the need. As a matter of fact, the old noble families had become extinct as a result of the wars or been weakened by the division of their family estates. Here was the chance for the upper layer of the free peasants to offer themselves for military services. Henry IV (1056–1106) had started building up a royal dominion around the Harz mountains, and he manned the castles that he erected in the Harz and Thuringian forest with Swabian servant-knights or *ministeriales*, that is, freemen who accepted service contracts without becoming feudal vassals. It was this policy that enraged the old German nobility and contributed greatly to making most of its members willing tools of the papacy and of the German princes in opposing the emperors during the Investiture Contest. Still, the demands of war compelled the princes to employ servant-knights. Soon these mingled with the old nobility and out of the two classes, the one dying, the other rising, a strong new German nobility emerged during the thirteenth century.

All over Germany castles grew up, built either by princes to make their position unassailable against the emperor as well as against foreign and internal enemies, or by noble knights assisting the princes but also making their own independence more secure. The conflict between the emperor and the princes had its counterpart in the conflict between the noblemen and the princes on the territorial level. For the vast majority of the German people, however, the radical feudalization of society meant dependence on the higher classes. Only the growth of towns and cities, which belonged to the same age, seemed to open prospects of a new freedom.

✍ Imperial Versus Princely Might

WITH THE ACCESSION to the throne of the Hohenstaufen Frederick I (1152–90), called by the Italians "Barbarossa" because of his auburn beard, internal conditions became peaceful and a new political order developed. His extraordinary wisdom and mature political judgment, coupled with his great military prowess, raised the imperial power to new heights. Small wonder that he became a legendary figure in later centuries. According to a popular legend he was not dead but asleep in a cave in one of Germany's wooded hills, and some day he would awaken and restore the magnificence of the medieval Empire—so the Germans fondly dreamed in long days of political adversity. Actually, Frederick's successes in a reign of almost four decades were earned not by superhuman gifts but by sober attention to all the various opportunities that were left to the crown. He accepted the new position of the princes which they had gained in the Investiture Contest and co-operated with them as the first among equals, but he carefully expanded his rights of feudal overlordship. Frederick I also conducted a deliberate policy of augmenting the royal demesne and establishing a closer relationship with the rising German cities, which offered a new chance for the consolidation of the emperor's influence in Germany. But his major efforts were exerted in an attempt to utilize the resources of Burgundy and Italy for the enhancement of his imperial power—a policy that, under his successors, brought the Hohenstaufen empire to catastrophe.

It is doubtful whether Frederick Barbarossa made much headway against the German princes; but there can be no doubt that when his heirs got more and more deeply enmeshed in their Italian policies, the independence of the princes increased. Frederick II (1212–50), who was more a Sicilian than a German ruler, formally recognized their authority in the "confederation with the ecclesiastical princes" of 1220 and the "statute in favor of princes" of 1232. The first law finally deprived the ecclesiastical principalities of the last traces of their old role as centers of royal administration. The emperor renounced the right to build castles in their territories, as well as the exercise of the right of coinage and the administration of justice. Royal officers were completely withdrawn from the ecclesiastical principalities. In the statute of 1232 these privileges were extended to all the princes. It was the abdication of the German monarchy and the recognition of the princes as the exclusive rulers of their territories and as equal partners with the emperor in the government of the Empire. The inability of the German emperors ever to establish the hereditary principle on a firm basis made the balance of power even more precarious. The concessions to the princes that had been made during the thirteenth century and earlier had been granted with a view to getting their approval of hereditary succession. Imperial laws assumed the character of treaties between the emperor and the princes, like the "electoral capitulations" of future centuries.

Two concessions granted by Frederick II illustrate the political strength of the princes. Under the terms of the confederation of 1220 the imperial ban, the terrifying thunderbolt of sovereign imperial jurisdiction, was linked to clerical authority. The imperial ban, which deprived a person of all civil rights, was henceforth to be pronounced automatically six weeks after a person had been excommunicated by a German bishop, without a prior hearing by the ordinary courts. Frederick II also yielded to the princes in his attitude toward the cities, an issue of great historical significance.

Henry IV had found support in the new urban communities not only against the princes but also against the Church; during his rule the German cities awakened to their potential power. In the tenth century most cities were ruled by bishops, but they pressed early for self-government under the king. In the days of the Investiture Contest the cities were establishing their own internal organization and gaining the recognition of their autonomy from their former city-lords. In the twelfth century secular princes founded cities, granting them "charters of liberty." The Hohenstaufen emperors gave many cities the freedom of the Empire, whereby, except for payment of an annual tax to the emperor, they governed themselves.

For the first time in medieval constitutional history the cities monopolized all power within a given territorial unit. Equally significant was the development of a common citizenship. "City air is free air" (*Stadtluft macht frei*) was the principle under which serfdom disappeared from the cities, and dependent persons moving to them were before long made burghers. The new law of citizenship spread even beyond the city walls, as the cities began to extend the protection of their urban law in various forms to the people of the neighboring countryside. If this movement had continued, Germany might have become reorganized both territorially and socially, as happened in Italy. Co-operation between the emperor and the cities might have laid the foundations of a modern German monarchy. In England and France the cities contributed immeasurably to the growth of modern national monarchies.

But although the Hohenstaufen emperors realized the political possibilities opened by the rise of the cities, the princes recognized the danger and forced the emperors into a course of action inimical to the cities. As late as 1226 Frederick II made the great Baltic emporium Lübeck, just then recovered from Denmark, an imperial city. Six years later he promised the princes that he would "build no more castles or *walled cities* in princely territories," nor were new royal markets to compete with the older markets under princely supervision. A good many other rules impeding the political growth of the cities were contained in the same statute of 1232. In spite of such rules, they continued to grow, but chiefly in economic power. Most cities finally remained under the territorial princes, though giving them a staunch fight before submitting to princely authority. It was ominous that the imperial government of the Hohenstaufens sided with the princes rather than with the cities, in which the potentially stronger seeds of German unity were to be found.

Foreign Intervention and Internal Chaos, 1250–1350

IN THE REIGN OF FREDERICK BARBAROSSA it became customary to speak of the Empire as the Holy Roman Empire. The new attribute was supposed to stress the divine origins of imperial dominion. But the *sacrum imperium* succumbed to the *sancta ecclesia*. The death of Frederick II, in 1250, enabled the popes to stamp out altogether "the nest of vipers," the Hohenstaufen dynasty. The century from 1250 to 1350 was one of an anemic and at times defunct central government. Foreign intervention in German affairs increased. It came originally both from the popes and from France. But the papacy had itself become secular in its struggle with the Empire and lost much of its saintly prestige. It had also nourished the national monarchies outside of Germany, and in 1303 it was defeated by the French king, Philip IV, and led to Avignon without much of a public outcry being raised over such violence against the Holy See. Thereafter it was France that intervened in Germany in order to keep any central power feeble and to extend direct domination over the western territories of the German Empire. The English victories of Crécy and Poitiers of 1346 and 1356 relieved Germany in the west. The Hundred Years' War between England and France, as well as the rise of a powerful Burgundian state between France and Germany, though infringing on Germany's western position, made the century between 1350 and 1450 an age of modest national consolidation, in spite of the losses in the east.

The breakdown of the Hohenstaufen Empire in 1250 created complete chaos in Germany. One would have expected that the princes would have assumed the leadership of Germany, but they were neither closely united among themselves nor strong enough in their own principalities. Feudalism dealt with them as it had with the German emperors. The cities and the nobility defended their privileges against them and closed ranks for this purpose. The princes were also not supreme over the bishops and prelates who represented the Church in their territories. In the period after 1250 confederations were formed to maintain the law and peace of the realm. They were mostly confederations of cities, or of cities and groups of the nobility. The distinctions between territorial and imperial cities as well as between territorial and imperial *ministeriales*, who now began to call themselves *milites*, i.e., knights, became exceedingly tenuous. Even the differentiation of princes and knights was not an absolute one, and many a knight could attain princely rank. As a result, the political map of Germany for more than five hundred years resembled a strange mosaic composed of a few large stones and innumerable small fragments.

✍ Lasting Effects of the High Middle Ages on German History

STILL, two lasting effects on German history were left by the High Middle Ages. First, in spite of all the internal divisions and dissensions that had made common national action impossible, a national consciousness had been created and was not lost in subsequent ages. Secondly, political action centered more and more around the particularist forces, among which the princes proved the most energetic, although their dominions seemed to stand on shaky grounds and economic trends favored the cities. Everywhere the princes had to recognize the power of the estates, usually consisting of prelates, nobility, and cities, to which in a few cases peasants were added. The need for money, increased by the currency depreciation of the century, often forced the princes to sell or pawn their own rights and domains. They were dependent on the estates, which in return for the grant of new taxes demanded a financial administration of their own and even participation in the conduct of foreign affairs. The territorial states followed the Empire by becoming "dualistic" states, in which prince and estates competed for the exercise of supreme political authority. The centuries from 1350 to 1650 saw the "dualistic state" (*Ständestaat*) everywhere except in the free imperial cities; in these all public authority was firmly in the hands of the city council, which had power over every person in the city and its territory.

✍ The Cities

THE CITIES WERE the first rationally administered political units in Germany. Written records were kept of all transactions, and administration was carried into fields that the feudal state could never have mastered, such as economic and welfare policies. Yet the gains of the cities in Empire politics were limited compared to their progressive administrative systems and economic wealth. In their use of certain military weapons they were clearly superior to the princes. This was true with regard to the naval forces of the northern sea cities, but also generally with regard to artillery, which was developed after the fourteenth century mainly in the cities. But federations of the cities, such as the Rhenish League of 1254 and the Swabian League of 1376, were soon checked by the territorial princes. The greatest federation of cities, both of free and territorial cities, the Hanseatic League, was not primarily a political alliance but an association for the common acquisition and use of trade privileges in the countries of the Baltic and North Seas. This League, which reached from the Zuider Zee to the Gulf of Riga and maintained establishments all over Scandinavia, as well as in Novgorod and in London, could not fail to exercise great political and at times even military power, but these were rather by-products of its economic enterprises.

If the German cities did not become the dominant power in the German Empire, this was largely due to their lack of common interests. The upper German cities, the Rhenish cities, and the northern sea cities were each united by a kindred political outlook, but not even the long-distance trade that all these cities carried on so successfully lifted the German burghers to the recognition of common nationwide objectives. A strong central power might have knit together these groups and infused them with a sense of political responsibility for the nation. But we have already seen that the Hohenstaufen emperors found such a task beyond their strength, and after their demise the princes could decide how much imperial power should be tolerated in Germany. After the dissipation of royal rights and of the crown property it was clear that an emperor who wanted to be more than a puppet in the hands of the German princes had to be the ruler of substantial princely territories of his own. The Swiss Count Rudolf von Habsburg, whose election in 1273 ended the Interregnum, had already realized the necessity for such a dynastic endowment and, by making himself duke of Austria, created the nucleus of one of the strongest territorial states in Germany. But the Habsburgs failed to capture the imperial title for their dynasty, since the princes jealously guarded the elective principle of the Empire.

✍ Codification of Relations Between Emperor and Princes

THE RELATIONS BETWEEN the emperor and the princes were formally codified by Charles IV (1347–78) who, secure in the possession of Bohemia, wished to make the imperial crown the property of his own family. Charles IV was a shrewd diplomat and a keen appraiser of political realities. He drew the final balance of German constitutional history in the Middle Ages, and thereby opened a new chapter of history. Charles IV recognized that the Italian and Burgundian policies of the medieval emperors could not produce a foundation of imperial power and that a drastic retrenchment of German political aims would relieve the Empire of costly foreign efforts and make it possible to concentrate on internal conditions. The changed European situation, particularly the weakness of France under the blows received from England, and the desire of the Avignonese papacy to extricate itself from French tutelage, enabled Charles IV to strengthen the German Empire.

✍ The Golden Bull of 1356

THE LARGEST single act of medieval legislation, which to the end of its existence formed the central piece of the German constitution, was the Golden Bull of 1356, so called after its golden seal. It was the result of negotiations between the emperor and those German princes who since 1257 had claimed the exclusive right to elect the emperor. They included the duke of Saxony, the margrave of Brandenburg, the king of Bohemia, the count palatine of the Rhine, and the three archbishops of Mainz, Cologne, and Trier. Their rights as imperial electors were now reaffirmed in spite of the fact that many historical accidents had led to the formation of this group, which from the outset excluded other equally strong princes, for example, the dukes of Austria and Bavaria. But the Golden Bull clarified the character of membership in the electoral college. It was not a dynastic property but a function to be exercised by the heads of states. Their principalities were now declared to be indivisible and under the law of primogeniture, so as to exclude the appearance of two claimants for a vote from the same princely family —in the preceding century this had often led to complete splits among the electors. Moreover, a simple majority was to settle elections.

The new electors received semiregal rights. In addition to full exemption from imperial jurisdiction, they received the rights of coinage, of levying custom duties, of mining, and of the protection of Jews. The application of the late Roman law of lèse-majesté to the electors elevated them as persons. It should be mentioned that the formal grant of these privileges strengthened the hands also of the other princes who soon received or usurped them. In this respect the Golden Bull became the magna charta of German particularism. But it provided also an orderly procedure for an imperial regime on a federative basis. No double elections ever took place after the promulgation of the Golden Bull. More important than the stable procedure was the silent exclusion of papal co-operation. The popes had asserted that the election of an emperor needed papal approbation and that the new rule could not begin before it had been given. They had also claimed the right to act as imperial vicars in the absence of a confirmed emperor. The Golden Bull designated the duke of Saxony and the Rhenish count palatine as imperial vicars and declared that the emperor entered upon his reign as soon as he had been elected by the electors. The Roman "emperor-elect" began to exercise the authority of his office in Germany irrespective of the papal coronation.

The Golden Bull conceived of the Empire as having its main center of gravity north of the Alps, and its organization resting on German bases. A decisive step was taken in the direction of a separation of national from universal political ideals. In the fifteenth century, after the Councils of Constance and Basel, this trend took deeper root among the people and it became customary to speak of Germany as the Holy Roman Empire of the German Nation. The formula has been strangely misinterpreted by nineteenth-century historians as expressing a German claim to rule Europe, whereas it was intended to denote that part of the Roman Empire which was inhabited by Germans.

But the shift of policy toward more limited and national aims which Charles IV initiated could have borne immediate fruit if the federation principle adopted by him had led to a strong federative organ. The Golden Bull mentioned annual meetings of the emperor and the electors for discussion of the affairs of the Empire. The electors, however, could not easily leave their own lands so often, nor did they care very much to become a council of the emperor. Preoccupied with their own territorial troubles, they demonstrated no great eagerness to organize as a special body and impose their will on the emperor. Occasionally attempts were made to transform the electoral college into a league of electors in order to correct supposedly mistaken policies of the emperor or even to depose a failing emperor. But these projects did not produce any lasting constitutional results. The electors, "pillars of the empire" as they were called, were eventually satisfied to become the leaders of all the princes of the Empire and form the first estate on the diet of the Empire (*Reichstag*). Between 1350 and 1450 the electors were mainly absorbed in struggling with their own estates and with neighboring princes and cities. They might have developed more enterprise in matters affecting the Empire if the emperors of the period had enhanced their own influence in Germany and thereby threatened the virtual independence of the princes.

But the successors of Charles IV, Emperor Wenzel (1378–1400) and Emperor Sigismund (1410–37), did not solidify the position that their ancestor had assumed. Quite apart from the personal shortcomings of the last Luxemburg rulers, the Hussite revolution blew up the Bohemian bulwark on which their whole strength had rested. Imperial power did not rise when, in 1438, the Habsburg dynasty, in the person of Albrecht II, succeeded to the throne of the Holy Roman Empire, which it was to occupy, with a brief intermission in the years 1742–45, to the end of the first German Empire in 1806. At the time of the accession of Frederick III the Austrian territories were divided, since primogeniture had been allowed to lapse. The long reign of the indolent Frederick III, from 1440 to 1493, did nothing to advance imperial authority in Germany. He was distracted from the Empire by his concern about dangers to the Habsburg possessions rising in Hungary, Bohemia, and more remotely in Turkey. His son Maximilian's marriage to Charles the Bold's daughter, Mary of Burgundy, in 1477, marked the beginning of the rise of the Habsburg dynasty to European pre-eminence. But since, as will be seen, the new Habsburg power did not really rest on Germany, it could not take as its foremost aim the reformation of the German constitution.

✑ Divided Lands and Classes in the Fifteenth Century

THROUGHOUT EUROPE the fifteenth century was characterized by violence and civil war, but nowhere was the chaos as great as in the divided lands and classes of Germany. The lawlessness that dominated public life seemed to engulf even its moral foundations; in 1378 the papal schism occurred, and after 1418 the Bohemian heretics defeated all German armies. The longing for a constitutional reform of the Empire was already apparent in the early fifteenth century and found expression in a large number of reform programs. Among them the *Concordantia Catholica* (1433) of Cardinal Nicholas of Cusa, one of the greatest philosophers of Germany, deserves mention. It anticipated the proposals for a council of regency formed by the estates of the Empire, which was to be attempted seven decades later. Another pamphlet by an anonymous author, known as the *Reformation of Emperor Sigismund*, reads like a document of the period of social revolution in the early years of the sixteenth-century Reformation. But it is difficult to estimate the influence of these and many similar writings on the actual course of events in the fifteenth century. Efforts for a reform of the German constitution were caught in the triangular struggle for power and independence among the emperor, the princes, and the cities. The main issues were the suppression of feuds, and the establishment of courts and a supporting organization for the execution of judicial decisions. The electors proposed a regional division of the Empire for achieving internal peace and order. But in their proposals they always aimed also at an expansion of their own jurisdiction and at the exclusion of direct contacts between the emperor and the lesser estates—i.e., the free imperial cities and the low nobility—which the emperor did not wish to lose. All attempts at a reform of the Empire were stalled after the Nürnberg Diet of 1438.

The Territorial States at the End of the Fifteenth Century

WHATEVER PROGRESS toward pacification and a more effective political organization was made in Germany before the end of the century was achieved in the princely territories. The more powerful princes began to overcome the enormous difficulties that lay in the way of the formation of territorial states. Nowhere was the "dualistic" nature of these budding states abolished. One could even say that only in this period did the dualistic state come into existence. The fundamental peril had been the complete dissolution of any territorial cohesion, since both the nobility and the cities refused to accept princely authority and in their own political schemes flouted any responsibility for the territorial welfare. The princes could never hope to make themselves absolute rulers of their principalities. All that they attempted to achieve was the unity of the two territorial authorities, prince and estates, in a co-ordinated system.

This objective could be accomplished only if the existing estates in the various sections of a territory were merged into an estates-general for the entire territory with power to enforce on all its members the resolutions passed by the representative body (*Landtag*). The nobility of the district of Straubing in Bavaria, for example, claimed special tax exemptions and formed a league to defend their rights. Rostock in Mecklenburg defied in 1480 a general tax passed by a meeting at which it had been represented; not for eleven years could the maritime city be forced to pay. The many-sided struggle that eventually compelled cities and noblemen to accept the rights and duties of membership in the territorial estates lasted a long time, but it was practically over by the end of the fifteenth century. Not everywhere did it end with the victory of the princes. In southwestern Germany—specifically, in the Trier district, the Palatinate, in Alsace, Hesse, Franconia, and Swabia—where the power of the territorial princes was relatively weak, large groups of the nobility successfully resisted absorption by territorial princes. They placed themselves directly under the emperor, to whom they paid "charitable subsidies," small voluntary taxes, which were the more graciously received since they did not require the assent of the Diet of the Empire. The freedom of action of these imperial knights was buttressed by their influence on the ecclesiastical principalities, which were so abundant in this region. Members of this class occupied most of the canonicates in the neighboring bishoprics and abbeys, benefices that gave their families added income and often enough enabled them to play hand in glove with the ecclesiastical rulers.

The south German princes also failed to subjugate the imperial cities. They stopped the city leagues, which the Golden Bull had already outlawed, but they could not overwhelm the free imperial cities. The Bavarian dukes made an attempt in 1488 to turn Regensburg into a Bavarian town; this attempt, however, was resisted, and for the most part the many imperial cities in upper Germany maintained themselves. A different situation prevailed in northern and, particularly, in "colonial" northeastern Germany. In the young country east of the Elbe the leadership of the princes had always extended to all groups of the people. Ecclesiastical authorities were not able to gain much secular power, and the nobility did not block all contacts between the common man and the princely ruler, whose activities, particularly in the military field, were more conspicuous than in the older parts of Germany. The state that the Teutonic Order had created in Prussia was, of course, in a unique category. It was an oligarchic regime of the nobility which, however, at the height of its development produced a strictly unified policy administered by officials appointed by the Grand Master of the Order. The Prussian cities, too, were under the supervision of the Order, irrespective of whether or not they belonged to the Hanseatic League.

At the beginning of the fifteenth century the two largest principalities in northeastern Germany entered upon a new stage of their history. In 1415, Emperor Sigismund gave the electorate and margravate of Brandenburg to his loyal lieutenant Frederick of Hohenzollern, burgrave of Nürnberg, and eight years later, the electorate and duchy of Saxony to Margrave Frederick of Meissen of the Wettin dynasty. The second event was immediately more important, since it brought the industrial regions of Thuringia and upper Saxony together. The princely revenue from metal mining and salt mining rights made the Saxon rulers financially stronger than most other German princes. The integration of the Saxon nobility and the Saxon cities into common territorial estates was achieved with comparatively little friction. For more than two centuries the electorate of Saxony remained the strongest of all the north German principalities. Brandenburg, poor in natural resources— she was derisively called the German Empire's "sandbox"—had a long way to go under the Hohenzollerns before she could measure up to her southern neighbor. The beginnings of the Hohenzollerns in Brandenburg were stormy. Still, Frederick I forced the obstreperous noblemen to abide by the rules of the dualistic state, and his successor, Frederick II, known as "Irontooth," brought the city of Berlin-Cölln under his control in 1442 and caused all the Brandenburg cities to leave the Hanseatic League.

A molecular relationship on a new territorial basis was thus created. The question as to which of the two powers, princes or estates, was to gain full ascendancy over the other, was only decided by the Thirty Years' War. Both groups represented retarding as well as progressive political elements and ideas in the evolution of a modern state organization. The princes were accustomed to conceive of their rule in terms of private ownership. The distinction made between their own private and public finances was at best tenuous—a fact that made understandable the resistance of the estates to new tax levies and their insistence upon participation in the collection and disbursement of such funds. An even greater obstacle to the formation of popular allegiance to the state was the division of territories among the sons of a ruling prince.

The estates, in their opposition to these practices, contributed to a more modern conception of the state as a public trust to be administered for the common welfare. It is doubtful, for example, whether the law of primogeniture, which the Golden Bull had already postulated for the electorates, would have been generally adopted if there had not been steady pressure from the estates. Even so, primogeniture was very slowly accepted. In the late fifteenth century many of the larger principalities, such as Brandenburg, Württemberg, Saxony, and Bavaria, issued "house laws" stipulating the indivisibility of the territories and the succession of the eldest son to the throne. But these laws were often challenged, and only around 1600 did a movement begin that stabilized the law of primogeniture in the large principalities. The small ones struggled with the problem well into the eighteenth century.

The estates aided the transformation of the German territories into territorial states, but the princes were practically everywhere the leaders, or at least the instigators, of this process. They took the initiative in the unification of their territories by abolishing the representative bodies in the old regional units and establishing the estates-general (*Landtage*). At the same time the princes began to consolidate their various rights with a view to building a supreme state authority extending evenly over the whole land. There is no question but that during the later fifteenth century a good many of the bold German princes had their sights set on the acquisition of absolute sovereignty, but they failed to reach this objective. Their demand that assemblies of the estates could only be held if they were convened by the princes was generally accepted, and the princes also presented "propositions" that formed the basis of the deliberations of the estates. The pre-eminent position of the "lord of the land" was thereby recognized.

But the right of the estates to grant taxes could not be challenged, nor could their right to criticize freely every princely action, including his personal conduct. Everywhere the estates participated in some form in the administration of taxes that they had approved. In all these matters the nobility proved to be the aggressive element, and noblemen dominated the agencies created for these purposes. Moreover, they insisted that posts in general administration which the princes set up should be reserved for members of the indigenous nobility. The princes could not disregard this pressure, particularly when the need for heavy new taxes became urgent, as happened in the sixteenth century, largely as a result of the much greater outlay required for the newly created mercenary armies. The power of the nobility in the territorial states of Germany was stronger in 1550 or 1600 than it was in 1500. But even at the later dates, the pre-eminence of the princely "lord of the land" (*Landesherr*) persisted.

∽ Establishment of Permanent State Governments

IN THE LAST YEARS of the fifteenth century the administrative system of the territorial states again reached a new stage. The rational organization of Burgundy had a great impact on Austria, to which it was joined under Maximilian I; and Austrian influence on the organization of governmental agencies in the German territories was noticeable down to the early seventeenth century, though the Burgundian-Austrian institutions were not blindly imitated but were grafted upon earlier native organs. There came into existence permanent state governments that could function even in the absence of the monarch. The territorial governments grew out of the council of secular and ecclesiastical nobles which the princes at their liberty had called together for consultation. The institution was turned into a permanent collegiate body by the appointment of trained lawyers as "daily" or professional councilors, and the nonresident councilors began to disappear. Though in theory and occasionally in practice the prince remained the president of the new permanent council, the actual direction of its business was soon placed in the hands of a high official, and strict rules of procedure were issued. The new permanent council originally dealt with every function of government, but financial affairs were early brought under a new office, the chamber or court chamber (*Hofkammer*). When the councils once more came increasingly under the influence of the nobility, the princes selected a few councilors as their privy councilors for the management of political matters. By the end of the sixteenth century the privy council was constituted as a special agency of the state, responsible under the prince for general state policies, while the old council was confined to the administration of justice. There were endless variations, not only in the names of these agencies, but also in the division of functions among them. However, the triad of offices—council, chamber, privy council—appeared in practically every German territorial state and formed the foundation of princely power. A fourth group of agencies, designed to administer the new taxes granted by the estates, was only partly under the control of the princes and sometimes entirely a preserve of the nobility. It is in the financial field that the dualism of the state organization found its clearest expression.

✒ *Activities of the New State Power*

As IMPORTANT AS the organization of the new state power was the scope of its activities, which was far-reaching. The model of the all-embracing government of the cities was infectious. The foremost single task of any German government at home was the administration of justice. The princes of the fifteenth and sixteenth centuries did not set themselves revolutionary aims in their governmental actions. In every field they wanted to defend what was the good old custom. But if one sought to define what the common law was, a great variety of often conflicting legal customs appeared in the component parts of the new territorial states. The councilors of the princes were trained in Roman law and were unable as well as unwilling to develop German law. The codification of positive law and legal procedures, which took place in the territorial states beginning in the last decades of the fifteenth century, were conceived in the spirit of the Roman law (which, incidentally, lent itself well to justification of the dominant role to which the princes aspired).

The economic policies of the princes were also conservative. Everybody's customary needs were to be satisfied; by this it was always understood that the needs of the members of the various classes were not, and ought not to be, identical. The preservation of the peculiar class distinctions was a definite objective of the economic and social policies of the German territorial state. To find the "just price" that the producer and the laborer could demand and the consumer afford was the main concern. Beyond this, disturbing influences from abroad had to be kept out. The export of wool was prohibited in order to keep the price of wool and indigenous cloth low, while the import of foreign cloth was hindered. The sale of victuals was strictly supervised, and middlemen were excluded in order to keep food prices cheap and stable. Similar emphasis was placed on the stabilization of wages. The output and wages of artisans were exactly prescribed; craft guilds were often dissolved so as to make price-fixing impossible. Where a shortage of day workers occurred, people who were idle were forced to work.

These economic policies have been referred to as mercantilistic practices, but the expansion of economic activities to gain additional political power was not yet a clearly envisaged aim. Commerce, irrespective of whether it was domestic or foreign, was not much favored, nor was luxury tolerated even if it benefited native production. The dominating trend was the stabilization of the traditional social order and the old customs. The nobility gained most freedom, since the state regiments could least enforce their ordinances against the most powerful social and political group in the land. Careful thought was given to seeing that the economy of the cities was not undermined, and the intention was to continue industries and commerce as a virtual monopoly of the cities, but the grain trade, even beyond territorial boundaries, had to be left in the hands of the nobility. The exacting sumptuary laws were not only intended as a means to avoid the import of luxury goods or to propagate Christian simplicity but also to keep differences in social rank visible. Elaborate rules concerning the amounts that it was permissible to spend on dress or on feasts for such occasions as carnivals, weddings, and funerals, affected the life of the lower classes more than that of the nobility. Of a more generally benevolent nature were the efforts of the governments to improve the welfare of the communities by training surgeons, apothecaries, and midwives.

The rise of the new territorial states in Germany during the fifteenth century is often described merely as the disintegration of the medieval Empire and the usurpation of the royal or imperial prerogatives by the princes. But the new power of the princes was only partly built on former royal rights. It was also based on the new political tasks that were boldly tackled for the first time in German history by the princes. The great breadth of their policies, which were called in Germany "*Polizei,*" i.e., activities directed toward a well-ordered polity, showed that an age had arrived in which a new intensification and rationalization of politics had been reached. The German territorial states had not only inherited and divided among themselves what had once been the authority of the medieval emperor, but had formed dynamic political centers of a novel type.

It was this progress toward new forms of political organization that made the territorial states such strong competitors with the Empire. By the end of the fifteenth century it had become clear that a strong imperial government could be reconstructed only if the German territorial states were willing to lend it new strength by federative arrangements, or if the emperor were to gain unforeseen new power that would enable him to reduce the princes and make himself master of German life. Both methods were tried at the beginnings of modern times.

CHAPTER 3

German Politics in the Sixteenth Century

✍ Population

IN THE YEARS AROUND 1500 Germany was the largest country in Europe, not only in area but also in population. All population figures for the sixteenth century—and, for that matter, for the seventeenth and most of the eighteenth—must be considered at best as critical estimates. It is assumed, however, that in the early sixteenth century France was more densely populated than Germany, probably at the rate of 3:2, but the German population, close to twenty million in size and settled over a wider area, outnumbered the French by about one fourth.

The soil of France was more fertile than that of Germany. Internal agrarian settlement in Germany had reached its natural limits by 1500. What was left of the vast woodlands of Germany, which had been cleared assiduously during the preceding five centuries, was unsuitable for agrarian cultivation. Not even modern technology has brought any great change in this respect. The remarkable expansion of German agricultural production in the nineteenth century was gained by intensified and scientific management rather than by the extension of the tilled acreage.

The German population, which continued to grow throughout the sixteenth century, was unevenly distributed over the Empire. Its density was greatest in the whole Rhine valley and in upper (south) Germany, less in Thuringia and Saxony, rather thin in the northwest, and weakest east of the Elbe. By 1500 the division of land in the south had already gone too far to permit an expansion of the peasant population, and the towns, though still adding to their industrial employment, could not fully absorb the new man power. Thus as early as the sixteenth century there appeared definite signs of relative overpopulation, especially in Alsace, Swabia, and Bavaria. A new industry, the formation of mercenary armies, solved the problem for the time being.

Germany possessed officially about 3,000 towns, but 2,800 did not have more than 1,000 inhabitants. They were merely prominent local places, depending for their livelihood on the surrounding countryside. These small communities were not producing for a distant market, since the size of their populations did not permit the division of labor or the development of skills required for the production of exports. Not even the towns of from 1,000 to 2,000 inhabitants, of which there were about 150, could have had a truly urban structure and influence. The remaining fifty communities were the centers of the urban civilization of Germany, so much admired by foreign visitors to the Empire. Of these, more than thirty had populations of between 2,000 and 10,000; only about fifteen had grown beyond this size, thereby becoming dominant centers.

In the thirteenth century Cologne was the greatest German metropolis, with a population of up to 60,000; by 1500 the number of inhabitants had fallen to under 40,000. By the early sixteenth century Augsburg had become the largest city in the Empire, approaching the 50,000 mark. Nürnberg, which grew more throughout the century than any other large German city, had more than 30,000 people in 1500, and about 40,000 in 1600. Magdeburg, its position on the Elbe comparable to that of Cologne on the Rhine, equaled Nürnberg in size. Strasbourg and Breslau were slightly smaller, while Erfurt and Lübeck were substantially behind these cities. Frankfurt on the Main, Ulm, and Regensburg had populations of about 15,000. The old cities on the upper Rhine—Mainz, Speyer, and Worms—had already unalterably declined, and less than 10,000 people were living within their walls. In contrast, it may be noted that Leipzig, at the beginning of the century still mainly the northeastern outpost of Nürnberg's trading system, grew, like Dresden, under the tutelage of the Saxon rulers, from under 5,000 to over 10,000 in the course of the century. Berlin, another territorial city, possessed in the early sixteenth century a population of 12,000.

✎ *Relative Strength of Princes, Prelates, Cities*

THE ACTUAL GOVERNMENT OF GERMANY was in the hands of less than 2,500 local and regional authorities. Among these were close to 2,000 imperial knights, who together owned less than 250 square miles of land. They did not recognize any overlord except the emperor but were not represented on the diet of the Empire. The list of assessments made by the diet of the Empire for certain taxes affords an idea of the comparative strength of the 50 ecclesiastical princes, 30 secular princes, over 100 counts, about 70 prelates, and 66 cities, though it must be borne in mind that at all times powerful people have the means to ease their own obligations and devolve their burdens upon the shoulders of the weak.

The archduke of Austria and the duke of Burgundy headed the list (*Matrikel*) with charges of 900 fl. (florin or gulden) each. The assessments of the next group, 600 fl. each, were far lower. This group consisted of the six electors of Mainz, Trier, Cologne, the Palatinate, Saxony, and Brandenburg, as well as the dukes of Bavaria, Württemberg, and Lorraine, and the landgrave of Hesse. In the category of 500 fl. were found the dukes of Saxony-Dresden, Pomerania, and Jülich-Cleves, the margrave of Brandenburg-Kulmbach, the archbishops of Magdeburg and Salzburg, and the bishop of Würzburg. Included among the greater princes, with assessments of between 300 and 450 fl., were the dukes of Mecklenburg and Brunswick-Lüneburg as well as the bishops of Bamberg, Münster, Liéges, and Utrecht. Few secular princes appeared in the 100–300 fl. bracket, but 13 bishops and 26 prelates were included— among them the imperial abbesses of Essen and Quedlinburg—as well as 14 imperial counts, for example those of East Friesland and Mansfeld. Three secular princes, 40 prelates, and over 100 counts were assessed under 100 fl.

Cologne, Nürnberg, and Ulm, with assessed payments of 600 fl., were the only imperial cities that measured up to the electors. Strasbourg and Lübeck, with 550 fl., and Augsburg, Frankfurt, and Metz, with 500 fl., were close followers. There were 10 other cities with payments of over 300 fl.; 40 others with payments of over 100 fl., and only a small number paid less than that. The list of tax assessments shows what great financial strength the German cities commanded. In general, foreign observers, including Niccolò Machiavelli, were profoundly impressed by the wealth of German resources, but they were also aware of the impossibility of employing these resources for common political ends on account of the internal disunity of the Empire.

✍ Recognition of the Need for Reform

THROUGHOUT THE FIFTEENTH CENTURY the Germans had clamored for a constitutional reform of the Empire. The smashing defeats at the hands of the Hussites, the political pressure from Charles the Bold on the western provinces, the fights among the territories and particularly among the princes and cities, the crying abuse of feuds for purposes of highway robbery by the lower nobility—these were only a few of the tribulations that kept alive the desire for a change of public conditions. The Councils of Constance and Basel, which had reformed the Church, seemed to many to be models for assemblies of the secular authorities that should deal with the reform of the Empire. During the fifteenth century one such organ had come into being on a more regular basis and had slowly evolved rules of procedure. The diet of the Empire (*Reichstag*), whose early history can be disregarded here, represented the estates of the Empire. It consisted of three curias. The first was formed by the electors, the second by the princes, and the third by the free imperial cities. In the council of princes the counts had two curial votes, the prelates one.

With the consent of the electors the emperor would call the diet, which in plenary session would listen to the propositions presented by him. Each curia would then deliberate separately, and after reaching agreement the electoral curia would consult with the curia of princes, finally both together with the cities. Whether the cities, in case of disagreement between the electors and princes, had the decisive vote, or whether their opinion was to be considered a mere counsel, was a controversial matter. The Peace of Westphalia of 1648 settled it in favor of the cities, but by that time the cities had become too weak to use the decisive vote for any important purpose.

The organization of the Imperial Diet shows that it was chiefly an instrument of the German princes led by the electors. The princes saw, in the lower nobility of the Empire, revolutionary elements that obstructed the steady growth of the territorial principalities, while they viewed the cities as their worst competitors. Thus, the princes kept the lower nobility out of the Imperial Diet, subordinated the counts and prelates to themselves in their own curia, and opposed the equal rank of the cities. The same ends were also sought by the princes in the movement for a reform of the Empire. They wanted to make their own position more secure by suppressing the lower nobility and by excluding the cities from participation in making far-reaching political decisions. In contrast, Emperor Frederick III and his successors saw no advantage in being separated entirely from contact with the lower estates, and this conflict of interests between Emperor and princes, which encumbered all the discussions of reform plans, was one of the major reasons for the largely negative outcome of the reform movement. Still, the fronts were not as tightly drawn and the issues not as clear-cut as might appear at first glance.

The marriage of Maximilian I to Mary of Burgundy and his successful military defense of the Burgundian heritage created a new political situation. The duchy of Burgundy itself was ceded to France, but the Netherlands and even the Franche-Comté were retained by Maximilian in the Peace of Senlis of 1493. So far the Habsburg rulers, with their eyes on the Danube and Moldau, had been unwilling to assume any obligations in western Germany and western Europe. Austria, on the contrary, had often played with France against the west German princes. It was obvious that French policy would always desire the return of the Franche-Comté and in general aim at moving the frontiers of France farther to the east. Consequently, Maximilian's acquisition of the former lands of Charles the Bold of Burgundy laid the foundation for the conflict of the houses of Habsburg and Valois which was to last for more than two hundred and fifty years. But during the reign of Maximilian the French kings directed their greatest efforts, not toward the north and northwest but toward the domination of Italy, which thereby became the proving ground for the modern system of European states.

Habsburg control of the Burgundian lands was advantageous for Germany in many respects, and imperial action against French rule over northern Italy would have deserved the full support of the German princes, but a deep gulf appeared between the emperor and the Empire. The formula *Kaiser und Reich,* once the proud motto of united strength, now became the expression of the contrast between the princes, claiming to represent the Empire, and the emperor, who was considered an outsider. The cleavage was not even superficially closed by the great popularity that Maximilian enjoyed among the German people. The contemporary Germans saw in him an ideal ruler and detected in him, "the last knight," many of the qualities of the legendary Frederick Barbarossa. Emperor Maximilian had much to recommend him. His aristocratic appearance and friendly manner inspired confidence. He proved himself to be a competent and brave soldier as well as an audacious hunter and mountaineer. Though not learned, he was a well-educated man, possessing great intellectual curiosity and artistic taste. His attitude toward the Church and religion was one of superficial devotion. The new Renaissance ideal of gaining immortality through winning glory by great deeds was the mainspring of his political actions, which he publicized widely in carefully styled manifestos.

Yet Maximilian's restless agility lacked clear and persistent objectives. This was not unusual among the statesmen of the period, but it was bound to be even more pronounced in the case of a monarch whose territories were widely scattered and characterized by disparate interests. Maximilian conceived of his task essentially as a dynastic enterprise. Though he always recommended his policies as tending to secure the greatness and welfare of the German nation, he was constantly motivated by a longing for the aggrandisement of the Habsburg dynasty, and always willing to abandon a German policy if an opportunity, however remote and even fantastic, appeared for the enlargement of the Habsburg possessions. Maximilian was successful in preparing the elevation of his grandson Charles to the throne of Spain, Naples, and Sicily through the marriage of his son, Philip the Fair, to Juana of Spain, and the elevation of his grandson Ferdinand to the thrones of Bohemia and Hungary.

> *Bella gerant alii, tu felix Austria nube*
> *Nam quae Mars aliis dat tibi dona Venus,*[1]

it was mockingly said of the nuptial diplomacy of the Habsburgs. And undoubtedly these achievements of Maximilian were more lasting than those of the wars he conducted to expand Habsburg rule.

It was the prevalent dynastic element in Maximilian's policy that made the princes suspicious and made constructive co-operation between them and the emperor impossible. There existed a general sentiment that the enforcement of internal peace in Germany, the defense of the Empire, and also a number of urgent economic policy problems could not be solved by the territorial authorities but called for action by the Empire. The feeling was strongest in the ecclesiastical principalities, which had fallen behind in the development of their internal political organizations. Regionally considered, the western and southwestern princes were most active in the movement for a reform of the Empire. To some extent it may be judged that the movement was a last attempt of the territories that had formed the heart of the medieval Empire to recapture some of the influence in Empire affairs which the young and strong territorial states in the east—Austria, Bavaria, Saxony, and Brandenburg—had acquired.

---

[1] Others may lead wars, you happy Austria marry,
The gifts that Mars gives others, you receive from Venus.

✍ The Imperial Cameral Tribunal, 1495

THE REFORM MOVEMENT found a leader in Berthold of Henneberg, archbishop of Mainz (1484–1504). A conservative ecclesiastical figure, this earnest and persistent imperial count could be called a conservative in politics as well. He was opposed to an active foreign policy as long as the Empire had not been consolidated internally. "Peace and Order" were his proclaimed aims, and in his opinion they could be realized only by the establishment of supreme imperial organs on a federal basis. Apart from improvements in the procedures of the diet of the Empire, the proclamation of the Eternal Peace and the founding of the Imperial Cameral Tribunal (*Reichskammergericht*) at the Imperial Diet of Worms in 1495 were the first concrete fruits of the reform movement. The Eternal Peace outlawed forever all personal feuds and enjoined the imperial estates to seek a settlement of conflicts by peaceful means.

For this purpose the Cameral Tribunal was created. It was a court of the Empire rather than of the emperor. The emperor appointed the chief justice, two presiding deputies, and two associate judges. The other twenty associate judges were nominated by the imperial estates; two by the emperor as the ruler of Austria and Burgundy; six by the German electors; and twelve by the other estates, which were grouped together in six "Circles of the Empire" (*Reichskreis*). Clearly the princes dominated the court. They financed the Tribunal and supervised its operations through regular visitations. The Tribunal had a great influence on German public life, in spite of the refusal of the large territories to permit appeal from their own courts to this court of the Empire. The fact that the Tribunal followed Roman law had a great effect upon the legal systems of the territories and thereby kept German juridical customs from falling completely apart. More immediately important: the Tribunal was a major element in stamping out, within a generation, feuds among the German estates.

It was originally planned that the funds for financing the Tribunal were to be derived from a general poll tax, the so-called Common Penny, which at the same time was to yield to the emperor the means for armed help. Naturally Emperor Maximilian was particularly anxious to see this direct tax introduced, as he would have liked to have a general military levy of men instituted. Both ideas, however, met with stubborn resistance on the part of the princes and cities. Neither wished the emperor to gain direct control of the actual raising of taxes and men within their own territories. Such grants would have given the emperor a power comparable to that of the French king and would have enabled him to disregard the liberties of the estates of the Empire. After a short and unsuccessful attempt at collection of the Common Penny and organization of an imperial army through the draft of every four hundredth man, the discussions returned to the creation of a general list of assessed contributions from the various estates. This *Matrikel* left the individual estates free to determine the method of tax collection and administration. It was the task of the emperors to raise the armed forces with the funds placed at their disposal.

During the early years of the sixteenth century a system slowly evolved under which the normal strength of the imperial army was computed at 20,000 men on foot and 4,000 horses. In 1521 the monthly pay of a foot soldier was fixed at 4 fl. and of a horseman at 12 fl.—or 128,000 fl. for the whole army. The cost was distributed among the estates according to a certain key. These "Roman Months," as the contributions were called—because the estates had granted them in the past to enable the emperors to gain the imperial crown in Rome—served in the future as the standard unit for all the money grants that the Imperial Diet might pass. The estates made regular payments only for maintaining the Imperial Cameral Tribunal, which was in their own interest, since it was so largely their own agency.

⌘ *The Imperial Governing Council, 1500*

BUT THE ESTATES FOUND it against their own interests to strengthen the monarchical authority of the emperor. In internal pacification as well as in matters of foreign policy the estates wanted to play an active role. Already the Diet of Worms of 1495 had planned to establish an Imperial Governing Council, a *Reichsregiment*, as it was named. But only the Diet of Augsburg of 1500 prevailed on Maximilian, who was just then in dire political straits, to accept such a federal organ. The Council consisted of the electors, of whom one was always to be present for a three-month turn, while the others would delegate a councilor. One secular and ecclesiastical prince also had to attend for a period of three months, in addition to one deputy from each of the six imperial "Circles," from Austria and Burgundy, from among the prelates and the counts. The imperial cities were to send two members. The Council was to be presided over by the emperor or by a deputy appointed by him.

The Imperial Governing Council claimed full authority in ruling the

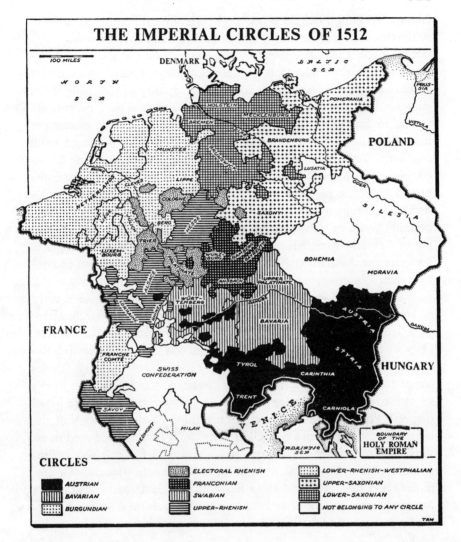

THE IMPERIAL CIRCLES OF 1512

Empire. Although certain procedural reservations were made in favor of the emperor, the Governing Council pretended to be able to act without his consent. A government by the estates took the place of monarchical rule by the emperor. It has been asserted that such a government would have been advantageous for the future unity of Germany if the emperor had co-operated with the group. But it would be entirely wrong to find fault only with the emperor. Actually the estates got more than they were prepared to shoulder. They never achieved a full representation of their own members on the Imperial Governing Council. Not even the electors, who could have dominated the Council, displayed eagerness to make it work. The Council lacked money and a staff of subordinate officials to impose its will throughout the Empire. Nothing could be done to interfere with the independent foreign policy of Emperor Maximilian or with his efforts to frustrate attempts to integrate the Austrian and Burgundian lands with the German territories under a common federal authority.

The Imperial Governing Council dissolved, a complete failure, early in 1502. But Maximilian's endeavor to strengthen the monarchical regime led to nothing in the non-Habsburg territories of the Empire. Only where he co-operated with the estates was he more successful. Between 1505 and 1512 he proposed to form four new Imperial Circles out of the Habsburg and the electoral territories, and add them to the six circles created earlier for the selection of members of the Imperial Cameral Tribunal and the Imperial Governing Council. In each of the ten circles a captain and a council of delegates was to be appointed to assume the enforcement of internal peace and of defense. It was an important scheme, but it was not put into operation in Maximilian's lifetime. The death of Archbishop Berthold of Mainz and Maximilian's foreign preoccupations after 1512 brought the reform movement practically to a standstill.

✎ The Election of Charles of Spain, 1519

THE PROBLEMS OF the constitutional order of the Empire came to the fore again with the approaching death of Emperor Maximilian. Since 1517 Maximilian had tried to gain the approval of the electors for the succession of his grandson, Charles of Spain. The negotiations begun by Maximilian and the struggle over the election after his death in January,

1519, raised fundamental issues not only of the German constitution but also of European politics. The attitude of the electors was also affected by the cash that the Habsburg government could distribute and by the show of military strength it displayed in Germany in 1519. Francis I of France coveted the imperial crown, and he had the support of Pope Leo X, who was rightly afraid that the ruler of Spain, Naples, Sicily, Burgundy, and Austria, if he assumed the imperial throne, would revive the universal aspirations of the medieval emperors. But the Italian and French agents did not arouse much enthusiasm for their candidate, while Charles' Burgundian and Austrian campaign managers knew how to sell the "young noble blood" as a German prince, though Charles was practically not even by blood a German.

Papal diplomacy realized its mistake in promoting Francis I and eventually tried to persuade the elector of Saxony, Frederick the Wise, to become a claimant to the imperial dignity. But Frederick and the other electors realized that only a prince who commanded large resources of his own could afford to accept the imperial position. The German electors and princes, however, were not willing to subordinate themselves to the future emperor, whatever his might would be. It was a sign of their feeling of security in their own consolidated power that, in spite of the protestation of the elector of Brandenburg, they all gave their vote on June 28, 1519, to Charles V. They also disregarded the fact that the third consecutive election of a Habsburg heir was bound to strengthen the claim of the hereditary character of the imperial office.

The German princes showed a greater personal deference to Charles V than had been seen in the dealings between the estates and the emperor in a long time. But they were far from making any substantial political concessions. They made Charles V accept a series of stipulations as preconditions of his election. This so-called "capitulation of election" aimed at the continuation of the existing constitutional order and at thwarting the use of the great foreign resources of the emperor for elevating himself above the German princes. He was held by the "capitulation" to rule the Empire in accordance with its laws and customs. The emperor was supposed to come to no major political decisions without consulting with the estates. German and Latin were to be considered the only official languages, and no foreigner was to be employed in German imperial offices. The emperor was not permitted to bring foreign troops into Germany or to employ the means of the Empire for the benefit of dynastic interests in his own territory.

✍ *The New Imperial Governing Council, 1522*

To INSURE THE EXECUTION of these and similar demands, Charles V had to concede the installation of a new Imperial Governing Council following the lines of the Council of 1500. Still, the young emperor, even before having attained full command of his wide kingdoms and lands, was not prepared to prejudice his monarchical pretensions. "It is not our mind and will to have many lords, but only one as it is the tradition of the sacred Empire," he proudly declared before the estates at the Diet of Worms in 1521. He tolerated an Imperial Governing Council only in times of his absence from Germany, when it was to act under the directorship of a chairman appointed by him.

It is possible that the distinction was more theoretical than practical, the more so since Charles V was not in Germany from 1521 to 1530. The Governing Council convening in Nürnberg in 1522 boldly tackled plans for a federal reform. An order for the enforcement of internal peace and of the judgments of the Imperial Cameral Tribunal was discussed. Financial problems—such as a common monetary system, and, in the field of revenue, the Common Penny and indirect income from an imperial customs system—were debated at length, and a permanent defense establishment was considered. But the Council suffered from the same weaknesses as its predecessor twenty years before. The lack of steady participation of the great princes and the division among princes and cities were further aggravated by religious conflict. By 1524 it was already obvious that the Governing Council would never be able to produce results; least of all could it create a federal authority independent of the emperor. After the return of Charles V to Germany in 1530, the quiet, official demise of the Council was hardly even noticed.

✍ *The Order of Imperial Execution, 1555*

A NEW PERIOD FOLLOWED, in which the emperor prepared to enhance his position as a monarchical ruler. The policy was now merged with Charles' fight against the Protestant heresy. The complete military defeat of the Protestant princes in 1547 seemed to lay the way open for a reform of the German constitution in a monarchical sense. But the hour was quickly lost, as will be seen later, and the old equilibrium between the emperor and the estates was restored. The Diet of Augsburg of 1555, by its official recognition of German Protestantism, blocked the rise of the monarchical power of the emperor as well as the evolution of strong federal organs. The only reform plan that the Diet of Augsburg turned into law, after it had been discussed for more than forty years, was the organization for the enforcement of the Eternal Peace and the execution of the sentences of the Cameral Tribunal.

Maximilian had already suggested entrusting these tasks to the Imperial Circles. In each of them a captain was to be appointed and imperial troops were to be placed at his disposal. The highest officer of the circle was conceived of as standing above the estates of the region and fulfilling his function in behalf of the Empire. But the "order of imperial execution" (*Reichsexecutionsordnung*) of 1555 recommended the appointment of the greatest secular prince in the circle as captain, who could only appeal to the individual estates for armed assistance. The circles were built exclusively on the estates, which formed a diet of the circle analogous to the Imperial Diet. In those regions of Germany in which strong territorial states could carry out the assigned actions, the new circle institutions never came fully to life. In the Rhineland, Swabia, and Franconia, where petty lords abounded, the circles were more significant as institutions that ameliorated the worst excesses of the regional fragmentation. They did not become imperial provinces, though they were given certain imperial functions, such as the supervision of the monetary system and, at the end of the century, the organization of military defense against the Turks. They also developed ambitions toward strengthening regional unity by drafting common police orders and supervising economic activities.

✍ *Evaluation of the Reform, 1495–1555*

THIS WAS THE END of the movement for the reform of the Empire which, particularly in its first and most important period, between 1495 and 1524, had been accompanied by considerable popular enthusiasm beyond the chancelleries. Neither a strong monarchical nor a strong federal power had come into being in the Empire. It can be said, however, that the reform activities, in spite of their meager practical results, halted the process of further dilapidation of the Empire, which seemed imminent in the fifteenth century. The few rules and institutions that were created did not enable Germany to engage in any sustained common political action but they gave her a passive pride of her peculiar political constitution. Peculiar it was, indeed. Jurists and political thinkers have never agreed as to whether the Empire should be classified as a monarchy, an aristocracy, or a mixed state. Nor did its few common institutions ever operate well. The Imperial Diet was an unwieldy body, which by itself could never have directed the affairs of the Empire, if for no other reason than because it could only assemble temporarily. If it granted the emperor matriculatory assistance, let us say for a campaign against the Turks, who was to insure the full payment of all the contributions from the estates? The Imperial Cameral Tribunal was, from its inception, overburdened with work, and the delay of lawsuits became worse and worse till the end of its existence in 1806. Even more damaging was the unwillingness of the powerful estates to tolerate appeals from their own courts to the Imperial Cameral Tribunal and a widespread refusal to accept judgments of the Tribunal by seeking revision from the Imperial Diet.

✍ The Swabian League

FOR ALL PRACTICAL PURPOSES the Holy Roman Empire had become at the beginnings of modern times a loose confederation of a large number of political entities of varying, and often negligible, internal and external strength. In international affairs the power of Germany could not assert itself, and it added to the might of the Habsburgs only to the extent that these rulers could tap some of the resources of the Empire. This they could do less through customary constitutional channels than through special political arrangements. The most important instrument of Habsburg policy in the Empire during the early sixteenth century was the Swabian League, a confederation of south German princes, cities, counts, and knights for the common defense of law and order. The maintenance of influence in upper Germany was a major object of Habsburg policy. Since the Swiss Confederation had defeated Maximilian's attempt, in the Swabian War of 1499–1500, to bring it back to the Empire, the Swabian League, though itself often suspected of separatist tendencies, was the only center of common action in southern Germany. And the land bridge between Tyrol and Burgundy was greatly needed. The Habsburgs held two outposts at the eastern and western banks of the upper Rhine, known as the *vorderösterreichische* lands (Anterior Austria). These dominions were the Breisgau, comprising the city of Freiburg and the region of the southern Black Forest, and the Sundgau in southern Alsace. But their strategic significance could be made fully effective only in conjunction with the neighboring territories. Thus there was active co-operation between the Habsburgs and the Swabian League, and it was a grievous loss when, at the end of the 1520's, religious conflict crippled the League.

Up to that time the Swabian League had been the mainstay of order in southern Germany. It achieved its greatest military triumph in 1519, when its armies occupied Württemberg, whose Duke Ulrich had tried by an audacious coup to seize the free city of Reutlingen. The duchy was placed under Habsburg administration, which continued for more than a decade—until in the days of the collapse of the League Duke Ulrich was brought back with the support of France and the Protestant German estates. The Swabian League also took a leading part in putting down the revolt of the imperial knights which Franz von Sickingen wanted to set off by his attack against the elector of Trier in 1523; and again in 1525 it was the League that crushed the revolution of the peasants in upper Germany.

There were also other reasons why southern Germany was of paramount importance to the Habsburgs. In addition to strategic considerations, the military and economic resources of the region counted uppermost. We shall confine our observations in this section to the military aspects.

✍ *The Revolution in Methods of Warfare*

THE REVOLUTION IN METHODS OF WARFARE which occurred in the late Middle Ages was a general European event. Technology did not by itself suddenly transform warfare in this period, as is often thought. It took many centuries to turn the early cannons into an effective field artillery, and the perfection of modern hand firearms was equally slow. Prior to the industrial age, startling inventions were rare, appearing only at long intervals.

During the Middle Ages military functions had been largely monopolized by a special class. The knight was deemed the ideal warrior and in return for his services was endowed with land and social rank. The conditions of natural economy made long absences from the estates impossible, and the king could call up his vassals annually only for a limited period of military service. With the disintegration of the old feudal system and the longer duration of campaigns, monetary stipends for the services of knights became common; knights came to be professional mercenaries on horseback.

A certain number of mercenary troops had existed all through the ages. They were to be found as guards of royal households or castles and at frontier posts. Towns, too, employed such forces for their normal security needs on a rather wide scale. It is known that in the Italian city-states the mercenary system prevailed. In Renaissance Italy warfare became an industry directed by the *condottieri*, military entrepreneurs, who often enough used their power for the overthrow of the republic they were supposed to defend. In Germany the use of mercenary troops increased during the fourteenth and fifteenth centuries, but the mercenary system was not general. The burghers were ready to man the walls themselves and even to accept occasional war duties outside the city. The knights were still considered to be the most powerful arm in land warfare.

Not bullets from modern guns but the primitive pikes of the Hussites and Swiss finally outdid horses on the battlefield. The victories of the Swiss peasant army over Charles the Bold in 1476 made infantry the "queen of battles" and ushered in the dawn of the new power of the disciplined mass. The Swiss did not excel in technology; their artillery was as poor as their cavalry. Their military prowess derived from the survival of an older social organization of Teutonic tribal life, which had been basically the order of relatively small groups of cattle raisers. Cattle raising remained the major Swiss industry. A large part of the country was still common property administered by the original village organization, in which political, social, economic, and military functions had been vested for many centuries. The pressure of overpopulation was felt by the Swiss early and acutely, since the mountains allowed only limited internal colonization. The Swiss found an outlet in becoming mercenary troops; such troops had been raised by their neighbors since the twelfth century. Many Swiss were used by the German emperors in their Italian wars, and groups of them continued to go to France, Germany, and Italy in the later Middle Ages. The Swiss acquired their military skill in foreign wars before, in the fourteenth century, they fought their own war of liberation from their old overlords, the Habsburgs.

The Swiss victories over the Burgundian knights' armies a century later not only revolutionized military tactics but also changed the internal character of states. The effect of the novel tactics was perhaps originally overrated. Horses were not in all circumstances useless against the Swiss array, as the shocked old school at first believed. The Swiss phalanx was not well adapted to subduing entrenchments, particularly if such positions were strengthened by artillery. But it took a good while to discover such countermeasures.

The military role of feudalism, which in the Middle Ages had decisively molded the whole structure of society, seemed doomed. Was it not time to fall back on the military levy of all classes, which no doubt would have had an equalizing influence on all social distinctions? A humanist like Machiavelli could argue that the Swiss battle order was a revival of the tactics of ancient Rome and that the Swiss communal spirit showed similarity to the republicanism of the Roman citizens who had formed the invincible legions. National armies were in his opinion the solution to the military problems of the age. Many fresh attempts were actually undertaken in Germany also to inject new life into the old Roman militia idea. Until the end of the Thirty Years' War, in 1648, a good many territorial princes vainly tried various schemes for the reactivation of the militia.

But the case of the Swiss was unique. They were not just peasants and townsfolk, but from the outset had in their ranks a considerable number of professional warriors who had served abroad. There existed as yet no training for warfare other than the actual pursuit of war itself. The sturdy and primitive mountaineers living closely together in their old communities could easily be fitted into a phalanx. Moreover, after their first successes as a group the Swiss found in soldiering a welcome outlet for their pent-up national energies and a golden opportunity for building up an industry. Except for the three years from 1512 to 1515, when they occupied Milan and seemed at the moment to have embarked upon empire building, war for them was, and remained, strictly an economic enterprise carried on abroad for profit.

In richer countries such as Germany people were unsuited to warfare of the new type, nor were they attracted to the military profession as a communal pursuit. In Germany, apart from some southern regions, overpopulation created no serious problems, and the growth of arts and industries held better prospects than war. The Swiss also had introduced a new ferocity into warfare. Losses in battle showed a sudden rise, and the unashamed cruelty of the fighting appalled contemporaries. The integrated members of town and country communities could not wish to enter into a world of such ruthlessness. Only the downtrodden, foot-loose, or adventurous could be induced to challenge fate.

It was not easy to see how such a medley could be welded into a disciplined body of men. The Swiss ruled themselves by councils, in war as in peace. No single general commanded the Swiss armies, but the captains of the individual units would go into a huddle before issuing the orders of the day. Unanimity was not always achieved, nor did the authority of the captains over their men always go unchallenged. But usually the Swiss bands held together, since the individual was not in the habit of wandering too far from the group. Swiss discipline, which was by no means perfect, was the natural outgrowth of ancient forms of communal life.

What had come to the Swiss as a heritage of their historical past and social conditions, other nations had to produce artificially by experiment and training. France could meet the demand for foot soldiers only by hiring the Swiss. Germany was the first country to emulate the Swiss model. Emperor Maximilian trained German mercenaries in Swiss tactics. The *Landsknechte*, as they were called, used social forms of the craft guilds to a large extent. The code of honor of the new German soldiers was that of a craft. The master exercised prerogatives of command but was not an absolute boss. Like journeymen in the old guilds, the soldiers exerted a strong influence on all operations, particularly on the maintenance of discipline among the troops. But in contrast to the Swiss, the position of commanders was greatly heightened.

The German *Landsknechte* were a success. Their first generation paid dearly for copying Swiss methods of warfare. The Swiss hated these impostors more than all their other adversaries, but the Germans soon became a match for them and, after the battle of Ravenna in 1512, won an edge over them. Machiavelli praised the Germans' fine stature in contrast to the small and unattractive appearance of the Swiss mountain folk. But the Germans gained superiority also by better leadership and discipline, which made new tactical developments possible and also strengthened the combined use of infantry, cavalry, and artillery. The *Landsknechte* made great progress in this direction under such military leaders as Georg von Frundsberg and Schärtlin von Burtenbach. It was in the period of transition from the age of chivalrous warfare to that of mercenary armies that members of the German nobility made a place for themselves in the new armies. The development of a distinct officer's career gave members of the old feudal classes their opportunity to securing a new social function, which in future days was to strengthen their political role as well. In Germany this was to last into the period of Hitler.

The growth of an officers' class was, accordingly, one of the institutions bequeathed by feudalism to the subsequent period, and among the noble officers many of the feudal ideas of honor and chivalry lived on. But quite apart from the distortion that the old ideas suffered in this transition, it should not be forgotten that feudalism as a fundamental principle of the military organization of society had lost its significance. The new noble officers exercised a technical function in a social order that depended on a moneyed economy. Still, the part played by noblemen in the development of modern armies was of decisive importance in maintaining a continuity of military tradition over the breach created by the Swiss military "revolution." The nonexistence of these feudal groups in Italy, or at least their weakness, is one of the major reasons for the relative inferiority of Italian troops.

From the early sixteenth century on, Germany could raise foot soldiers who were reckoned among the best troops of Europe. She also produced a good cavalry, though it was less distinguished than the French mounted troops. But in the late sixteenth century Germany trained the first pistol-armed horsemen, the black riders, or as the French called them, the *reîtres* or *pistoliers*. All through the century the German cities gave the manufacture and use of guns great attention.

The military potential of Germany was enormous, but it could not be mobilized for common national purposes. This was due not only to the political division of the Empire but also to the weakness of the territorial states. German soldiers soon served in many foreign armies. German political authorities could not inculcate in the *Landsknechte* national or patriotic loyalties, the less so since the princes themselves disregarded any national sentiments in their foreign policy and warfare.

CHAPTER 4

German Economic Life in the Sixteenth Century

✍ Effects of the Black Death

IN THE SECOND HALF of the fourteenth century the Black Death and other plagues wiped out large sections of the population all over Europe. The economic history of the next two centuries was overshadowed by these events. We must assume that Germany lost at least 20 per cent, and more probably 30 per cent, of her population. On the whole the pestilence mowed down the people in the towns more fiercely than those of the countryside. Still, many villages disappeared and cultivated land became waste. Migration to eastern Germany dropped to a trickle. Labor on the farms became scarce, the more so since the cities attracted the rural people and offered them freedom. Small wonder then that throughout the fifteenth century the peasants were able to improve their social position with regard to their lords.

But the peasants did not profit economically from their social advance, as the consumers of their produce had been decimated. Grain prices fell drastically and remained depressed till the middle of the sixteenth century. At the same time the prices for all the products of urban industry rose steadily. This viselike movement of prices narrowed the income not only of the peasant but also of the nobility, which during this same period had lost in addition its decisive place in military service. The slow rise of princely power in the territorial states was certainly not unconnected with the economic difficulties of the noblemen. Even more obvious was their loss, to the cities, of influence in public affairs.

In contrast to the Thirty Years' War, which devoured both men and goods, the Black Death of the fourteenth century did not destroy the assets held by the cities. These were accumulated by the groups of survivors. New fortunes were created and with them a high demand for consumers' goods and luxury articles, which stimulated crafts and industry. The cities attracted new population and entered upon a period of vast expansion of their commercial and industrial activities. They constituted, at least to the middle of the sixteenth century, the dynamic element in the economic life of Germany. In German history the age before and during the Reformation was more of a burghers' age than any other age before the nineteenth century. The civilization of the period grew and was molded largely by what happened in the cities. Even the territorial princes, developing their modern administration, took a clue from the cities and drafted many of their learned councilors from among the burgher class. After 1500 the prices of agricultural products began to rise and in the later part of the century they became very high. Simultaneously the expansive energies of the cities ebbed slowly. Thus in the second half of the century the economic position of both the peasants and landed noble lords became stabilized, but the nobility also consolidated its social and political power. The bourgeoisie exercised only a limited influence on German life in the seventeenth and eighteenth centuries.

ᴈᴑ The Transformation of Agriculture in "Old" Germany

BUT SIXTEENTH-CENTURY GERMANY, in spite of her prosperous cities, was a predominantly agrarian country. More than three quarters of the German people lived in the country, and even in the cities and towns many still practiced agriculture. The organization of agriculture and of agrarian society was different in the various regions of Germany. The sharpest contrast existed between the old Germany and the "colonial" Germany east of the Elbe. It was during this period that this division, which was to have profound consequences for the general history of modern Germany, hardened most drastically. But even within old Germany, to which we will direct our attention first, the transformation of agriculture which was caused by the agrarian crisis of the fifteenth century led to highly differentiated forms; this was to have a bearing on the social and political conditions of modern Germany.

Most of the land was owned by princes, by the Church, and by noblemen. Free and independent peasants survived into the modern age, particularly in Friesland, western Holstein, and lower Saxony, but also in Tyrol, in the Black Forest, and a few other places. Historians have been inclined to trace this freedom back to ancient Germanic times, but it is more likely that the peasants gained their freedom in the High Middle Ages as colonists who cleared the forests in difficult mountain areas or drained the sea marshes or swampy river lands. Not very large numbers were involved, and the free peasants did not determine the general course of agrarian history in Germany. It was everywhere dominated by the development of controls exercised by lords.

Three types of controls existed: control over land, over person and family, and over justice. The peasant could, therefore, have three different lords or, if one lord combined two or three of these authorities, two or only a single lord. The interplay of such traditions and forces was bound to produce a great variety of conditions. Five regions of old Germany can be distinguished according to the agrarian structure that prevailed in them till the end of the eighteenth century.

The first region to be considered is the northwest, that is, the land between the Rhine and the Elbe as far south as the Teutoburg Forest and the Harz Mountains. Here the landowners, aiming at the preservation of their property rights and at receiving the maximum rent from their holdings, succeeded in depriving the peasants of any personal rights in land. They rented the land, usually merging four of the older peasant holdings, to peasants who came to be called *Meiers*. These newly aggrandized peasants became freed from practically all the shackles of medieval bondage, but at the price of losing all hereditary rights. They could be removed from the land at the lord's pleasure. The new *Meier* tenure did not become prevalent all over the northwest; in the north around Bremen and Lüneburg, and particularly in Westphalia, medieval forms of land tenure were not so radically changed. The peasant retained an inheritable right of land use, but older forms of bondage also survived. In practice the differences in legal rights became rather negligible. Where bondage was not abolished, it was transformed into dues, and the tenure of *Meiers*, originally limited in time, became during the sixteenth century unlimited and hereditary unless the peasant failed in his contractual obligations.

The latter development might not have occurred if the judicial power had been in the hands of the landlords. In the fifteenth and sixteenth centuries the noblemen pressed for higher rents in order to maintain their own incomes. Moreover, with the decline of knightly military service they withdrew to their own country places, where they had usually maintained home farms of their own, normally not much larger in size than those of the *Meiers*. Now the interest in building a desmesne led to the eviction of peasants, as happened at the same time east of the

Elbe. But the princes, who had kept all or at least most of the judicial power in their hands and with it the means of interfering with local conditions, stopped this eviction. They wished to tax the peasants and consequently were opposed to their exploitation by the nobility. The policy of the princes promoted the undisturbed possession and finally the heritable nature of leases and tenures. In the seventeenth century the peasants' holdings were declared indivisible units.

Northwestern Germany was characterized by the continued existence of a large class of peasants holding sizable farms and enjoying stable conditions of rights and duties. But the creation of large peasants' estates made some peasants landless. In the regions of the *Meier* law these migrated to eastern Germany or to the cities or became *Kossates*, small landholders who had to work on the larger peasant estates to make a living. In Westphalia the peasants did not gain the same independence but remained under the former landlord to whom they paid dues. Without these dependent peasants the larger estates could not have been worked. These small peasants also carried on handicrafts and rural industries. In Westphalia these activities were extensive and produced textiles and metalwares that reached far beyond the local market.

Other forms of organization existed in the Germany of the left bank of the Rhine north of the Moselle. Here the early growth of towns and cities had dissolved the medieval structure more thoroughly than elsewhere. Many peasants had become simple leaseholders, but even the mass of the peasants held their land simply by the payment of regular dues to the landlord. Where personal servitude continued at all, it took the form of payment rather than subservience to the arbitrary will of a lord.

A third region of peculiar agrarian organization was the part of central Germany bounded by the Harz Mountains in the north, the Thuringian Forest and Erzgebirge in the south. Thuringia and Saxony were settled by colonists who either cleared woods or placed new land under the plow. A free tenure prevailed from the beginning and unfree peasants were few. No seignorial system ever developed fully. The absence of personal freedom was unknown. The obligations of the peasants were derived from their land holdings, irrespective of whether they took the form of dues or services.

Again conditions were different in (old) Bavaria and in the Austrian territories. There was a small group of proprietary peasants in Bavaria, but the bulk of the soil was owned by the Church—that is, by bishops, chapters, monasteries, church parishes—and by the nobility and territorial princes. Among the noblemen there were great lords with hundreds of farms as well as small lords with no more than a single farm. Many noblemen managed their own farms themselves. Hereditable tenure of land by the peasants was widespread, but lifetime tenures, terminating upon the death of the peasant or landlord, and temporary tenures were also common. The ecclesiastical owners of land were particularly stubborn in defense of their property rights through the continuance of lifetime and temporary tenures, which incidentally offered a chance to extract additional tributes at the time of the renewal of tenures. Monastic foundations had an even greater interest than many noblemen in maintaining farm cultures for their own immediate sustenance. They, therefore, clung firmly to the preservation of bondage. Bondsmen worked the desmesnes and played a part also in working the large peasant farms. The survival of bondage was facilitated by the judicial power, which had to some extent come into the possession of the secular and ecclesiastical nobility. But the territorial princes, the dukes, held judicial authority over half of the peasants; this helped to stem excesses of bondage.

The same chequered system as in Bavaria prevailed in most of the German sections of Austria. Better conditions, however, characterized Tyrol, which, like Thuringia and Saxony, was a country settled by the colonists who were attracted by the reward of freedom in exchange for the hard work of clearing mountainous woodland. In practice this amounted to a system of small dues and hereditary tenures. But around 1500 free tenures were actually on the increase, and the general conditions of the Tyrolese peasants were improved further. It was important that here in Tyrol the peasants were represented, in addition to the clergy, nobility, and towns, in the estates of the duchy—a rare case in Germany.

The last region with a separate structure was the populous southwest, broadly the region bound by the upper Rhine between Basel and Heidelberg and the Lech river. Here in Swabia and Rhenish Franconia many of Germany's rich cities had sprung up, but these lands had also been the basis of the imperial policy of the High Middle Ages. The southwest was beset with ecclesiastical dominions, small principalities, countships, and estates of imperial knights. Nowhere else in Germany did there emerge such a large number of territorial authorities who, within their mostly tiny orbits, claimed the plenitude of princely power. These lords did not care about landownership but about land rents and increased income from dues. The land tenures, mostly hereditary and with fixed rents, were so favorable to the peasant as to make him a virtual proprietor. He could divide his estate or sell it, and needed only the formal consent of the lord for these transactions. But the new "princes" or princelings who were the great landlords could advance their greedy claims by pointing to their public function, which, as a rule, rested on their old judicial power. The numerous obligations, as far as they had come down from seignorial days, were no longer justified by customary law but were enforced like tax payments, and since the new "sovereignty" tended to equalize all subjects, they were often extended to all the members of a community. Thus the petrified forms of a much older legal order were used to serve modern political objectives.

∽ Restlessness of the Peasants

IT WAS CLEAR that this system was too inflexible to fit the changing economic circumstances of future centuries, though in the early sixteenth century the economic situation of the southwestern peasants was, on the average, improved. But there were places where economic conditions deteriorated, either as a result of the shrinkage of farms in consequence of the division of family holdings, or as the outcome of the arbitrary oppression of individual lords. Still, although revolts in these territories served as triggers to launch larger revolts, the dissatisfaction and restlessness that could be sensed all over the countryside in the southwest was not so much economic as social and political in character. It was felt that a new order was coming into existence in which the peasant had no participation in proportion to the services he gave to the community. Actually his proprietary rights had become more secure, and since many of his personal obligations had been turned into dues, they no longer interfered with his personal life. But these dues, collected to assert the validity of claims for past services and duties, seemed unrelated to the new realities. They were felt to be obnoxious intrusions by authorities who were departing from customary law and imposing an unjust jurisdiction.

The peasants of this age were more completely dominated by traditionalist sentiment than any other class. They had often reacted against changes of legal controls with fierce rebellions. Thus in the fourteenth century the free Dithmarschen peasants in western Holstein had fought successfully against the encroachment of the neighboring princes and noblemen; in 1559 they finally had to accept the overlordship of the kings of Denmark and dukes of Holstein. The war that the Swiss waged in the fourteenth century against the Habsburgs was the peasant revolt of the most lasting consequences, since it was ultimately to lead to the creation of a new nation. The Swiss revolt, too, was originally a movement of resistance against the threats of a system governed by territorial princes. The unrest noticeable in southwestern Germany in the beginning of the sixteenth century was chiefly caused by a deep opposition to the innovations introduced by the new territorial princes. The first larger banding together of peasants for revolutionary purposes occurred in the *Bundschuh* movement of 1502–17, so called after the symbol chosen by its followers—the low shoe of the peasant that was bound with a string above the ankle, in contrast to the riding boots of the nobleman. Outbreaks of violence occurred and serious plots were discovered in many places in the upper Rhine region and Swabia.

In all these revolts there appeared expressions of memories of former days in which the peasants had enjoyed conditions of greater human dignity. The peasants rose to restore the "old law" that had been customary in the time of their fathers, before it had become undermined by the new territorial princes. It was in these peasant groups that there lingered on a vague nationalism of Empire, in which, incidentally, some of the small nobility joined. Constitutional reform and strengthening of the emperor's power was a popular demand in this heartland of the Holy Empire. But in the Middle Ages law was based not only upon custom but upon Christian commandment as well. The medieval Church had accepted the Stoic doctrine that men are created equal but had added that inequality in power and wealth had come into being as the penalty of original sin. This compromise between ancient natural law and Christian ideas had been challenged loudly in the later Middle Ages, and a new search for the "divine law" had begun. Was the law of God and the law of the fathers identical, or was the social order of the world to be rebuilt without regard to traditions and in following the Gospel literally understood? Traditionalist programs of restoration and radical projects of new construction were not far apart in the thinking of this period.

This explains the fact that, once Luther's preaching had challenged the religious and social teachings of the old Church, and had in addition made the secular power and property of the Church suspect, much larger masses could stand up against social and political abuses or even demand the realization of the "divine" or, as it was called now, "evangelical law." A considerable group of peasants faced the Church most concretely in the persons of the new overlords. The *Bundschuh* revolts, though spread over a wide area, produced only local outbursts, and a connection between them was maintained only through a small number of conspirators. These were easily suppressed. But it was another matter when in 1525 the majority of the peasants of Swabia and Franconia rose and managed to organize revolutionary armies numbering many tens of thousands. This time they found some leaders among the Protestant clerics and even among noblemen, and in their own ranks there were many *Landsknechte*. In their clearly defined demands, opposition to the territorial princes and nobility, together with the hope for a rebirth of the Empire and the Church, were as essential as the complaints about economic conditions. The great Peasants' War of 1525 was an uprising not only of desperately miserable people, but also of many who wanted, beyond their own security, a share in the order of society.

The Peasants' War, was, as we shall see later, more than a mere peasants' revolution, and it was not entirely confined to southwestern Germany. It was defeated by the princes and followed by bloody punishment and cruel reprisals. It is interesting, however, to note that the peasants had no difficulty in paying the money fines imposed on this occasion and, more important, that no change occurred in the general status of the peasants of old Germany. The Peasants' War blocked any attempt of the peasants to improve their social and political position. The impact of these events on the character of modern German history can hardly be overrated. The vast majority of the German people were cut off from any active participation in public affairs, and their own style of life was warped by the will and whims of other classes. The peasant remained a mere beast of burden. Sebastian Franck said in 1534 that the peasant was everybody's "foot-rag."

The attitude of the other classes toward the peasants was contemptuous and hostile. The urban classes, including the educated groups, were as inconsiderate as the noblemen. It was probably the burghers who made stupidity a by-word for the peasant in Germany. It was true that the peasants had little to recommend them. Frank described them as not being given to innocent piety but "wild, treacherous, and untamed." Yet the existence of such uncouthness and beastliness did not prove that it was an irredeemable curse. What freer social conditions could produce was shown by the culture of the Westphalian and the Frisian peasants, but they remained the exception. As a rule the peasants were mere objects of exploitation and manipulation. How completely the world of education was alienated from rural life could still be sensed in Karl Marx, to whom the villages were places beyond redemption. An agrarian existence seemed stupid to him. This social rift, perpetuated from the fifteenth century onward, was profound in most of old Germany and chilled the natural human relations among the members of the nation.

Economically, as has been said before, the situation of the peasants improved owing to rising prices in the latter part of the sixteenth century. Agriculture was carried on in primitive fashion. The three-field system generally prevailed and grain crops were planted almost exclusively. Poor harvests proved doubly calamitous in an age without potato and beet cultivation. Cattle breeding was limited. Few meadows were kept in Germany; forests, and in the fall, the empty fields, were used for grazing. As a result there was little manure, and this was only poorly utilized. Fertilizers were hardly known. Yields, therefore, were small. The increase in agricultural labor led to an intensification of cultivation in the course of the sixteenth century, but the Thirty Years' War destroyed this, as well as many older achievements of German rural society.

✑ The Transformation of Agriculture in "Colonial" Germany

AN EVEN WORSE SITUATION was brewing in the country east of the Elbe. During the High Middle Ages the colonist-peasants, coming from all parts of the Empire and beyond—from Flanders to lower Saxony, Swabia, or Franconia—had enjoyed special freedoms and privileges. At the same time the nobility, which had acted as the military arm in the crusading wars against the Slavs, had been defeated by the Christianized Slavs and superseded as a warrior class by the innovations in warfare. Frustrated in their bellicose exploits, the knights turned to the management of their own estates.

In the colonial settlement of eastern Germany the knights had usually received estates four to six times larger than the peasants' farms. But their incomes rested chiefly on dues and taxes. Originally they had not even been overly anxious to add to their own estates when peasant lands fell vacant owing to death or to migration to the towns. But after their military services had ended, they became agriculturists and agrarian entrepreneurs. From the early thirteenth century on, the eastern provinces of Germany had exported grain to western Germany, the Netherlands, and England. After 1500 rising prices and growing demand made this trade even more attractive. But the extension of landed property as such did not produce larger crops as long as labor was scarce, as was also capital for investment. Thus, the nobility sought not only to acquire peasants' lands but also to make the peasants lend their labor and tools to the working of the lord's demesne. It was of decisive importance that the nobility east of the Elbe had acquired—or was about to acquire —judicial power over the peasants. It was equally significant that in these territories many Slav bondsmen survived and their lesser state tended to serve as a model for detracting from the conditions of the German peasants. Nowhere were the territorial princes able for any length of time to interfere with the *Junkers*, as the members of the gentry in northeastern Germany were called, in their policy of making the peasants *gutsuntertänig*, that is, dependent on and subservient to their own large agrarian enterprises. The growth of these self-managed *Junker* estates (*Gutswirtschaft*) and the simultaneous extension of control over the peasants (*Gutsherrschaft*, in contrast to the west German and western European *Grundherrschaft*) was fully under way in the sixteenth century in Prussia, Pomerania, Mecklenburg, Brandenburg, Lusatia, and eastern Holstein. Only the Thirty Years' War was to bring this system to its sad conclusion. These "east-Elbian" *Junkers* have been said to be early representatives of modern capitalism. The desire for profit is, however, not confined to capitalism. Possibly their attempt at large-scale calculation displayed something of the new capitalistic temper. But their economic operations were based not on the employment of their own capital but rather that of the peasants—that is, their labor as well as their draft animals and plows. The economic position of the *Junkers* was built by political means, and the ruthless use of politics for economic ends remained typical of the *Junkers* to their demise in the twentieth century.

✍ The New Importance of Craft Guilds in the Cities

Cities had sprung up throughout Germany. During the High Middle Ages their function within the general economy had rested relatively more on trade than on industry. But the new situation caused by the population decline in the late fourteenth century led to a greater concentration of industry in the cities. With the renewed population growth in the fifteenth century, considerable expansion of both commercial and industrial activities became possible. The new importance of the craft guilds found expression in their pressure for representation in the city government, which led to many revolts and revolutions. Nowhere in Germany did the craft guilds become the rulers of the cities, but their members were in most places admitted to the charmed circle of the "better people" (*cives meliores*), as the old ruling families were called. The north German cities showed greater resistance to the admission of new social groups than did those of the south, but even in the latter area, differences existed, as for example between the conservative constitution of Nürnberg and the more liberal order of Augsburg.

Yet no sharp distinction should be drawn between aristocratic and democratic groups in these governments. Recently admitted members from the craft guilds soon became patricians themselves, eager to defend their special rank and interests. The republican governments of the German cities were regimes of the dominant economic groups, which were, however, sensitive to the demands and sentiments of the majority of the burghers. Internal strife, they knew, was a threat to the autonomy of the city, since it would invite intervention from the outside. The appearance of tyranny and corruption had to be avoided, while all aspects of the lives of the citizens had to be brought under control. There was little privacy in the narrowly built and overcrowded cities, and nothing escaped for long the watchful eyes of the town fathers. A major part of personal life came under authoritative regulation; the enforcement of laws was stringent, and the inculcation of a common spirit, all-pervasive. The princes, in their ambition for absolute power, could and did learn a great deal from these republics about the objectives and methods of government.

The most elementary prerequisite for the existence of all cities was the maintenance of their food supplies. The larger the city, the more it depended on food imports from distant parts. The free imperial cities acquired areas of the surrounding countryside, but these were never even remotely large enough to provide for their entire consumer demands. Cities located in areas of small farm surpluses—most of the cities of western and southern Germany—were particularly under the necessity of bringing in large quantities of food from distant places. Such supplies could easily fail, either because of bad harvests or war at the source, or war around the receiving city. The storing of grain in city granaries had to be adopted on a large scale as a public policy. But beyond the management of vital food provisions, the cities left the direction of economic activities to the guilds, though under the strictest supervision by the civic authorities. Prices and wages were set, and the domestic market was protected against foreign competition. In stark contrast to the far-flung economic connections and the special privileges that German merchants had acquired in foreign lands, the German city was treated as a closed economy. One may find in this a certain prelude to the mercantilistic policies of the future.

✎ *Trade with Foreign Countries*

THE GERMAN CITIES REACHED the peak of their productive energies in the half century between 1480 and 1530, though the expansion of the Hanseatic cities of the north had been arrested somewhat earlier. Broadly speaking, the grandiose unfolding of urban prosperity was favored by the new opportunities which arose during this period and which were ably grasped and diligently cultivated by this generation of German merchants and craftsmen. Because of chaotic conditions in France in the fifteenth century much of the northbound Mediterranean trade shifted from the old Rhone route to the passes of the eastern Alps. The disturbances in Italy since the end of the century had weakened, and finally wrecked, the supremacy of the Italians in long-distance trade. Europe's chronic deficit in its balance of trade with the Levant and the new power politics of the nations with their inflated military expenditures created a sharply increased demand for precious metal, of which the Empire was the greatest producer. Moreover, the development of the whole eastern belt of Europe from the Baltic to the middle Danube created markets for goods and sources of raw materials of greater dimensions than had existed in the High Middle Ages.

Within the system of Western economy, Germany around 1500 was in a central position, which it was to regain only once in the century after 1850. Germany's contacts with the Levant through Italy were old. Subsequently the Hanseatic towns, knitting together the northern economy from the Netherlands to the northeastern Baltic, had made the Scandinavian countries as well as Russia, Poland, and England their customers. In spite of her political divisions, Germany was economically more integrated in 1500 than would again be true for a long time. The traffic in goods, particularly in mass commodities, still moved mostly by water. But the German river system did not link together all the regions of Germany, not to mention the linking of Germany with the rest of Europe. A road system was called for, not only because of a parsimonious nature, but also because of the avarice of the lords and princes, who, through the imposition of tolls and dues, preyed upon the movement of commerce and might have choked it if no alternative transportation had been available. The roads were, of course, primitive, but Germany's roads were in a better state in the sixteenth century than in the century after 1648. A complete abolition of all internal customs would no doubt have given trade a tremendous boost, but such a course, discussed at length at the Imperial Diet of Worms in 1521 and in the years thereafter, failed, as did other reform projects of the Empire. The chaotic currency and money conditions were equally handicapping to German commerce.

Nevertheless, the amount of traffic was astounding. One can distinguish various basic transactions. The simplest form was the exchange of different types of foodstuffs. Fish, one of the great commodities of the sea towns, was traded in places as far away as northern Italy; it might be used to buy grain or wine, and also to pay for imports of raw materials. More important for the general economy was the exchange of both food and raw materials between the countries with sizable surpluses and those of high consumption and production. Finally, there was a vigorous exchange of half-finished and finished goods within all of Germany and between Germany and other countries. It was in this field that southern and western Germany were much more active than the north. The trade of the Hanseatic cities was not substantially an export of industrial products of their own; it was predominantly a trade in goods produced by others. Trade in grain was the main Hanseatic business, while the catching and distributing of herring was its own main contribution. Otherwise the Hanseatic cities had to rely largely on the industrial production of other regions to meet the balance of trade with countries from which they purchased not only grain but also many other raw materials.

✥ Commodities of German Trade

GERMAN TRADE OF THE EARLY SIXTEENTH CENTURY was already concerned with a great variety of commodities. Grain trade was, if not the most extensive, the most essential. Grain was needed to satisfy not only the hunger, but also the thirst, of the densely populated German regions. Grain meant bread, as well as cattle feed and meat. Furthermore, it was the base for beer, the most widely used beverage in an age which, rightly, distrusted water and milk, quite apart from the fact that the Germans loved to indulge in drinking. Closely related to the grain trade was the cattle trade, in which again the east was the chief supplier, although certain regions of northern Germany contributed heavily. Some major distributing centers developed. Cologne, for example, was the chief receiver and distributor in the Rhineland, not only of eastern grain, but also of cattle, which, in herds of many hundreds, were driven over the roads from Frisia. In an age of regular fasting, the distribution of fish assumed large proportions. In the ports of origin this helped to create a large cooperage industry, which worked also for the large beer trade, concentrated chiefly in northwestern Germany. Wine was shipped to distant places from the Rhine and Moselle, as well as from Alsace and Tyrol. It was even imported from France, Italy, Hungary, and Portugal. Honey, still the main sweetening stuff, was imported chiefly from Lithuania and Poland; the small amount of cane sugar from southern Italy and Sicily served as medicine rather than as an article of general consumption. Only later did the importation of cane sugar from the West Indies make it common. Spices, dyestuffs, and a small amount of colonial fruits continued to come from the Levant and the Mediterranean. The lumber trade was carried on actively. The rich forests of Germany provided not only for the manifold needs of Germany, including charcoal, but also for exports. In addition, the Hanseatic cities traded Baltic lumber in Flanders and England. Special wood of high quality, required for arms and for shipbuilding, was also brought from the Baltic.

The large trade in these products was augmented by the distribution and import of industrial raw materials. Wool and flax, to meet the needs of home production, were available in most places, but where textiles were made for wider markets and for exports, the raw materials had to be imported from England and the Netherlands, as well as from Spain and Hungary. The supplementary demand for flax was met in the east. Danzig, the largest port for the import of grain from Poland, also shipped large quantities of flax to southern Germany as well as to Scandinavia, the Netherlands, and England. Silk, which on a small scale was woven in Augsburg and in large quantities in Cologne, came from the Levant and Italy. Cotton, needed particularly by the large fustian industry of Ulm, was imported from Sicily and south Italy. However, foreign textiles found a large and growing market in Germany; this was particularly true of English fabrics. Among other products imported from the east by sea and by land, and sold again as raw or finished goods, were skins and furs. During the sixteenth century Leipzig was already well on its way to becoming the center of the continental fur trade. Germany's metal trade was based largely on her own production. Raw or half-finished metal and fabricated metal goods were valuable parts of national and international trade.

✍ Changes in the Role of the Guilds

THIS CONDENSED LIST OF TRADING GOODS indicates the extent to which by 1500 the local economy of even the small towns and villages was being integrated into a larger system of economic exchange which, through the cities, reached far beyond the national boundaries. It is easy to grasp the intimate and essential interrelation that existed between the industrial and commercial activities of this age, often called the "age of early capitalism." The organizational forms of production were of course deeply affected by the new conditions of trade. The regular organization of all industrial work was still the medieval guild. With functions transcending economic purposes, the guild was in many respects the projection of the natural form of human association, the family, into the life of society. It was the grouping of a number of large familylike groups, which not only worked together, but also lived under a single roof. The guilds were conceived of also as organs for the realization of a higher order. Most immediately they were members of their political community and were bound to exert their energies toward achieving its material and spiritual health. The materialistic aspects had to be judged and ordered by Christian ideals. Acquisitive desire was sinful and had to be transformed into the mere demand for earning enough to gain the necessities customary to one's station. Everybody was to work for his upkeep, but not at the expense of his fellow man or of his fellow class. There was a "just price" for all the products of labor, and the regulation of prices by the authorities was considered to be as normal as their rules for the spending habits of the various social classes. The Church sanctioned this order, and as she endeavored to lead all social organizations to a Christian life, the guilds naturally became agencies for the stimulation of prayer and worship. The many chapels and altars given by guilds testify to their consciousness of spiritual partnership.

While it is clear that the guilds were animated by the ideals of an organic Christian order, it is much more difficult to say how completely they managed to realize them. The sermons against the taking of interest, expounding an integral part of the Church's social theory, were clearly of little avail, and the laws against luxury were constantly broken. However there is no doubt but that the social and economic ideas prevalent in the craft guilds exercised great influence far into the modern world.

In the large cities of Germany ever more specialized guilds, each concentrating on the production of particular items, sprang into existence. This proliferation of guilds was caused by the growing volume of trade beyond the city. Specialization meant greater output and a stronger competitive position. But it was also a sign of the hardening of the guild system. The guilds could no longer absorb the growing mass of urban people. To rise from apprentice to master became difficult unless one married the master's widow or was born a master's child. A special class of journeymen came into being. Married journeymen, living outside the master's house, were not uncommon, and fraternal orders of journeymen were formed to cultivate a common spirit and common diversions, and to represent social interests of the group to the authorities. Other fissures appeared in the guild organization. Scarcity of work, which occurred readily in the overspecialized guilds, forced journeymen to look for additional employment, and they found it as toll collectors, gate wardens, hawkers, and in other uncertain jobs. The unity of life and productive work broke down. The journeymen became laborers.

✍ Spread of the Capitalist Organization of Business

WHILE IN THESE CASES the guild system proved inadequate to cope with the social and economic problems of its own members, it was threatened in its very existence by the spread of the capitalistic organization of business. A merchant or financier might commission guilds to produce goods in certain quantities and might even provide the raw materials and tools required. This separation of the producer from the market was increasingly carried a step further—by excluding the guild altogether and by farming work out directly to a group of individuals working at home. The merchant or financier superseded the craftsman as director of production.

The expansion of mining led to similar forms of organization. Originally mining had been carried on by small miners' companies under a concession from the territorial prince. In coal mining—which was pursued only in a small way though some Rhenish coal was exported as far as Flanders—this system continued. But the great demand for metals resulted in the introduction of expensive machinery in the mining and metallurgical industries. The princes did not have the funds needed for such development and were happy to give mining concessions to capitalists, who naturally planned to manage the mines with a view to the greatest possible profit. Among the German craftsmen, miners had enjoyed a certain social distinction, and they were famous the world over for their high skill. Charles V estimated in 1525 that 100,000 people in the Empire were employed in mining and metallurgy, and there is much evidence to support his statement. But at the moment when mining had its triumph, the miners themselves had lost their control over production and management, and become dependent on impersonal contractual arrangements. Inevitably, social tension was brewing. The revolt led by Thomas Münzer in 1525, which is usually considered merely as the central German eruption of the great Peasants' War of that year, drew much of its strength and character from the dissatisfaction of the Saxon and Thuringian miners and textile workers.

While the new economic conditions unsettled the traditional forms of the industrial order of the Middle Ages, even more startling changes appeared in the organization of commerce and finance. In earlier centuries merchants had formed companies. But usually these had been arranged on a temporary basis for bringing together the necessary capital or spreading the risk in specific business ventures. Such arrangements continued into the sixteenth century, and they remained typical of Hanseatic practices. In southern Germany standing companies had come into existence. The biggest one was founded by a large group of families in the imperial cities around the Lake of Constance, and its headquarters were in Ravensburg. During the fifteenth century few, if any, European trading firms measured up to this great Ravensburg Trading Company, which carried on trade in almost every commodity practically all over the continent. This company was in existence from 1380 to 1530. It was one of many such companies. But most others were in the hands of individual families, and in these companies operation might be shared by brothers, cousins, uncles, and other relatives. Such family firms often accepted capital from outsiders at a fixed rate of interest.

Firms of this sort were found in all southern German cities, small and large, but they flourished particularly in Augsburg and Nürnberg. Some of them, such as those of the Tuchers and Imhofs of Nürnberg, continued to concentrate on trading, but others added money changing, financial credit operations, and banking to their original business activities. The connecting link between all these enterprises lay in the metal trade and the mining industry. Augsburg became, in the last third of the fifteenth century, the main seat of the new companies, of which the houses of Fugger, Welser, and Höchstetter were the greatest among a cluster of lesser firms. The peak of their power was reached in the first three decades of the sixteenth century. The bankruptcy of the Höchstetters in 1528, though probably the consequence of reckless business practices, sounded the first major warning. After 1557 there was a rapid decline in the big commercial houses, which for two generations had been among the actual rulers not only of Germany but also of Europe and the world.

The Fugger family engaged in the textile industry and in trade. By 1400 it already belonged to the *Fondaco dei Tedesci,* the hall of German merchants in Venice, and was represented in other trading centers of the continent. During the century it made its first contacts with the Roman Curia and established connections with the Habsburgs through a loan to Emperor Frederick III. Jacob Fugger, "the Rich," led the house to its dazzling height. With cautious circumspection and bold vision he directed the firm from 1478 to his death in 1525—during the earlier years with his two elder brothers—and his golden touch made it by far the most prosperous business in existence. The vast variety of trading ventures engaged in by the Augsburg merchants defies description. The Augsburg merchants were quick to shift some of their activities to Lisbon, once the discovery of the sea route to East India turned much of the Oriental imports, particularly spices, from Venice to Portugal. When the Portuguese began to bring their goods to Antwerp, the Augsburgers built up their trading and banking position in the Netherland emporium. Thus the change of trade routes did not at first interfere with the expansion of Augsburg's trade, and in the beginning relations with the rulers of Spain seemed auspicious for German co-operation in the American trade.

The extension of the Fugger enterprises into the mining industry and metal trade was the most decisive cause of their fabulous rise. From the Habsburg princes they acquired concessions in the copper and silver mines of Tyrol. Later they proceeded to launch large operations in the copper fields of Neusohl in Hungary. They also acquired the Silesian gold mines in Reichenstein. Finally they received a lease on the quicksilver mines of Almaden from Charles V. They acquired further influence on metal production because of the discovery of the *Saiger* technique. This method of extracting silver from copper ore required large installations, thereby excluding the small entrepreneur. On this foundation the Fuggers erected their position in the metal trade, which was not a monopoly, but which served to lift them beyond their competitors. In an age that remained hungry for precious metals the output was greatly expanded. It has been estimated that central European production of silver and copper multiplied five times between 1460 and 1530.

ᔍ *Political Strength of the Large Commercial Houses*

CRUCIAL AS THE MINING INDUSTRY and metal trade were in the commercial empire building of the Fuggers, these interests tied the merchants to the chariot of the kings and princes, from whom they received their economic rights. The Hanseatic merchants, in an age that was just drawing to its close, carried on their trade within a political setting that they themselves were able to master. As late as 1522 the Hanse Towns, under Lübeck's leadership, could defeat King Christian II of Denmark and Norway, and keep him from annexing Sweden to his realm. In contrast, the south German merchants had no political power, nor did they ever try to acquire more political influence than was needed for their business transactions. But in this age merchants could not trade without the protection of the authorities, who in turn wanted to profit. Nowhere was this expressed more sharply than in the mining industry. The princes claimed mining as a regalian right, and though they did not have the capital to develop it, they knew that it was one of their main sources of income. They wished not only to share profits but even to anticipate them in the form of loans and credits. Thus, while mining was one of the chief sources of the great financial wealth of the Fuggers, it bound them to the political fortunes of the Habsburgs.

There is no doubt that Jacob Fugger, as well as his descendants, felt a genuine loyalty to the imperial house, and their devotion to the old Church was sincere. Jacob often enough gave prudent advice to Emperor Maximilian, but his delight about the successful conclusion of the marriage pact that was to bring the crowns of Hungary and Bohemia to the Habsburg dynasty was obviously heightened by the favorable prospects it opened to the Fugger interests. In counseling that the conflict with Poland over the Teutonic Order in Prussia be discontinued, he was clearly motivated by business reasons. Sentiment and cool reasoning were undoubtedly combined in Jacob Fugger's decision to secure the election of Charles V in 1519. The electors of the Holy Roman Empire demonstrated a brazen importunity in pressing for money. Francis I was generous in promises, but the electors demanded 850,000 fl., guaranteed by German financiers. It was then that the Fuggers offered

543,000 fl. and the Welsers 143,000 fl. When the balance of the sum was promised by some Italian bankers, the electors unanimously gave their votes to Charles V in St. Bartholomew's Church in Frankfurt on June 28, 1519.

This was only the prelude to much greater financial exertions. Without the moneyed wealth of the Fuggers the whole policy of the emperor would have been impossible. The tax revenues that Charles V could collect from his own dominions were too small to pay for the never-ending wars during his reign. As the Fugger loans piled up, it began to be doubtful whether they were economically sound. The concessions and privileges that the Fuggers received had, no doubt, originally been lucrative, but by 1525 the firm was already hesitant to take on the lease of the huge Spanish crown estates, the *Maestrazgos*, to settle old debts and to guarantee a new loan. The original balance between trade and credit business, on which the health of the firm largely depended, was slipping. The Fugger capital grew from 200,000 fl. in 1510 to 2,000,000 fl. in 1526 and reached its towering peak, of around 5,000,000 fl., in 1546. Still, the annual profit fluctuated greatly. Between 1511 and 1527 the average profit was more than 50 per cent; between 1534 and 1536, only 2⅕ per cent; between 1540 and 1546 it was 19 per cent; between 1547 and 1553 it was 5⅝ per cent. Thereafter a decline began, and it could only be covered by the surrender of capital.

The development of the Fugger business in later years was determined partly by the general historical changes that took place during the period after 1530 or 1550, about which more will be said in Chapter 9. The Fuggers had given, or had been compelled to give, vital hostages to the fortunes of high politics which they could not hope to control. In 1557 they suffered a terrible initial blow with the first default in payments by Philip of Spain. In a compromise settlement five years later they had to accept huge losses, and the same happened again at the time of the second Spanish bankruptcy in 1575. In spite of this, the Spanish government expected the financial assistance of the Fuggers in the war against the Netherlands. The third Spanish state bankruptcy, in 1607, finally ruined the firm, and the Fuggers of the next generation settled on their Swabian estates as imperial counts. The total losses suffered by the Fuggers because of Habsburg loans amounted to 9 million fl.

The history of the Welser family runs absolutely parallel to that of the Fuggers, though on a smaller scale. Among its most interesting, if not its most profitable, ventures was the attempt to gain a foothold in the Spanish colonies. In the early 1520's the Welsers ran ships from Antwerp to the West Indies, where they founded a base in San Domingo. In 1526 they received a charter from the Spanish crown for the exploitation of a colony, which, characteristically, they called "Little Venice," that is, Venezuela. They were permitted to open mines with German miners and granted the right to import 4,000 Negro slaves. Probably more than a thousand German colonists were brought over, but the results did not live up to expectations, and some bitter arguments started with the Spanish colonial administration over custom duties. After 1550 the first German colonial enterprise had to be written off.

Apart from the Fuggers and Welsers there were a large number of merchants of lesser capital but considerable distinction, not only in Augsburg and Nürnberg, but also in Ulm and Constance. Many of them went out of business in the second half of the century, and those who survived lost their place in international commerce. It did not matter whether these firms had cultivated French rather than Spanish business, since the French government defaulted equally on its payments. Nor were houses that had confined their activities to trade immune to decline. Before discussing the reasons for the general shrinkage of trade in the later sixteenth century, let us consider some aspects of the period of high prosperity.

✍ Growing Popular Interest in Economics

THE RISE OF THE BIG COMMERCIAL HOUSES led to the full separation of wholesalers and retailers. Whereas the former usually remained outside the guild organization, the latter joined local merchant guilds. But there remained traders of lower rank, hawkers and pedlars—a sign that the trade guilds, like the crafts, had become closed. This was one of the more lasting social consequences of the commercial boom of the age. The public did not seem to notice the growth of these semiproletarian groups, although it had raised a great outcry against another phenomenon that was not new but merely accentuated by the activities of the new international merchant class.

The drive against "monopolies"—a term that was at that time applied to monopolies, cartels, syndicates, and often to speculative buying— might as well have been directed against the traditional economic system. All the "regalian" rights had led to monopolies in the Middle Ages. The salt monopolies of the princes were particularly old, but metal monopolies were not much newer. At the beginning of the six-teenth century King Manuel of Portugal ruled over his monopoly in spices; the pope built up his alum monopoly, which was protected by sales cartels; the Duke of Prussia formed an amber monopoly; and Frederick the Wise tried to develop a monopolistic trade organization for pepper in Thuringia. Many of the monopolies that were derived from regalian rights fell into private hands, and there is no question but that cartels mushroomed under the conditions of the time, all at-tempting to increase prices even when they were not direct price car-tels but agreements on the volume of production or partition of mar-kets. But it could be argued that none of them succeeded in exclud-ing competition to the extent of affording control over the general price structure, and that, with high production costs and the likelihood of market interference by local authorities, such agreements were nec-essary in order to expand and stabilize production. No answer can be given to the problem, since the people of the times failed to discuss it in economic terms. Their complaint that monopolies and all the new busi-ness practices—which even outside of Germany were dubbed "fug-gery" (*Fuggerei*)—were responsible for the steep rise in the general price level, proved, as we shall see, to be untenable.

It was the first time in German history that the people discussed economics, which till then had been in the domain of scholastics. But like the latter, they approached economic questions as moral issues. They saw prices going up and felt the social and political changes, presumably brought about by new economic forces. It was easy then to jump to the conclusion that the big merchants must have caused the perversion of the traditional economic order. Since this had been in conformity with religious teaching and customs, it was believed that modern practices were obnoxious because they were immoral or plain "usury." The clamor was further swollen by Luther's demands for re-forms, and the imperial diets began legislating against monopolies. The Diet of Cologne of 1512 passed the first law against restraints of trade. In the "capitulation of election" of 1519 Charles V had to promise to limit the activities of the big merchants. Additional legislation against price cartels and speculative trading was passed by the diets of 1524, 1526, 1529, 1530, 1532, and 1541. But in spite of the obvious popular anger, nothing seems to have been achieved. When the fiscal of the Empire proceeded in 1523 against the Fuggers, Welsers, Höchstetters, and others, Charles V issued imperial letter patents exempting them from prosecution. In 1525 he issued a new law that made the drive against monopolies rather illusory. In their own granting of monopolies the territorial princes did not pay any attention to the legislation of the Empire. With the lesser prominence of the big merchants in the second half of the century, popular irritation about monopolies subsided. In the period of mercantilism, monopolies appeared in a new form.

✍ *The Rise in Prices*

THE RISE IN PRICES during the sixteenth century occurred throughout Europe. Prices in Germany rose to the end of the century by about 300 per cent. The movement was not advancing on an even front. Agrarian prices rose only after 1525, and there remained at all times substantial variations among different cities. The most obvious cause was the vast increase in coined money, made possible by the production of metals from the German mines. Between 1493 and 1520, the annual production of silver was 35,100 kilograms in the Empire, chiefly in Saxony, Bohemia, Tyrol, and Alsace, as compared with 10,000 kg. in the rest of Europe. Between 1521 and 1544 the figures were 50,000 kg. and 10,500 kg. respectively, but the new American production amounted to 13,300 kg. The next fifteen years yielded 53,200 in Germany; 11,500 in the rest of Europe; and 199,200 kg. in America. Thereafter American silver production rose fast and by 1581 was beyond the 300,000 mark, but during this same period many German mines began to give out and only 21,400 kg. were manufactured annually in Germany between 1601 and 1620.

It is impossible to say how much of the silver that was mined found its way into the mints. We may safely assume, however, that a substantial part did, and that its inflationary impact was further enhanced by the expansion of uncoined money in the form of credit notes. The relation between the amount of money in circulation and prices remained hidden in the sixteenth century. Even after Jean Bodin, in 1568, put his finger on the connection, it was a long time before it was generally accepted as a theory. We shall no doubt be inclined to accept it as a reasonable explanation if properly qualified. Nevertheless it is difficult to see why grain prices finally should have risen much higher in Germany than in France or England. Apparently the national product, particularly after 1550, did not expand sufficiently to take care of a growing population, and consequently the living standard of the masses declined. Moreover, with a large population in the countryside, a smaller farm surplus had to feed a larger urban population. In this situation prices for agrarian products were bound to increase faster than those for industrial commodities. A further consequence was the fall of industrial wages. How great the actual decline was is difficult to determine. But it is clear that there was not only a time lag in the adjustment of nominal and real wages, characteristic of inflationary periods, but also a leveling down of real wages, which continued into the period of the Thirty Years' War. Some of the pressures operating can be discerned in the closing of the guilds and the growth of the commission business with its employment of cheaper labor.

✎ *The Decline of Germany's Foreign Trade*

IN THESE DEVELOPMENTS the beginning of the hardening of the arteries of German economic life can be diagnosed. The standstill of economic productivity after 1550 was not entirely due to the changes in economic geography, or to the political forces abroad, which the German merchant could no longer overcome, but also to a weaker sense of enterprise. Both in the south and in the north there were signs of an inability to adopt new mercantile practices and to give up old privileges which could not be defended by the Germans and only provoked resistance among the Hanse's customers, driving them into the arms of competitors. Greater advantage could have been taken of the influx of religious refugees from western Europe and Italy to develop new industries, for many of them were skilled in arts that were not as well developed in Germany as elsewhere. But practically everywhere the cities were too conservative and too parochial to bother with aliens. The new international situation, however, would probably have overtaxed the strength of an even more energetic generation than the one living in the later part of the sixteenth century.

The evolution of "early capitalism" in Germany after 1500 took place at a time when the progress of the Turks and the discovery of the sea route to East India had already revolutionized Mediterranean commerce. The eastern Mediterranean and Venice lost immediately in importance, while Portugal and, after the opening of the West Indies, Spain and the western Mediterranean became the strategic trading areas. But simultaneously France came to the fore, and after the conclusion of its alliance with Turkey in 1535–36, it dominated the Levantine and north African trade. We have already seen how successfully the Germans had shifted their business contacts toward southwestern Europe early in the century, but that developments worked against them after

1550. The Turkish advance into Hungary broke the trade with the lower Danube basin which could have been considerably expanded in time.

But additional losses were suffered in the northeast, north, and northwest. The Hanseatic League was most immediately shaken by them, though events in the Netherlands had a direct reaction on southern Germany as well. During the High Middle Ages the northern German cities had enjoyed the advantage for their trade of wide regions, rich in raw materials but poor in industrial and commercial development. The rulers of these non-German regions in the north and northeast had been anxious to obtain the personal profits that the merchants offered, and had been too weak to oppose exploitation of their countries. The threat of an abortive Scandinavian unification had brought the north German cities together in the Hanseatic League during the late fourteenth century. For more than a century the Hanse proved a powerful instrument of further economic expansion and colonialist policy. Built on its supremacy in the Baltic and Scandinavian world, the League made itself an imposing force in the foreign trade of England and the Netherlands. Actually the Hanseatic merchants entered even the Iberian and Mediterranean trade.

It was unlikely that the open field in the north would continue to be theirs indefinitely, or even that England and the Netherlands would permanently accept an unequal status. As a matter of fact, the English had made a strong bid to enter the Baltic trade as early as the fifteenth century. But Edward IV renewed in 1474 the old privileges of the Hanse without insisting upon special rights for English merchants in the Baltic. The English exporters, eager to gain full profits from English cloth manufacture, were compelled to confine their intensive commerce to the Netherlands. The corporation of the Merchant Adventurers, spearheading this drive, made Antwerp its base.

In the Netherlands, Bruges had served as the trading center of the League. The highly developed industrial cities of Flanders were satisfied to leave the import and export trade in German hands. Though Bruges itself was not a member of the League, the Hanse boasted of extraordinary privileges in that city. But the seaway to Bruges silted up during the fifteenth century, and Antwerp became the great port instead. When the League belatedly opened its offices in Antwerp, the Scheldt city was not willing to grant it special privileges. Antwerp was set on winning commerce from everyone and from everywhere. It gave merchants unprecedented freedom from restrictions and thereby attracted the Italians, Portuguese, south Germans, and English. Early in the sixteenth century Antwerp became the greatest commercial center, as it had the first modern exchange. But while the Hanseatic merchants had to meet strong competition in Antwerp, the Scheldt port did not enter upon the old hunting grounds of the League in the north and the Baltic. Antwerp citizens lived on brokerage in the widest sense.

But the Dutch in the Rhine estuary, depending on eastern grain, even on eastern wood, hemp, and tar for shipbuilding, were early driven out to sea to make a living. When the herring shoals discontinued their appearances in the Baltic in the second half of the fifteenth century and spawned off the coast of Norway, they gained a great advantage over the Germans in fishing. But the Dutch ships began to invade the Baltic as well. Probably all through the century the Dutch served in the Baltic more as sailors than as traders. They were welcomed particularly by those Hanseatic cities, such as Reval or Danzig, that had to ship many bulky products. By about 1500 the Dutch carrier trade in the Baltic had already surpassed Hanseatic shipping in number of ships, though not necessarily in amount of goods carried.

These events showed that the Hanseatic League could not close its ranks as effectively as formerly. The "Wendish" cities, as the group around Lübeck, Hamburg, Wismar, and Rostock was called, could not always rely on the support of the other League members against Denmark, although the Danish kings, through their control of the Sound, had the League literally by its throat. Reval and Riga were apprehensive about relations with Russia; the Westphalian cities, such as Dortmund, Soest, Herford, or Münster, about those with the Netherlands. Lübeck's leadership was often challenged, and it was further weakened by internal tension. The patriciate, worried by the common people, often looked to the Danish king and the Holstein nobility for protection. The whole League concept was placed in jeopardy by the magnetic pull of the new regional forces. The Netherlands were still in the Holy Roman Empire, but it was the deliberate policy of Charles V to keep them as separate as possible from the German Empire. Charles also did his best to further the commercial interests of this wealthiest of his domains. But the "Wendish" cities were too far removed geographically, and, after turning Protestant, also ideologically, to give special concern to the emperor. As early as 1512 the Dutch had acquired free passage for their traders through the Danish Sound. Twenty years later Lübeck regained her own privileges, but in 1544 Charles V saw to it that the Sound was opened to the Dutch. The toll register of the Sound showed that around 1500 the ratio of German to Dutch ships was 40 to 51; around 1600, it was 17.5 to 70.

The advent of the Dutch to the Baltic gave the people of that region the chance to wreck the Hanseatic trade monopoly in the Baltic. In 1499 Czar Ivan III closed the St. Peter's court, the commercial settlement of the Hanse in Novgorod. It was temporarily reopened a few years later, but the Russian trade of the League did not recover from the attack. Soon thereafter national resistance to the Hanse stiffened in all the Scandinavian countries. Sweden, under Gustavus Vasa, began a systematic development of her own economy and imposed heavy duties on Hanseatic goods. With the building of a Swedish navy was laid the foundation of power that would ultimately lead to the attempt to bring the southern shore of the Baltic under Swedish control and thus win the *dominium maris Baltici*. Denmark waited longer, since her Norwegian dependencies were still more dependent on the deliveries and purchases of the League. But the intensification of Norwegian-Dutch trade brought the end. In 1560 the Hanseatic center in Bergen was placed under Norwegian administration.

The last country to deprive the Hanseatic League of her old privileges was England. The Merchant Adventurers tried to extend their trading bases on the Continent, and also to whittle down the privileges of the Germans in England. In 1556 the Hanseatic merchants lost those privileges in England that they had enjoyed above Englishmen; in 1579 they were classified among the foreign merchants. But the struggle between the Merchant Adventurers and the Hanse was fought at the same time on the German side. The English merchants demanded reciprocity in Germany; this meant the right to maintain commercial establishments and staples in the German cities. Emden accepted them in 1564. Then Hamburg, in a jealous and acquisitive mood, trespassed and invited the English in 1567, though only for a period of ten years. When, at the instigation of the other Hanseatic cities, the Imperial Diet forbade the renewal of the arrangement and Hamburg complied, the English went back to Emden, and in the following years English traders swarmed over Germany, offering their fine English cloth.

These were the years when the whole economic scene was thrown into chaos by the fall of Antwerp to its Spanish beleaguerers, with the subsequent sack of this commercial metropolis. German losses from the disaster were great, and all German trade connections with Brabant and Antwerp were broken. German commercial groups were divided as to whether the situation made stern action against the English intruders more urgent or whether it would be advantageous to do business with them. The Imperial Diet of 1582 demanded the expulsion of the English from the Empire, but little was done to execute the ruling. Emden, the most immediate neighbor of Holland, could not easily be coerced. Thus Queen Elizabeth could close the Hanseatic center, the Steelyard in London, in August, 1589. When the Empire finally issued a general order for the expulsion of the English merchants in 1597, the English government replied with the exclusion of traders from their island.

But the German edict was hardly enforceable, since too many Germans were eager to deal with the foreigners. In 1607 the emperor himself departed from the law by granting to Stade, a small town in the Elbe estuary, the right to have an English staple. Hamburg was truly alarmed. The latter city, which in the Middle Ages had not belonged to the first rank of German or Hanseatic cities, had made great progress all through the century. Beer trade and the export of Brandenburg grain, which reached the port over the Havel and Elbe rivers, had been important items in the Hamburg trade list, but the new significance that trade along the Atlantic coast assumed made growth in volume and variety of goods possible. During the Dutch-Spanish War, Hamburg as a neutral had carried much of the exports from the Iberian peninsula to the north. But with the end of the war this opportunity had passed, and Hamburg eagerly welcomed the Merchant Adventurers.

When the English returned to Hamburg in 1611, they received privileges that raised them not only above other foreign merchants but also above the local merchants, placing them in a position similar to that which Hanseatic merchants had formerly enjoyed in England. The monopolistic privileges from which the Hanse had profited in the first hundred and fifty years of its existence were, no doubt, bound to become dead letters once the Baltic region developed national powers and national commercial classes. But if even reciprocity was lost, this was due to the fact that the German cities were divided among themselves, had no support from a national state, and were also separated from the new territorial states. To this extent political forces had a decisive impact on the disastrous changes in the international position of German trade. The often-heard contention that Germany's commerce was wrecked by the discovery of America and the growth of western trade across the Atlantic does not carry conviction. Except for Spanish silver, trade on the high seas did not for two centuries bring imports of vital significance. The sixteenth- and seventeenth-century expansion in the volume of international trade took place on the seas that break upon German shores.

✎ *The Rise of Certain Cities to a New Importance*

BY 1600 GERMANY WAS IRREVOCABLY on the way to becoming an economic inland realm. The Hanseatic League, less than a shadow of its former self, lingered on till 1669, when it held its last diet. Of its sea cities, only Danzig and Hamburg demonstrated a continuing capacity for growth. Danzig remained for a long period the greatest grain port, but German merchants handled chiefly the harvests of Poland, and grain left the Vistula in Dutch bottoms. The mainstay of Hamburg's position was its service to English and Dutch trade. But Hamburg also systematically built up its commercial relations with the rest of Germany. As early as 1558 an exchange had been founded. It was followed in 1619 by a bank, which enabled the Elbe city to play an important role in the history of German currencies. (The modern German money unit, the "mark" of 1873, must be traced back to Hamburg.) Hamburg was liberal in the admission of foreigners. She took the Jews expelled from Portugal and the Lutherans from the Netherlands; this helped both her international trade connections and her home production.

Among the inland cities, the commerce of the Rhenish cities was particularly damaged. With the fall of Antwerp in 1585 communications with the Scheldt were broken, not to be restored till 1792. The Rhine estuary was in the hands of the Dutch, who thereafter controlled Rhenish commerce. Cologne, rigid in her admission policies for social and religious reasons, sank to a provincial level. Cologne was confined to regional trade on a commission basis and to carrier services. The development of textile and other industries, which the Protestant refugees from Flanders and Brabant might have brought to the old city, went to smaller places, such as Krefeld, and to localities in what was to become the modern Ruhr district.

Frankfurt could attract a great deal of the trade in commodities that had been transacted in Antwerp. In the course of the seventeenth century Frankfurt became firmly tied to Amsterdam, but its magnificent geographical location made the city an ideal distributing point for a large area of central Europe. Its trade fairs were great events, and it became an important money market. Its internal administration was, in terms of the age, tolerant toward Jews and gave refuge to the Protestants from the Netherlands. Leipzig, the other developing inland center of German trade, was not as generous in its normal practices, but during its large spring and autumn fairs every visiting merchant had equal rights with the Leipzigers. Unlike the Hanseatic cities and Frankfurt, Leipzig was not a free city. It was the first "territorial" city to reach prominence; it was favored by the good administration that Saxony enjoyed in the later half of the sixteenth century and by the silver-mining in neighboring Freiberg, where the mines, in contrast to all the other German metal mines, only then reached their highest output. But Leipzig never became an eminent banking center.

In spite of all the sure signs of economic decline between 1550 and 1620, for which the rise of Hamburg, Frankfurt, Leipzig, and Danzig could not compensate, the period was not one of poverty and dearth. Although the giant fortunes were lost, much of the accumulated wealth remained in the hands of the surviving families. Many of the proudest town houses and halls, guild centers and residences, were created in this age. These structures reveal the attitude of a generation of heirs more apt to spend gracefully than to acquire laboriously. Certainly their properties were standing on the books higher than their true value warranted. Yet in those generally peaceful days there was still much well-being among the rich classes. If the Hanseatic merchants drew their balance, they could still find, even at the threshold of the seventeenth century, that their shipping and the volume of their trade was increasing. Commerce in the Baltic multiplied seven times during the sixteenth century; this gave the Germans a chance to hold their own or to do a little better in absolute figures. No German ship entered the Mediterranean after 1609, but though the number of Dutch ships dwarfed that of German vessels, German shipping was larger than English shipping up to the days of Cromwell. It was the Thirty Years' War that turned the steady decline of German shipping into a complete collapse, and through the annihilation of German capital and assets made necessary the subsequent launching of a restoration under new auspices and with new methods.

It was one of the national misfortunes that most of the capital formation of the sixteenth century went into consumption rather than investment. The large capital resources of Augsburg were largely deflected to drive the bloody mills of power politics, and no new opportunities for an expansion of industrial productivity were found in the later half of the century. An intensification of the national economy with a view to strengthening the home market might theoretically have been advisable. But this again would have required greater political unity, of which even less existed after 1555 than before. Thus all the great achievements of German economic history, created by the burghers, ended in failure.

CHAPTER 5

The Church, Religion, and Cultural Life on the Eve of the Reformation

✍ *Religious Tradition of the Church*

IN 1500 THE ROMAN CHURCH had proclaimed a jubilee indulgence, and from all corners of the Western world people had gone to Rome to gain comfort for their souls. Among the pilgrims Germans had been very numerous, for the religious authority of the Church, which had nursed ·German thinking from barbarity to civilization during a full millennium, was unbroken in Germany, where not only were the fundamental principles of religion unchallenged but also where the Church's political power was more far-reaching than in any other country. This pilgrimage ironically began the century in which the institutions and ideas of the Roman Church were to come close to extinction in Germany, eventually to survive only with great difficulty in about half of the Empire, not to speak of other countries which, as a consequence of the German revolt, were totally or partially lost to the Roman Church. The actual catholicity of the Church has been challenged ever since. Soon there were competing and warring churches; no longer did a common ecclesiastical roof cover Western Christendom.

Catholicity had had a meaning not only in space but also in time; it had meant the continuous tradition of all the generations. But the word was still used to describe other dimensions. The militant church on earth was united with the triumphant church in heaven. And closely related to this metaphysical aspect was its general philosophical application. The Church was believed to preserve the divine truth, able to absorb everything good and beautiful, and to give it a harmonious and wise order. The universalism of the Roman Church was grounded in belief in the divine nature of creation and in God's revelation manifesting itself in the totality of life. Roman Catholicism has often been described as a *complexio oppositorum*. The Church, in its grandiose career of missionizing among the Jews and pagans, displayed no reluctance to assimilate religious forms from Jewish ritualism, Hellenistic mystery cults, asceticism, mysticism, and Germanic folklore. For the demonstration of its doctrine, ancient philosophy, Platonism, Aristotelianism, and Stoicism had provided the intellectual molds. For the development of its institutions, Roman law was absorbed, as was Roman statecraft for the practical conduct of the militant Church.

The Church's capacity for incorporating these seemingly disparate forces explains its strength and its dangers. It could speak to all races and to people in all stages of spiritual and intellectual development, but it also had to accept ideas and practices incompatible with the highest Christian mission, or at least likely to deflect the eyes of her members from the supreme truth. Needless to say, the Church was by no means arbitrarily adopting extraneous elements. It had condemned many a heretic movement and learned in such crises to define the substance of its own doctrine more distinctly than before. But the Church had equally rejected every attempt to question its authority in making the choice between admission and exclusion of ideas, and in setting the key of the harmony that would combine its manifold aspirations. The latter consideration always determined to some extent the response of the Church to the reform movements aimed at leading the Church back to its major Christian function, which arose in quick succession in its own ranks.

The Roman Church handed to the Latin-Germanic peoples of the Middle Ages the cultural synthesis, combining Jewish-Christian and Greco-Roman forms and forces, which had been fused in the first five Christian centuries, and which had found its greatest expression in the figure and work of St. Augustine. His thought and religion were too profound and comprehensive to be directly carried forward by the lesser theologians and church leaders who followed him. Still, his personality towered above the centuries of the Middle Ages as did no other. Both the internal and external history of the Church were deeply affected by the seeds he had planted, while there remained on the other hand Augustinian ideas which, because unfulfilled, acted as a stimulus of criticism. Petrarch, the leader of the Italian Renaissance,

Erasmus, and other humanists, as well as Luther, could find in St. Augustine encouragement for their opposition to scholasticism.

The creation of the fundamental Christian doctrinal system belonged to the ancient period. The medieval Church promulgated formally only one additional dogma, that of transubstantiation (1215). The basic character of the ecclesiastical organization was also settled before the destruction of the Roman Empire, but the Church had to cope thereafter with an entirely different political and social reality. With the disappearance of the Roman state and of the remnants of an autonomous classical education, the Church became the only treasure house of higher cultural life in a primitive world, and the model of strong political and social integration. Technology, art, education, and scholarship were preserved in the monasteries, and the administrative capacities of ecclesiastical officialdom were vastly superior to the loose and uncontrollable feudalistic methods.

✎ Political Influence of the Church

THUS THE ROMAN CHURCH was inevitably drawn into the political world. It gave aid to the growth of the new states that merged from the tribal era, and lent a hand in all fields of public endeavor. In return, the secular rulers led their peoples into the Church and supported its religious work. State and Church merged into a single commonwealth, the *respublica Christiana*. One should probably not use the term "state" with reference to the medieval political forces, since the modern state is so largely characterized by its autonomy and sovereignty. Medieval kingship was, however, bound by its moral duties to the Church and religion, while the Church recognized and supported the social order and the execution of a ruler's work. The concept of the *respublica Christiana*, which exercised an influence on Western thought and institutions well into the seventeenth century, assumed the unity of the religious and political objectives of society, which were one and the same, since logically membership in the Church was a prerequisite of any civic right.

The dangers arising from the combination of political and ecclesiastical authority were tremendous. The Church became deeply involved in secular commitments and struggles. Its bishops and clerics, serving as political leaders and advisers, tended to minister more to the secular rulers than to the Christian Church. No doubt, the high clergy was permeated by people who were politicians and warriors rather than priests. If they assumed in addition to their episcopal duties the functions of actual secular princes, as happened in Germany, the whole structure of the ecclesiastical hierarchy was threatened. Vassalage to a king and obedience to the Church produced conflicting loyalties. By demanding from its clergy the fulfillment of certain monastic ideals, among which celibacy served as the foremost symbol, the Church attempted to maintain ecclesiastical discipline. But asceticism could not repair the conditions that were created by the vague co-ordination of the two parallel authorities. The earnest desire of the religious reformers of the twelfth century to sanctify the Church and, through a saintly Church, to purify mundane conditions provided the moral energies behind the bold policies of Gregory VII and Innocent III.

The so-called Investiture Contest was waged by these popes to abolish the parallelism of authorities and to erect in its place a papal monarchy over the *respublica Christiana*. It is well known that the papacy destroyed the German Empire by its theocratic ambitions, only to be overpowered and made captive in 1378 by the French kingdom, which the popes had favored, together with other national forces, against the Empire. But for our purpose it is important to remember that the hope of the reformers of bringing the Church back to its religious mission through papal monarchy failed. In the attempt to exclude secular influences, or what was then called "simony," from the Church, the papacy itself became more and more of a political power organization, compelled to amass the financial and political resources needed in the world-shaking conflict fought by a greatly inflated and centralized body of officials. How deeply secularism was already rooted in the papacy was shown by the full growth of the fiscal system of the papacy in Avignon at a time when the papacy could no longer expect to realize its universal reform plan.

✑ Curtailment of the Church's Secular Power

THE FINANCIAL PRACTICES OF THE PAPACY aroused criticism and opposition, as did the claims of the Curia to an absolute monarchical power over Christendom, which were carried forward after the popes had fallen under the power of the French crown. Everywhere the secular authorities tried to counter the papal policy, and they found support even among the devout, who felt that a papacy void of its universality and ridden with secularism could not guarantee the common welfare.

Where national kings wielded power, as in England and France, popular support took on a distinctly national character. But even in Germany the prestige of the princes was strengthened. It was symptomatic that they began to found universities, as this function had until then been strictly in the ecclesiastical domain.

The election of two popes in 1378 and the ensuing schism, which lasted for practically forty years, threatened to take the government of the Church out of the hands of the Curia. With the Councils of Constance and Basel, the monarchical rule of the Church seemed to be superseded by an episcopalian and synodal regime. Emperor Sigismund convened the Council of Constance in 1414, and the princes—and, incidentally, also the academic theologians—had a strong voice in the deliberations, particularly in the early period. The Council of Constance voted in four "nations"; this rule had been introduced to outvote the papalist Italians. But the conflicting interests of France, England, and the Empire broke up the co-operation of these three nations, and the restored papacy was able to extricate itself from conciliar control and resume its former policy after its return to Rome. England preserved the exemption from papal intervention in the administration of Church affairs in that country which she had gained during the Avignonese period. France, in the Pragmatic Sanction of 1438, promulgated the Gallican principles that practically cut the pope off from the government of the Church in France. Germany received papal promises for similar privileges, but the Empire was not able to realize them. Only the most powerful territorial princes, first in Austria, than in Saxony, Brandenburg, and Jülich-Cleves, were appeased by special concordats; these gave far lesser rights to the secular government than those enjoyed by the English, French, or later Spanish governments. Still, a beginning was made for the extension of Church supervision by the territorial princes, and they steadily expanded their control. The diets of the Empire continued to complain about the exercise of papal jurisdiction and fiscalism. The "grievances (*gravamina*) of the German nation" were listed and passed by many diets after 1461, among them those of Augsburg in 1518, and Worms in 1521.

These grievances, however, were concerned not only with legal and financial relationships with Rome, but also with the moral reform of the Church. If the conciliar movement did not gather great strength after the Councils of Constance and Basel, this was partly due to the disappointment of earnest men regarding the work of the two councils. The Council of Constance had on its agenda three points: unity, faith, reformation. It had given back to the Church a single head—as had the Council of Basel—although after its convention it had almost produced a new schism. With the trial and burning of Huss, the Council of Constance had satisfied faith, but the disheartening Hussite wars followed, and the long-protracted Council of Basel (1431–49) achieved peace only by compromise. Much debate had taken place concerning a reform of the Church, but neither council had achieved anything. The conciliar theory was not forgotten, but with its practicality in question, it became in the later half of the fifteenth century a secondary weapon of chancelleries and lawyers in gaining concessions here and there from the Curia.

The papacy could disregard the arguments for the superiority of councils and could concentrate upon rebuilding and completing its own regimental supremacy. The task was conceived almost entirely as a political enterprise, and the temptation to deal with religion according to political convenience and to exploit the devotion of church members for fiscal and political ends became irresistible. The conditions of the papacy were made worse by the necessity of regaining the government of the Church state, and by the ensuing involvement in the lethal conflicts of Italian factions and states. The secularization of the Italian Renaissance civilization, which saw the popes as leaders and patrons of immortal art, made them also the practitioners of the worst immorality of Renaissance Italy. In 1500 the tiara adorned the head of Alexander VI Borgia.

✍ *Religious Teaching of the Church*

WHILE AT THE BEGINNING of the sixteenth century the Roman curialists, who considered the Church an empire to be ruled by the forceful imposition of monarchical laws and ordinances, constituted the most powerful single force in Catholicism, the Church had not ceased to be to its millions of followers a deep and heartfelt religious concern. Christian religion had inherited from Judaism the idea of God as the austere judge, who would pass judgment on the value of each individual. In Jesus' message the judgment had been interpreted as a demand for a conduct of life aimed at the realization of the highest ethical norms. Such norms had to transcend those of daily life and could ultimately be derived only from the perfection of God. But in Jesus' teaching God was not only the stern judge but also the father who wished to save the sinner. Grace and justice were then, and have remained, the fundamental characteristics of the Christian conception of God, or, as seen from the point of view of the individual believer, the problem of human sin and divine grace has been the burning issue of Christian religion and ethics.

From its inception, however, the Christian Church was a community of people who wanted not only to listen to Christ's words but also to share, through cultic devotion, in the spiritual benefits of Christ's suffering and death. The Judaism of Jesus' time was already permeated with Greek thought, but contacts with the religious and philosophical schools of Greece and Rome multiplied when the Church spread over the Roman Empire. If the Church wanted to communicate with the Greco-Roman world, it had to state its own aspirations in the language of the philosophers. In this process of Hellenization the concept of God was clad in metaphysical terms. God was represented as dwelling far beyond the universe, a pure spirit, and removed from man. In this setting His love for man appeared even greater, if more miraculous. But at the same time when the absolute and sole might of God was fully developed, an opposite movement was gaining. The Gospels had already spoken of rewards for certain human actions and attitudes, as can be seen in the Sermon on the Mount or in the blunt advice of Jesus to embrace poverty in order to collect treasures in heaven. But, characteristically, it was the first great Roman father, Tertullian, who suggested the legal terms "merit" and "satisfaction" for the rationalization of this relationship.

Man was considered to rise, at least partially, beyond his sinfulness and thereby to win the consideration of God. The same aim was behind asceticism, which also had roots in original Christianity but won further strength and distinction from the teachings of the Cynic and Stoic schools about the self-discipline of mind and body. It assumed much wider scope in the Church as a break with the congenital nature of man and a parting from the secular order for a life exclusively devoted to God. Asceticism in the Western world had two aims, which occasionally tended to be separate but on the whole were present together, and which were linked by a considerable number of intermediary objectives. The discipline of the human will could result in a contemplative-mystic vision of God or in a greater desire and capacity .for doing the "work of God" in this world. Chastity, poverty, and humility were the main virtues to be practiced in an ascetic religion. Whether more activistic or quietistic in outlook, asceticism assumed a dualism of the universe, in which the other world, the world of God and of the spirit, was the only fully real one because it contained absolute truth, perfection, and eternity.

Yet in spite of this metaphysical dualism, there was in the idea of merit and satisfaction, and also in asceticism, the tendency to ascribe to man the ability to progress toward the good, a notion that was in conflict with the concept of God's omnipotence. The ancient Church wrestled with this profound antinomy and gave its final answers through the creation of the ecumenic symbols that it bequeathed to medieval and modern Catholicism and also to official Protestantism. They comprised the Apostolic, Nicene, and Athanasian creeds. The last, which bore its name for no good reason, has also been popularly known as the "whosoever will" creed, after its opening words, which introduce in unmistakable language the solemn purpose of these Christian symbols. "Whosoever will be saved" must keep the Catholic faith, for "he who does not keep the faith pure and inviolate will undoubtedly perish in eternity."

✍ Scholasticism

IT FELL TO THE MEDIEVAL SCHOLARS to expound, systematize, and pass on through the schools this faith of the Fathers. Little original theological work was done in the early medieval centuries, but scholasticism began to flourish in large schools from the eleventh century onward. It reached its highest and most representative expression in St. Thomas Aquinas, who accomplished in the philosophical realm what Innocent III had done in the field of practical policy. In the writing of St. Thomas, nature and spirit were harmonized to the satisfaction of faith and reason. In his system the relation of sin and grace was balanced, and on this foundation an elaborate individual and social ethics was constructed. To Thomas Aquinas, religion was essentially an experience of the speculative mind. With the help of Aristotle, Thomas overcame the older scholastic "realism," which had contended that ideas have reality and are given to us in the actual world. In school language this was expressed in the formula *universalia ante res*. St. Thomas taught that ideas were real only within things and had no reality above them, *universalia in rebus*.

The logic of St. Thomas displayed an appreciation of the difference between natural reason and divine truth. Though reason cannot measure out revelation, he believed that it could demonstrate the rational possibility of revelation and that through critical elucidation of the doctrine and practice of the Church, the true vision of God, the aim of all religion, could be achieved. St. Thomas also endeavored not to impair the omnipotence of God, but again the philosophical dualism was not carried to extremes. Man has no capacity for gaining salvation, or even for acquiring merits in the eyes of God, but to the extent that he conforms to natural morals, he is not sinning. God may even reward the good actions of a pagan or of a Christian sinner not because he deserves it, but because God is benevolent. True meritorious works are beyond the capacity of man, since they require a supernatural quality, which is received through the sacraments of baptism and penance. This "infused grace" creates a "habit" of love of God, which is the source of meritorious acts. But St. Thomas did not deny that in order to achieve good works, the Christian must raise the sentiment of love of God to clear consciousness. To this extent a co-operation of the human will with God's grace was postulated. As reason and revelation were conceived as complementary, so nature and grace were not entirely opposed to each other. "Grace presupposes nature; grace does not dispose of nature, but perfects it," was the keynote of the whole speculation of Thomas.

St. Thomas was more careful than any other schoolman not to abolish the distinction between the natural and supernatural, but he saw an underlying unity of the world, which was moreover not only symbolized but fully guaranteed by the actual presence of the Church. The Church was the kingdom of God on earth, and its head the vicar of Christ. Truth, justice, and peace, the divine and eternal, were present in the Church, which was the mystical body of Christ and at the same time, in its visible order, an organization to rule the world and, through its laws and powers, to direct its members toward God. God was the demanding judge, but also the God of love, who through Christ had entered the world, expunged the guilt of man, overcome death, and thereby built a Jacob's ladder connecting heaven and earth, which will hold to the last day. He has also left to the world His grace and love, not only in His word but also in holy sacraments that dispense real love and eternal life. If the Christian accepts the word of God as truth and follows it, if he places his faith in Christ and uses the sacraments, sins will be forgiven and he may hope for eternal life. No one may rely on his own merits, but through divine grace man gains increasing freedom from the world and sin. Through the love with which he is endowed he wins merits that may permit him to survive the last judgment.

But St. Thomas went further. In this objective world order, which linked heaven and earth under the rule of God, the individual could not conduct his life and religion without guides of special holiness. A priest-hood was demanded to tutor souls, and in its hands was laid the ad-ministration of the legacy of Christ, the word and sacraments. There was no doubt that the priest brought about the miracle contained in the sacraments, irrespective of the attitude of the Christian layman, though there remained controversies about the requirements needed to make the imparted grace fully effective in the heart of the individual. All priests were understood to stand under the pope, whose voice was the voice of Christ. Beyond the narrow confines of the Church he was the vicar of Christ on earth, and that meant also the regent of Christ on earth. The teachings of the Church said that the Christian could marry and remain in the normal occupations of secular life without suf-fering damage to his soul, but that it was more advisable to become a monk and prepare oneself through asceticism for the gift of eternity.

All these characteristics of the Church were reflected in the pro-found systematic thought of St. Thomas, the towering intellectual achievement of the age of Gothic art. It is clear, however, what dominant function the actual Church held in Thomas' vision of the world. The hierarchical and sacramental Church was the place in which the meeting of the natural and supernatural was objectified, but for that reason it left no room for personal decisions of faith. As the sacraments are objectively fulfilled by their proper ritual performance through the priest, so the faith is determined by the Church. "The Church is the faith and the sacraments of the faith," said St. Thomas. What is demanded from the Christian is the unconditional acceptance of the ecclesiastical doctrine as divine truth. In other words, the faith of the individual is basically an act of obedience and as such is de-clared to be meritorious. This led to the contention that it is not neces-sary to know "explicitly" the doctrine of the Church. For a general determination to believe the teachings of the Church, an "implicit faith" is sufficient.

✎ *Nominalism*

THE SACRAMENTAL-PRIESTLY CHURCH was given an imposing authority by the *doctor ecclesiae*. But the Church of the fifteenth and sixteenth centuries was far more regimental and much less spiritual than St. Thomas. His systematic interpretation of theological realism interfered with an authoritarian interpretation that wished to act according to practical convenience. The official Church was, therefore, not unhappy about the rise of a school competing with realism and usually called "nominalism." The name is explained by the new epistemology, which, however, the founder of the new scholastic school, John Duns Scotus, did not as yet employ. But William of Occam (died 1356) taught that ideas were *nomina*, names or conceptual terms, with which the human mind organized its experience and which had no reality outside the human mind. Scholastically, this was expressed: *universalia post res.* Applied to theology, this led to the denial of harmony between reason and revelation which St. Thomas had established. The realism of human reason was confined to the world of which we have knowledge through sense impressions, whereas we have no knowledge of the supernatural. Occam became thereby the father of philosophical criticism, pragmatism, or positivism, and it is easy to see why Occamism could contribute to the development of an empiricist science.

The Occamist approach might have been complemented by a religious and metaphysical skepticism. But the opposite was the case. Occam declared the attempt to reflect the whole universe in a rational system impossible, and consequently religion and philosophy were separated, but only in the sense that two forms of truth existed, for Occam never questioned that religion contained truth, though one that did not follow the rules of rational logic. One can paraphrase Tertullian's famous statement, *"Credo quia absurdum,"* in Occam's case by: "I have faith not in spite but because of the irrationality and arbitrariness of religious propositions." But here, even more emphatically than in Thomism, faith was an act of obedience to the authority of the Church, and the power of priests and the reliance on sacraments were further enhanced. The abdication of theology from the active definition of the substantive faith resulted in an internal corrosion of theology. Nominalists, however, could not resist the temptation of tampering with Christian doctrine either by imposing their rationalistic ethics or by justifying the principles of convenience which the Curia followed. Casuistry had already been strong in realism; now it led theology into a desert of formalistic and hair-splitting arguments or a morass of absurdities.

In its inception nominalism was viewed with grave suspicion by the Church. The personal anti-curialist opinions of Occam were largely responsible for this original resistance, but from the end of the fourteenth century Occamism became ever more widely accepted. When Wycliff and Huss championed realism, nominalism lost its political stigma. The fifteenth century was dominated by the "new method" (*via moderna*), particularly in Germany. The Dominicans saw to it that the old theological method (*via antiqua*) was not lost, and the stirrings of Thomistic reactions to "modernism" could be felt through the century, although they were concerned mostly with details. A subcurrent of Augustinian thought was also noticeable. But the Scotists held the advantage over the Thomists.

Nominalism, weak as it was as a Christian theology, contained elements of a new understanding of religion. Through the denial of a simple identification of religion with thinking, which was the inheritance of Greek philosophy, religion received autonomy. Occam, following ideas presented by Duns Scotus, explained God not as the highest essence but as the supreme will, to be experienced by the will power of man. He changed the emphasis in religion from metaphysics to ethics and thereby awakened a novel interest in psychology and the forces of history. To be sure, among these historical forces, in Occam's opinion, was also the Church as it had come down through the ages. But in Occamistic criticism at least beginnings were made in differentiating between the sources of ecclesiastical authority and in placing the Bible above later tradition. The new psychology, however, was soon dissatisfied with the magic aspects of the operation of sacramental grace. Those were the ideas with which Occamism prepared the way for Luther's religious development, as will be seen later.

But the main impact of nominalism on the Church of the fifteenth century was the strengthening of its hierarchical and sacramental system at the expense of the spiritual and personal forms of piety. The terrifying reality of the Last Judgment, so magnificently expressed in the *Dies irae, dies illa,* was always in the mind of the Christian; and before his eyes stood the glory of heaven and the intermediary sphere of the apostles and saints, but purgatory and hell were also there. Deadly sins would lead to hell, venial sins to purgatory, and there could be no doubt that even the temporary penalties of purgatory were dreadful. As heaven was clearly projected into this world, so was hell. In nature, which could only be envisaged as animated by superhuman forces, the devil and evil forces played mischief, but they did so even more in the life of man. To gain assurance of salvation was the highest desire of every frightened soul, but this security the Church did not give its members. It offered itself only as a way toward sanctification, provided the individual would submit obediently to the laws and teachings of the Church. The greatest practical significance rested in the administration of penance. The sacrament of penance gave the priest the power to restore a sinner to the standing before God that he had received in baptism. Absolution was given if the sinner showed penitence, confessed, and paid the penalties. But whereas penitence had originally included a conscious faith and true repentance, scholasticism demanded only "implicit" faith, and instead of contrition a lower form of penitence, "attrition," as the theologians called it.

The Church could, however, in addition help the sinner to free himself of the temporal penalties of purgatory, since it had at its disposal the treasury of good works which Christ and the saints had bestowed on it. The indulgences which the Church had introduced at the time of the crusades were open to grave abuses, particularly if the Church used them for filling its coffers. The tendency toward weakening the character of penitence still further, and toward loosening the connection of ecclesiastical indulgences with the sacrament of penance, was strong from the outset, and it was resisted in practice even less than in theory. Under the Renaissance popes the reckless use of indulgences reached a climax and brought on Luther's attack against Rome.

That a theologian, such as Luther, could win the ear of the masses was surprising, at a time after theology had fallen from public esteem, as it had during the fifteenth century. Disregarding for a moment the fact that the printing presses had not yet created as large a reading public as in Luther's day, one does not have the impression that seekers of intellectual and religious truth after the conciliar period found in theology the representation of their own vital problems. The period did not produce great thinkers, and the nominalistic epigoni busied themselves with sophistic and trivial questions in the service of the Church. This might simply have produced a return to older forms of theology, to either St. Thomas or St. Augustine, and such movements were actually not uncommon. But a lack of interest in theology was even more characteristic of the time, though practically nowhere in Germany was it coupled with a disregard for religion.

Theology, as we have mentioned before, had come into existence in the ancient world and had been an integral cause of the victory of the Christian Church over ancient paganism and philosophy. The political motives that led to the adoption of the Church by Constantine should not be underrated, and political motives were entirely predominant in the Christianization of the Germanic peoples in the age of transition to the Middle Ages. The Teutonic races submitted to the Roman Church not because the speculation about the two natures of Christ, or the fine reasoning on the Trinity, expressed their deepest longings, but because they saw in the Church a power for civilizing the world. The intellectual analysis of faith meant little, though of course the Christian religion had to prove its supernatural quality, if possible in objective or material signs. This explains the great stress on the sacraments, which figured as the most prominent problem of theological discussion in the early Middle Ages. It also makes it understandable why the regimental and hierarchical trends in the Church could gather such momentum.

✍ *The Influence of Medieval Society on Religion*

THE MEDIEVAL CHURCH was an aristocratic church, not only in its own internal structure, but also in the sense that it had to deal chiefly with the nobility, the only class that had the potential strength to defend its style of life against Christian ethics. The social standards of the feudal nobility, with their pugnaciousness and contempt for the weak, stemmed wholly from a tribal and pagan past. This serious challenge the Church met either by winning noblemen for direct service in the hierarchy of the Church or by a redirection of the ideals of the noblemen. The warrior instincts were channeled into the sacrifice for the cross, and asceticism was shown as a force for training a better disciplined fighter as well as a better Christian. As far as the ideal of the *militia Christi* did not produce the Christian knight, this was another example of worldly sin and had to be coped with by the practice of penance and church penalties. Still, between the Church and the feudal nobility there remained an inner antagonism, which not even far-reaching concessions by the Church could extinguish. The attempt of the Church, for example, to raise the sex morals of the class through the cult of St. Mary resulted often enough in painful confusion.

But with the growth of medieval society the character of medieval religion changed. The social differentiation brought new groups into being, and the spread of lay culture made these more vocal. Among them the towns and cities were most important, and here the Church found much that was more congenial to Christian religion than among the restless feudal nobility. St. Thomas, though himself a son of the high nobility, had great praise for the cities. They were places of peace and communities in which the rank of the individual was determined by the peaceful work he did, not by inheritance and prowess. The great cathedrals were likewise community buildings given to peace and to devotion before the altars of the Church, and the urban corporations, guilds, and crafts, too, cultivated Christian religion and ethics. The cities also became the foremost centers of learning and carried schooling beyond the nobility and clergy into at least some of the groups of the laity. The Church, the real Jerusalem, could see in the cities the closest approximation to new Jerusalems on earth.

From Bernard of Clairvaux to St. Francis and St. Dominic, the Church experienced among its members a deepening and intensification of religious faith which made its home more and more in the cities. This new piety formed the background of the rise of the scholastic systems. The need was felt to prove the truth of the Christian religion in philosophical terms, to protect it against skepticism and deviations caused by formless sentiment. This theology had to throw its nets far out to bring in not only nature, of which this age was more conscious than its predecessors, but also an elaboration of moral rules suitable to guide man in a more complex social world. Scholasticism was, however, burdened by the tradition of an earlier stage, and thereby prevented from coming fully to grips with the ideal contents of its own age. Moreover, if scholasticism wanted to command the respect of the people to whose lives it proposed to give meaning and direction, it would have needed a much greater influence on the Church itself than it ever had. The authority, and eventually the inner backbone, of scholasticism was largely destroyed by curialism.

✆ *Mysticism*

THERE WAS, however, still another form of Catholic religion, less definite in form and expression and therefore less likely to be easily regimented. Mysticism has often been described by Protestant scholars as a separation from Roman Catholicism, if not as a decisive preparation for Luther's religion. It has also often been called the first clear expression of a peculiarly German national spirit. None of these contentions seems justified by historical facts. Mystical elements were already present in original Christianity, and mysticism, under the influence of neo-Platonic thought, had a rich history in the ancient Church. In St. Augustine mysticism appeared as the sublimest form of individual piety, but it was in full harmony with his faith in the Church and its doctrine. Mysticism gained a general renascence through Bernard of Clairvaux and St. Francis of Assisi, as well as through St. Thomas.

Undoubtedly, it was of great significance that beginning in the fourteenth century southern Germany became the productive center of mysticism, which spread from there to the Netherlands and central Germany. The first great representative was Master Eckhart (d. 1327), followed by Heinrich Suso (d. 1361), Johannes Tauler (d. 1361), Thomas a Kempis (1380–1471), and the anonymous author of the *German Theology* (around 1480). Among the lesser figures Ludolf of Saxony (ca. 1460) may be mentioned, since through his writings Ignatius Loyola became acquainted with German mystical thought. This literature was written in German and denoted a new stage in the history of the German language, particularly once the printing presses carried these writings, in numerous editions, beyond the monasteries. Next to the Bible, the *Imitatio Christi* of Thomas a Kempis has remained to our own days the most widely distributed book.

Impressive as this mystical literature was, beyond a certain elaboration and a fresh power of expression, it did not add new ideas to those already accumulated in the earlier history of the Church. St. Augustine once epitomized his religious aspirations in the words: "God and the soul I want to recognize; nothing else." The fundamental intention of mystical experience was to restore the direct relationship between the soul and God which was spoiled and dimmed by the world. The soul must seek purification and illumination to ascend to a union with God. This required an abnegation of the self produced by a life of humility, poverty, and suffering. It called for a contemplation of the world as God's creation, and the signs of His work and presence had to be found. Here the sacraments, particularly penance and the eucharist, had their important place, but minor symbols, from holy relics to mere amulets, also served as stimulants for the elevation of the soul to the highest experience of the one-ness of the supreme being, in whom all differences are overcome, and in whom the soul, which has extinguished the consciousness of personality, receives the mysterious cognition of the identity of God and world.

Both imaginative and rational contemplation were demanded and immensely developed by mysticism. The imaginary observation of Christ's humble and suffering life on earth in all its details was the surest way to the recognition of his divine nature. Man must follow Christ and emulate him, then Christ will be reborn in him. New insights were hereby gained for the analysis of man, his mind and passions. The ascetic exercise was originally to culminate in the bliss of the pure vision of God. But it was the influence of Duns Scotus, and probably of the wider knowledge of psychology, which shifted the

focus of mystical life. If God was will, the conflict was not one between finite being and absolute essence, but one between partial and
supreme will. The highest stage that the soul could reach was, in this
case, to come to rest in God through love, and to be absolved of all
interest in the nondivine, including all human sentiments, even those
of bliss.

Mysticism was quite compatible with both scholastic philosophy and
with Catholic piety, which was more comprehensive than its theological rationalization. Eckhart, for example, was not only the author of
German mysticism but also of many Latin scholastic tracts. But in spite
of the orthodoxy of the German mystics, the increase of mystical
thought and practice showed a growing demand for a personal participation in religion. This was shown also by the greater emphasis in
the fifteenth century on preaching and, particularly in Germany, by
the sprouting of all sorts of lay fraternities dedicated to religious devotion, teaching, and charity. Italy, too, had her revivalist preachers,
among whom a few extended their activities into Germany. But in Germany the "Brethren of Common Life" and many other groups practiced their *devotio moderna*. All this may be taken as a healthy sign of
the religious vitality of the Church, and indeed the brotherhoods in
Cologne saved some Catholic life through the storms of the Protestant
Reformation.

But mystical religion could produce results that went beyond the
customary ecclesiastical piety. Mysticism sublimated the doctrine of
man's capacity for co-operation with God in his own salvation by
stressing the struggle against the self. Yet, was not man by mystical
training able to acquire by himself the full cognition of God? The
correct explanation was, of course, that such ability was the gift of a
gracious God. But was this explanation always adhered to? This became
the more questionable since at the same time the priesthood was moved
to the background, while the sacraments, even if recommended, were
only subsidiary to the genuine mystical experience. With a relative
disregard for the hierarchy and the sacraments of the Church, a way
could open to a straightforward pantheism. But nowhere in the Germany of the fifteenth century were such conclusions drawn. Only one
great thinker, Nicholas of Cusa, formulated a philosophical system
designed to understand the coincidence of the finite and the infinite,
of the parts and the whole, in a Platonistic method that departed
from all scholastic reasoning. This man from the land of the Moselle,
who rose to the purple, was a strong churchman, and as bishop of

Brixen he conducted a relentless fight with the neighboring duke of Tyrol, which was widely noted. But the cardinal's speculative system had no visible influence on German thought. It found responsive minds only in Italy, where it was readily absorbed by the Florentine Academy.

✍ The Development of a Secular Culture

GERMAN MYSTICISM OF THE FIFTEENTH CENTURY continued to live within scholastic metaphysics and to cherish the ideals of the medieval *respublica Christiana,* which it was anxious to rejuvenate. Such hidden seeds of future secularization as it contained did not take deep root in Germany. Only in a society that had gained a certain independence from the Church was this likely to happen. But other forces were needed to produce such social life. In the Italy, France, and England of 1500 they were clearly at work, and in all these countries it was the rise of the state around which a new system of moral values and loyalties could be built. The three nations were of course still in very different stages of development. The renascence of the natural man was in its infancy in France and England, while in its bloom in Italy. But the national monarchies in France and England had at least excluded Rome from intervention in the affairs of their churches, and their national governments had established themselves not only as actual political superiors but also as centers of cultural life.

In Italy the city-states had subdued feudalism, and to many Italians the papacy had become just another, if somewhat irregular, state. The life of the modern city communes was the soil of the Italian Renaissance. The Renaissance was by no means so unified a civilization as it appeared in Jacob Burckhardt's classic description. Even under the brilliant surface of a secular culture there remained much of the old religious feeling. It is sufficient to mention the volcanic power with which it erupted during Savonarola's regime in Florence. But it is perhaps even more important to remember that the old ideas appeared not only in such reactions to the new education, but also in the intellectual representatives of the Renaissance culture. Pico della Mirandola, together with Marsilio Ficino, the leading philosopher of the Academy of Florence, wrestled incessantly with the problem of how to find a synthesis of Platonism and scholasticism. These forces enabled Italy after the middle of the sixteenth century to return to a reformed

Roman Catholicism, which, in the form of the Counter Reformation, was to stop and reverse the Protestant movement in Germany.

If the old ideas were only subdued but not lost in Renaissance Italy, how could one expect the sudden outburst of a secular culture in sixteenth-century Germany? The Empire and its people were, in their religion and most of their political and social institutions, still profoundly motivated by traditional ideals. The forms of Italian civilization could be adopted or imitated, but a real transformation of German thinking did not result and, as far as we can judge, would never have taken place even if Lutheranism—in Goethe's much-quoted words—had not "pushed back quiet education everywhere." However, even within these limitations, a German humanism that was highly significant added to German life new notes that were never forgotten, and were to become dominant in later stages of German history.

To call any attempt to improve Latin style and expression humanistic, is rather misleading. Such efforts were widespread in Germany as well as in France and England and could well be undertaken by thorough schoolmen. Nor can the search for classic texts as such be called humanism. The expansion of knowledge of antiquity had gone on for many centuries. Only where these pursuits were undertaken with the intention of winning a distinct philosophy of life, or at least norms for the regulation of human affairs, does it make sense to speak of humanism. This had occurred in Italy. The study of antiquity was the means of organizing and making meaningful the conduct and aspirations of the cultured groups in the Italian city-states. Classic studies were to lead to the fulfillment of the greatest potentialities of man; for this reason Leonardo Bruni had called them the *studia humanitatis*, and Erasmus in the first years of the sixteenth century, the *litterae humanae* or *studia humaniora*. But this Ciceronian ideal of *humanitas* could aim at very different things. To the Platonic philosopher, an ordered *humanitas* could be the reflection of *divinitas;* to Machiavelli, it was a disciplined manliness, for which even religion became a mere means of political planning; for others it was nothing but an aesthetically draped paganism or sensualism. Italian humanism always avoided criticizing the traditional religion directly. As a rule, it simply disregarded the old forms of Christian piety and expected them to wither away, as humanists replaced the scholastics in the positions of ecclesiastical authority. When Lorenzo Valla showed, in 1440, that the theory which had served as the justification of the papal claim for secular rule over the Church state was based on forged historical evidence, this was not done to attack the foundations of religious faith. Valla's *Donation of Constantine* was chiefly a political design to embarrass the papacy.

✎ *German Humanism*

GERMAN HUMANISM COULD GROW only at the courts, among the higher classes in the cities, and in the universities. After the middle of the fourteenth century Germany had founded universities of her own. The first was created by Emperor Charles IV in Prague (1348); fifteen others followed in the next hundred and fifty years. First among these were: Vienna (1365), Heidelberg (1386), Cologne (1388), Erfurt (1392). When the Hussite storm drove the German scholars from Prague, they found shelter in the new university of Leipzig (1409), and shortly thereafter Rostock came into existence (1419). After 1450 a host of new universities was launched: Greifswald (1456), Freiburg and Trier (1457), Basel (1460), Ingolstadt (1472), Tübingen and Mainz (1477), Wittenberg (1502) and Frankfurt on the Oder (1506). It was not surprising that, with the exception of Cologne, the south German universities reached in this period a higher rank than those of the less-developed northern Germany. But altogether the German universities remained small, conservative, and somewhat provincial institutions.

Although the German universities were created by princes in the age of political conflict within the Church to minimize the influence of the French and Italian universities on the future members of the German clergy and court service, they were dominated by a strictly orthodox spirit. In all of them, with the single exception of Cologne, where the *via antiqua* prevailed, Occamism dominated. But it was an Occamism without teeth, and adjusted to the official teachings of the Church. The universities were in the beginning almost entirely theological institutions. Though provisions for a law, medical, and liberal arts faculty were made, the last was only considered propaedeutic to the other faculties, while medicine and law were inadequately represented. The study of canon law prevailed. When Roman law became increasingly important in preparation for a public career, a law degree from Pisa, Bologna, or Padua would still outshine work in a German university, and the study of law by German students in Italy increased the import of Italian ideas into Germany.

During the later half of the fifteenth century the standing of the law faculties as against that of the divinity faculties rose, and the faculties of liberal arts served less exclusively as preparatory schools for theologians and took greater initiative in defining their own objectives and standards of instruction. Through them humanism began to infiltrate the universities. In the beginning itinerant scholars offered occasional lectures or courses within or outside of the regular curriculum. Some of them, like Peter Luder, often called the first German humanist, were rather loose in character, and used the classics as a wordy excuse for their licentiousness. The resistance of orthodox professors against such bibulous pagans was natural. But during the last quarter of the century representatives of the new learning and new poetry gained regular positions and chairs. Everywhere the Latin of the schoolmen was beaten into retreat and soon held up to ridicule as "kitchen Latin" by the humanists.

The new "poetry" and "eloquence" was in most cases only a cloak for old customs and ideas. Historians have often spoken of a "scholastic humanism" in Germany, and it is true that many professors in all faculties adopted the new forms and subjects without giving up any of the traditional metaphysical notions, though they might at times call God "the immortal ruler of Olympus" or Christ "Hercules." In a few personalities, however, the Christian ideas were moved into a side chapel to give room to the glorification of man. Conrad Celtis, the most gifted and enthusiastic of the German poets, began as an itinerant scholar and ended as a professor of poetry in Vienna (d. 1508). Most of his verses were imitations of Horace and Ovid displaying a frank sensualism, but at the same time he sought after new rules of life and education. Humanistic eloquence, he felt certain, could, with the help of the ancients, reveal the knowledge of the universe. With great joy of discovery, the libraries of the monasteries were combed for manuscripts of the classic authors and the texts were published in rapid succession by the Italian and German presses. Much of the belief in the power of the word and of language stemmed from the fact that the art of printing seemed to give words a higher validity as well as a much wider distribution. With a naïve pride, Celtis and other poets offered their Latin hexameters to patrons as an assured way to win immortal fame.

North of the Alps the new art did not reach the elegance achieved by the Italians. The humor of the Germans was blunt and their wit stilted. It was remarkable how many of the poets were sons of simple peasants: not only the Franconian, Celtis; but also the Hessians, Eobanus and Crotus Rubeanus; the Swabian, Heinrich Bebel; and the Swiss, Glareanus. Much more no doubt than in subsequent centuries the German universities of this age were places where talent from all classes could gather and gain advancement. But these children of the people had to cover a long distance from the beech woods of the mother country to the olive groves of the south. The revival of antiquity was for the Italians the revival of their own glorious past. *Humanitas* was *Romanitas*. North of the Alps it could not have the same meaning. Outside of Italy humanism, by looking at the classic model, was forced to compare its own character and history with what the Italians called the nature of the Roman and Italian nation. Thus the study of a foreign civilization led to curiosity about the German past.

Enea Silvio Piccolomini, while at the court of Frederick III, had given the Germans the first modern description of Germany in the style of the new humanistic historiography of Italy. He had also reminded the Germans of the information they could gather from classic sources, such as Caesar, Tacitus, Pliny, and Strabo, on their original history. The German humanists made their best scholarly contribution in the field of historical study. Celtis and Heinrich Bebel made Tacitus' *Germania* the key book of German humanism, and the other sources were subjected to critical scrutiny. The extension of interest in German history led to the discovery and publication of some of the great sources of medieval history, such as Einhard's *Life of Charlemagne,* and the works of the historian of the Hohenstaufen era, Otto of Freising. In the pursuit of these studies close contacts were formed among the humanists. Celtis' boldest hope was the production of a work that would depict on a broad canvas the history of Germany in all its regions and ages, and he succeeded in stimulating other humanists to undertake the writing of histories of individual sections. The first significant work, still largely reflecting a medieval scheme of history, was the *World Chronicle* of Nauclerus, church provost of Tübingen. Celtis died before the Reformation, but the historical interests that he had aroused were little affected by the Lutheran revolt, and it was after 1517 that the Bavarian Aventinus, the Alsatian Beatus Rhenanus, and the Hanseatic Albert Krantz produced the best works of which this school was capable.

Krantz was a diplomat in the service of Lübeck and Hamburg, and as a man of affairs he gave to his books a more realistic touch than academic scholars could display. The favor of princes, which the latter came to enjoy, did not carry them that far, though it galvanized their industry. Emperor Maximilian patronized the humanists because they seemed useful in spreading his greatness. This man, who lived in the world of the chivalrous legends of the Middle Ages, liked to be presented to Italy and the world at large as the new Augustus. In 1487, he crowned Conrad Celtis *poeta laureatus;* in 1500, Cuspinianus, Celtis' successor in Vienna; in 1518, Ulrich von Hutten. Following the example that France and Burgundy had set, he also appointed the first German court historian. It seemed to be politic not only to set down secular deeds for future memory, but also to broadcast one's fame among one's contemporaries.

Maximilian's support of the humanists had ambiguous results. He drew them away from mere academic exercises and closer to the political arena, but he wanted them to glorify the Habsburg dynasty and his personal policies. Thereby he hindered the progress of the humanist historians toward the aims that these early students of Clio had tried, if somewhat vaguely, to reach. They wished to understand German history as the reflection of lasting moral and cultural traits. Their critical equipment was too poor to accomplish this end, and frequently, in place of the many legends of the past which they destroyed, they merely introduced new myths. But the attempts to demonstrate the unity of German history and civilization might have served as the foundation of a national patriotism that would have counterbalanced the centrifugal forces of German political life.

This, however, would have required political leadership and a commitment to clear and specific spiritual ideals. It was not enough to contend that through Tacitus the ancients had bestowed their approval on the German ancestors; or to say, as Heinrich Bebel did, that the Germans had in their native adages as much wisdom as the Greeks; or, to assert, as every humanist did, that the Germans were the intellectual equals of the Italians, as shown by their learning, not to mention the invention of gunpowder and printing. These were expressions of pride, but not political programs; even less were they convictions that could bring on a general renovation of religion and the Church. Exactly those men who were most experienced in public life took the greatest care not to extend the political claims of the new history too far. The historical writings of Cuspinianus, who served Maximilian also on diplomatic missions, were done entirely in furtherance of the emperor's dynastic projects. The friends and converts whom the humanists had made among the patriciate did not inject an independent political note either. Conrad Peutinger of Augsburg, the legal counsel of the Fuggers and defender of the monopolies, found his main interest in geography rather than history, as did also Willibald Pirkheimer. From the latter, who was one of the first citizens of Nürnberg, we have a short historical description of the Swiss War of 1499, in which he participated.

The German humanism that was represented by Celtis and his group of followers was proof that the liberal arts had become more independent of theology, and that the new "eloquence" reformed the style of life of its devotees, among whom were a good many lawyers and princely councilors. They began to feel superior to the contemporary theologians, though theology itself was hardly anywhere questioned. But a few of the German humanists turned to the philosophy of Florence. In Mutianus Rufus (1471–1526), who in his youth had been a classmate of Erasmus at the school of the Brethren of Common Life, a new philosophy appeared for the first time in Germany. Jewish religion, Greek and Roman philosophy, and Christianity were to him emanations of a single God, who was to be made the object of contemplation and worship. To this theism, a universal natural ethics corresponded, in which Church, sacraments, and hierarchy had lost all meaning. Mutianus thought his ideas unfit for the masses, but suitable to serve as the philosophy of an initiated elite. He did not publish his thought, and spoke his mind only in correspondence with intimate friends, or in conversation with visitors welcomed at his retreat.

✆ German Humanism and Reform of the Church

IN CONTRAST TO THE PHILOSOPHY of the esoteric Mutianus, Johann Reuchlin's learned studies were intended to reform the old Church, to which he was devoted. This Swabian scholar (1455–1522) was a Latinist of rank and the first fully accomplished Greek scholar. The systematic cultivation and teaching of Greek among scholars were to his credit. But he made an even more original contribution by placing the study of Hebrew on a secure level. Yet the languages were to Reuchlin only the key to the mysteries of ultimate truth. Under the influence of Pico della Mirandola, he proceeded from Plato and Pythagoras to the study of the cabala, desirous of gleaning hidden knowledge from the occult lore of the Jews. It was strange that this irenic man should have become, in the last decade of his life, the center of furious controversies.

In this age in which economic rivalry and religious superstition had resulted in acts of violence against the Jews, a Jewish renegade, Pfefferkorn, tried to win the favor of the Church and public by demanding the destruction of the dangerous Jewish literature. In 1511 Reuchlin published a tract (*The Eyeglasses*) defending the scholarly value of Jewish writings. The University of Cologne disapproved, and the superiors of the Dominican Order, in whose hands the power of inquisition rested, opened proceedings against him. They could not convict him for many years, since Reuchlin had many protectors among the clergy, at the imperial court, and even in Rome. But the power of the Dominican Order was formidable too, and in 1520 the Curia, already under the shadow of Luther's revolt, finally decided against the senescent scholar, who was burdened with frightful legal expenses.

The Reuchlin case led to the formation of fronts in Germany. The prosecution of Reuchlin brought humanists of every point of view together for the defense of the new studies. The Dominican proceedings were taken as an attack on the dignity of scholars by barbarian zealots. The unity of the humanists seemed suddenly complete. The world, in the words of Mutianus, was divided between the Reuchlinists and the stupid people. But even more impressive was the belligerent spirit that was grounded in a magnified pride and a growing hostility against the Church authorities. Here voices of a young generation could be heard, and if they could not in the end save Reuchlin, they could make the contemporary monasteries contemptible through derision. In 1514, Reuchlin published *Letters of Famous Men,* a collection of letters written in support of his case by eminent men. In the fall of 1515, and during the two following years in augmented editions, an anonymous collection appeared—the *Letters of Obscure Men,* purporting to contain the correspondence of the inquisitors and their scholastic friends. They proved to be a work of literary fiction, lampooning the dubious personalities, bad morals, sinister scholarship, and corrupt Latin diction of the power-greedy persecutors of Reuchlin. With their inimitable ribaldry and persiflage they were a unique piece of satire, which succeeded in foisting the label of obscurantism upon the scholastic brethren.

The *Letters of Obscure Men* were written by Crotus Rubeanus and Ulrich von Hutten. Crotus displayed a gift of humorous caricature, whereas his friend Hutten added a strong dose of invective to his sarcastic portraits. Hutten (1488–1523), the scion of a noble Franconian family, had chosen the path of an itinerant scholar and had absorbed the new poetry and eloquence. He was just about to mature into the best writer of Latin that Germany was to produce in this period. But it was not in his blood to settle in academic temples. He transferred the warring instincts of knighthood to the literary arena and became the political publicist of German humanism. Hutten was an outright "imperialist"—that is, he was convinced that the emperor was supreme above the pope in Christendom. But the emperor was, in Hutten's view, the representative of the German nation, and if Germany had lost her universal position, it was due to the evil machinations of the Italian papacy, which had extended its domination over all Church life, politics, and education. The political fight for a reform of the Church and the Empire was to go with a revival of learning. While Hutten merged the popular resentment against Rome, as expressed in the "grievances of the German nation," with the humanistic opposition to the theologians, he was in his heart not unmindful of the need for a more comprehensive spiritual power to broaden the basis of the struggle with the Romanists. This feeling was to place him in 1519 on Luther's side, but before that it made him one of the most admiring and vociferous apostles of Erasmus when the great Dutchman appeared on the German scene.

Desiderius Erasmus of Rotterdam (1465–1536) came to Germany in 1514. He wanted to publish on the Continent his Greek New Testament, a job that the small presses of England could not handle. It was done by Froben in Basel during the next two years. Except for two brief visits to England, he lived in Louvain from 1517 to 1521, and thereafter in Basel until the Reformation drove him to the neighboring Freiburg, the chief city of the Breisgau, which was under Habsburg rule. Although his life was closely connected with Germany, he did not feel fully at home among Germans. He was a cosmopolitan at heart, and the national movements of the age seemed to him to interfere with the reform of the universal Christian society for which he hoped. His influence was worldwide, and it was deep and lasting also in Germany, though in his later years it seemed to have been blotted out by the rise of the Reformation.

Erasmus, the illegitimate child of a cleric, was brought up in a school of the Brethren of Common Life. Largely under the influence of his relatives, he entered a monastery, but his urge for individual freedom soon made it a prison to him. He gained permission to leave for study in Paris. Then he went to England, where he found in John Colet the guide to what became his Christian humanism, and in Colet's circle, youths, such as Thomas More, who shared his ideals of a new education. Among the Oxford reformers Erasmus came in contact with the ideas of the Academy of Florence and with an earnest Biblical study; this, together with memories of the simple mystical piety and studious industry of his early school years, determined the direction of his thought and work. Already when he came to Germany, his fame in Europe was unexcelled, and his edition of the New Testament was only the capstone of a program of reform which he had outlined earlier in a number of books, such as the *Enchiridion Militis Christiani* (*Handbook and/or Dagger of the Christian Soldier*), the *Adages,* and the *Praise of Folly.*

Erasmus was not a systematic philosopher or a predominantly religious figure but a moralist and philologist who presented his ideas in a Latin prose of choicest form and with a wit and irony that delighted the reader while dodging the traps of censorship. Erasmus believed that the Gospels and the Pauline letters contained the highest wisdom, but that in antiquity Christian truth had already been foreshadowed by such men as Socrates, Plutarch, and Cicero. Christian religion was the culmination of ancient civilization, as its simple essence had been best interpreted by the ancient Fathers, among them Jerome, Ambrose, and Augustine. Thereafter simplicity had been buried under theological subtleties and defiled by barbarousness of expression. The way to the sources in which the profoundest knowledge was enshrined was the study of the original languages, which alone could lead to a full understanding and a renewed realization of the highest ideas.

Christian religion was seen by Erasmus as the perfect ethics. He liked to speak of it as the "philosophy of Christ," which could be learned, like Socratic philosophizing, by the application of a natural mind trained in the interpretation of literary texts. Out of the great classics and Holy Scripture the individual could derive directly a body of rules for the conduct of his private life and for the good of society. Erasmus was convinced that the Christian virtues, once clearly grasped, would reform not only the individual but also the political world. As man, prodded by the admonitions of Christ and the philosophers, could rise to a Christlike life, the outer order of the world could be improved by the morality of good people. Excessive wealth, rigid class distinctions, factionalism, and the suppression of women were to him examples of the weakness of practical religion. Most of all, he was concerned about the denial of Christian love to be found in war. Observing the vicar of Christ, Julius II, turning into a war lord, he wrote, if anonymously, a polemic dialogue against him. But after 1515, when the war between the emperor and Francis I over Italy seemed to have come to an end and a humanistic Medici, who accepted Erasmus' dedication of the New Testament edition, was on the papal throne, Erasmus became more hopeful for a reform of the Church. The young Charles of Spain made him a councilor in 1516, and through Cardinal Wolsey humanism gained influence at the English court. The years after 1516 saw Erasmus busy projecting his moral program into politics.

A new type of Christian piety found its representative in Erasmus. His faith in the supremacy of Christian ideals was beyond question. What he selected from antiquity was chosen with a view to its compatibility with Christian ethics. He did not believe that human reason could fathom all the riddles of life, and skepticism with regard to nonessential matters was the proper attitude of a mature and therefore humble mind. But man had the capacity for intellectual and moral growth, and consequently for building a more habitable world. Ideas and hopes that the European Enlightenment was to develop into mighty forces were cautiously, and not without some incongruity, uttered by Erasmus.

Though not openly asserted, some very revolutionary ideas were implied in his program. Erasmus never tired of castigating as Judaism any work done only to fulfill an outward law or to collect merit. Good works ought to be a spontaneous outflow of a good heart and judged by the personal motive that produced them. Asceticism, too, if practiced as mere obedience to institutional orders, was of doubtful value, though it was laudable when adopted freely as an act of self-discipline and humility. Essentially, the piety of Erasmus was based on the personal experience of the individual and therefore not dependent upon the intercession of priests. It was at the same time the conscious recognition of ethical ideals that could be rationally stated, and consequently no room was left for the operation of sacraments. Erasmus himself never challenged the validity of the sacraments, but called the exaggerated veneration of saints and relics superstitious. It was in the logic of his teaching that the role of the hierarchy and of sacraments in the Church was no longer a primary concern.

Erasmus, however, cared about the Church as the great educational institution of mankind and felt that as such it was deserving of a much higher place than the states and political authorities, which catered to the lower needs of men. The priests and bishops had to become scholars in order to be able to set a model by action and word for the simple moral life of all believers. Such a reform he hoped to set in motion by the persuasion of correct learning, and he could compare his edition of the Greek New Testament to the building of the new metropolitan church of the *respublica Christiana*, St. Peter's in Rome. But was not thereby the whole Christian theology, as it had been understood through the centuries, discarded? Contemporary theologians were quick to point out that if Holy Scripture was the highest source of faith, a grammarian became the arbiter of religion if he took it upon himself to emendate the text of the Bible. One could also say, as the Protestants did later, that the interpretations of Erasmus were colored by his general preconceptions. He used metaphorical interpretation very liberally in order to get around sections of Scripture, for example much of the Old Testament, which conflicted with his own philosophy.

In Erasmus the age reached the most advanced rationalistic conception of Christian faith that was possible under the conditions of the time, and well into the eighteenth century his Christian humanism remained a leaven of civilization. But we must distinguish between the various aspects of his work. As a teacher of languages and style his success was immediate and general. Luther used Erasmus' New Testament as early as 1517, when he lectured to his students on the Epistle to the Romans. In the same year the young nephew of Reuchlin, Philipp Melanchthon, was brought to Wittenberg as professor of Greek. Four years later Luther was to begin his German translation of the Bible from Erasmus' text. The revision of the text of the Vulgate ordered by the Council of Trent also originated in the impulse given by Erasmus. His editions of the Fathers intensified the study of the history of the ancient Church, from which the Protestants derived ammunition for criticizing scholasticism, but which also enabled Catholic scholars before long to show the organic links between the medieval and ancient Church.

The impact of Erasmus' rationalistic theology and ethics was felt less directly. Luther rejected them entirely, but they were potent elements in Melanchthon's thinking and therefore in Lutheranism. Ulrich Zwingli was from the outset open to Erasmian thought, and the so-called Swiss, or "reformed," Protestantism was permeated with the ideas of Erasmus. Sixteenth-century Catholicism, though it placed many of the writings of Erasmus on its index of prohibited books, proved not immune to his teachings. In none of these groups, however, was Erasmian theology the dominant note. Only in the eighteenth century did this change; only then was the optimistic aspect of the faith of Erasmus turned into a secular philosophy of progress.

From 1515 to 1520 Erasmus of Rotterdam gained the widest public fame and support in Germany, though his followers were naturally found only among the educated people at the courts, in the cities, and at the universities. There can be no question, as his orthodox critics contended, but that he alienated the feelings of many in the Church, particularly as it existed in Germany. His attempt to reduce the tremendous ecclesiastical and theological apparatus to simple personal forms had a wide appeal. But if the admirers of Erasmus saw in him the leader of an active reform, they were mistaken. He knew that neither temperament nor intellectual gifts had marked him as a practical reformer. He also knew that the reform which he envisioned could be achieved only through education and persuasive exhortation in a long evolutionary process, in which feuds and open divisions would be of most dubious assistance.

∽ The Religious and Cultural Scene at the Beginning of the Sixteenth Century

IF ONE SURVEYS the German religious and cultural scene at the beginning of the sixteenth century, one is struck by the vast variety of disparate phenomena. The Germans of all classes were profoundly concerned with religion. No one openly asserted the rightfulness of an unreformed pagan life, but such living was quite general. Sensuality was certainly as widespread as in any other country; gluttony and drunkenness were, according to native and foreign testimony, much worse than elsewhere. A certain virtue was made of the coarseness and rudeness of some German customs. "Grobianism" became a cultivated literary style as an expression of forthrightness and realism. In general, however, the Germans looked for divine forgiveness of their sins and followed the recommendations of the Church to gain assurance of such forgiveness.

Foreign visitors often expressed amazement at how well kept and decorated German churches and chapels were, even in the smallest villages. The religious life was active, perhaps often to the point of nervous excitement, in order to gain heavenly salvation by all the methods that the Church offered, or at least tolerated. These methods ranged from the sublimest mystical piety to the primitive belief in miracles, from sensitive ethical feeling to gross legalistic conceptions such as indulgences. In between stood all those devotional practices, such as veneration of saints, belief in relics, and pilgrimages, that sprang from lesser or higher Christian motives. Not much is explained by saying that the danger of perverting religion into magic and superstition was greatest among the illiterate, since the vast majority of the people were illiterate. Thus the character of public thought depended largely on the state of the clergy. Superstitions not only welled up from the people but were also imposed by clerics. The worst example was the persecution of witches. In France it had appeared as early as the thirteenth century, while in Germany the first witch trials occurred about the middle of the fifteenth century. When in the 1470's two papal inquisitors, Heinrich Institoris and Jacob Sprenger, wanted to extend the hideous obsession, they ran into strong popular opposition and had to take recourse to the Curia. In 1484 Pope Innocent VIII issued a bull that authorized the inquisition to proceed against witches, and in 1487 these two professors published their *Witches' Hammer* (*Malleus Maleficarum*), which supplied the new madness with theological and juridical theories. For two centuries this plague devoured its innocent victims, raging most fiercely during the Thirty Years' War. Protestantism carried the evil practice to somewhat greater lengths.

Superstition and the abuse of religion could not be assigned to any special groups. One can notice, however, many signs of the growing intensification and deepening of religious feeling toward the end of the fifteenth century. No writer or poet has given adequate expression to the range of thought and imagination of which the Germans of the age were capable. Only the arts give us a chance to adumbrate their deepest aspirations.

It is unnecessary to enumerate the galaxy of artists at work in Germany around 1500. In this period Germany was, next to Italy, the main center of creative art, a position she was not to occupy again in all her history. Architecture, however, played a small part in the flowering of the arts. The cessation of all great building activities in the first two decades of the sixteenth century may simply have been caused by the abundance of churches which had been constructed by preceding generations. It may have been produced, as Georg Dehio suggested, by a loss of the sense of the monumental, which in turn was a result of the great variety of active artistic exploration, as this was not easily brought into the more abstract synthesis demanded by architecture. Patronage and consumption of art had changed, too. Among the German princes only two stand out as liberal connoisseurs: Emperor Maximilian and Albert, the elector of Mainz. On the other hand, rich burghers appeared as supporters at the side of noblemen, and beyond them even the simple people showed an appetite for art. The graphic arts and sculpture thus became the characteristic German arts of the early sixteenth century.

The artistic forms remained in the tradition of Gothic art, which Germany had adopted and developed in her own way. The influence of the Italian Renaissance was not strong, particularly before 1520, and it served to enlarge the field of artistic vision rather than to transform the style. More important than style was the object of art. In general, the exposition of religion remained at the center of all artistic effort. This was quite compatible with the realistic mastery of nature, which was carried to greater perfection. But the transcendental was more directly related to the natural life of this world, and in the method for accomplishing this aim the individual personality of the artist expressed itself with an unprecedented force. Although the artists were still bound by the craft-guild tradition, they emerged as individuals.

We must confine our remarks to the three greatest painters produced by Germany in this age. About Mathis the Painter we know very little. Not even his name, Matthias Grünewald, is well documented. He was presumably born about 1480 and died in 1529. Albert of Mainz was his protector in later years. In the eight paintings of his that have survived we certainly have only a small part of his work, of which the greatest achievement was the altar of 1516 in Isenheim in Alsace. In the forms of expression, Mathis was the most revolutionary artist of this generation, and at the same time the least affected by the secular side of life. His chief concern was to show the suffering of Christ incarnated in the world—a world that was, at the same time, under the stern judgment of God. No painter has portrayed so vividly the world in all its gruesome horror, doubly terrifying in the defiling power it seems to have even over the divine. But his world, depicted in stark realism, simultaneously appears transfigured by the transparence of a heavenly order to which man is drawn with overwhelming force. In Grünewald's genius the deepest religious motives of the Middle Ages found a new and grandiose expression.

But Grünewald as a person remained hidden behind his creations. It was different with Albrecht Dürer (1471–1528), whose personality aroused interest and admiration among his contemporaries. The use of woodcuts and copper engravings gave him a much wider public than former artists had attained. It also gave him the means to bring a much wider and more varied reality and human experience into artistic view. Nor did the world of Christian piety alone find a poetic realization in his works; his sharp and thoughtful eye also explored nature and the secular order with critical delight. Although Dürer's artistic creations were the natural outpourings of an industrious genius, he was, like Goethe, both artist and thinker. Following suggestions of Italian Renaissance philosophy, he searched for a theory of art, but he also reflected with deep personal concern on the important religious, intellectual, and political movements. He was a member of a closely knit sodality to which belonged the leaders of the Nürnberg patriciate: the mayor, Caspar Nützel; Willibald Pirkheimer; and the city secretary,

Lazarus Spengler. Together they devoted themselves to the study of the ancients, of Augustine, and eventually of Luther. The practical application of ideas to the ethical conduct of life was obviously their main interest, and the emphasis on personality was mirrored in Dürer's portraits of his fellow citizens and of the eminent personages of his age. From this angle Luther's message seems to have captured him. In his last great work, the Four Apostles, he showed the potential power of the new religion in the formation of great human character.

Hans Holbein, Jr. (1497–1543), was a member of a different generation, and since he went to England from 1526–28, and after 1532 permanently, it is doubtful to what extent this Swabian is fully representative of German developments. But within limits he indicated at least the other possibilities that existed in the growth of German civilization. Religious subjects, which he treated in his early years, displayed only an unconsoled skepticism about life. Later on he dropped Gothic forms entirely and became a Renaissance artist and the portrayer of a secular society.

II

The Rise *of* Protestantism

CHAPTER 6

Luther and the Beginnings of Protestantism

✍ The Sale of Indulgences

THE SECULARIZATION OF THE CHURCH in the fifteenth century led to the most dubious practices in financial matters, dubious because they exploited the religious devotion of the masses for the mere enrichment of the papacy. The sale of indulgences, though probably the most profitable, was only one method for obtaining such gains. It is not necessary to go into the history of indulgences, which had come into the Church only at the time of the crusades. Their theological justification remained somewhat controversial, though the curialistic theologians tended to strain their application to ever greater lengths. But the practice with regard to the sale of indulgences had gone far beyond any theological consideration. It was lightly adopted by popes for materialistic ends, and promoted by salesmen with a cold-blooded disregard for religious values.

In 1507 Julius II had again announced an indulgence, the income from which was to be used for the building of the new St. Peter's Church in Rome. Pope Leo X had in 1513 continued the action of his predecessor. It was this indulgence that was used for a deal with the new archbishop of Mainz, the twenty-four year old prince Albert of Brandenburg. This Hohenzollern prince had become in 1513 archbishop of Magdeburg and bishop of Halberstadt, where he succeeded a member of the Wettin dynasty of Saxony. In 1514 Albert was elected archbishop and elector of Mainz. It was the third time in a decade that a vacancy in Mainz had occurred, and each time the new bishop had had to pay large sums for papal confirmation. Albert had promised to pay the cost of his confirmation out of his own pocket. But the accumulation of three episcopal dignities was strictly forbidden by canon law, and

Leo X demanded a special sum for the appeasement of his conscience. He offered, however, to assist the archbishop-elector in the mobilization of funds through the sale of indulgences. The Fuggers, who acted in this period as the foremost bankers of the Curia, were the intermediaries in the business. They advanced 29,000 Rhenish fl. to Albert and were granted a handsome commission for the financial management of an indulgence sale, whose income was to be divided between Pope Leo X and Albert.

The campaign was delayed, and not all the princes gave their permission for it to be carried on in their territories. Particularly Frederick the Wise, elector of Saxony, frowned upon the sale, because it served the political aims of the Hohenzollern family. Thus, when John Tetzel, a Dominican monk, opened the drive in 1517, he did not receive permission to enter Saxony, and had to confine his activities to neighboring Brandenburg. Here he appeared with the usual noise and display, attracting people to buy the "Papal letters" which promised easy forgiveness of sins on conditions that were frivolous even in terms of the most liberal official doctrines on penance. A Fugger clerk accompanied the party, emptied the boxes, and kept the cash accounts. While Tetzel operated in Jüterbog in the proximity of Wittenberg in Saxony, people from Saxony went there to purchase the "easy conscience tickets" and on returning insisted on having the remission of their sins validated by their local priest. It was in his capacity as confessor in Wittenberg that Martin Luther was faced with the issue of papal indulgences. Prompted by his feeling of responsibility, he undertook to clarify the theological problems that had never been dogmatically settled. It seemed a challenge to the scholar, and being a professor, Luther intended to launch an academic debate on what seemed to him the doubtful points of the matter.

On October 31, 1517, this young professor affixed 95 theses on indulgences, in Latin, on the door of the court church of Wittenberg, inviting scholars in good medieval fashion to dispute them. He was quite unconcerned that it was the eve of All Souls' day, when the people would flock to the church to receive the benefits that flowed from veneration of the huge collection of holy relics assembled by the faith of Elector Frederick, the benefactor and patron of the recently founded university. Luther was not expecting any publicity outside of academic circles and was completely taken by surprise when his theses became a sensation not only in the universities but also in the Church at large, even among the laymen. Printed in Latin and German, they were spread throughout Germany in an amazingly short time. As an early Protestant writer put it, "It was as if the heavenly angels had played messengers." A simple monk from the provinces or, as he himself said, from the dirty outskirts of the west, became a public figure overnight and made the order of the *respublica Christiana* tremble. Who was the man who was destined to wreck the religious foundations of the Western world and with it the religious unity of the German people?

✍ *Early History of Martin Luther*

MARTIN LUTHER was born in Eisleben on November 11, 1483. His father Hans, the son of a Thuringian peasant, had come to this mining district south of the Harz mountains to make a living, and through hard work rose to a comfortable and respected position in the neighboring Mansfeld, to which the family moved soon after Martin's birth. His father hoped that Martin would do even better, and, by acquiring a law degree, gain a secure social rank. As soon as Martin had completed elementary school at Mansfeld, he was sent to schools at Magdeburg and Eisenach. In 1501 he went to the University of Erfurt and in four years completed the prescribed liberal arts course, moving up to second in his class when he received his magister title in 1505. His father rejoiced, expecting his son to enter the study of law and enjoy a prosperous law career, when Martin suddenly decided, in 1505, to become a monk. After a novitiate of a year he took the vows of an Augustinian friar.

There is little testimony on the religious influences of his early youth. We must assume that in family, school, and university he was surrounded by the regular piety of the age, which ranged from formal obedience to ecclesiastical rulings to earnest personal devotion. What special experiences impelled him to aim at a higher state of Christian perfection, which according to the Church could be gained through monastic life, we do not know, and it would be of doubtful validity to construe the events in the light of modern psychology. One of his friends died in the summer of 1505. Shortly thereafter Luther was caught in a storm. Lightning struck close to him and threw him to the ground. In terror he called out to St. Anne, the patron saint of the Mansfeld miners, and promised to become a monk. No doubt this was the occasion rather than the cause of his conversion. If he was surrendering to a hallucination instead of following an inner calling, as his bitterly disappointed father suggested, he could easily have retraced his steps during his novitiate. But he never wished to turn back. The convent of the

Augustinian brothers, which he selected from among the Erfurt monasteries, had an excellent reputation for strict asceticism, and it accepted him after a year's probation.

His fellow monks and superiors took pride in Luther, and he was selected to become a theologian. Already in 1507 he was consecrated a priest and thereafter he devoted himself to the study of divinity. In 1508 he was loaned as a lecturer in philosophy to Wittenberg, but was quickly brought back for theological teaching in Erfurt. The following year he was active in the organizational problems of his convent, and was sent by his brethren to Rome on the affairs of the order. He went to the Christian capital as a devout member of the Church and returned unshaken in his faith in the papacy, though his mission had been unsuccessful. In 1511 he went to Wittenberg. The following year he received his theological doctorate and became professor of Holy Scriptures, which he remained to the end of his life. In addition, he was made the preacher of the convent and, in 1514, also of one of the Wittenberg churches. Moreover he acted as superior and regent of studies in the so-called "black" Wittenberg monastery and rose to the office of supervisor of eleven cloisters in 1515. Small wonder that he soon complained that he could easily employ two secretaries to assist him in his many duties. By this time he had also become a very popular professor.

Altogether this was a very successful career within the modest setting of the provincial world of Germany, and it provided ample proof of the friendship and recognition accorded Luther by his fellow monks. But in all these years deeper developments were taking place in the heart and soul of this growing monk and scholar. Their ultimate import was concealed not only from his friends but also from himself.

✍ *The Development of Luther's Thought*

MARTIN LUTHER had entered the monastery to take the highest path of Christian life that the Church recommended, knowing also the Church's warning against its austere demands. But he had also come to the cloister to meet squarely the problem that the Church proclaimed to be the center of all Christian endeavor: how can man become just under the judgment of an exacting God? We have already seen not only how the medieval Church had kept this question alive, and how its whole educational system was directed toward awakening the people to the urgency of this matter, but also how it had developed a solution that offered a relative assurance of ultimate salvation. According to every witness, Luther was an earnest monk. As a matter of fact, he carried ascetic exercises, such as fasting, castigations, prayer, and use of the sacraments, to extremes. There was no need to sharpen Luther's sense of guilt or intensify his burning eagerness to do penance. But the help that the ecclesiastical system afforded to the faithful in gaining a relative assurance of peace and salvation, failed in Luther's case.

Monastic life was designed to strengthen awareness of human sin, but also to endow the individual with those qualities required for reaching the goal of the human pilgrimage. By the very act of his profession, the monk acquired a higher perfection, and his calling enabled him to come much closer to fulfillment of the supreme Christian commandment to love God and one's neighbor with all one's soul. There were times when Luther praised the life of the cloister, and the years from 1505 to 1512 were not a single chain of personal crises. But they were punctuated by recurring inner conflicts of the greatest intensity, and it was during these periods of extreme anguish and agony that Luther achieved step by step a radical re-evaluation of the Christian religion. He was driven into it by the extreme sensitivity of his moral judgment. In the face of the absolute God, he felt completely unworthy. Man could not hope ever to overcome his sinfulness by his own efforts. The ancient Church, including St. Paul and St. Augustine, saw corruption chiefly in man's sensual nature, and, in accordance with theological tradition, Luther used the theological term "concupiscence" to describe sinfulness. But sensuality was to him only one aspect of human reprobation. He was obviously little affected by such temptations, as he continued for a good many years after his break with the Roman Church in a state of celibacy. Human unworthiness was for him grounded in the ineradicable selfishness of human motives, which assert themselves not only in all actions of practical life but also in the individual's relations with God. Good works, even the desire for salvation itself, stemmed from man's desire for personal happiness. Human self-assurance caused the incapacity to love God with all one's heart and soul.

Luther was and remained a child of his time, or for that matter of the Middle Ages, in his firm belief in the reality of God and the actual presence of the transcendental in this world. God was present everywhere, in every creature and plant, in every event, even in the mischievous operations of the devil. This sounds like pantheism, but it was the very opposite for Luther. He was trained by Occamist theologians, and con-

sequently God was will and dynamic force behind and above all appearance. Luther started also from an Occamist position in his conviction
that philosophy could not understand the mysteries of divine revelation.
All through his life we hear him inveigh against Aristotle and against
that "whore," human reason. But he departed from scholasticism in refusing to see in the hierarchical and sacramental Church the dispenser
of an objective transcendental reality. Religion, he once said, is not
"doctrinal knowledge," but wisdom born of personal experience.

The power of God could be experienced only in the heart. This
sounded like mysticism, and in self-analysis and in the expression of religious feeling Luther undoubtedly learned from the mystics. But the
way of the mystics seemed to him ultimately fallacious. Even where it
took the form of the full abnegation of the individual, there remained
self-seeking pleasure in the mystical longing, and in the idea of man
rising to the level of God the majesty of the divine was slighted. Moreover, the consummation of mystical experiences was temporary. Moments of union with God were followed by times of separation and uncertainty. Luther wanted certainty of salvation and a religious experience that proved its reality by transforming the total existence of man.

From a Catholic point of view Luther's demand for certainty of salvation, achieved through direct experience, must inevitably appear as
proof of a heretical disposition. It was *hubris*, sheer presumption, and a
dangerous subjectivism to set up such a goal and form of faith. Two
spiritual principles are here placed in opposition to each other, and it is
true that in the person of Luther a new historic type of consciousness
came to life which was incompatible with the dominant piety. But Luther is certainly misjudged when his struggle for faith is called the outgrowth of what has been termed "scrupulosity" by Catholic confes-
sors, and such pronouncements become more misleading if they are
considered together with the state of Luther's health.

Luther was not scrupulous, since he wanted to, and eventually did,
overcome the scruples that had originally moved him to exaggerated
ascetic and confessional practices. The range of his moods and temper
reached from recurring fits of deep melancholy to moments of high
joy, but these were not regular states of mind; rather, they were signs
of the intensity of personal feelings in a man who lived in continuous
activity and production. Physical ailments occurred mainly after his
monastic period and were probably worsened by his exertions. His ailments were vexing and reacted on his moodiness, particularly in later
years. But Luther was one who could derive strength even from the

weaknesses of his psychic and physical nature. These do not explain the bent of his ideas.

What is bound to appear to Catholics as mere presumption and immodest self-assertion, will in Protestant eyes be a sign of the earnestness and purity of the religion of the Thuringian monk. It was his moral conscience that could not be appeased by all the advice that contemporary piety offered. In his visions God was always the stern judge, whom man could not hope to propitiate, since the perversion of human nature allowed at best a natural morality that was still infinitely removed from the absoluteness of the eternal. Rejection and damnation were inescapable if one had to understand God as just. Because Luther never questioned the reality of the divine majesty, the word of the justice of God fell upon him like a terrorizing blow, and it was almost as frightful a torture to be tempted to bypass the demand of God, since it was clear that in such moments the devil tried to ensnare one. These were what Luther called his *Anfechtungen* (assaults), "temptations," which threw him into states of panic and anxiety that threatened to turn his bones into ashes.

Scholasticism, as we have seen, had, with more or less logical consistency, taught that man could do good works only with God's assistance, which however was given through the sacraments. Occam, by assuming that God's will predestined some for damnation, others for salvation, by an arbitrary and even capricious decision that left the individual in complete doubt about his fate, saw the actions of God more directly pointed toward the individual. Still, the development of Luther's thinking ought to be seen against this background. He proceeded to the assumption that mortal perfection could only be a gift from God. But what do we know of God? What He is in the absolute, we never could know, for He is a "hidden God" (*deus absconditus*). Men could know, however, what He is for men, since God has revealed himself to them in the work of Christ and in the Scripture as a God of mercy and grace. By arousing fear and trembling in their hearts and consciences, He calls upon men to recognize their perversions and impotence and accept from Him a new strength that makes them able and happy to serve Him. Man becomes righteous only in the eyes of God, since it would be impossible for Him to establish any relationship with sinners. One has said that God, like an artist, already recognizes the completed sculpture in the unhewn block of marble. The modern metaphor is not quite adequate for a description of Luther's thought. To him the moving force was Christ and the Word of God operating in man.

The *gratia infusa*, "the love that is shed abroad in our hearts," was transformed from a sacramental event, effective by its very performance with the proper ritual, into a personal experience that became meaningful only through a personal affirmation. This affirmation had two stages, the admission of complete unworthiness and the placing of trust in God's plan. Luther accepted predestination, but not in Occam's sense. God was not capricious, and what He had started He would not drop. On the other hand, Luther, in contrast to Calvin, his greatest student, did not move the doctrine of predestination to the center of his theology. It seemed undesirable to him that man should delve more than was necessary into the mind of God, which he would know fully only in heaven. It was far more important in this connection that he should derive from his religious experience a confident joy that would fill his whole existence. Luther believed that a justified man still remained in a state of sin but won the strength to progress toward the good. Most of all, he gained a personal relationship with God, which freed him from his lonely terrors. Godlessness or hell was for Luther literally being without God, and community with God was heaven. Even if the individual who had once found God was damned, he was obliged to love God for such hours of blessedness as he had known. Man ought to love God as his creator, but a hundred times more as the merciful giver of grace through Christ and His Word.

✆ *Certain Misconceptions Concerning Luther's Thought*

LUTHER'S RELIGION has been much misunderstood in modern times. For most of the nineteenth-century liberals it was the religious parallel to the secular Renaissance movement in laying the foundations of modern individualism. Modern individualism and secularism were actually not so simple an outgrowth of the civilization of the Renaissance as former historians believed, and the Reformation of Luther was even less an outgrowth of this time. His religion was more than the culmination of the historical trend toward a more personalistic piety, and remained separated by a deep gulf from Renaissance individualism, as well as from the idealism of Kant and Hegel. It was a tremendous step to find the essence of religion entirely in the personal conscience, to admit, at least in principle, no other authority than personal faith, and to expect the individual to apply this faith in a creative manner to the solution of all the problems of life. When Luther says, "The person precedes the [religious] work," or "You have as much as you believe," the individual seems to be elevated to the rank of the true religious artificer and the doors seem wide open to subjectivism.

But Luther's intention becomes clearer when he remarks, "I, too, must be present, otherwise it does not work, but I cannot contribute anything to justification." Luther was a world apart from any modern conception under which man has within himself the capacity to reach for the stars. Man's faith is produced by God, and what he grasps in his faith, be it called God, Christ, or Word, is a supernatural reality in which the true Christian is allowed to participate to the extent that he overcomes his natural thinking, and this also includes his personality. The human spirit is "flesh," too, only God is spirit, and Luther did more than anyone after him till Sören Kierkegaard to describe the radical "otherness" of God. It seemed preposterous and sacrilegious to Luther to believe that God was the concept of man. Religion, too, was not mere sentiment, its validity was dependent on the sincerity of devotion. The Word determined the contents of faith, and Luther was absolutely convinced that the Word of God was clear. He was, therefore, not prepared to tolerate unorthodox people. "If it is said that Emperor Charles for his part was certain that Papal doctrine was correct and that he should act in justice after the same commandments of God . . . to suppress our doctrine, the answer is: let this go and let God act as judge. But we know that he cannot be certain of it and never will be, since we know that he is in error while we have God's Word with us. He ought to recognize God's Word and promote it, like ourselves, with all his powers." The certainty of having in his personal struggle for faith broken through to an absolute transcendental order was the source of Luther's heroism in the years after 1517.

✍ Individual Stages of Luther's Inner Development

IN EXPLAINING THE NATURE of Luther's religious experiences between 1505 and 1517 we have not paid attention to the individual stages of his inner development. We have only occasional insights into his early monastic years, but from 1512 onward we can follow the unfolding of his thought in great detail, particularly through his university lectures. He early became an avid reader of the Bible, and he is reported to have known the Latin Bible by heart in 1509. From his solitary life and from study, he was drawn through his various posts to growing activity.

Once he had become a professor, he was compelled to organize his thoughts in a systematic way, to broaden and compare them with the scholarship of the present and the past. Just before he began to teach his first academic course, he discovered a new interpretation of St. Paul's definition of God's "justice," which became a capstone of his own faith. Yet he was not aware of presenting to his students a radically new theology, though he used sharp words against the pagan Aristotle and the schoolmen. Luther, who by 1516 had become the leading academic figure of the young university, helped to change the theological curriculum to emphasize Biblical studies. But he felt no revolt against the Church, or contempt or derision for its representatives and institutions. Doctor Luther resented the *Epistles of Obscure Men* and called the unknown author a charlatan. He wished and hoped, however, to improve academic theology in some directions. In the summer of 1517 he wrote 97 theses on scholasticism and distributed them, even outside Wittenberg. Although the 97 theses were more advanced in the exposition of his new approach than the 95 theses on indulgences of October 31 of that same year, few people read them, and nobody cared to discuss these exercises. The 95 theses proved a bombshell, because they raised issues in which many people were profoundly interested. They induced people to look into the theology of this audacious monk, and under the prodding of sympathizers and the criticism of foes, Luther became, to his own astonishment, fully conscious of the immensity of his conflict with tradition and custom. Not before 1520 did he succeed in realizing the full consequences of his personal religious experience and in envisaging the practical application of his faith to the problems of the age.

It would not be difficult to read into the 95 theses the full theology of the mature Luther, though many aspects appear still in an embryonic and abbreviated form. Even many of the approving remarks on existing ecclesiastical institutions turn out on closer scrutiny to be untoward deviations from the essential norms of the Church. Luther asserted, in thesis seven, for example, that the authority of priests was instrumental in the remission of sin. But the authority of priests was clearly deprived of any juridical power; priests were made messengers of the good tidings of God's forgiveness to the truly repenting. The pope was no exception, and was conceived of as the first officer of the Church rather than as the holder of the key to heaven. Together with the religious meaning of special indulgences, that of the hierarchical system in general was abandoned. Still, Luther felt that he fought only abuses and believed that the pope and bishops did not know what their official theologians and salesmen of indulgences were doing. He sent his 95 theses to the archbishop of Mainz.

∾ Conflict with Rome

FROM MAINZ the first denunciation was sent to Rome, where it was thought appropriate at first to use the discipline of Luther's order to refute him. In April, 1518, he appeared before the provincial chapter of the Augustinians in Heidelberg. It was here that he won his first theological students and allies outside of Wittenberg. The young Martin Bucer, future reformer of Strasbourg, Johann Brenz of Württemberg, and others, saw Luther and were spellbound by his personality and ideas. Officially the Heidelberg disputation did not lead to any result. But another denunciation of Luther came to Rome in March, 1518, from the German Dominicans, who tried to bring succor to Tetzel. A judicial committee was appointed and reached the decision to summon the German monk to Rome. On August 7, Luther received the order to appear within 60 days before the Curia in Rome. The next day Luther approached Elector Frederick, asking him to use his influence with the pope and emperor in order to have his case adjudged by a German court.

Greater danger, however, was already brewing. Emperor Maximilian, busy paving the way for the succession of his grandson Charles to the imperial throne, had expressed his willingness to co-operate with the pope in the suppression of Luther. It seemed possible then to deal with Luther in summary fashion, and the papal legate, Cardinal Cajetan (Tommaso de Vio of Gaeta), who represented the Curia at the diet of the Empire in Augsburg, was instructed on August 23 to call Luther before him. If Luther refused to recant, the cardinal was to have him arrested and extradited to Rome; if Luther failed to appear, excommunication was to be pronounced against him and his supporters, and the secular authorities were to be compelled to imprison the "notorious heretic." But the instructions were changed out of political considerations. The papacy had been rightly alarmed by the threatening progress of the Turks and, together with the emperor, had urged a sacred war against the infidels. With few exceptions, among whom Elector Frederick was the most eminent, members of the estates had turned down the whole project. They were unwilling to grant a tax for a political enterprise in which the papacy would have played a leading role. The diet, whose meeting closed officially on September 28, had shown a passionate aversion toward Rome. Obviously it was not wise for the Curia to disregard German sentiment by settling the Luther case through non-German agencies.

Frederick the Wise insisted on keeping his professor in Germany, and there was additional cause for taking his wishes seriously. Apart from the Turkish problem, the question of succession to Maximilian began to cast its shadow over the scene. Leo X had decided against the candidacy of Charles. It was for this reason that Cajetan had received new orders. He was to do his best to make Luther retract but was to let him go if he did not do so. Luther came to Augsburg and had three audiences with the cardinal on October 12–14, 1518. Cajetan, the general of the Dominican order, was one of the most earnest theologians, a scholar fully versed in Thomistic thought, and a man of irreproachable conduct. He tried to win Luther by friendliness, then by objective discussion. But what did objectivity mean in this situation? Luther appeared humble in the beginning but became surprised when he heard stated for the first time from one of the princes of the Church, theological ideas that he had rejected as un-Christian and therefore considered excluded from the thinking of the leaders of the Church. He was stubborn and not without pride in the superior theology of Wittenberg. The treasure of grace administered by the Church and the certainty of faith were the focal points of the discussion. When Cajetan got exasperated with Luther's tenacity, and tried to impress him with his high rank and unimpeachable Roman theology, Luther forgot his own humility and warned the cardinal not to assume that the Germans did not understand "grammar." The meeting was broken off.

While still in Augsburg, Luther appealed officially "from an ill-informed" pope to one who "ought to be better informed." Rumor had it that his arrest was imminent, and his friends urged him to leave the city hurriedly and secretly in the night of October 20. In Nürnberg he was shown a copy of the Roman instructions to Cajetan of August 23, which had called him a "notorious heretic." He could not know that they had been superseded by other directives and felt certain that he could not expect an open and judicious hearing from the pope. After his return to Saxony he prepared a digest of the Augsburg proceedings for publication and now demanded that his case be settled by a general Christian council. It seems that the Saxon court advised him against taking this step, but Luther was willing to save the elector embarrassment by leaving Saxony, to go to France and place himself under the protection of the Sorbonne, which was considered the staunch defender of the conciliar theory of the Church. These thoughts did not display political realism but were clear evidence that national sentiment was a subordinate element in Luther's opposition to Rome.

But the Curia delayed action against Luther, and the death of Emperor Maximilian on January 12, 1519, led to a further deliberate postponement of his prosecution, which proved of far-reaching consequence to the Church. In order to avoid the election of King Charles I of Spain, which would bring together Spain, Burgundy and the Netherlands, Naples-Sicily, and the Austrian lands under the imperial crown and force the papacy into submission, Leo X promoted the election of the French king, or of Frederick the Wise. To gain either end, the co-operation of the foremost German prince on the electoral college was vital. Various favors were showered on the Saxon ruler. His famous collection of religious relics was endowed with additional indulgences, and he was selected a recipient of the Golden Rose, the highest honor the pope could bestow upon a secular prince, while the Luther case was soft-pedaled. A Saxon nobleman, Karl von Miltitz, was sent on a diplomatic mission to the north to create good will. Miltitz was a friendly and inept diplomat who on the one hand exceeded his instructions by overemphasizing the pope's intentions for a reconciliation, and on the other aroused, through his sanguine reports, comforting hopes about the possibility of Luther's willingness to return to obedience. At this juncture, however, the pope wanted to be reassured, whereas Luther was inclined not to aggravate the situation by any unprovoked action.

The Leipzig Disputation

BUT SOON THE ZEAL of an academic opponent brought Luther into the open again. Dr. Johann Eck, professor at the Bavarian university of Ingolstadt, had been one of the first persons to discover in the 95 theses an alarming deviation from the orthodox doctrine of the Church, and he had at once commented on this, his action leading to one of Luther's early literary feuds. Eck was a learned man with an extraordinary gift of memory and great forensic talent. To the time of his death, in 1543, he was the most active and the ablest German theologian to defend the old Church against Luther and his followers. His personal conduct in his younger years had made him many enemies, and he was, not without reason, suspected of personal ambition. In later life he outgrew his boisterousness and desire for preferment, but he could never overcome the original limitations of his mind, which lacked originality and, more important, any deep religious sense.

Eck challenged Andreas Carlstadt, Luther's colleague in Wittenberg, and Luther to a disputation, which was held in June, 1519, in Leipzig. Luther's experiences in Augsburg had led him into studies of canon law, and he had reached the conclusion that as late as the fourth century the bishop of Rome had not been recognized as head of the universal Church. Luther had gone even further at times by asserting that the whole jurisdictional authority of the papacy was not established before the twelfth century. Such opinions made Eck's defense of the apostolic succession rather easy, and in terms of academic learning Eck scored heavily not only over Carlstadt, who was a poor debater, but also over Luther. Eck seemed to win even more drastically when he moved the debate toward the central religious issues concerning the Church's essential position as mediator and the nature of Christian faith. Luther took the view that no Christian could or should believe anything outside of the Scripture. Eck switched to Huss and drew from Luther the reluctant admission that among the articles condemned by the Council of Constance some had been Christian. Eck pushed further, demanding from Luther a clear statement as to whether councils could err. Luther conceded that they could. His opponent was well satisfied to have shown him off as a heretic and as having compromised his authority in Germany, where people were proud of the Council of Constance and resented the Czechs.

The Leipzig Disputation completed Luther's development as a Church reformer. So far he had felt himself to be a restorer of Christian piety and a fighter against individual abuses in the Church. Now he realized fully that what he called the restored gospel implied a total reoganization of all authority. Recognition of the need for universal reform fell heavily on his heart, but he went to work courageously. In the great reformatory writings issued in 1520 he presented a comprehensive program of ecclesiastical and social reform based on his fundamental faith. The Leipzig event aroused almost as much attention as the 95 theses and brought him many new supporters. It is most difficult to gauge the popular succor that Luther enjoyed in these years. The general applause that his early deeds and writings evoked was certainly an ample demonstration of the existing dissatisfaction with the condition of the Church in Germany, but no one could say whether criticism stemmed more from religious motives or from anger at the interventions of Rome in the public life of Germany, and to what lengths people wished to see the reform carried.

✍ *Luther's Following*

MANY PEOPLE WERE SIMPLY EXCITED by the sensational element. The mob turning up to see Luther in Augsburg wanted to have a look at the "new Herostratus," and even on Luther's way to Worms people put pictures of Savonarola in his hands. If the old Church of the time had had in its ranks enthusiastic popular preachers, the spread of Luther's influence might have been stemmed. It is also possible that the Church might still have stamped out the fire if it had fully enforced its law in 1519. But with every day that passed such enforcement became more precarious, since Luther gained an ever wider audience and more collaborators. The reaction to the Leipzig Disputation encouraged him to address himself to the whole nation in German, and the printing presses gave wings to his ideas.

In the past the presses had published mainly learned and ecclesiastical books, largely in Latin. The heavy tomes were expensive and could be distributed only among churchmen and scholars. Luther made the pamphlet a common form of publishing. Small-sized pamphlets, often containing not more than six or eight pages, could be widely sold for little money. As a rule they displayed on the title page a woodcut, which gave even the illiterate a notion of the content. Between 1518 and 1524 the publication of books in Germany increased sevenfold, and the number of copies printed showed an even greater expansion. Luther's thirty writings between 1517 and 1520 were distributed in more than one-third of a million copies, with the great reform tracts reaching between fifteen and eighteen editions. One could think that every German was reading Luther, an impression that is strengthened by the fact that already by 1521 anti-Lutheran or non-Lutheran writers incurred great difficulties in getting their writings printed. Publishers preferred marketable goods even then.

But the overwhelming mass of the people could not read and had to be read to. In the propagation of Luther's teachings members of the clergy undoubtedly were active above all others. To some extent the pride of the academic graduates set itself against the feudal or political appointees to ecclesiastical positions. Luther's attack on the hierarchical Church gave the theologically interested clerics, and in general the scholars, a significant place in religious and public life, and many of them were eager to assume an intellectual leadership of the social groups from which they themselves had come. The academically trained clerics carried Luther's ideas to every corner of society and gave the Lutheran cause a prestige in the eyes of the common people which it might not easily have gained otherwise. At no other time in their history did the German universities exercise such an intensive influence on all classes of German society. First among them was, of course, Wittenberg. As early as the summer of 1519 this small school had almost as many students as Cologne and Leipzig, the largest German universities of the time, and this provincial place attracted students from every part of Germany as well as from Switzerland, Bohemia, and Scotland. It was rather unusual that even masters gave up their church offices and went to Wittenberg to study. Thomas Münzer was the first of these advanced scholars.

From these theological and clerical groups sprang Luther's closest followers. They were the persons who carried his ideas into the other provinces and to all classes and, after 1521, became the founders of the new congregations and churches. But the leading classes of the cities and the learned councilors of the princes were also directly reached by Luther's writings. It was important to them that at this moment the humanists took sides with Luther or, like Erasmus, seemed to see in him a positive force. Thus the majority of the intellectual elements in Germany were joined in sympathy with Luther, at least to the extent that they wished to have his cause treated with utmost consideration. To the extent that they held positions of influence in the councils of the secular and spiritual territorial states or cities, they did their best to obstruct the administration of ecclesiastical justice. Few committed themselves at this moment to Luther both in religion and politics. But in Lazarus Spengler, the secretary of the city council of Nürnberg, who, in 1520, published his *Plea in Defense of Martin Luther* (*Schutzrede*), we find a man who made the basic ideas of Luther fully his own and was clearly directed by them in his political plans. The relations between Nürnberg and the University of Wittenberg, which had existed since the founding of the latter, became close and intimate in these years.

Georg Spalatin, the secretary of Frederick the Wise, was chiefly responsible for winning the protection of the elector for Luther, and other councilors supported him. It is unfortunate that the available sources do not permit a clear picture of the motives of this man, who, more than any other person, was responsible for Luther's survival. Frederick was an astute politician, but shy and reticent in personal contacts and conversations. He was a conscientious ruler, used to deliberation with his councilors. He took special care in the administration of Church affairs and asserted his prerogatives as prince not only in financial but also in disciplinary matters in a way that foreshadowed the Church policies of future Protestant lords. But in religious matters he gave every evidence of traditional orthodoxy. His protection of Luther, with whom he never exchanged more than twenty words, arose largely from his wish to tolerate as little intervention from Rome in his country as possible, and particularly in his beloved Wittenberg University, of which Luther was the best-known professor. Only slowly did he give up his own devotion to sacred relics, and how far this phlegmatic and silent man adopted a Lutheran faith in his last years is not known. But in him, pope and emperor met a territorial prince who took advantage of any political turn to defend his own position and who was a master at diplomatic and legalistic procrastination. Frederick, however, was wise not only on account of his gift for silence but also in that he recognized the limitations of his own political power. The best proof of this was his refusal to become a pretender to the imperial throne in 1519. He would not have had the means to establish an independent authority against the Habsburg family and many other competing forces.

Besides those who welcomed Luther, but abstained from trying to direct his course, there were others who wished to drag him directly into the political arena. The moment was auspicious for such attempts. Luther had just reached the point where he saw the need for the reform of public conditions; moreover, the crisis of his personal fate was visibly approaching. If he had been one to capitalize on his outward success, he might have conducted his own fight by placing the emphasis chiefly on a political attack against the papal system, to which both the people and the authorities would have been receptive, and might have accepted support from any quarter. He was genuinely impressed by the political hopes that the imperial election of 1519 aroused and he could talk about Charles V as "the young, noble, German blood." But even when he devoted his attention to national problems, he remained primarily in his own religious realm.

✎ *Luther's Opposition to Rome Given Patriotic Meaning*

THE TEMPTATION TO GIVE Luther's opposition to Rome a predominantly patriotic meaning was brought home most distinctly by Ulrich von

Hutten, who reached in these years the height of his productivity. What distinguished Hutten among German humanists was his activism. He was no schoolmaster or mere poet, nor were humanistic interests a mere embellishment of his social existence. To him ideas were weapons for a political fight. As a descendant of imperial knights he had imbibed a strong Empire patriotism. His studies of the *Germany* of Tacitus had given this patriotism a new justification in the continuity of popular virtues. The Germans were noble, courageous, and freedom-loving. Humanistic education was to make them fully aware of their national heritage and to enable them to restore the full might of the Empire.

Originally liberty had meant to Hutten the freedom that the individual members of the Empire enjoyed under the chaotic constitutional conditions of Germany. But in these years it began to assume for him an additional significance as freedom from foreign influence. While in his younger years he had pamphleteered for Emperor Maximilian against the popes, as ecclesiastical heads perverting the proper division of secular and spiritual authority in Christendom, the conflict now assumed in his eyes a national character. The Roman popes were the successors of the ancient Caesars who had tried to subjugate the Teutons. The struggle between the Latins and Germans had continued in the clashes of medieval popes and emperors, and could be resolved only through a relentless war against all the secular powers of the Roman Church, particularly in Germany, and through the simultaneous victory of humanism over stale scholasticism, the intellectual twin of the Roman lust for domination. From the recently rediscovered parts of Tacitus' *Annals* he developed the legend of the heroic German fighter opposing Roman ambition. The tribal prince Arminius, who in A.D. 9 had annihilated a Roman legion in the Teutoburg Forest, became the model of German prowess and virtue.

Latin humanism became in the hands of Hutten the instrument of anti-Latin nationalism. But in spite of some pagan overtones, Hutten's ideas of an ethical reform were sincere. With deep passion he had thrown himself into the Reuchlin feud, but he was determined to carry the fight against the "obscure men" from the literary into the political arena. The question was whether he could gather some political support from among the imperial knights. Dissatisfaction with the conditions of the age was rife among them, but the knights were bound to the German Church through many ties. Bishop's sees and chapters were largely occupied by them. Educational reform was beyond the ken of these "centaurs," as Hutten himself occasionally described them. But Hutten succeeded in winning the friendship of the one knight who had risen to a position of personal influence greater than that of many German princes.

Franz von Sickingen (1481–1523) had become a power in German politics as a cunning soldier and merchant of war. In the chaotic political circumstances he had succeeded in gathering considerable capital and in acquiring a military reputation, which made him a big military entrepreneur and captain. In the years from 1518 to 1521 this German *condottiere* had made himself an indispensable tool of Habsburg policy. The army of Sickingen, encamped in the neighborhood of Frankfurt during the summer of 1519, had hung like a warning cloud on the horizon when the German electors voted for the Habsburg heir. Ulrich von Hutten had persuaded Sickingen to take an interest in Reuchlin's affairs, and when he began to recognize the general significance of Luther's struggle, he prevailed on Sickingen to support Luther. Soon Martin Bucer became Sickingen's priest. Hutten had judged the beginnings of the controversy on indulgences to be another miserable squabble among the schoolmen, to be welcomed as a sign of their bent toward self-destruction. The Leipzig Disputation turned the literary knight into an unreserved admirer of the Wittenberg monk, and he decided to carry his own polemics against the papacy to radical extremes. In a number of extraordinary satirical dialogues he called upon the Germans to free themselves from the yoke of the Roman Church. But before the writings made their appearance in print during the spring of 1520, Hutten had contacted Luther and offered him Sickingen's protection. It is not clear whether an almost simultaneous invitation that Sylvester von Schaumburg tendered to Luther on behalf of a hundred Franconian knights was, at least indirectly, connected with Hutten's agitation and actions.

✷ Luther's Rift with Rome Widened

LUTHER HAD NO REASON for leaving Saxony, nor was he willing to involve his cause in any political scheme. But Hutten's fight for "German freedom" impressed on his mind the inevitable connection between religious and political reform. He could not fail to see that it would have been easy for him to win the enthusiastic support of all of Germany if he had declared himself the champion of the political grievances of the nation. But he was not swerved from his own path. For the clarification of his own thought at this moment, Hutten did him a real service by the publication of Lorenzo Valla's *Donation of Constantine*. Since the Leipzig Disputation and under the shadow of the approaching resumption of his trial, Luther had been studying the legal and theological foundations of Church authority. Valla's demonstration that the Roman bishops had not received the rule over the Church states from Emperor Constantine convinced Luther that the Roman Church was not only partially affected by abuse and superstition, but was perverted to its heart. In this case the pope was the Antichrist himself, and the present age a gruesome prelude to the last day. Apocalyptic and eschatological visions filled Luther with grim expectations, which at times led him to wish for open revolt. "If we punish thieves with the gallows, robbers with the sword, heretics with fire—why do we not attack with all arms these teachers of perdition, these cardinals and popes, and that whole worms' heap of the Roman Sodom . . . , and wash our hands in their blood."

Yet such pronouncements were made in passing moments of fiery anger, while Luther remained convinced that the kingdom of the Antichrist would fall before the Word of God, and that as far as reforms of the world were needed, they should be enacted by the proper authority. In this spirit he wrote in 1520, when threatened by the papal ban, his reformatory writings, *The Sermon on Good Works, Address to the German Nobility, On Christian Liberty*, and *The Babylonian Captivity of the Church*. The first of these brief books unfolded the consequences of Luther's new ethics. There were no works that could make man better in God's judgment. Man was enabled to do good works through the strength of the faith that God instilled in him. Faith in God would compel man to prove his love of his neighbor. It was vain to attach the label of merit to individual actions, since morality was nothing but an attitude of heart. Monasticism, celibacy, or any other fulfillment of duties and services imposed from above was morally meaningless, since a Christian required no law other than the Decalogue and the Sermon on the Mount, from which a faith could be derived that was realizable in ethical conduct by everyone, be he priest, layman, prince, or shoemaker. In other words, there were no higher and lesser states of perfection, but in every occupation man could live up to a vocation from God, or, put differently, every Christian believer was a priest. In his most popular and influential tract on *Christian Liberty*, Luther once more expressed, in powerful language, the idea that every

Christian was above any law, was "a master of all things" because he was "a serf of God."

Hierarchy hereby received a new meaning, but at the same time was attacked from the sacramental angle. Luther's *Babylonian Captivity of the Church* contended that the true Church had been taken away from the believers by the doctrine of sacraments, which had placed the distribution of grace in the hands of a select group of people. Luther found no special priesthood in the New Testament, and only three sacraments—baptism, the Lord's Supper, and penance—but even these sacraments conveyed grace only to the faithful and were not effective by their mere performance. This denial of the traditional doctrine of sacraments proved scandalous to many who had sympathized with Luther. Surprisingly, it was most resented by the humanists, who had always placed little emphasis upon the sacramental institutions of the Church. But Luther's destruction of Catholic sacraments threatened the very existence of a universal Church led by an intellectual elite. Most of the humanists were willing to sacrifice neither universality nor the continuation of a corps of leaders dedicated exclusively to spiritual tasks. Erasmus, who had been working, so far behind the scene, to protect Luther, discontinued his efforts after the publication of the *Babylonian Captivity*, and even Crotus Rubeanus, the author of the *Epistles of Obscure Men*, made his peace with the old authorities.

✍ Luther's Program for Reform of Public Life

ONCE HIERARCHY AND SACRAMENTS WERE THROWN out as elements irrelevant to the Christian Church, and the faith of all believers was made the exclusive substance of religion, the reformation of Christianity could not be confined to the rebuilding of ecclesiastical institutions or to the mere reform of education; the whole of Christian life within the *respublica Christiana* had to be reoriented. The dualism between spiritual and secular authority had to be abolished as well as the whole system of gradations from low to high stages of perfection. The dichotomy between the realms of grace and nature was bridged only in acts of faith, and the Church was formed by the believers past and present, a mystical community of saints, in which the Word was kept alive. Canon law was invalid in secular affairs. No sanction of force, no secular dominion and property belonged to the Church, whose only function was the propagation of the Gospel. If the Church was, in such a radical manner, removed from the direction of public and private life, the secular world had to be reorganized in order to give Christians a free way for the realization of the divine commandments. For this purpose Luther added to his general program of Church reform an agenda for the reform of public life. He demanded a thorough revision of education at all levels, as well as the enforcement of public mores through sumptuary laws, abolition of public houses, and rules against begging. He represented nothing new in his moralistic demands and remained even more traditionalistic in his suggestions concerning economic life. As a child of a predominantly agrarian society he believed that it was better to stimulate agriculture than the merchant's trade and that the capitalistic practices of the Fuggers should be suppressed as usury.

Luther addressed himself to "the German nobility," and this meant to the emperor and the estates of the Empire, as the foremost authorities within Christendom. He was not inclined to turn over to them the government of the Church, and, least of all, the decision on matters of faith. But he argued in terms of late medieval theory that in an emergency the secular arm had the right and duty to restore the Church to its proper order. Thus he wanted the emperor and the estates to intervene by calling a Christian council. What he had in mind, however, was not exactly a new Council of Nicea, for although the emperor was to act as had Emperor Constantine, the council was not to be composed exclusively of bishops; other theologians, and even secular representatives, were to be present.

∽ Papal Action Against Luther

WHILE LUTHER, during the year 1520, explained his own position to the authorities and to the whole nation, the papal see at last took action against him. Not only politics had delayed disciplinary measures but also the ineptitude of the papal legate, Karl von Miltitz, a loquacious Saxon, who had kept everyone confused for many months. The delay was, however, also a sign that Rome misjudged the intensity of the storm that was brewing north of the Alps. New legal proceedings against Luther were not opened in Rome until January, 1520, and the deliberations, in which Johann Eck participated, lasted till June. The forty-one statements of Luther over which the anathema was pronounced contained some of the most glaring heresies, but at the same time a number of minor deviations, while the writings of the months after the Leipzig Disputation were not taken into consideration. In spite of the time spent in deliberation, the final document, signed as a papal bull on June 15, 1520, was rather unsatisfactory. Luther was given sixty days to recant. If he refused, the Church would pronounce judgment on him. Meanwhile his writings were to be burned.

Dr. Eck was dispatched as papal nuncio to publish this bull, *Exsurge Domine*, in central Germany, while a papal diplomat, the Italian humanist Hieronymus Aleander, was sent out to the imperial court and charged with the execution of the bull in the western parts of the Empire. Eck was not a particularly happy choice. He was widely disliked, and the bull was suspected to be a work of personal vindictiveness. The execution of a bull was not a simple legal transaction, particularly if the secular authorities wished to raise difficulties against its official announcement. Excommunication had become a blunt weapon during the fifteenth century. At one time three popes had excommunicated one another. On other occasions the papal excommunication had been rashly applied and lifted again for political ends. It had lost its efficacy against princes and rulers; now it could not be set in operation against a churchman. Only in three places, Meissen, Merseburg, and Brandenburg, did Eck succeed in having the bull officially posted. Even in the place of his recent academic triumphs, in Leipzig, the university refused to publish the bull. In many towns the people showed a threatening attitude, and the authorities, depending on their inclinations, were either too cowed or too much in sympathy with Luther to act against popular opposition.

Friendly jurists questioned the legality of Luther's trial. It was asserted that he had never had a real hearing and that he was ready to defend his case before a correctly appointed court. Luther, probably on the advice of the Saxon councilors, expressed doubts regarding the authenticity of the bull, but added on his own that the bull was the product of Satan. After he had heard that in Louvain and Cologne his books had been burned, he took the revolutionary step of burning a copy of the bull together with a copy of the code of canon law and a few scholastic treatises. The brief ceremony took place on December 10, 1520, before the gates of Wittenberg in the presence of students and professors. It was an audacious gesture, undertaken with a trembling heart, but with a clear awareness that there could be no retreat from this ultimate challenge of the politico-ecclesiastical order of universal Christendom. Luther was not eager to suffer martyrdom, nor did he count on political protection. Not even his own ruler, he felt, should be obeyed in these matters. But Frederick the Wise tolerated even this outrage and, more than that, employed every diplomatic and legal device to save his professor from the pyre.

Aleander had better success than Eck with the publication of the bull. Meeting the young emperor in the Netherlands, he persuaded him in Antwerp on September 28 to issue an order for the suppression of the Lutheran heresy in his Burgundian realm. On October 8, 1520, the nuncio presided over the first book-burning in Louvain. A week later he prevailed on the bishop of Liége, a prince of the Holy Roman Empire, to emulate the active devotion of the emperor. But when the imperial court on its travels reached the Rhineland, it encountered a very different atmosphere. On October 23 Charles was crowned German King with great display in Aachen, the old city of Charlemagne. Three days later, with the permission of Pope Leo X, he assumed the title of Roman Emperor Elect. At the same time the political conversations started between him and the German princes, who had tried to bind him to constitutional conditions before the election in the preceding year.

Charles V was reluctant to agree to a hearing for Martin Luther, even more so after the Vatican issued a new and final bull, *Decet Romanum Pontificem,* in condemnation of Luther. Charles V had readily permitted the execution of a papal sentence in his own countries. Brought up as a devout son of the Church by Bishop Hadrian of Utrecht, subsequently Pope Hadrian VI, he was willing to place the power of secular government behind the persecution of a declared heretic. But he had to give in to the German princes, and particularly to Frederick the Wise, who argued that in view of popular sentiment it would be impossible to proceed against Luther unless he had first received a hearing. A long tug of war ensued. It lasted till March 6, 1521, when Charles V issued, from his first diet of the Empire, which was officially opened in Worms on January 27, an invitation to Luther to appear before the diet, granting him safe conduct.

Politics compelled Charles V to make this concession, the first and most important accommodation that he made in the Luther case. The power of the new ruler was by no means as imposing as it seemed. Spain was in internal revolt, political relations with the pope since the election were tense and uncertain, and conflict with France was likely. It was desirable to get from the Empire the funds for gaining the imperial crown and, beyond this, to establish as much predominance over the recalcitrant estates of the Empire as could be gained. But there was a question of right as well. According to Article 24 of the capitulation of election, which Charles V had again sworn to on the eve of his coronation in Aachen, he was not to permit a German of any class to be placed under the ban "without cause" and "without hearing." The stipulation showed how far even orthodox German princes were aroused before Luther's case had become a national issue to oppose the jurisdiction of the papacy in Germany. Nobody had thought that the diet of the Empire might assume authority in religious matters, but once the idea had been presented, it came to be seen that a German diet, with its large membership of ecclesiastical lords, was a sort of national church council.

From the point of view of the papacy, of course, such an argument reviving the conciliar theory made things worse. The papal nuncio fought with all his might to keep Luther from appearing before the diet. Even the imperial councilors would have preferred to arrange a less formal and less conspicuous hearing for Luther; and when it became impossible not to invite him to the diet, they would have liked to frighten him from appearing or, as a last resort, limit the hearing in such a way that the diet would not look like a court on matters of faith. The endless intrigues, which at a decisive moment enveloped even Hutten, were overcome by the firm policy of the Saxon elector. He could not assure Luther, however, that he would not meet with the same fate as Huss in Constance. But Luther was determined to testify before the world to the righteousness of his faith.

His journey to Worms was a triumphant progress. Everywhere he was surrounded by jubilant crowds and welcomed by friendly hosts. If Aleander in his colorful reports to Rome said that three quarters of the people of Germany were Lutherans, this was probably true, though it was almost impossible to say exactly what "Lutheran" meant. No doubt, Luther's personality impressed the Germans, and he seemed to them the very embodiment of the people with his homely language, straightforward manner, and boundless courage. The Spaniards in Worms found him awkward in his gestures and lacking in form. The lean monk of former years showed at this time the first signs of stoutness, but his deep, dark eyes had not lost their radiating glow, and he proved the fire in him as a preacher on his way to Worms. Many must have found in his sermons the confirmation of their admiration for the man, who by his writings, particularly by his German writings, had enabled the layman to participate in religious speculation, formerly a domain of the learned or of a privileged class.

But even in the spring of 1521 it was doubtful whether the support of Luther did not rest to an even larger degree on anti-Roman sentiment. Hutten's program of a fight for German freedom was closely related to Luther's idea of Christian liberty, and Hutten had become, next to Luther, the most influential writer in these months. He had followed Luther's example at the end of 1519 by turning to writing in German, first by translating his Latin invectives against the papacy and Roman power, then by pouring forth in German verse and prose his loud accusations against the exploiters of the nation.

✍ *Luther's Appearance Before the Diet of the Empire*

LUTHER APPEARED before the emperor and princes for the first time on the evening of April 17. Up to the last moment the proceedings of the occasion had been subject to negotiations behind the scene. The imperial councilors insisted that only two questions be directed to Luther, namely whether he confirmed the authorship of his books and whether he was prepared to recant all or part of them. The judgment of the Church was thus implicitly declared valid, and in order to tone down the unusual intervention of a political body in religious affairs, a clerical person was designated as speaker. Dr. Johann von der Eck (not to be confused with Luther's academic opponent, Johann Eck), an official of the archbishop of Trier, placed the two questions before Luther. It came as an anticlimax when Luther accepted the authenticity of his books but requested time for consideration of his reply to the second question. He was granted one day. Whether he was taken aback by the nature of the proceedings, since he had expected a real hearing, whether he was flustered by the great audience, or whether he was simply eager to put his fateful answer in unexceptional language, we do not know. But the apprehension of his friends and the satisfaction of his enemies were unjustified.

Luther appeared again before the assembly of the diet on the evening of April 18, the hall lighted by torches. He began to speak in a firm voice before a tense audience. In a German speech of about ten minutes, later repeated in Latin, he divided his writings into three groups. The first comprised those of a simple devotional character which even many of his opponents had called unobjectionable, and which he could not revoke. The second group consisted of his writings against the "papal tyranny under which particularly the German nation was suffering." He declared that he would stand by these teachings. With regard to the third group, his polemic pamphlets against persons, Luther conceded that he had used language more bellicose than was becoming to his vocation, but felt that he could not recant these writings either, since a recantation would make the tyrants overbold. But Luther admitted that he was an erring human being and that he would be the first to throw his books into the fire if he was shown evidence of error through the Bible. The argument that he was throwing the Christian world into immeasurable conflict, he met with the reference that Christ had not come to bring peace but the sword. God's ways were miraculous and beyond human comprehension. It would be dangerous to establish peace by suppression of the Word of God, who was above the pharaohs and the kings of Babylon and Israel. It would be a bad beginning for the reign of the young emperor if it opened with such an action.

Luther's statement still left one door open. He had declared that he would be willing to reconsider his position if it were refuted by Biblical evidence. But for the diet this would have meant entering into a discussion with him. On the other hand, if they did nothing about Luther's demand, he and his friends could maintain that he had not only been refused a hearing but also that he had not been allowed to express his views fully. Therefore it was decided to request from him a brief and unequivocal reply to the main question. These were Luther's decisive words: "Unless I am convicted by testimonies of the Scripture and clear reason—for I do neither believe the pope nor the councils alone, since it is obvious that they have contradicted each other—my conscience is bound by the Holy Scripture and a captive of the Word of God. Therefore I cannot and will not recant anything, for to go against conscience is neither right nor safe: God help me, Amen."

Quickly von der Eck shot back, "Let your conscience go, Martin, your conscience is in error." But the emperor stopped any further exchange of words, and the meeting broke up noisily. When Luther passed the Spanish horsemen at the street gate, they were heard to jibe at him yelling, "Into the fire!" and the sentiment of Charles V was substantially the same. He called the electors and princes together the following morning, asked them what should be done next, and when they wanted time to ponder the issue, this seemingly slow youth read and translated to them a statement that he had written in French. It was both a confession of his own personal faith and a statement of the policy to which he was to adhere all his life: As a descendant of the Christian emperors of Germany, the Catholic kings of Spain, the archdukes of Austria, and the dukes of Burgundy, "who without exception had been loyal to their deaths to the Roman Church, defenders of the Catholic faith, the sacred customs, decretals, and traditions of worship," he was determined to cling to the legacy of his ancestors and to stake his "kingdoms and dominions, friends, body and blood, life and soul." "It would be a disgrace for me," he said, "and for you, members of the noble German nation, if in our age by our negligence even the appearance of heresy and any curtailment of Christian religion would sink into the hearts of men." Listening to Luther's speech the day before, he continued, he had felt sorry to have hesitated so long. He would not hear Luther again, though he would abide by his guarantee of safe conduct. He would henceforth consider Luther a notorious heretic, and he hoped that they, as good Christians, would do their part.

∽ Informal Meetings of April 23–25

EVERYONE WAS IMPRESSED, but it took much to spur German princes into haste. While they discussed the imperial proposition for another day, ominous signs of popular dissatisfaction with the proceedings of the diet were noted. The German princes, among them the archbishop of Mainz, were sufficiently frightened to arrange another meeting with Luther so that he could not assert that he had not received a hearing, and so that the people would not get the impression that Luther had been condemned without debate. The emperor objected, but he had to tolerate the appointment of a select committee of the diet consisting of two electors, two bishops, two princes, two city representatives, and one imperial count, under the direction of the elector-archbishop of Trier. The committee was appointed on the same day that the diet passed a resolution concerning "the grievances of the German nation against the Holy See." The chancellor or Baden, Hieronymus Vehus, one of the princely advisers who was quite active in passing this resolution, was chosen as counsel for the committee. The meeting with Luther on April 23 and less official negotiations thereafter were friendly conversations, in which, in addition to Vehus and von der Eck, the Augsburg plenipotentiary Conrad Peutinger as well as the Trier elector did their utmost to find a compromise. But all the difficulties that were to frustrate the many attempts at a reunification of the old and new religion in the decades and centuries to come had already appeared in the discussions of April 23–25. Luther was attracted by the proposal that some of his opinions should be reserved for the decision of a Christian council, but he was not prepared to accept such a procedure unconditionally. He was determined "not to give the Bible out of his fist." No common ground on matters of substance was found and even fewer common authorities to which both parties might bow.

These conversations must have been a greater strain on Luther than his appearances before the assembly of the diet. The consequences of his stand were brought home to him more fully both with regard to the universal Church and the future of Germany. If he had been concerned only with the political welfare of his country, he would have made concessions in the strictly religious field, for example, leaving a ruling on sacraments to a future council. In that case he would have found support for his fight against Rome among the estates of the Empire. Actually, the fate of Germany was for Luther only incidental to his sense of obligation to the Church of God, and he conceived even of this in absolutely transcendental terms. Any accommodation to secular conditions would have seemed to him a betrayal of Christ, and had he had any prescience of the bloodshed and crime to be committed in the name of Christianity during the following century, he would probably have considered it a vision raised by the devil. When in the last moments the archbishop of Trier asked him what suggestions he would make about the settlement of the issues, Luther quoted: "If this counsel or this work be of men, it will come to nought: but if it be of God, ye cannot overthrow it; lest haply ye be found even to fight against God" (Acts 5:38-9). Within three or perhaps two years, he felt, this would become manifest.

The representatives of the German estates had to recognize that Luther was inflexible and that they could not get anything from him that would allow them to deflect the emperor from his outright opposition to the friar. Most of them certainly were relieved in their own conscience, which was in any event awakened not so much by the compunction of their hearts as by the trouble expected in the enforcement of the law against Luther. Luther left Worms on April 26. Just before his departure with an imperial safe conduct of three weeks, the Saxon elector let him know that he had decided "to put him away," that is, to remove him to a secret place. With great reluctance Luther agreed. On May 3, 1521, Luther was kidnapped by horsemen of the elector in Thuringia and conducted to a castle, the Wartburg close to Eisenach, where he lived for the next ten months, disguised as a *Junker*.

Frederick the Wise had disavowed in Worms any personal interest in Luther. He was most eager not to arouse the ire of the emperor. When finally the diet went to work on an edict against Luther, he removed himself from Worms. On May 8 the edict was approved by the imperial cabinet, but for political reasons Charles V delayed its presentation to the estates and his final signature. When the edict was passed by the diet on May 25, the ranks of the estates had been thinned by the departure of many princes, and this was to be used later, quite incorrectly, if effectively, as an argument against the legality of the edict. On May 26, 1521, the edict, which added the imperial to the papal ban, became law. Charles V asked the attending nuncio Aleander whether he was now content, and the latter happily agreed that he was. Whatever dissension existed between the two supreme authorities of the *respublica Christiana*, they did not entertain any doubts that their common fiat would put an end to any rebellion. But the fire was not that easily stifled.

The Edict of Worms branded Luther as a devil in the habit of a monk, who had defiled the sacraments and made them dependent on the faith of the recipient. He was characterized as a pagan because of his denial of free will and depicted as an enemy of the hierarchy, as well as of secular authority. A special point was made of the fact that attempts had been made to reason with him "but he recognizes only the authority of the Scripture, which he interprets in his own sense." Harsh as the language of the edict was, it was quite logical from the point of view of the old order. Even its prediction of civil disorder was well justified. The new conception of Christian religion was bound to revolutionize the old political system and possibly also the old social system. But neither the traditional order nor the faith on which it lived rested on firm foundations. The old institutions, customs, and beliefs were dear to the age but no longer commanded absolute moral respect. Luther would not have aroused popular support if he had not attacked conditions under which the people chafed, but few would have followed him into the inner realm of his religion if, in their opinion, he had not promised a solution to the moral and spiritual conflicts under which they suffered. In the days of Worms, Luther showed them what prodigious courage could spring from the new faith.

CHAPTER 7

Reformation and Revolution,
1521–25

✆ *Charles' Struggles for European Supremacy, 1521–30*

FOR AN UNDERSTANDING of the events that took place in Germany in the next decade, it is of the greatest importance to realize that the imperial power was never able to make its full impact felt in Germany. Charles V left Worms in 1521 to go to war against France and to return to Spain. He did not come back to the Empire until 1530. During this period he devoted himself to gaining control of his own dominions and stabilizing his imperial position in Europe. It was in these years, too, that he fully awakened as an individual and acquired his ultimate stature.

Charles had been brought up in Burgundy, and although in his twenties he became more familiar with Spain and felt more at home in this, his mother's, country, his youth in the Netherlands had formed his personal character. The ideals of Christian chivalry, the cult of dynasty, and the desire for glory gained by meritorious deeds, stemmed from the saturated culture of the Burgundian court. Although Charles had an unbending pride in his imperial dignity, he was not given to the ostentatiousness of his ancestors. There was in him great humility, a genuine religious devotion, and an amazing self-discipline. His personal moral character towered far above that of the princes of his age, particularly the German princes. He was cautious and slow in his policies, partly because he was so much given to examining political actions in the light of his ideals. When in 1527 Pope Clement VII, who had double-crossed him more than once, became his captive, Charles V was incapable of taking full political advantage of the crucial event, as he felt embarrassed to lay down the law to the pontiff. At the same time, Charles was a good judge of men, but too rigid in his bearing to impress them with more than his lofty majesty. This was especially true in his dealings with Germans. He never mastered the German language, and apart from his native French spoke only Spanish.

Charles' political plans were originally based on Burgundy. The full restoration of the empire of Charles the Bold under his crown was his chief aim. Conflict with France was, therefore, inevitable. It was fought in Navarre, Flanders, and on the Rhine, but above all in Italy. Mercurino Gattinara was till his death in 1530 the chief political adviser and guide of Charles V. Serving as grand chancellor, he broadened the political vision of the emperor by making him see the Burgundian problem in its wider European context. A Piedmontese, though with long experience in Burgundian councils, he directed the emperor's attention to the supremacy of Italy, and the latter came to see that it was only by driving out the French and subjecting Italy to his own will that he could hope to rise above Francis I and to induce the papacy to support his imperial rule. Gattinara guided Charles toward a policy of restoring medieval universalism, and in this the conquest of Italy was the most important and immediate objective.

What distinguished Charles' policy from that of the German emperors of the Middle Ages, was the fact that Germany played a minor role in its execution. Spain, the Italian possessions, and the Netherlands were the true bases of Charles' universal policy. Spain had received this foreign prince as her king with deep suspicion in 1516, and his acquisition of the imperial dignity was disliked. The Spaniards were afraid that their welfare might suffer from an imperialistic policy. When Charles left Spain in 1520, it rose in rebellion. The dangerous revolution was defeated in 1522. Although Charles was careful not to abolish old institutions, after that time he governed Spain as an absolutist ruler and largely succeeded in converting the nobility to his imperialism, which assumed more and more a Spanish hue.

The Netherlands were ruled by two strong-willed and shrewd lady relatives of Charles: his aunt Margaret, and after her death in 1530 his sister Mary, the widowed queen of Hungary. The prosperous society of the Lowlands enjoyed much greater freedoms—"German freedoms," they were called—than Spain. Both the nobility and the cities were proud of them. They also approved of Charles' endeavor to keep Burgundy separate from the German Empire. The incipient national feeling was not averse to the dynastic character of the government, while the mercantile interests were boosted by the connection with Spain and the support of the imperial government. The rich Netherlands contributed far more money to Charles' political undertakings than any of his other dominions. The Holy Roman Empire did not provide any fiscal revenue. The "Roman Months," [1] granted by the diet for the acquisition of the imperial crown in Italy, had to be used together with the revenue from Austria for defense against the Turks. Of more immediate significance was the help provided by loans from German bankers and the possibility of raising soldiers in Germany if the imperial purse contained money. In contrast to the Empire, Naples, Sicily, and at a later date Milan contributed substantially to the financing of Charles' policies.

Nevertheless, the revenues from all his possessions, as well as the credit he received, proved inadequate for the gigantic task Charles set himself. He was in a continuous state of penury. When Italy finally lay at his feet and he wished to sail from Spain to his coronation in Bologna in 1529, he had to wait for the arrival of his wife's dowry from Portugal before he could proceed. Then, going from Bologna to Augsburg, he found himself again stranded for want of cash, this time in Innsbruck. All during his reign his armies were every so often stopped by the drying up of the sinews of war. His two greatest military victories, however, the battle of Pavia of 1525, in which King Francis I was captured, and the conquest of Rome in 1527, were also conditioned by financial difficulties. The imperial generals probably would not have attacked at Pavia if they had been able to pay their soldiers; and in 1527 the commanders of the imperial forces were powerless to discipline their unpaid and ragged soldiers and keep them from marching to Rome, this leading to the cruelty of the German and Spanish soldiers in the Eternal City.

The discrepancy between means and ends shows the weakness of the administrative systems of the states that were just emerging from the feudal age. King Francis was beset by similar troubles, but by and large the administration of his compact realm was more advanced, and many of its shortcomings were made up for by the patriotism of the French nation. The dominions of Charles V were a loose chain compared to the French kingdom. Charles V recognized that he had to respect in all his possessions the peculiar traditions and customs of the various countries. In view of their diversity, he thought it impossible to create so much as a common upper council from among them. The ties that bound his possessions together were exclusively dynastic. A deeper community of sentiment only the Church could create. This was the

[1] See page 44.

chief political cause of Charles' loyal defense of orthodoxy and his desire for a true co-operation between emperor and pope on a universal scale. However, it was also the reason for the pope's power over the emperor, which could never be completely blotted out by mere military and political conquest.

The history of Charles' struggles for European supremacy is not part of German history. Suffice it to say that by 1529 he had succeeded in driving the French out of Italy, but he had not defeated France to the extent of compelling her to support his policies aimed at restoration of the religious and political unity of Christendom. France would always try to drive a wedge between pope and emperor, but she went much further in her denial of a common responsibility for the *respublica Christiana* by her alliance with Turkey of 1535–36 and through a steadily growing liaison with the German Protestant princes. England, too, went her own way, at least after 1530, and all the attempts of Charles V to gain some hold on Denmark and Scandinavia failed completely early in his reign. In view of the great strength of these national forces one may wonder whether Charles' political program was not utopian from the beginning. But considering what a reformed Catholic Church was able to achieve in the world after 1550, we must again acknowledge the significance of the role played by the papal attitude in the first half of the century. If the papacy had risen earlier from its religious coma and its preoccupation with Italian politics, the emperor might have stemmed the tide that, in his lifetime, was running against the unity of the Western world.

ᔜ *Division of Habsburg Dominions*

WITH THESE GENERAL EUROPEAN DEVELOPMENTS in mind, let us turn our attention back to Germany. Shortly after he was elected ruler of the Empire of the German Nation, Charles V turned the regency of his German domains over to his brother Ferdinand (1503–64). Ferdinand was supposed to marry the sister and heiress of King Ludwig of Bohemia and Hungary, while the latter was to receive the hand of Mary, sister of Charles and Ferdinand. This double marriage, like all royal unions, was a political project, and it would probably not have come off if King Ludwig had not been convinced that he needed the backing of the rulers of the German lands in order to defend Hungary against the Turks. But the promising match required the endowment of Ferdinand with dominions of his own, which naturally were found in the old Austrian duchies. On April 28, 1521, two months before the two weddings were solemnized in Linz, Charles V ceded, in Worms, the ducal powers over Upper and Lower Austria, Styria, Carinthia, and Carniola to his brother.

In January and February, 1522, in agreements made in Brussels, the partition was carried further. The archduke was made regent of all the German Habsburg possessions, which meant Tyrol, Vorarlberg, and the whole Anterior Austria, including at this time, in addition to the Breisgau and Alsace, the duchy of Württemberg. In an agreement that was to be kept secret until Charles' imperial coronation, Ferdinand was raised to the hereditary rulership of all these territories with the exception of Alsace, which, after his death, was to fall to the Burgundian crown. Nothing showed so clearly as this last stipulation the preoccupation of Charles V with Burgundy, while the provision of secrecy indicated his concern about the German reaction to these agreements. Charles felt that Ferdinand could not effectively rule all the German possessions as long as he himself had not become emperor through papal coronation and the way thereby been opened for Ferdinand's election to the kingship by the German electors.

For all practical purposes a new German branch of the Habsburg family, besides the Burgundian-Spanish branch, was set up by the Brussels agreements. Charles V planned the partition in the confident hope that his magnanimity would cement the common rule of the Habsburgs over a united Europe. Ferdinand never failed to recognize his brother's position and greater political vision. He also shared with him an unshakable loyalty to the religion of their fathers. Ferdinand had spent most of his youth in Spain and was originally an even greater stranger to things German than Charles V. But as time went on, he not only learned German but also identified himself with German interests, the more so as events compelled him to look to the German princes for help.

King Ludwig of Hungary was killed in the battle of Mohács in 1526, and Archduke Ferdinand became King of Bohemia and Hungary. Yet the victories of Suleiman II, supported by the indigenous Magyar forces under Zápolya, left little authority over Hungarian territories to Ferdinand, and, worse than that, left Austria open to Turkish invasion. Naturally, Ferdinand always viewed German affairs with an eye to the urgent problems of southeastern Europe. Fraternal bonds, though never broken, proved inadequate to overcome the centrifugal powers of Europe. Ferdinand's youth and the weakness of his authority with regard to the Austrian estates did not enable him to conduct a policy of his own in the years after the Diet of Worms.

✂ *The Imperial Governing Council of Nürnberg, 1522–24*

IT HAS ALREADY BEEN MENTIONED that in these years the movement of the estates for a reform of the Empire again gained strength. The negotiations of the diet of 1521 were largely concerned with the problems of reform. Most important among them was the establishment of a new Imperial Governing Council.[2] Charles V succeeded in reaching an agreement with the princes, whereby such a Council was created only for the period of his own absences from Germany. The fundamental issue of the German constitution—whether the Empire was represented by the emperor or by the emperor *and* the estates—was left in the balance. The Council proved incapable of solving this problem—or any of the major reform projects discussed at Worms. The German estates were too lukewarm in their intention to develop a common policy and too diversified in their interests to achieve such an objective when they made the attempt. But in the religious affairs of the Empire a new policy was inaugurated by the Imperial Governing Council and the three diets that were convened in Nürnberg between 1522 and 1524.

After the publication of the Edict of Worms, the Lutheran movement seemed to spread with irresistible force. With the possible exception of the electorate of Saxony, no government was fully won over, though a good many wavered. Most important was the fact that Frederick, the first imperial regent and brother of Elector Ludwig of the Palatinate, was attracted by Protestant teachings. But there were other princes, such as Duke George of Saxony and Elector Joachim of Brandenburg, who did not falter for a moment in their allegiance to the Church. But no German prince played a decisive role in the tedious deliberations of the Imperial Governing Council, if for no other reason than because the princes attended very irregularly. Count Palatine Frederick, for example, was soon replaced by Archduke Ferdinand. An element of continuity was brought into the whole proceedings chiefly by the learned councilors of the princes. It was the first time in German

[2] See pages 44–8.

history that these legally trained officials as a group played such a great role. Most of the councilors were noblemen, but there were some burghers as well.

Johann von Schwarzenberg was the most eminent of these new public servants. This Franconian nobleman represented the bishop of Bamberg and was not yet a Lutheran, though he later died in the service of the Protestant ruler of Ansbach. In 1507 he had codified and reformed the penal law of Bamberg, and his penal code was to serve as the model of the Penal Code (*Peinliche Hals-und Gerichtsordnung*, or simply *Carolina*) that Charles V issued for the Empire in 1530. He had also attempted to derive a modern political ethics from Cicero's moral writings. This endeavor had a certain similarity with Italian efforts. But there was in Germany not a single political philosopher or analytical thinker comparable in intent to Machiavelli. The approach of these German professional public servants was practical and moralistic. "Justice and the common welfare," was the motto in which Schwarzenberg expressed his philosophy, and it was shared by others, such as Hans von der Planitz, the representative of the electorate of Saxony, and Lazarus Spengler, the secretary of the city council of Nürnberg. In the absence of big political figures and of any initiative on the part of the majority of the princes, the councilors could gain unusual influence.

One thing seemed evident: enforcement of the Edict of Worms was a task that might be accomplished in one territory, but was impossible in another, even if the full authority of the Empire was placed behind the territorial lord. The edict had met with a general hostility among the people and had done nothing to stop the continuous spread of Lutheran teachings into every locality and every class. Moreover, the people were now demanding action in the field of ecclesiastical reform, and radical social demands were raised. Literal execution of the Edict of Worms would have wrecked all the gains that had been made in a generation toward suppressing feuds and wars among members of the Empire. It would also have brought on the danger of popular revolt and revolution, and the German princes had to admit that their governments were ill-equipped for coping with such contingencies. Religious inclinations mattered little in this respect; actually, the ecclesiastical princes were most apprehensive. The maintenance of peace and ultimate religious harmony in Germany were strongly desired by the political leaders of the Imperial Governing Council in Nürnberg.

↷ *Proposed Reforms of Pope Hadrian VI*

IT WAS OF THE GREATEST CONSEQUENCE that these efforts received unintentional support from the head of the universal Church. In December, 1521, Pope Leo X had died, and in a surprising election the former teacher of Charles V, Bishop Hadrian, a Dutchman, was chosen pope. Pope Hadrian VI had grown up in the world of the *devotio moderna*, though he became a good scholastic theologian as professor of Louvain and bishop of Utrecht. Since 1516 he had served as trusted regent of Charles V in Spain. This earnest and ascetic bishop from the Netherlands found in the Spanish Church, which had been reformed by the great Cardinal Ximenes, a congenial atmosphere, but he was horrified by the moral depravity of the Holy See. He also was aware of the abuses rampant in Germany. With a pious zeal and with little circumstance and circumlocution, he attacked the glaring corruption of the Roman Church. In a way this was the opening of the Catholic Reformation, but it remained a short and premature episode. Hadrian's holy passion for freeing the Church from the embrace of low politics and finance, for bringing back the heroic days of Bernard of Clairvaux, and for rekindling the flame of a pure common faith could not cut through the web that secular interests and religious indolence had woven. When he died in September, 1522, he was already haunted by feelings of failure.

Unity of religion seemed to Hadrian, as to most of his contemporaries, the natural prerequisite of peace and the vital factor in the defense of Christianity against the hordes of Suleiman, who had taken Belgrade in 1521 and Rhodes in 1522. Therefore, Nuncio Chieregati, who was sent to the second Diet of Nürnberg, was instructed to demand the full execution of the Edict of Worms, but he was also to convey to the diet the pope's admission of the terrible abuses that threatened to strangle Church and religion, together with Hadrian's determination to launch a radical reform of the Roman Church on all levels. On January 3, 1522, in a dramatic speech, Chieregati presented the official confession of ecclesiastical sins and the promise of reform, pleading at the same time for the immediate enforcement of the Edict of Worms. But the estates argued that the abuses should be remedied before the edict of 1521 was enforced. They recommended that the pope, together with the emperor, call "a free Christian council in a convenient center of the German nation," and that the elector of Saxony see to it that Luther not write and publish anything new. Meanwhile ministers were to expound the Christian faith according to the oldest authorities.

Since the cities took exception to the economic legislation of the diet of 1522–23, no final resolution was passed, but the third Diet of Nürnberg, which opened in January, 1524, continued in the same direction, and the representative of the new pope, the learned and moderate Nuncio Campeggio, was as unsuccessful as his predecessor. The diet voted that its members would act "as much as possible" according to the Edict of Worms. But at the same time it was said that a council should be held, so that "the good would not be suppressed with the evil, and finally a discussion should take place on what everyone in future should adhere to." The diet did more than use delaying tactics. It demanded the convention of "a general assembly of the German nation" in November to decide what should be done till a universal council was convened. This was the closest approach to a settlement of religious and ecclesiastical issues through common action on the part of the political authorities of the Empire. It was also the last demonstration of the national reform movement that Archbishop Berthold of Mainz had led in the belief that Germany's ills could be overcome by the free co-operation of the estates of the Empire.

But the Imperial Governing Council was a weak organ for undertaking a national solution of the reform of the Church. It protested when the emperor forbade a national assembly for the discussion of Church reform, but was powerless to execute its own plan. The Council was divided on many basic issues. Uncertainty prevailed in attitudes toward the most urgent problem of foreign policy, the Turkish war, as well as toward relations with France. The conflict between princes and cities on economic and financial matters was unresolved. The Council also proved itself impotent to exercise leadership in the protection of internal security. The revolt of Sickingen and his knights, which occurred at this time,[3] was suppressed by the Swabian League and some individual princes. These circumstances made it quite impossible to steer the Governing Council into open opposition to the emperor. On close inspection, unity in Church affairs stood on shaky ground. Agreement among the members of the Council was achieved by the use of the lowest common denominator, the hope of the majority of the princes to keep Lutheran teaching from spreading any further. Such a temporizing rather than positive policy did not cement understanding.

[3] See page 51.

✎ *The Popular Movement for Reform*

THE REMOVAL OF LUTHER from the scene, though it did not last long and though Luther, from the Wartburg, resumed correspondence with his friends and publication of his writings, put popular sympathies and attitudes to a new and decisive test. Before Worms everyone had hoped that reform of the Church would be carried out, if not by the Church itself, by the emperor and Empire. Now not only the emperor but also the majority of the German princes were ranged against Luther's cause, and its future depended on the action of the people themselves. Practically everywhere the movement depended on leaders who in these few years had become students and followers of Luther, or who had been spurred into action by Luther's example. A good many of them had originally been led to a critical attitude by humanist ideas. The great mass were clerics, priests, and friars, a few among them prelates, but the majority preachers. Apart from natural differences of character, they also represented diversified trends of practical reform, largely conditioned by the various social and political forces with which the Lutheran movement had to grapple. As a matter of fact, even Luther was to modify his position in the course of the struggle.

Religious and political pamphleteering reached its greatest intensity in these years. Writings were largely in German and, insofar as generalizations can be made, the most effective pamphlets were apparently those that took up the position of whole classes, such as the peasants, burghers, or knights, in order not only to instill a new faith but also to inflame them to action. But the voices of defenders of the old Church were also heard. They were few. Johann Eck was joined by Johannes Cochlaeus, a humanist and former friend of Hutten. Yet he placed the Catholic faith higher than the liberal arts, and its preservation seemed to him a patriotic as well as a religious duty. In these early years Hieronymus Emser, secretary of Duke George of Saxony, and the Fransiscan Thomas Murner of Strasbourg, learned master of German satire, entered the fray. The polemics were fought with cudgels and flails. The German writers took great pleasure in their command of filthy epithets. Luther retaliated in the same coin, and although a good many persons were pained by these uncouth methods, they apparently did not displease the mass of the people. The weakness of the literary polemics of the Catholics was their predominantly negative nature. None of these apologists and controversialists had the religious depth or the theological knowledge to restate the Catholic faith in a form that would have given the thought and sentiment of this generation of Germans a clear focus. The movement of reform, therefore, could roll on.

✍ *Ulrich Zwingli*

AMONG THE LOCAL LEADERS who came into the open, the most original was Ulrich Zwingli in Zurich. Strangely enough, the same man who through his personality and public activities profoundly stamped the Swiss national character, thereby perfecting the political separation of the Swiss cantons from the Empire, was, through his response to Luther and his subsequent planning of common Protestant action, responsible for the establishment of close cultural ties between modern Switzerland and Germany. Zwingli (1484–1531) was, like Luther, a peasant's son, but he grew up in the air of a free community whose members impressed all of Europe by their military prowess. He had accompanied the Swiss *Landsknechte* on Italian campaigns, and his first attempts at reform were directed against the demoralizing consequences of the commerce in soldiers. His early education was humanistic rather than theological. The return to the Bible, and also to the ancients, prepared him for the teachings of Erasmus, whom he came to admire. Still, he was distinguished from Erasmus not only by his greater trust in politics but also by his personal need for a deeper religious experience. Zwingli, who looked at the world with bright eyes, was both more political and more religious than the rationalistic Erasmus. Although this preacher at the Münster of Zurich had never gone through the same abyss of despair as Luther, his own faith was the genuine expression of his warmhearted and manly nature.

Zwingli has often testified that Luther's writings capped his own religious growth. The doctrine of justification by faith became the core of Zwingli's religion, but it stood in a new context of spiritual and intellectual ideas. In Luther's view original sin had fully corrupted man, who even after justification could live only by the mercy of the Lord. Zwingli was no less emphatic in asserting the omnipotence of God, but original sin created a weakness—rather than an indelible corruption of human nature—which not even faith could restore to righteousness. And he who had been predestined for faith by God was also selected to serve as an organ for the realization of the divine objectives of creation in this world. Zwingli's faith, like Luther's, was essentially confidence in God, but it was not incompatible with a strong confidence in man's capacity to organize the world according to God's commandments. From this viewpoint, Zwingli did not find it difficult to consider the republican communities that he saw around him as centers for a reform according to the divine law and Holy Scripture. Whereas for Luther religion dealt essentially—to use St. Augustine's famous formula—"with God and the soul and nothing else," it was for Zwingli concerned equally with God and his chosen people. The realization of a social order under a Christian law was a vital task for Zwingli, as it was for the churches in Switzerland, England, Scotland, and America which started from the same religious basis. Political activism, as well as a pronounced legalism, characterized the "Reformed" Protestantism.

But faith implied for Zwingli the clear consciousness of a lucid truth that could stand up to philosophical critique. Luther's hostility toward philosophy was alien to Zwingli. This religious humanist found in ancient philosophy early signs of a revelation, and philosophy was for him the critical means for preservation of the spiritual character of Christianity. Consequently, he went much further than Luther in his criticism of the sacraments, which became to him mere symbols, and he was a puritan in banning the arts from Christian worship and from the churches. Around these principles Zwingli built his Church in Zurich after 1519. The Reformation was introduced in 1523 by religious debates that were held under the auspices of the city government, an unprecedented event in that the secular authority sat in judgment over matters of faith.

Zwingli was the most independent figure among the new leaders of the Protestant Reformation, and most of the others were more deeply molded by Luther's theology. These leaders represented variously shaded theologies and, beyond their theology, attacked the problems of practical ecclesiastical reform by different methods. It was not surprising that in the southern German cities the reformation of Zurich made a great impression. Basel, under Johannes Oecolampadius, became a bridge from Switzerland to the upper Rhine. Strasbourg was particularly rich in theologians who were active in reform. Caspar Hedio, Wolfgang Capito, and Martin Bucer transformed this imperial city, while Urbanus Rhegius pressed the cause forward in Augsburg, as did the Blarer brothers in Constance, and Johann Brenz in Schwäbisch-Hall. Beginning in 1522, Andreas Osiander preached in Nürnberg right under the eyes of the Imperial Governing Council and the papal nuncio.

The Nürnberg city council, after the adjournment of the Governing Council in 1524, proceeded to hold a religious disputation. As had been the case in Zurich, its outcome was a foregone conclusion, and Nürnberg became the first city in Germany with an officially established Lutheran Church.

✍ *Events in Wittenberg*

BUT IN ALL THESE YEARS the center of the Protestant movement remained in Wittenberg, and events in Saxony and Thuringia were the most crucial. Martin Luther was originally removed, as he himself put it, to "the realm of the birds." From the Wartburg castle he looked over the crowns of the trees that covered the Thuringian hills. His gigantic energy even then found no rest. In addition to his lively correspondence with many people he managed to write more than ten tracts, but beyond that he did the ground work for his two most influential works, the collection of his sermons on the epistles of the church year (*Kirchenpostille*) and his German translation of the Bible. The former remained for centuries the great book of evangelical comfort and instruction, and Luther himself called it his best book. He accomplished the translation of the New Testament in three months. Although he consulted at least one older translation, his translation was altogether his work, his new interpretation of Christian faith in a new language, which only a genius could conceive. In a Germany that was still a country of dialects, Luther created a standard that became the foundation of national communication in religion, literature, and politics. Luther's New Testament of 1522, to which by 1534 his translation of the Old Testament was added, could not have achieved this result if he had not succeeded in bringing the sources of Christian religion before the modern reader with the power of a creative artist. Luther's Bible has had a strong influence on non-German translations of the Bible, especially the English. At first it had to be issued in editions adapted to the vernacular dialects, for example in lower Germany, but after a few decades the original was accepted all over Germany as well as in Switzerland, which thereby remained in the realm of German literature.

While Luther still concentrated his own labors on the building of a restored devotional life, news of growing unrest came to the Wartburg. In Luther's absence the members of the university, the clergy, and the townsfolk of Wittenberg began to draw certain practical conclusions from his teachings. With the holy mass declared a perversion of religion, with the whole sacramental and hierarchical system of the Church challenged, and with good works and external penance questioned, how should the Church organization and the conduct of the individual Christian be reformed? Priests and monks got married, and the dissolution of monasteries and chapters raised the question of what should be done with the properties of all the ecclesiastical foundations. At the same time, as gifts for private masses, indulgences, and payment of fines ceased, the living of ministers was jeopardized. Once one started with a single reform, the need for others seemed to become only too obvious. Changes in arrangements for worship were equally complex. Was the mass to be replaced by the Lord's Supper, and wine and bread to be offered? What should be done with the high altar, with altars devoted to saints, and with relics, statues, and pictures? The Latin service was thrown in doubt, as was also, in view of the universal priesthood of all Christians, the requirement of theological study for ministers.

Under strong pressure from town and gown, the town council of Wittenberg assumed some leadership in the financial field. Following suggestions made by Luther in his tract *To the German Nobility*, it issued, in January, 1522, an order for the establishment of a "community chest," which was to administer all Church property and income. The chest was also to provide for the poor. At the same time begging was forbidden and public houses were closed. This action indicated that in practice it was not easy to separate external from internal Church reform. As far as can be judged, the move of the Wittenberg council was not prompted by acquisitive motives. But a desire for actual control of the possessions of the Church no doubt encouraged many cities, noblemen, and princes to promote the Protestant cause. Wittenberg, however, was swept by other convulsions; for a while these threatened every kind of order.

In the university Andreas Carlstadt (1480–1541) became the most prominent professor. He was a poor theologian and a rather unstable character. Slightly older than Luther, he attempted to make up in radicalism what he lacked in originality, but he posed questions and rushed developments that the new movement under Luther's influence was inclined to postpone or neglect. During the Christmas season, 1521, Carlstadt distributed bread and wine at the Lord's Supper, dispensing with the ornate dress of a priest. A day later he got married. But soon he preached new Christian laws: he who received only the host at the Lord's Supper was committing a sin; unmarried and childless priests should not be tolerated. Eventually, Carlstadt advised the students to leave the university for practical occupations, since Christian wisdom was given to the simple people. He himself went to the uneducated and asked for their help in the interpretation of the Gospel.

While Carlstadt promoted his prescriptions for a new Jerusalem, the town population and students committed iconoclastic acts in the churches and threatened with violence the continuation of most of the old religious customs. The upheaval was heightened further when, late in 1521, the first representatives of a new apocalyptic sectarianism, the so-called "Zwickau prophets," made their appearance in Wittenberg. In the Saxon town of Zwickau where the germs of Hussite ideas from neighboring Bohemia were alive, the activities of Luther had produced among the craftsmen a laicist radicalism. Nicolaus Storch, an impoverished master clothier, taught a mystical approach to God, based on a peculiar interpretation of the Bible; it led through the suppression of sensuality to a direct contact with God in which the ultimate sanctification and certainty of selection was achieved. A prophetic gift and mission sprang from this community. The secular order seemed sinful and deserving of extermination if the inner voice commanded it. In Thomas Münzer, who was for a while a preacher in Zwickau, arose a champion of such total destruction.

Nobody in Wittenberg proved able to stem the flood. Young Philip Melanchthon was particularly disturbed. The Zwickau prophets, for example, frightened but impressed him. Elector Frederick, in his customary inability to take an open stand, intervened with orders against any innovations, but was unwilling to enforce his rulings against religious movements. He requested Luther's advice, though he insisted that Luther remain in hiding. But in open defiance of the elector's orders, Luther returned to Wittenberg early in March, 1522. For a full week he preached to the crowd every day and succeeded in calming the storm. Luther had not worried about minor excesses and occasional outbreaks of violence. He had derided the fears of the elector and his councilors about the breach of public peace and had told them that, as Christians, they should be concerned only with their peace with God. He had not wished them to intervene with force.

But Luther did not want to see the Gospel perverted and imposed as a new law by church leaders. Believing that the truth was on his side, he entered the public debate, and the people in Wittenberg and other neighboring places accepted his demand that no one be pushed into a new faith or into giving up religious customs dear to him. Luther trusted that the transformation of souls would bring on automatically a reform of institutions. Thus, for the time being, all radical innovations were abolished under his influence. A change in Luther's attitude toward secular authority was noticeable in these years. In 1520, when he wrote *To the German Nobility*, he had hoped that the princes would take the leadership in the reform of the Church. It is true that not even to them did he assign the task of direct reform of the Church; they were mainly supposed to call a Christian council, which in turn was to settle the reform of the Church. But the events of Worms had persuaded him that the secular authorities of the Empire, both emperor and estates, could not be relied upon in the religious struggle. Luther therefore stressed the injustice of any governmental intervention in religious affairs and the right of the faithful to organize their religious life.

Watching the political scheming of the Imperial Governing Council, as well as the first execution of Lutheran "heretics" in the Netherlands, Bavaria, and Austria, his low opinion of princes turned into outright condemnation. A shrewd prince was a rare bird, he said, but a pious prince rare beyond measure. The attempts of the princes to interfere in religious matters aroused his anger: "These drunken and mad princes. . . . May God deliver us from them and graciously give us other regents. Amen." Luther's special ire was directed against the ecclesiastical princes. "It would be better that all bishops would be murdered, all chapters and monasteries uprooted than that a single soul should perish, let alone all souls, on account of these useless fetishes." These and other remarks sounded like calls for revolution and were undoubtedly understood as such by a good many people. But they were not meant to justify any disobedience except in matters of conscience. Yet was it possible to draw a clear line between religious and political criticism?

✧ *The Revolt of the Imperial Knights*

WITH REGARD TO ECCLESIASTICAL PRINCIPALITIES, such a division was most difficult, and the argument that it was not possible to draw a clear line between them was used by those forces that expected to gain most from an extension of religious reform into the political field. Hutten had been the first imperial knight to advocate open war against the priests of the Roman Church by the right of medieval feud, and he had found some response among the Franconian knights. But as a class the imperial knights were divided. Their relatives occupied most of the chapter posts and a good many ecclesiastical sees. Moreover, alone or as a group, the knights did not command enough political or military power to revolutionize the German constitution. Only Franz von Sickingen, the successful German *condottiere,* had acquired a fortune and position that made him a formidable political figure. We have already seen that Hutten gained influence over him and that Sickingen did much to protect and encourage Protestant theologians. But during the summer of 1522 plans for political action matured; these had as their ultimate aim the complete secularization of all ecclesiastical dominions. A "fraternal union of the nobility" was founded, and it was open to cities as well as to princes.

A beginning in secularization was to be made in Trier, whose elector had favored, in 1519, the election of Francis I and had appeared in Worms as the chief opponent of Luther. In the last days of August, 1522, the "fraternal union" declared feud against Archbishop Richard von Greiffenklau; in September his bishopric was invaded, his forces surprised, and siege laid to his capital. But the archbishop, an imperial knight, was an experienced military man and defended Trier most ably. Sickingen had to lift the siege and retreat. On October 1, 1522, Sickingen was declared an outlaw by the Imperial Governing Council, as a disturber of peace. The hope of Sickingen and Hutten that some princes and cities would join their holy war proved an idle dream. The conflict of interests between the truculent knights and both cities and princes was too deeply rooted to be overcome by evangelical principles. Instead, princes and cities joined forces to suppress the knights. In the spring of 1523, the electors of the Palatinate and Trier, together with the landgrave of Hesse subdued Sickingen and his fellow knights along the Rhine. Sickingen was killed during the siege of his castle Landstuhl on May 6, 1523. During the summer the Swabian League mobilized an army that razed twenty-three castles in eastern Franconia. Shortly afterward Ulrich von Hutten died, a fugitive in Switzerland.

This was the end of any attempt on the part of the imperial knights to play an independent role in German politics. It was at the same time the event that for the time being, and, as it turned out, for the next centuries, saved the ecclesiastical principalities as prominent institutions of public life in Germany. The most immediate impact of the revolt of the knights was a growing fear that the Lutheran movement, as the Edict of Worms had predicted, would undermine orderly government.

This feeling had already driven the representatives of the old system into more determined action. Leonhard von Eck, the Bavarian chancellor was the most clear-headed among them. It was this strong-willed and shrewd statesman, rather than the two colorless Bavarian dukes, who was responsible for Bavaria's remaining, from the beginning, the staunch defender of the old faith. He built up Archduke Ferdinand's resistance, and the mandate of Charles V against the meeting of the national council in Speyer, which the Diet of Nürnberg had called, corresponded to his thinking. He paved the way for the convention of a group of princes which was held in Regensburg in June, 1524. At this meeting the archduke, the Bavarian dukes, and twelve prince-bishops, in the presence of the nuncio Campeggio, agreed to execute the Edict of Worms in their territories and jointly to oppose the Lutheran heresy. They found it necessary, however, to work toward a "reformation" of the Church, which, in their opinion, would include not only improvement in the discipline of the clergy and of morals in general, but also the termination of abuses and clarification of doctrine. The Regensburg Convention was the first step in the direction of a Catholic reformation, but, as the future was to show, German Catholicism was not able to achieve such a reformation by itself. It was also the first separate alliance of members of the Empire in the brewing religious conflict.

The emperor's mandate against the national council and the Regensburg Convention increased the internal tension immensely. The south German cities, which had chosen the cause of reform, decided to stand their ground, but the shadow of possible suppression lay over the countryside. At this moment the villages became alive, and as early as 1524 peasant riots and revolts occurred, particularly in Swabia. Early in 1525, the revolutionary movement spread from Alsace to the land south of Bavaria (Allgäu, Tyrol, Styria) and soon engulfed all of Franconia and the Palatinate. Finally, it reached Thuringia as well. It became the largest and fiercest revolutionary mass movement in German history.

✑ The Peasants' War, 1524–26

THE FRENCH REVOLUTION was not caused by the philosophy of the Enlightenment, nor was the so-called Great Peasants' War caused by Lutheranism. We have already discussed the social conditions that had promoted unrest and revolts among the peasantry of southern Germany before the Reformation.[4] But the new religious ideas gave the peasants' movement principles that enabled it to organize beyond the local sphere and to present its aims as part of a universal and national reform. The demands for Church reform were genuine and formed an important element in setting the spark to the revolts. It is significant that the Peasants' War started in the region studded with imperial cities, in which the Reformation had been carried through in recent months, often enough after much popular tumult. This region was also the area closest to Switzerland, and Swiss republicanism had just found expression in Zwingli's reform in Zurich. However, this was the part of Germany where the clash between the old and the new was most likely to occur. Here Habsburg power weighed most heavily on the lands from Austria to Alsace, particularly at this moment when Württemberg was in the hands of the imperial house. In the town of Waldshut on the upper Rhine, the Habsburg government had already undone the work of the Protestant reformers and forced the Lutheran minister Balthasar Hubmaier to flight.

The desire was general among the peasants to spread the Reformation, already accepted in many cities, throughout the country at large. The election of ministers by congregations had always been a point in the peasants' demands, as had the idea of a community chest. These were good Lutheran aims, as were also the peasants' claims for the abolition of ecclesiastical principalities and monasteries. But along with these demands for Church reform, plans for social reform for the peasant class were advanced. These varied, depending upon local conditions, but all tended to urge a greater measure of equality, in conformity with "divine" or "evangelical" law. Finally, a number of economic demands were made and usually justified as expressions of a fraternal Christian attitude.

The peasants' programs were amazingly modest. The most widely distributed and accepted program, the famous *Twelve Articles of the Peasantry*, clearly showed that Lutheran ideas exerted a strong influence toward moderation. Obedience to a rightful government was strongly reaffirmed, and it was made clear that equality should not mean the complete disappearance of classes and social ranks, only of serfdom and bondage. In view of the general tenor of this and similar documents, the attempt to base general hunting and fishing rights on the Biblical paradise seemed rather irrelevant. For there was willing-

[4] See pages 60–3.

ness to debate and compromise. The use of violence was frowned upon in the beginning.

But although a number of small potentates, such as Count Wertheim and Count Hohenlohe, did compromise with the peasants, the larger states were not prepared to make any concessions. In fact, the same princes who had come together in Regensburg saw in the uprising of the peasants the ultimate corruption caused by Lutheranism, but at the same time the opportunity for suppressing it. All the negotiations with the peasants that were carried on by the government of Archduke Ferdinand or by the Swabian League were conducted simply to gain time for the mobilization of troops.

Thus the revolt became more intense and also more widespread. The peasants formed regional organizations or "groups," such as the "lake group" around Lake Constance (*Seehaufe*), and these groups formed a "fraternal union." A corresponding military organization was created; colonels and captains were elected. In the villages of southern Germany there were many former or idle *Landsknechte*, and fighting with pikes and shotguns was a practiced art. But the peasants did not find adequate leaders, nor did they prove themselves particularly brave in final showdowns. None of their elected captains demonstrated military skill or political acumen. Both in battle and in negotiations they were easily outmaneuvered. More impressive were the Lutheran ministers who were advising leaders of the movement, but neither from the ranks of the peasants nor from among the ministers did a leader comparable to the Hussite Žižka arise. The peasants built up some sort of central organization but continued to deal with the individual governmental authorities of the territories. The peasants' program actually called for a political reform of the Empire, and some of the intellectual leaders and sympathizers felt this keenly. But any attempt to change the constitution of the Empire by revolution would have brought emperor, princes, and cities together in joint opposition, in spite of the dissension that existed among them.

Because of the chaotic dispersion of political power in Germany the peasants' movement was without a central target of attack. Thus its leaders hesitated and gave it enemies time to get ready for the kill. Meanwhile in many places compromises on reforms were concluded, and pressure was brought upon monasteries and chapters to desist from any support of the opposing elements. The churches suffered the same depradation that had characterized the Wittenberg riots of 1522. Considering the breakdown of the old organs of internal security, acts of violence and brutality against persons were rare. But rowdyism was widespread, and, as had occurred among the tumults in the cities, a contempt for what had only a day earlier been venerated as holy came into the open; there appeared, too, a sodden hatred of anything connected with learning, for example, libraries and books. Perhaps nothing demonstrates so clearly as the blind acts of destruction that occurred how far removed the downtrodden sons of the nation were from the civilization of the age.

As the movement gained strength and the fire engulfed Franconia and spread down the Rhine as far as Cologne, Osnabrück, and Münster, religious aims became somewhat threadbare, and economic and political demands began to dominate. In its northward march the revolutionary movement changed its social composition. In a number of towns the lower classes gained control of the municipal government and made common cause with the peasants. The imperial city of Heilbronn, which subsequently became the seat of a "federal chancellery" of the peasants, and Rothenburg were among the new allies of the peasants, as were the bishops' cities of Bamberg and Würzburg. The soldiers of the bishop of Würzburg, however, defended the Marienburg, the castle of the city, and it became one of the main centers of actual warfare in the Peasants' War. In Franconia the movement attracted the last representatives of a revolutionary knighthood. Götz von Berlichingen and Florian Geyer acquired legendary fame by their participation in the war.

In Thuringia the collaboration of the small townsfolk with the peasants was even more pronounced. Here the movement, under the influence of Thomas Münzer, assumed a character comparable to the Taboritism of Bohemia. But Münzer, who acted in Mühlhausen like a new Gideon, was greater as a preacher and agitator than as an organizer. Although his religious ideas, about which more will be said later, gave events in Thuringia a peculiar note, he failed to extend his theocratic leadership over the whole region.

It was estimated that by late April, 1525, 300,000 peasants were under arms. In addition to the whole northeast and northwest of Germany, there were notable regions in the south not struck by the revolt, for example most of Bavaria and the big imperial cities, such as Nürnberg and Augsburg. Even where the territories were in an uproar, as happened in Austria and Hesse, the princes were not left without resources. Count George Truchsess, captain of the Swabian League, achieved his first successes in Swabia in April, partly by trickery, partly by fighting. Landgrave Philip of Hesse subdued the Hessian peasants and marched into Thuringia, where, on May 15, Thomas Münzer and 8,000 men were overwhelmed in the town of Frankenhausen by Philip, Duke George of Saxony, and the duke of Brunswick. Münzer was executed two days after the battle, which, in fact, was a one-sided slaughter. On May 12, Count Truchsess defeated the peasants of Württemberg, and in the following six weeks the movement was suppressed everywhere in central and southern Germany. Fighting continued into the next year only in the Alps, where it came to assume merely a local significance.

✍ *Aftermath of the Peasants' War*

THE CRUELTY OF THE PUNISHMENT that followed defies description. The criminal justice of the time, with its penalties in the form of sinister modes of torture and mutilation of which decapitation was the most humane, celebrated its wildest orgies. It is estimated that 100,000 peasants lost their lives in the course of the war, and we do not know how many maimed or blinded people lingered on for years in villages and towns as a result of this, one of the most shameful chapters in German history.

Only one German prince, old Elector Frederick the Wise, had clung to hope of a peaceful compromise with the peasants. In his hesitant, if considerate, manner, he said, on April 14, "Perhaps we have given the poor people cause for their revolt, in particular with the prohibition of the Word of God. The poor are in many ways oppressed by us, the secular and ecclesiastical authorities. . . ." And on May 4, the day before his death, he still recommended that a man be sought who could inspire confidence among the peasants and negotiate a peaceful settlement.

Luther could no longer have been the man for such an attempt. In the early phase of the war the peasants had looked to him for endorsement and support. The *Twelve Articles* were no doubt written with the hope of finding his approval. Actually Luther wrote, late in April, his *Admonition for Peace on the Twelve Articles*, which seemingly tried to mediate between the governments and peasants, but did so in a curious fashion. The *Admonition* declared both parties to be wrong. Luther inveighed bitterly against the princes and lords, whom he made responsible for the revolt. "The sword is at your neck, though you think you are firmly in the saddle. This conceit will break your necks

. . . not the peasants, God himself is set against you." He urged them to give in to the equitable economic demands of the peasants instead of continuing in their tyrannical mood. Luther advanced, however, as his chief argument for practical moderation, the specious assertion that even a "hay wagon would give right of way to a drunkard." With still more passionate acerbity he criticized the attitude of the peasants. He accused them of using the Gospel as a sad subterfuge for their social ambitions. He told them further that even if some of their aims were reasonable, they had no right to press them through revolt. Christians could pray to God, but had to accept the government that was set over them; likewise, they had to accept in patience the suffering it might entail. The princes would be damned by God for their injustice, but nobody who fought their injustice would enter heaven either. Christian liberty was a spiritual good, and the kingdom of heaven and of the world were to be held strictly apart.

Thus the *Admonition*, though threatening not only the peasants but also the princes with the anger of God, was weighted in favor of the princes, whose government all were to obey "with hand, mouth, and heart." But if one accepted Luther's spiritual conception of Christian liberty and followed him in his criticism of the use of evangelical truth for the justification of economic and social programs, it was doubtful whether one was justified in defending the necessity of serfdom with Biblical testimony, as Luther did. It was surprising that even in the field of worship and faith Luther did not make an effort to meet the demands of the peasants, who, as we have seen, wanted to adopt the reforms of the cities in the villages. Luther decreed that it was impossible that "such a big mob would consist entirely of good Christians," and that the majority wanted to exploit the piety of the others in an arbitrary fashion. The same argument could of course be used against a reform movement of any class. If Luther declared the demand in the *Twelve Articles* for some limitations of the tithe as "sheer robbery," and because of it called the leaders of the peasants "mean prophets of murder and gangsters," one could not help but sense behind the theological pleading a strong social bias against *hoi polloi*. "The donkey wants to be beaten, and the mob wants to be governed with violence."

There seemed to be in Luther no awareness of the consequences of his own actions and words. To be sure, Luther had always declined to turn the restoration of the Gospel into a secular war, but his obedience to established authority had not been one of "mouth and heart." The destruction of the old Church, its doctrine and law, on which an integral part of all public life was grounded, could not fail to unravel the whole fabric of society. Nor could the wild language Luther had used against the papacy, bishops, and priests as well as the princes be passed over lightly. Luther was unwilling to admit that his angry words were bound to raise a distorted echo from every corner of society. The social and political world was alien to him. In this respect it could be said that he remained an ascetic monk. What moved him in these weeks was not a physical fear but deep concern for the purity of spiritual religion. It seemed that religion, in frightful labors, might be drawn into the struggle of human ambitions and interests. With passionate determination Luther threw himself against the flood.

As he had done in 1522, Luther went out to speak to the revolutionary masses. But he found the whole land south of the Harz mountains, through which he traveled, in revolt, and the panic in his heart was heightened by his personal observation of the widespread influence of Münzer's ideas. He did not find any response this time. When he preached in Nordhausen, people rang tocsin and almost slew him. It was in these days that he wrote his pamphlet *Against the Robbing and Murderous Peasants' Gangs* in which he admonished the princes to end the revolution through a blood bath. "Therefore must here smite, choke, and stab . . . whoever can be conscious that there is nothing more poisonous, obnoxious, and devilish than a revolutionary man, as one must kill a mad dog." And so the pamphlet ran on in pained and painful disregard of all humaneness. The peasants, hundreds of thousands of them, were now "robbers and murderers." In a letter written at the same time he said, "If there are innocent people, God will save them. But since they do not obey, no mercy ought to be shown."

The princes did not need Luther's incitement to butchery. Indeed, in general Luther's actions had little impact on the course of external events. He could not have changed the defeat of the peasants if he had taken their side. But his stand had consequences that could be felt in German history for centuries. Luther himself was shocked by the tragic crisis, but he defended himself afterward in statements no less violent than those he had used during the conflict. He hastened, however, to recommend clemency and mercy to the princes after victory, and when they showed none, he called upon them the future judgment of God. These were no empty words with Luther, but they could not undo the gruesome devastation wrought by the revengeful lords or the icy chill that Luther's ire had thrown into the souls of the masses. Here ended the days when it had seemed that the Protestant Reformation would be embraced by all classes of the German nation and would give to the subjected groups some sense of participation in the great issues of public life. These groups now fell back into apathy or rather superficial conformity. Bitter jibes at religion were heard, and even stronger thrusts were taken at Luther as the pseudo-prophet who could twist the Scriptures to suit his own ends even more than the old priests. It is symptomatic that the tidal wave of popular pamphlets that had flooded Germany since 1518 suddenly subsided. The masses became sullen, and the theologians worried about their co-operation in reforms.

The Growth of Sectarianism

STILL, THE FIRE WAS NOT SO EASILY STAMPED OUT. Politically, the cards were badly stacked against the possibility of a continuation of the general revolutionary movement. But the intensity of religious feeling among earnest people could not be broken overnight. It led to the growth of a free sectarianism. The "free sectarians" (*Schwärmer*) represented a large variety of religious doctrines and practices, and they are described only inadequately if they are grouped together. But all of them were no doubt originally determined by both their obligation to and differences with Luther. They based their beliefs on the certainty of salvation and on a universal priesthood, ideas that Luther had given them. The authority of the Church and tradition meant nothing to them. And they also attacked the authority of the Scriptures. They asked how a pagan could ever be converted if faith could be acquired only through a book. Beyond a simple faith in the Word, which Münzer called "literal," "fictitious," or even a "monkey faith," there was the direct contact with God. According to Münzer, a true Christian faith was not acquired by intellectual contemplation of the suffering of Christ, but by the actual acceptance of superhuman suffering. By the infliction of such a cross upon man, God awakens in him the word that is already hidden in his heart. It is this "inner word" that gives the individual the strength to bear the impossible and "to hope against despair." Faith is built by this ever-continuing revelation. It is not created by the Scriptures, which are only a testimony of faith to be understood by the faithful rather than the learned. And new prophecies are definitely possible.

The doctrines of the "inner word" or "inner light" presupposed some positive capacity in man, and, indeed, Luther's denial of free will was rejected by the sectarians. Men, conscious of their election, are not free of sin, but they have both the urge and the general power for the realization of a Christ-like life. There were innumerable differences among the sectarians in their understanding of what the law of such a life was to be. The Sermon on the Mount was emphasized, but although acquisitive practices were usually frowned upon, communism was not demanded by all the sectarian groups. The attitude toward the state varied greatly among them. Münzer called on Christians to destroy the godless princes because they burdened and oppressed people so much that they could not devote themselves to religion at all. But Münzer did not plan to abolish political government as such, rather he wanted to restore it to the people. After the disaster that befell Münzer, nonresistance to evil became the rule among the sectarians. This usually meant the refusal to hold any political office or to participate in war, court litigation, oath-taking, the holding of servants, and the collection of interest.

✎ *Anabaptism*

THE NEW LIFE FOUND ITS CENTER in new churches; these, under persecution by enemies, often amounted to nothing more than the smallest conventicles. Their members separated from the official churches voluntarily to form their own communities of "friends of God." As the symbol of their new faith and their decision to live up to it, most of them chose adult baptism. After the spring of 1525 the great majority of the sectarians were Anabaptists. We cannot trace Münzer's influence on the beginnings of Anabaptism very clearly. We know that he advocated it from 1522 and that he was in Swabia and Zurich in 1524. But Anabaptism as an organized movement took its origins from Zurich after the debacle of the Peasants' War. Friends of Zwingli, such as Conrad Grebel, were the leaders there. Grebel was a humanist and a person of rank in the community. What appealed to him and to many similar figures in the German cities was the emphasis that Anabaptism placed upon a strictly spiritual interpretation of religion, on man's own power and activity, and they also may have been attracted by the elite character of the new groups. The mass of followers, however, consisted of lowly people, peasants, and even more the poorer classes in cities and towns. The oppressed found in Anabaptism the reflection of their own situation of human suffering.

Sectarianism spread fast, as migrant preachers presented the gospel of the imitation of Christ instead of the justification by faith. These preachers were great and courageous persons. Among them was Balthasar Hubmaier, the Lutheran minister of Waldshut and possibly the author of the *Twelve Articles*. He became an Anabaptist on Easter, 1525, and finally carried the new message to Moravia, where he died a martyr's death in Nicolsburg in 1528. Hans Denk, Hans Hut, and Ludwig Hetzer were outstanding figures in their own right. Nürnberg early expelled Denk; for a while Augsburg served as a center of agitation, and finally Strasbourg, until even there fierce persecution began. Everywhere the congregations displayed an extraordinary purity of morals which impressed even their enemies. Their worship combined popularity with depth of religious feeling; their hymns were among the finest religious lyrics. The weakness of the movement was its lack of a common spiritual authority. The "inner word" and new prophecy made for division into splinter groups. And although these "children of God" proved their Christian love among themselves, they became indifferent to their fellow men outside their own sect.

The persecution of Anabaptism by all political and ecclesiastical—Catholic, Lutheran, and Reformed—authorities was cruel, even beyond the usual measure of the century. In Zurich, where the first large congregation was formed in 1525, Anabaptists were first fined, then jailed, and after 1527 drowned. Following an imperial mandate of 1528, the Diet of Speyer of 1529 passed a law under which all adult Anabaptists were to be condemned to death without special trial. An ancient law of Emperor Constantine the Great, issued for the protection of the Nicean dogmas, was resuscitated for this end. The calm defiance that the great mass of the sectarians showed in the face of death demonstrated the wealth of individual character and inner life that existed in these groups. But the human dignity displayed by the victims only led their torturers to greater excesses. It was demanded that the tongues of Anabaptists be torn out to keep them from confessing their faith in public.

Except for a few underground groups, Anabaptism was actually suppressed in southern Germany, Austria, and Switzerland within a few years after 1525, but the movement gained fresh strength in the region of the Empire that had not been affected by the Peasants' War and had been exposed to the strongest repressive measures against any religious innovation. The government of the Netherlands had prosecuted any deviation from the line of orthodox religion with pitiless logic. The Lutheran and Zwinglian sympathizers, who were apparently numerous, particularly among the upper classes of the towns and cities, were kept at bay for the time being, but Anabaptism found ardent followers among the lower classes. Anabaptists were known in the Netherlands as Melchiorites, so named after the Swabian Melchior Hofmann, whose missionary travels had led him to Livonia, Sweden, northern Germany, and the Lowlands, where he found his most enthusiastic followers. After his imprisonment in Strasbourg, Anabaptism in the Netherlands, in an atmosphere of strong social tensions, took a turn toward active revolution. Jan Mathys, a baker in Harlem, became a prophet urging the violent destruction of the godless and the establishment of the kingdom of God.

In neighboring parts of Germany, on the lower Rhine and in Westphalia, social conflicts, magnified by the inflation of prices and taxes, led to serious revolts in the towns after 1529. Originally, Lutherans, Zwinglians, and Anabaptists had co-operated, as had been the case in Münster, in overthrowing the power of the bishops. As early as 1531 the bishop of Münster had had to leave the city to burghers set on a radical reformation. It was to this new Jerusalem that the Dutch Anabaptists flocked under the leadership of Jan Mathys and young Jan Bokelson of Leyden. In February, 1534, the Anabaptists won out in the internal struggles for power and, under the kingship of Jan van Leyden, established in Münster their heaven on earth, which did away with all the works and institutions of man, including family and property. Their heaven was in reality a communist camp, and its members had to fight for their lives from the beginning. But for almost a year Bishop Franz von Waldeck fought against them in vain. In June, 1535, the rulers of Cologne, Cleves, Saxony, and Hesse, disregarding their own religious differences, conquered the city together.

This last revolutionary outburst of Anabaptism, accompanied by fantastic abuses and scurrilous excesses, threatened not only its existence but also the honesty of its religious principles. David Joris (d. 1556), the chief leader of the Melchiorites, who exercised a great influence throughout Switzerland, the Rhineland, and the Netherlands, rejected revolution but preached chiliastic principles. This glass painter from Flanders lived the life of a rich burgher in Basel under an assumed name, acquiring a fortune through gifts from his followers all over Europe. The Council of Basel had him disinterred and burned when his identity became known after his death.

The Frisian Menno Simons (1492–1559) organized the fragments of the Anabaptist groups in the Netherlands and East Friesland into "congregations of Christ." By removing the enthusiastic and eschatological elements from Anabaptist teaching and centering it on the development of an apostolic life of pure morals, Simons launched the free sectarianism that later played such a great role in English history. The Mennonite movement, as it came to be called, had a strong national Dutch character, and it was carried beyond the Netherlands mainly through Dutch exiles and traders. Thus groups were found as far east as Gothland, Danzig, and Wismar. In 1577 the Dutch congregations received freedom from William of Orange, and in East Friesland their situation remained tolerable.

✍ *The End of Sectarianism as a Force in Germany*

BUT SECTARIANISM CEASED TO BE A FORCE in the history of Germany. What survived of it was confined to local cells; these had little contact with one another and, in the absence of intellectual leaders, found it hard to perpetuate themselves. While sectarianism failed to make a lasting contribution to the social and political history of Germany, it created in some of its thinkers an intellectual subcurrent that at a later date helped the growth of new German philosophies. The Silesian nobleman Kaspar Schwenkfeld (d. 1561) and his mystical interpretation of Lutheran ideas struck notes that prelude Pietism. In Sebastian Franck of Donauwörth (c. 1500–43) appeared a religious and historical thinker of genius, who wove Lutheranism, German mysticism, Renaissance speculation, and the thoughts of the ancient Fathers into a pantheistic world view: God was absolute goodness and was in all creation. But in contrast to nature, which followed God's will, man was endowed with moral freedom. This freedom was not an absolute one. Man was given by God the freedom to choose, without which, in Franck's opinion, no sin or penalty could be justified nor could any teaching be sensible. Human will had a choice, but its efficacy was limited by God's power, which directed the universal course of events. In this universal course even bad acts could contribute to a good end.

Franck saw history moved by the conflict between God's power and the free individual will of man. The latter was dominated by egotism, but also could follow the "light of nature" which had been implanted in every human being. This Stoic concept made Franck declare reason to be the fountain of all human rights and "above all written laws." What ancient philosophers had called the light of nature, reason, *logos*, was in theology the Word of the invisible Christ. But Plato and Seneca had known the Word as much as had St. Paul. The Word was nothing but the moral nature of man communicated to him by God. The struggle against egotism or the old Adam was to lead to the confident obeying of the light of nature, the spirit, Christ. Through the hatred and abnegation of one's own self and through the acceptance of Christ as the rule of life, man was justified.

Franck followed Erasmus in seeing in Christ the wisest teacher, who by his own words and actions had revealed the nature of all religion. Salvation by God, however, was not tied to a unique event in mid-history, for otherwise all those would be damned who, for reasons of time and space, had no chance literally to listen to the Word. As the fall of man was a universal event, so was justification, and consequently it had to be conceived of as an inward and spiritual act. Whereas for Luther justification was an objective act of God, it was for Franck a subjective transformation of individual consciousness. Franck achieved a novel construction of history. God was always the same, and history, too, did not change its fundamental character, because it was determined by God. But the Adam-like nature of man created changes on the surface. Egotism led to dominion, wars, and suppression; limited human intelligence, to the materialization of religion through the invention of dividing doctrines and ceremonies. Although Franck was close to Anabaptism, he saw in it eventually the faults of all churches. But since there were more bad and foolish people than pious ones, Franck expected the world to go on as it always had, in a succession of narrow churches and ambitious states. The true historian could look at historical events with pessimism and tragic irony, which might at times turn into full satire. From observing the Reformation, Franck drew the sad conclusion: "The world will and must have a Pope, whom it will reverently believe in everything . . . if one takes from it one every day, it will soon look for another." But men of good heart and spirit belonged to the invisible Church of God, which over the ages and over the civilizations had comforted them.

This profound religious philosopher and historian was a deeply lonely and isolated figure. Community, as could be seen, had no place in his thought, which was an individualism that found its intellectual home in the universality of God and the world. With true bravery he went through life, hunted from place to place by suspicious ministers. For a while he made a living as soapmaker and printer. He was a master of the written language, and next to Luther, the best writer of German prose of the sixteenth century. Among other books, he managed to write a universal history (*Chronika, Zeitbuch und Geschichtsbibel*, 1531), a cosmography (*Weltbuch*, 1534), and a German history (*Germaniae Chronicon*, 1538). These works formed a bridge to the age of Kant, Hegel, and Schleiermacher.

CHAPTER 8

The Growth of Protestant Territorial Churches

THE YEARS FROM 1517 to 1525 afford a penetrating insight into the moving forces of German history and into the thoughts and feelings of the people of all classes. In these years decisions were reached that proved of the most far-reaching influence on German life in subsequent centuries. The awakening of the lower classes, which had taken place under the impulse of Luther's ideas, was brought to a standstill. The old powers took control, and the new ideas could survive only insofar as they received the support of this group. Luther had called the princes to combat the social revolution and to save pure religion. Once the princes had beaten down the revolution, they became the masters of religion as well. The Catholic princes who fought the peasants believed that the subjugation of the peasants would allow them to restore the old Church, and in some Catholic territories the Peasants' War was followed by acts of religious suppression.

But Lutheranism lived on, though no longer a free movement, but organized and directed by governments. The Reformation gave them the opportunity to extend their power very considerably. The Reformation in the cities has been called the final chapter in the old struggle of the cities for independence from their original lords, the bishops. The last exemptions from the jurisdiction of the cities were abolished; this meant that monasteries and cathedral chapters now came under their control. Moreover, the judicial authority of the Church in family law was turned over to indigenous courts. The same happened in the territorial principalities. Here, however, the Reformation affected the balance of power between prince and estates. The subjection of the peasants had made the noblemen more secure than before. Everywhere in the reformed territories they claimed privileges in the new Church organization. Actually, a great slice of Church properties fell into their hands, and they also secured a dominant position as patrons of local churches. These noble rights of patronage, which lasted into the twentieth century, established a close connection between the Lutheran churches and the *Junkers.*

✍ *Later Influence of Luther*

IT WAS IN THIS GENERAL SOCIAL FRAMEWORK that Protestant churches were established in many territories after 1525. But before looking at their history, we must direct our attention once more to Luther, who still remained the most powerful single figure in the religious realm and whose spirit was to stamp the internal life of these churches. We have seen that Luther's whole personal concern had been the restoration of the Christian faith, and that he had very reluctantly accepted the necessity of fundamental reforms of the Church. By 1520 he had in substance outlined his theological position, which was not affected by the polemics with Erasmus in 1524. But the conflict with Münzer and the Anabaptists changed his ideas in a conservative direction. In modern times Luther has often been misunderstood as defending the freedom of religious convictions. This he never did. In Worms he asserted his faith by calling his conscience a captive of the Word of God, which he considered an objective authority. He speculated deeply on the interpretation of the Scriptures. He had a feeling that the books of the New Testament were not of equal value, and that for a full understanding of the New Testament the reader had to look at the essence of the whole rather than at the literal meaning of parts. But the difficulty of guarding against an unlimited subjectivism drove him back toward the assumption of the literal inspiration of the Scriptures. Faced with the sectarian doctrine of the "inner word," this became his dominant attitude.

✍ *Authorities of Lutheran Doctrine*

ORIGINALLY LUTHER HAD ABOLISHED all sacraments but one: the faith-producing Word. On this he had grounded two symbols, baptism and the Lord's Supper, which received their meaning from the Word and man's faith. But the Anabaptists made him anxious to give these symbols an objective supranatural validity. In this desire he fell back upon a great deal of scholastic thought, which he had otherwise excluded from his mind. He defended this new conception of the sacraments with such passionate tenacity as to make the co-operation between German and Swiss Protestantism impossible. But even more was involved. The search for objective sources or props of faith led him to emphasize strongly the continuity that existed between his religion and the Church of the first seven centuries. Luther never intended to found a new Church, rather he wished to restore the original Church, which had been perverted by the Roman papacy. To his death, he maintained that he represented the true Christian Church. The fact that his theological fight was fought almost exclusively against scholasticism, as well as lack of sufficient historical knowledge, induced him to accept the dogma and doctrine of the ancient Church. This was made easier for him because the ancient dogma did not talk about good works or about papal primacy. But it reflected Christian religion in the form of Greek metaphysical speculation and was ages apart from Luther's joyful confidence in God, who had revealed himself in Jesus Christ and given men the understanding of Christ through the Holy Spirit. To retain the ancient dogmas necessitated elaborate interpretations, and for this difficult task a special class of theologians was required.

An important transformation of Luther's religion was thereby prepared, and his successors and epigoni furthered this development. Luther had originally conceived the Christian faith as an attitude of heart which was gained in a personal relationship with the divine. But with the introduction of the new authorities, faith tended to become the acceptance of doctrines. The Church became a school in which articles of faith were taught as the prerequisite of true religion. The essential ideas, such as Luther's teaching on justification by faith, were then easily beleaguered or obscured by a large variety of lesser doctrines, and, in any event, theological leadership alone could guide the faithful through the complexities of doctrine. If the Lutheran churches became largely the churches of ministers rather than of the people, Luther's ultimate presentation of his religion was an important element in this process.

✑ Luther's Idea of the Church

IT HAS BEEN SAID that the Lutheran churches did not deserve the name of churches, and there is much truth in this contention. There was only one Church in Luther's opinion, namely the community of saints, universal in space and time. This Church was not only a metaphysical entity. It was real in this world, too, insofar as it had living witnesses, and its lights were shining in the darkness wherever the Word of God was preached and the sacraments were rightly administered. But in a strict sense, this kingdom of God was not a visible Church, and certainly not one meant to intervene in the world by other than spiritual means. Luther rejected the idea of building a visible Church around true Christians, since he denied that adequate criteria could be found for singling out true Christians from the vast majority of pseudo-Christians. And he did not even think it necessary to assemble true Christians as a special group, since nothing was required but arrangements for the preaching of the right Christian doctrine. Luther was not inclined to call this a church, as he avoided, in his translation of the Bible, rendering *ekklēsia* as church, but he was willing to turn over the organization of the Christian "congregation" to the princes and secular authorities.

Luther believed essentially that once the Word would be left unimpeded, it would regenerate the world. The visible Church, in his opinion, should not be confined to a group of elect; the Word should reach everyone. He continued, therefore, the medieval idea of general membership in the Church. With it he retained the idea of the uniformity of faith within a civic community. He did not wish to have religion imposed by force, but different religions within a single community seemed to him to endanger the public peace, and therefore the dissenter had to go elsewhere. Luther also felt that the congregation should have a right, if not to elect, at least to approve its ministers, and he was willing to give the individual congregation great freedom in its internal life, including the forms of worship. But popular sentiment could not express itself very well, or even establish a congregation, without some democratic procedures. For Luther, the congregation was always identical with the political community, and he expected the superiors of the political community to take the initiative in the organization of the congregations as well.

The "Territorial Church"

LUTHER DID NOT IDENTIFY secular with ecclesiastical government. In ecclesiastical affairs the princes or magistrates were not to act as secular rulers, but as the most eminent members of the congregation. In this he followed a conception that had been developed in the late Middle Ages, namely that in the case of a breakdown of order in the Church the secular authorities had the right to act as temporary bishops for the restoration of normal conditions. When Luther, in 1527, invited Elector John of Saxony to hold a visitation of church conditions, he made the distinction between the power of the political government in secular and in religious affairs. But it was too finely drawn to stand up against realities. The visitors, electoral councilors and ministers, appeared as officials appointed by the elector on the strength of his princely authority, and they examined not only the financial and physical needs of the congregations but also doctrinal matters, such as the forms of worship and the schools. Luther, though protesting, eventually tolerated the extension of political authority into religious affairs. The "territorial church," in which the territorial ruler acted as the highest bishop (*summus episcopus*), became the normal type of the visible Lutheran Church.

Princes usually construed this authority as a duty and not as a right, whereas in the cities it was often declared as the natural right of the city government. In any event, the exercise of Church government enhanced the dignity of the princes enormously. The care of both the physical and spiritual welfare of their subjects was placed in their hands. The definition of doctrine was not supposed to be a part of Church government, but the princes could not avoid intervening once the theologians were unable to agree on the interpretation of the Word of God. Thus the Lutheran churches became a branch of the state administration; not only were the mass of church members excluded from taking an active role in church affairs but the ministers were supervised and dependent on the prince and his nearest advisers. The adulating court chaplain could be found again and again through the centuries; no less important were the legal officials, who took over much more than administration of the marriage law.

✧ The Relation of State and Church

MORE WAS LOST than the autonomy of the Church. The medieval Church had aimed at ruling society and permeating it with its spirit. For this purpose the Church had demanded privileges and exemptions and had built its own corporate organization. Even modern Catholics would probably agree that it went too far in the direction of a state-like organization. But the Christian principle, if it is to set itself against a secular civilization, requires the embodiment in a self-centered institution. Calvin was able to separate his Church from the secular community, and to assert Christian principles with great force against it. In his Church of Geneva he followed to some extent suggestions that he had received in the first Protestant church he had seen after his conversion, the church of Martin Bucer in Strasbourg.

Calvin's Church, with its four offices of ministers, elders, deacons, and teachers, gave church members a part in church life. Beyond the preaching of the Word, it also kept social welfare and schools in the hands of the Church. We have already seen that Luther turned social activities over to the state, and it also took over the schools. Luther was, in fact, very effective in stamping out begging and indigence, and he made a great contribution to the reform of German schools. "We are called by all the world German beasts," he wrote; "we have been too long German beasts. Let us for once use reason, so that God may feel the gratitude of his creatures, and other lands see that we are human people who can learn something useful from them or teach them something, so that the world is improved by us, too." But social welfare and education were assigned to the state and administered thereafter in Protestant Germany from above, while voluntary Christian or humane activities suffered. Luther's Church was confined exclusively to the Word and to the spiritual comfort of the individual.

Luther's concept of the Christian Church was closely related to his ideas about this world. The existing political and social order expressed, in his opinion, the eternal will of God. God had created government by secular authorities for the enforcement of law and order, in which neither the individual nor the group was to meddle. Without an imposed order, man, corrupted by original sin, would lead the world into chaos, which would terminate the very existence of the world. In particular, the untamed human beast would murder the small minority of true Christians and thus make the spread of the Gospel impossible. The secular order, which Luther liked to describe as analogous to conditions depicted in the Old Testament, implied property, inequality, and serfdom, and had to be managed according to natural reason or worldly wisdom. Although ordained by God, the state as an institution was to Luther by no means a Christian state. In many respects it was directly opposed to Christian ideals, chiefly because it rested on force. Luther could understand that a Christian might hesitate to participate in the functions of governments as rulers, judges, soldiers, or hangmen. A true Christian could live in harmony with the ethics of Christian love. But the natural world, St. Augustine's *civitas terrena*, could not be expected to live according to the rules of the kingdom of God (*civitas dei*).

Luther wanted to have the two kingdoms strictly separated, the first being one of mercy and love, the other of anger and punishment. But since they were both willed by God, a Christian had to fulfill his duty in both realms. The contrast was eased by knowledge that the secular order was not only a penalty for sin, but also contained a promise of ultimate mercy. Since government made dissemination of the Word possible, and thereby access to salvation, this instrument of God's world rule was surrounded with a certain Christian aura after all. The whole conception led to a characteristic dichotomy in ethics. A true Christian was bound by his conscience to an ethics of love, but as a prince or ordinary officeholder he had to adhere to the secular law. The ensuing conflict of heart was harmonized by the assurance that preservation of the natural order was ordained by God, and consequently adhering to the secular law was a service to Him and to one's neighbor. In this perspective Luther could call strict execution of the law by a prince, or relentless fighting on the part of a soldier, true worship of God.

Luther nevertheless expected that there would be a difference in the attitude of a true Christian and that of a pseudo-Christian or pagan to political affairs. The true Christian, knowing not only about the sinfulness of the secular order but also about its transitory nature, would not participate in it for egotistical reasons but would conceive of his role as a commission received from God and as a service to his fellow men. The princes were "God's officeholders" and "servants of the people." As such they were obliged not to go further in the use of force than was necessary for the maintenance of law and order, and to remain conscious of the ultimate purpose of the secular order, which was the promotion of the right religion and life. Luther was never quite satisfied with the mere execution of the written law, and suggested that princes or judges be guided by equity (*epieikeia*) rather than by the letter of the law. However, he failed to develop these ideas, which would have humanized the political practices of his age. When he spoke of higher justice, he had in mind chiefly paternal generosity given voluntarily and arbitrarily by a superior, and not to be claimed as a matter of right by the subject.

If the rulers were just deputizing in the execution of a divine plan, there was no room for rights of the individual. The recommendation of clemency was directed exclusively to those rulers who wanted to be Christians. In Luther's opinion, few of them were Christians, and few of them ever would be, but in spite of this situation, their subjects were not released from obedience to the divinely ordained secular authorities.

A Christian owed obedience even to the sultan, and a prisoner of war in the hands of the Turks who escaped from his captivity was committing a crime, since he deprived his lord of a legitimate price. In Luther's thinking there was no place for any conception of a corporate or organic state in which, irrespective of its constitutional forms, the individual would have a personal role. The individual had nothing but duties to be accepted and suffered by him on account of the wretched state of the world.

Luther has often been praised as a liberator of the natural world, and particularly of the modern state. Actually, this is true only in a negative sense. He denied that the natural orders of life could be generally transformed, as the medieval Church had attempted, or that they could be renounced, as medieval asceticism had pretended. For Luther, the world remained thoroughly bad, and also a passing stage of human life, since beyond the short duration of earthly existence the timeless bliss of heaven extended. Luther could call the world "the front porch of hell," or say, "We serve in an inn in which the devil is the master and the world mistress," or, "The world is a stable crowded with bad boys; consequently, we must have laws and government, judges, executioners, swords and gallows and what not, to suppress the rascals." The sinfulness, as well as the approaching doom of the world and the certainty of God's kingdom as the only true reality, made Luther wary of attaching any significance to details of a secular order. The individual had to suffer the wrath of God in this world, and there could be no claim for personal rights. The embryonic conceptions of the sovereignty of the people which had been developed in the later Middle Ages, not only by Marsilius of Padua but also by St. Thomas, were completely eradicated by Luther and his successors. Opposition to tyrants was never heard of in Lutheranism, and human rights were not promoted. If a prince or magistrate acted in a tyrannical manner, the subjects had to suffer his actions as manifestations of God's unfathomable will, which, in any event, had not planned this world as the pleasure ground of humanity, although the carpet of God's creation revealed many golden threads to the attentive eye.

Submission with complete obedience was the supreme and absolute law that Luther preached, in all matters except one, namely religious conviction. Adherence to and open confession of the Christian faith could not be limited by any secular authority. But this faith could not establish any right of the individual either. Martyrdom and death hung over the head of every true Christian. Originally, Luther was convinced that not even the German princes had the right to oppose the emperor on religious grounds. He was persuaded only with difficulty by the Saxon jurists in the years 1532–34 that the law of the Empire gave the German princes such power. But Luther had no doubts that suffering was the fate of the Christian on earth.

The function of the state, according to Luther, was then to maintain a rough order in this sinful world of mortals so as to enable the chosen few to prepare for the kingdom of God. What little could be done by human effort to ease the conflict between the two realms could only be derived from recognition of the transcendental world. Clearly the Word of God should be unimpeded in a good state, the individual should be trained to receive it and to lead a life that would not misdirect his ideas to sinful purposes. In other words, government could gain moral objectives by emphasizing the church, school, and general welfare. The latter was not understood in any modern, materialistic sense as internal prosperity or outward power, but was interpreted in terms of medieval Christian customs as the preservation of conditions most conducive to the cultivation of piety. In the main the state had an educational task. The idea of the state as a power organism craving for aggrandisement was totally alien to Luther, and he also refused to give the state a religious mission in its foreign relations. He shocked his contemporaries when, in 1518, he opposed any war against the Turks and proclaimed their successes a just penalty inflicted by God on Christendom. After 1530 he modified his opinion to the extent of allowing the emperor to conduct a war in defense of the Empire, but he firmly denied that such a war could be undertaken as a crusade in the name of religion. In general, only wars of defense could be tolerated, and Christian princes who would bear injustices rather than go to war were to be commended. Defeat in war might be a wholesome castigation at the hands of God, which could bring men back to humility and right worship. Luther even advised Christians not to serve superiors who conducted aggressive wars, though they might have to suffer the consequences of such disobedience.

✍ The Individual's Social Responsibility

IN THIS RESPECT Luther was far from leaving politics uncensured and, even less, from permitting man to lose his consciousness of the extreme moral perils of secular life. The various economic occupations were in Luther's view not distinguished from political functions, insofar as all of them only served to keep the world going. A prince, a shoemaker, the father of a family, represented functions necessary for the continuation of the world. None of these states could be called Christian as such, though in each the individual could prove his Christian faith. Since these orders were God-willed, they were in fact the only ones in which a Christian could live. Withdrawal from the world would not lead to a life of higher sanctity; on the contrary, the presumed merits of celibacy or monasticism were fallacious and outright pernicious. There was no special Christian vocation. As every Christian was a priest, every honest natural occupation was a Christian vocation if carried on with devotion to its inherent natural purposes and in a spirit of true religion —this meant if one pursued one's occupation as a duty in the service of God and one's fellow man, and not for personal profit. Hard work turned any natural occupation into a Christian calling or vocation.

Social and economic life could not be Christianized, although a Christian could, and was obliged to, participate in it. It was an angry God who had created this world of toil and discomfort. Although by the right attitude it might become a place of purification for the individual, this general order was basically unchangeable. The conception of a static society conformed to Luther's religious interpretation of the world, and he resented changes like those produced by the new capitalism of the Fuggers or of the neighboring Saxon mining industries. Essentially, Luther thought of an agrarian society, in which agriculture and handiwork constituted the main occupations and in which little social mobility existed. The individual was born to his state, and it was his duty to fulfill its obligations throughout his life.

✍ The Influence of Luther's Social Ethics on Germany

IT HAS BEEN NECESSARY to describe Luther's social ethics in detail, because its influence on modern German history and on the formation of the German character can hardly be overrated. It is not surprising, however, that Luther's position has been much misunderstood by friend and foe alike. In this connection it is important to realize that he did not create the character of the German states in the period after 1525. Their institutions were of much longer standing, and they did not change very drastically because of the Protestant Reformation. Even their inclination to assume the direction of Church life had been prepared by the strong tendency of governments in the late Middle Ages to intervene in ecclesiastical affairs. The development of absolutist trends, which undoubtedly received support from Lutheranism, was by no means confined to the Lutheran parts of Germany. Austria and Bavaria, the most Catholic states, developed absolutist practices before all other German states. Luther's teachings had of course only a subsidiary influence on the actual growth of the German territorial state. But Luther's social philosophy was not merely a rationalization or, in Marxian terms, an ideological superstructure of existing economic and political conditions. Luther took issue with the ambitions of both the princes and the burghers. To this extent his theories were the outflow of the religious conceptions of a former monk.

Yet Luther's ideas lent the state a halo that it had not had before. The state's responsibility for Church organization, in addition to the physical welfare of its subjects, and the submission of the individual to political authority had never been carried to such extremes before. The Lutheran state was an authoritarian state (*Obrigkeitsstaat*) and, within limits, even a "Christian" state. It was not a power state (*Machtstaat*); the Lutheran states, under the influence of Luther's teachings, actually became incapable of conducting an active foreign policy. Luther was not concerned with the form of government either. Although monarchy was most familiar to him, he did not consider it the universal form of government. The republican governments that he saw in the German cities appeared equally legitimate to him. Conservative Lutheranism was compatible also with democratic forces and ideas, as can be seen from its history in Scandinavia, as well as in America. In a small way it could be seen to work harmoniously with such forces also in Württemberg. If the German imperial cities had not lost their influence on national life by the end of the sixteenth century, the virtual identification of Lutheranism with the monarchical state might not have become general in Germany.

But in spite of Luther's recognition of the secular character of the state and of the natural function of economic occupations, his contempt for the world and its sinful and transitory nature made him distrustful of any human capacity for changing the perennial order of history. Obedience and suffering were accordingly the lot of the Christian. Moreover, the existing secular authorities received through his doctrines an unusual dignity, and all deliberate opposition to them was banned. With no appeal to any higher authority left, the existing political and social order naturally became the divine order. And insofar as the modern *Machtstaat*, or power state, required the subordination of the individual to the absolute power of the government, Lutheranism helped to pave the way for it. But Luther was not faced by the modern state and had no conception of it, so he cannot be accused of bringing on a situation that he did not foresee and that was created by the rise of new forces. He did, however, glorify the *Obrigkeitsstaat,* or authoritarian state, and made it difficult to reform German political institutions, even at a time when the old order was being challenged. Civil rights and constitutional reforms had to develop in Protestant Germany independently of, if not against, the old Protestantism. Protestantism, however, having curtailed the influence of the Church over the state, had no means by which to oppose the state once it became indifferent to the confessional or even religious beliefs of its citizens after the eighteenth century. What Lutheranism became under these conditions, will be seen later.

It would be wrong to assume that the Lutheran movement in the century after 1525 can be exclusively traced to the domination of Luther's spirit. As we have already indicated, the Lutheran movement after 1525 was deeply influenced by the existing political powers, and its religious nature was profoundly modified by Luther's pupils and friends. Luther's writings were almost without exception fragments of a great confession of his own soul-shaking religious experiences, and most of them were written in response to challenges of the hour or of individual adversaries. His most systematic piece was actually his reply to Erasmus' polemic treatise of 1524, *On Free Will,* which he countered with his *Serfdom of Human Will.* But Luther, alive with the feeling of liberation from rigid and narrow dogma, was unfit to present his views in a systematic fashion. Moreover, many of the basic problems were bound to appear in a new light to the next generation, which had not gone through his historically peculiar struggles, though they profited from his solutions. At the same time, the next generation was more sensitive to new political pressures than Luther.

✍ *Philip Melanchthon*

THIS WAS PARTICULARLY TRUE of Philip Melanchthon, who, next to Luther, had the greatest influence on the formation of the Lutheran churches. This young humanistic prodigy, a nephew of Reuchlin, had come to Wittenberg as professor of Greek, in 1518, at the age of 21, and he had soon been won over by Luther's interpretation of Pauline Christianity. With the eclipse of Carlstadt and with Luther's far-reaching preoccupations, Melanchthon became the most eminent teacher of

Wittenberg University and, after 1525, the foremost theological representative of Lutheranism in the councils of the world. He was neither an original religious figure or philosophical thinker; his eminence rested on his encyclopedic scholarship and his extraordinary lucidity of presentation. This in itself would not have given him fame as *praeceptor Germaniae*, if there had not been a strong and distinctive character behind all his activities. He set the personal style for the members of the "academic groups," as they have been commonly called in Germany; these included not only the professors but also all those directly or partly educated by them, such as ministers of the church, government officials, lawyers, or other professionals. Melanchthon's contribution to the creation of these characteristic social types was great, through his leadership in the reorganization of higher education in Protestant Germany, no less than through the model that he set by his life and thought. His influence on German social history can be called greater than that of Luther, whose personality, both earthy and prophetic, had an inimitable uniqueness.

In his early years in Wittenberg Melanchthon seemed inclined to abjure humanism and make himself the loyal apostle of Luther. Had he not been touched in his heart by Luther's teachings, he would not have stayed in Wittenberg but would have gone back to Swabia and his Greek studies. In 1521, he published the first systematic presentation of the Lutheran faith, the *Loci Communes Rerum Theologicarum* (*Main Topics of Theology*). Luther called the *Loci* a book worthy of immortality and canonic validity. It was a masterful exposition of Luther's religion. But the year 1525 brought the differences between the two reformers more clearly into the open. In his controversy with Erasmus Luther had reasserted his doctrine of human impotence with a theological radicalism that frightened Melanchthon. Even more terrifying, however, was the revolution of the peasants, the widespread breakdown of morals and education, the appearance of the Anabaptists, the divisions among the Protestants, and the threat to the coherence of the Empire and to the unity of Christendom. Faced with these dangers, Melanchthon drew strength not only from Luther but also from his own humanistic education.

Whether Melanchthon was of a religious nature in the truest sense, is debatable. At least he was not religious in the exclusive manner of Luther. "I know," Melanchthon said, "that I have never been a theologian except in order to reform life." The humanization and civilization of mankind was his deepest desire. He did not believe that perfection could be the result merely of moral education. Man needed the strength derived from a God-given faith to reach this goal. But by divine creation man was endowed with a "natural light," which allowed him to grasp the fundamental practical and theoretical truths. This natural reason had found full expression in classic philosophy except for an understanding of the right inner disposition of the human heart, which human beings, blinded by original sin, could not perceive properly. Moral philosophy, consequently, dealt merely with external orders and actions; only the Christian message clarified the attitudes of men. The omnipotence of God was safeguarded in this system of thought, and Melanchthon followed Luther also in his rejection of metaphysics as the approach to an understanding of the divine essence. In contrast to the speculation of the schoolmen, Melanchthon centered his systematic treatment of Christian religion on the experience of faith and on the conditions of human consciousness which made such faith a reality.

But although human reason or ancient philosophy did not penetrate into the secrets of revelation, Christian religion and natural reason were not at loggerheads with each other. For example, the Decalogue only augmented and threw into bolder relief the ethical doctrines of Aristotle. The Christian message capped the building for which God had laid the foundations, and which, through the natural light, He had made His dwelling place. In other words, the two worlds that Luther had set poles apart were reunited by Melanchthon into one cosmos; in this world view, antiquity and Christianity were brought into a harmonious balance. The consequences were far-reaching, both with regard to the form and content of Protestant thought. The strong rationalistic character of Melanchthon's thinking stood out in contrast to Luther's emphasis on both sentiment and will. The younger man lived in a clearer, but more anemic, world. Melanchthon also wanted a tidy and neatly organized intellectual structure. The paradoxes that did not disturb Luther, since he saw in them the expression of a divine wisdom transcending human reason, offended Melanchthon's intellectual outlook.

Melanchthon was naturally inclined to seize upon those elements of Luther's religion which identified faith with doctrine. As he attempted, in a Ciceronian fashion, to abstract and summarize Greek philosophy in a unified classic creed, so the Christian view of life was to be codified in a system of unalterable doctrines. The proof of the identity of modern evangelical teaching not only with the Gospel but also with the dogma of the ancient Church became, therefore, one of the central chapters of Protestant theology. But more was implied in Melanchthon's teaching.

While at first he had taken pains not to mix philosophy and religion, as the schoolmen had done, as time went on he introduced more and more philosophical arguments. Insistence on the ancient dogma, as well as his own intellectual scheme, led to this. In the edition of the *Loci* of 1535 he openly denied the serfdom of the will and absolute predestination. Instead, he assigned to the human will a definite role in Christian conversion, and thereby was moved closer to a scholastic approach.

Melanchthon went along with Luther in defending the latter's doctrine of sacraments in the years after 1525. But finally, after 1540, his wish for unity among the Protestants as well as his revulsion against Luther's exclusion of reason made him modify his own position. As a consequence of these differences, deep rifts opened in the Lutheran camp. Most of the details of these theological controversies can safely be left to oblivion, but some of them point to a basic dilemma with which young Protestantism was faced. Luther had grown up in the medieval Church, which had aroused in its earnest members an acute awareness of human sinfulness. To those who, like Luther, had come out of the school of the traditional system of Christian penitence, the doctrine of justification was delivery from the anguish of a pained conscience. But to a new generation that had heard the soothing message from its infancy, the process of justification inevitably appeared in a new light. If the consciousness of sin and the trust in divine grace were from the beginning experienced simultaneously, these sentiments were bound to weaken each other. Obviously, they would be experienced one after the other, in which case, however, the problems arose of what constituted proper contrition of the heart, and of who could consider himself justified and at what moment?

Closely interwoven with these questions was the urgent need of maintaining strict ethical standards of Christian life after good works as a prerequisite of salvation had been abolished. From the beginning the Catholics accused Protestantism of opening the gates to moral laxity, and in the years after 1520, and even more after 1525, the decline of morals was, indeed, quite alarming. Melanchthon was willing to weaken Luther's conception of justification as the exclusive gift of God and the accompanying theory of good works as the natural fruits of justification, and to assert the necessity of good works for salvation. However, he was opposed and prevented from doing so by staunch students of Luther's, but only on the theological level. In practice, morality was enforced by the new churches and by the political authorities behind them. The criteria of ethical conduct were simple and almost identical with the needs of a paternalistic state. Obedience and enduring the hardships of life, including stupid and tyrannical lords, were the main tests of moral behavior.

The paternalistic state found its most powerful support in Melanchthon's social philosophy. He accepted all of Luther's social teachings on the state, the family, the individual's social duties, and on economic life. But Luther's whole social ethics was made absolutely rigid by Melanchthon's practical identification of the law of God with the law of nature. While Luther had retained a practical attitude of Christian skepticism about the realization of justice in this world, Melanchthon, in his desire for order, did not. Social ethics was for him a legal system, and this made the Christian authoritarian state, with its paternal police powers, fully supreme. Melanchthon was not a champion of arbitrary power; for him the state was based on laws. For this reason he preferred an aristocratic regime such as that of the German cities to monarchical government, which seemed more likely to produce tyranny. But he knew of no self-help against the abuse of power, since the laws of a state were the codification of eternal inequality and absolutism.

During the Peasant's War, Melanchthon outdid Luther in ascribing to the princes sweeping authority and in admonishing them to enforce the law relentlessly. A prince could demand any amount of dues and taxes from his subjects without accounting to them for the use of the money. In his judicial role he had an unlimited right to impose punishment. With regard to the serfdom of the peasants Melanchthon found any doubts irresponsible. This serfdom, he said was "rather too mild for such a wild and untamed people as Germans are." It was not only love of order and peace that made him authoritarian, but also the pride of education. By a strange twist of fate this man, who loved nothing better than the fellowship of scholars of like mind and the company of his students, was forced to act as the chief theological statesman of Lutheranism after 1530. The task crushed him at times, and certainly went beyond the strength of his sensitive nature. It might be admitted that not only his lack of a realistic appreciation of political forces but also a certain doctrinairism led him into great suffering. His willingness to compromise the Protestant cause exasperated his original friends. In their eyes this would have been bad enough had it been done out of conviction, but they pointed out that occasionally Melanchthon's attitude was warped by fear. And this was not altogether untrue. Particularly in the negotiations of the Diet of Augsburg of 1530, he was driven at times far beyond any position that he could have defended in good faith, even if one admits the genuineness of his wish for the preservation of the unity of the Christian Church. Again in the dark days after the defeat of the Protestant princes in 1546 he proved himself timid and unheroic.

It was amazing that Luther, who disliked Erasmian characters and who was resentful of any deviation, kept "Magister Philip" in high esteem all through his life. He was aware of the complete unselfishness of his colleague and of the inestimable services that Melanchthon rendered to a reformed Christian religion. While Luther thought of himself as a trail blazer, he admired Melanchthon for his ability to turn the forest into a well-kept garden. Luther was fully conscious of the fact that Melanchthon's didactic talent and his gift for relating religion to the total knowledge of the age made the systematic propagation and spread of the new faith possible. Although the relationship between the two men lost some of its warmth in the course of the years, their friendship was never broken. This protected Melanchthon for a time against attacks by eager followers of Luther. But after Luther's death the wrath of the zealous students of the late doctor of the Church fell upon the preceptor, and Melanchthon, who had always longed for Christian unity, found himself the center of furious battles that threatened to break up the German Protestant churches. In his old age he prayed to be saved from the *"rabies theologorum."*

Yet no one, apart from Luther himself, left as deep an imprint of his personality on the Lutheran churches as Melanchthon. Many of his younger critics failed to realize to what extent they were standing on his shoulders. While he certainly brought, with some of his ideas, serious differences into the Protestant world of Germany, he gave it unity in creating the forms and methods of transmitting the Lutheran faith and a specifically Lutheran civilization. In spite of all the theological wrangling of the generation that followed him Melanchthon transformed Luther's faith into a doctrine and was the founder of what has been called, in contrast to the early creative years of the Reformation, the age of Lutheran orthodoxy. He was entirely successful, too, in introducing not only elements of classical antiquity, which had been kept alive by the schoolmen, but also some of the new thoughts of sixteenth-century humanism. Humanism and philosophy remained in the new Protestant theology handmaidens of theology; antiquity was of course studied not for the beauty it revealed but for the intellectual instruction it provided. In this respect it was important that Melanchthon's encyclopedic interest included physics. The strange mixture of Greek science and Christian speculation made him not only reject Copernicus' refutation of Ptolemy as scurrilous but also discover in this world the devil, ghosts, demons, and witches, and accept astrological influences. But at least science found a place in the academic curriculum, as did also history, which, however, was chiefly used to provide illustrations of Christian ethics. Although at the end of the seventeenth century the methods and contents of study began to change, a field of worthwhile academic study had been laid out, and it served for 250 years as the arena for German intellectual effort.

CHAPTER 9

Empire and Reformation, 1526–55

❦

THE EVENTS OF 1525 and their aftermath ended the youthful stage of the Protestant Reformation. Compelled to establish itself amidst the hard realities of this world and the stubborn forces of the German political scene, German Protestantism forewent many potentialities of religious development which had been present in its early creative years. Few of them were taken up by later generations in Germany, while some of them bore fruit outside the country. But perhaps even more important for future German history than the contraction of the world of inner experience was the decision to leave to the secular government the organization of the empirical church, or rather churches, and to turn over to the political community many functions which, up to that time, had been fulfilled by the Church. Some of the consequences of these historic events were slow in making their full impact felt, but the new predominance of political forces over religious movements became apparent immediately after 1525. The territorial governments appeared as the leaders of the reform movement, while the theologians were confined to serving as advisers to the princes and their diplomats and jurists.

The Peasants' War seemed to support the opinion of all those who had seen in Lutheranism only the harbinger of social revolution, and it encouraged the defenders of the old Church to follow up the suppression of the peasants with the extermination of the Lutheran "sect." For this purpose an alliance was concluded in July, 1525, by the Catholic princes of north Germany: George of Saxony, Albert of Mainz and Magdeburg, his brother Joachim of Brandenburg, Duke Henry of Brunswick-Wolfenbüttel, and Duke Erich of Brunswick. The Protestant princes hesitated to join together openly. Among them were two Hohenzollern princes who had been won to the Lutheran side. Both be-

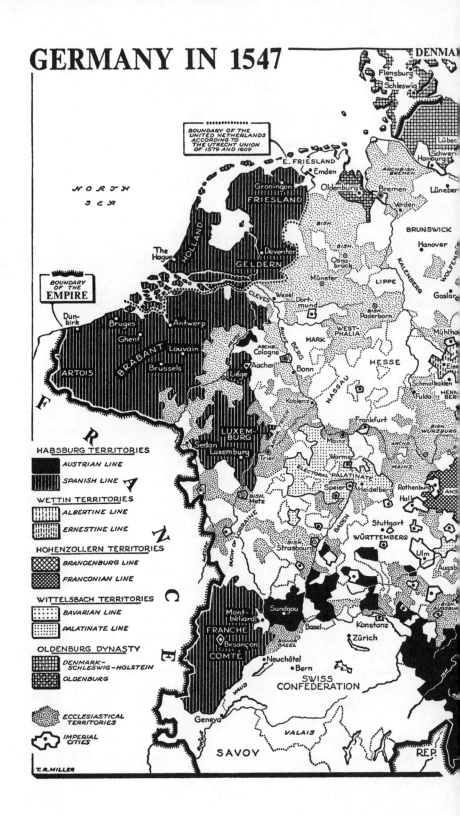

GERMANY IN 1547

BOUNDARY OF THE
UNITED NETHERLANDS
ACCORDING TO
THE UTRECHT UNION
OF 1579 AND 1609

BOUNDARY
OF THE
EMPIRE

NORTH
SEA

DENMA

Flensburg
Schleswig

Lübec
Schweri
Hamburg

E. FRIESLAND
Emden

Groningen
FRIESLAND

Oldenburg
Bremen
Verden

ARCHBISH.
BREMEN

Lüneber

BRUNSWICK

Hanover

WOLFEN

The
Hague
HOLLAND

Deventer

GELDERN

BISH.
Osna-
brück

Münster

BISH.

LIPPE

KALENBURG

Goslar

CLEVES
Wesel
Dort-
mund

BISH.
Paderborn

WEST-
PHALIA

Mühlha

Dun-
kirk

Bruges

Ghent

Antwerp

Louvain

Brussels

ARTOIS

BRABANT

ARCHB.
Cologne

Aachen

Bonn

BERG

MARK

Liége

NASSAU

HESSE

Eise

Schmalkalden
Fulda
HENN-
BER

Koblenz

Frankfurt

BISH.
WÜRZBURG

Bar

LUXEM-
BURG

Sedan
Luxemburg

Trier

ARCH

Mai

Worms

MAINZ

ELECTORAL PALATINATE

Speier Heidelberg

Rothenburg

ANS

Hall

HABSBURG TERRITORIES

AUSTRIAN LINE

SPANISH LINE

WETTIN TERRITORIES

ALBERTINE LINE

ERNESTINE LINE

HOHENZOLLERN TERRITORIES

BRANDENBURG LINE

FRANCONIAN LINE

WITTELSBACH TERRITORIES

BAVARIAN LINE

PALATINATE LINE

OLDENBURG DYNASTY

DENMARK-
SCHLESWIG-HOLSTEIN

OLDENBURG

ECCLESIASTICAL
TERRITORIES

IMPERIAL
CITIES

F
R
A
N
C
E

BISH.
Metz

DUCHY OF LORRAINE

BISH.
Strasbourg

BADEN

Stuttgart

WÜRTTEMBERG

Ulm

Augsb

BISH
REGENSBU

Mont-
béliard

FRANCHE
Besançon
COMTÉ

Sundgau

Basel

BISH.
BASEL

Neuchâtel

Bern

VAUD

Geneva

Konstanz

Zürich

SWISS
CONFEDERATION

VALAIS

SAVOY

REP.

T. R. MILLER

150 MILES

BALTIC SEA

RÜGEN

Rostock Stralsund

Kolberg BISHOP KAMMIN

Stolp Lauenburg Königsberg

Heilsberg

Danzig Elbing BISHOP ERMLAND

Marienburg

P O M E R A N I A

Kammin

DUCHY OF MECKLENBURG

Stettin

Graudenz

P R U S S I A

Bromberg

Thorn

VISTULA

ELECTORATE OF BRANDENBURG

Berlin Kustrin

Brandenburg Frankfurt

Schwiebus

Gnesen

Posen

WARTHE

KINGDOM OF POLAND

Stendal

Wittenberg LOWER LUSATIA

Kottbus UPPER LUSATIA

Glogau

Kalisch

ANHALT

Torgau Leipzig

ELECTORATE OF SAXONY

Dresden

Chemnitz

Liegnitz Breslau

S I L E S I A

ODER

Oppeln

Czenstochau

REUSS

Plauen

Eger

Cracow

VISTULA

BAYREUTH

Prague

KINGDOM OF BOHEMIA

MORAVIA

ELBE

nberg

UPPER PALATINATE

Brünn

MOLDAU

Regensburg DANUBE

BISHOP PASSAU

Budweis

DUCHY OF BAVARIA

Passau

ARCHDUCHY

OF

Vienna

Pressburg

H U N G A R Y

Munich

Linz

AUSTRIA

ABOVE THE ENNS BELOW THE ENNS

ENNS

Budapest

DANUBE

ARCHB SALZBURG

nsbruck

Graz

STYRIA

A U S T R I A N

H U N G A R Y

ROL

CARINTHIA

Klagenfurt

OTTOMAN EMPIRE

ozen

Laibach

T U R K I S H

OF VENICE

Udine

GORIZIA CARNIOLA

Agram

Trieste

SAVE

longed to the Franconian line; Casimir of Ansbach was the ruler of the principality neighboring on Nürnberg, and Albert was the grandmaster of the Order of Teutonic Knights. On Luther's advice Albert left his clerical calling and made himself Duke of Prussia. Duke Albert, who through his marriage to a Danish princess, established the first political connection between Lutheranism and the Scandinavian countries, was not a prince of the Holy Roman Empire but a vassal of the king of Poland.

✍ *The Protestant Cause After 1525*

THE PROTESTANT CAUSE IN GERMANY was chiefly represented by Electoral Saxony and Hesse. On the death of Frederick the Wise, his brother John (1526–32) succeeded him as elector of Saxony. He and his son John Frederick (1532–47; d. 1554) were deeply devoted to Luther and willing to act with less caution than the first protector of Luther. But the political initiative in the Protestant camp was in the hands of young Landgrave Philip of Hesse (b. 1504; d. 1567), who had assumed the reins of government in 1520 and declared himself a Lutheran four years later. Among the German princes Philip did not excel in moral standards of conduct, but he had a more active mind and greater political vision than most of his titled cousins, and his enthusiasm for the religious Reformation was genuine. In the winter of 1525–26 he concluded an understanding with the rulers in Wittenberg by which they would act in complete concert in the defense of the Gospel at the forthcoming diet of the Empire. This first coalition on the Protestant side was an important act. It was also a bold step in view of the fact that Emperor Charles V, through the victory of Pavia and the capture of the French king, seemed to have gained freedom of action. But at the time of the opening of the Diet of Speyer the political situation had already changed. Francis I had returned to France and, together with the slippery Pope Clement VII and other Italian rulers, was back in arms against the emperor. Turkish armies had broken into Hungary, and co-operation among the Catholic princes in Germany had weakened. The confident mood of Landgrave Philip helped to win time for the further strengthening of German Protestantism.

No one at this time wanted to break away from the Church, or even from a papal church. Everyone was in addition animated by the feeling that the national unity of the Empire was endangered by the strain of religious dissonance. Essentially, most people wished for both national harmony and the restoration of a universal religious and political order. All groups agreed, however, that this restoration could not be merely a return to the desolate state of the Church before 1517, and that distinctions had to be drawn between the eternal verities of religion and the human rules of ecclesiastical organization. It was with regard to the external state of the Church that the demand was first raised to settle them by national legislation, while true Christian doctrine was to be defined by universal consensus. The division seemed simple if stated in principle, but difficult if applied concretely. Faith, doctrine, ceremonies, customs, and laws of the Church were so closely interwoven that they could not easily be separated from one another. The separation of the essentials of faith from mere theology or of devotional worship from ritual required a comprehensive understanding of the living unity of the Roman Catholic Church. Charles V was fully aware of this when he advised his brother not to tolerate the discussion of certain special reforms by a national assembly and insisted that only a general council was qualified to make decisions in these matters. Charles believed, too, that a general council of the Christian Church should be convoked by the pope.

✆ *The Speyer Resolution of 1526*

WHEN ARCHDUKE FERDINAND REVEALED these instructions of the emperor to the estates in Speyer, the common effort to find for Germany a special order within the old Church was blunted, but unanimous agreement was reached that the Edict of Worms could not be executed nationally, and that until the convocation of a council the estates "with their subjects, would live, govern, and act in such a way as everyone trusted to justify before God and the Imperial Majesty." It was the burial of the attempt to anchor national unity in a community of religious institutions, although there was still a profound desire to maintain the papal Church and the traditional order of the Empire. It was tragic that two days after the conclusion of the Diet of Speyer King Ludwig II of Hungary and Bohemia was killed in the battle of Mohács, and Ferdinand was drawn completely into the struggles of succession in the southeastern kingdom. But of decisive importance was the break between pope and emperor, who, together, could no doubt have saved much of the universal order. Renewal of the fratricidal conflict between Clement VII and Charles V gave the Protestants the opportunity to consolidate their strength and build their own church organization.

Moreover, the battle between the emperor and the pope, which culminated in the sack of Rome in 1527, weakened the prestige of the Church.

In these circumstances the Speyer formula, which had been intended rather as a standstill agreement, became the basis for affirmative action among the Protestants. It is quite impossible to describe the actual step-by-step progress of Protestantism in Germany. In many cases the reform of the Church was brought about by the territorial governments, often enough in the face of considerable opposition within the territories. However, action on the part of the secular or ecclesiastical princes was at other times frustrated not by the territory as such, but by members of the estates, sometimes a town and often individual members of the nobility. Of the greatest consequence was the official reformation of Hesse, begun in October, 1526, when Landgrave Philip held a diet of the Hessian estates at Homberg, which was meant to act at the same time as a church synod. Francis Lambert, a French Franciscan friar from Avignon, who had studied in Zurich and Wittenberg, presented a memorable plan for the organization of the Church. It was to be built on the voluntary membership of believers, forming democratic congregations, which in turn would elect a synod to govern the Church. Emphasis was placed not only on the disciplinary power of the congregations but also on the social and educational mission of the Church. Luther warned against the adoption of such a constitution, which seemed to him too liberal, and actually the final organization of the Hessian church followed largely the Saxon example. But Lambert's recommendation for the establishment of a university was accepted, and in 1527 the first Protestant university came into being in Marburg.

In northern Germany before 1529 the countship of Mansfeld and the duchy of Brunswick-Lüneburg became officially Protestant, and Schleswig, Holstein, Brunswick-Calenberg, and East Friesland were also virtually Protestant. In Bremen the Reformation proceeded steadily after 1525 and was completed by 1528; it reached its conclusion in Hamburg a year later. The cities of Brunswick, Goslar, Flensburg, and Husum turned Protestant at the same time. In south Germany the Swabian cities of Reutlingen, Memmingen, Kempten, and Lindau had followed the example of Strasbourg, Nürnberg, and Ansbach by 1528. In Schwäbisch-Hall, Heilbronn, and Biberach at least the city governments were Protestant by that time. Small wonder that the neighboring duchy of Württemberg, then under Habsburg administration, was permeated by Protestant influences. But everywhere in the Empire Protestantism raised its head. A Church visitation of Styria in 1528 showed many towns and large sections of the nobility won over by the Reformation.

✎ Protestant Fear of Suppression

THE MOVEMENT HAD BECOME so widespread that it would seem to have been impossible to halt it by force. Nevertheless, the Protestants were fearful of an attempt by the emperor and the Catholic princes to suppress the Reformation by violent means. In this atmosphere Philip of Hesse fell an easy victim to the forgeries of Otto von Pack, a bankrupt councilor of the Catholic Duke George of Saxony. Pack persuaded Philip that Archduke Ferdinand, in early 1528, had concluded an offensive alliance with the electors of Brandenburg and Mainz, the dukes of Saxony and Bavaria, and the bishops of Bamberg and Würzburg in order to exterminate the new heresy. Philip wished to thwart such attempts by taking the initiative in attacking. He took soundings in France, and with Zápolya in Hungary, and he won over Elector John of Saxony for a projected action against the prince-bishoprics on the Main. Philip actually assembled a large force, but the Wittenberg government began to drag its feet, the Catholic princes declared Pack a swindler, and no fighting took place. Philip, however, blackmailed the bishops of Würzburg and Bamberg into reimbursing him for his mobilization, and he gained from the archbishop of Mainz the renunciation of his ecclesiastical jurisdiction over Hesse.

The "Pack affairs" were no credit to Philip, but they showed clearly the intensity of mutual suspicion that existed and how easily swords might be brandished. For the first time a prince of the Empire had scored in matters of ecclesiastical reform through the display of force. Might not the other side retaliate in kind, once it felt ready to act? As the payments and concessions to Philip indicated, the Catholic princes had been found unprepared, but they were stirred to greater activity. The defection of the pope in the years after 1526 had driven even Charles into a strong antipapalist policy. Imperial propaganda had freely used the conciliar theory in bitter literary attacks against the Curia, which could have struck contemporaries as hardly distinguishable from the attacks of the Lutherans. But the occupation and sack of Rome in 1527 by Spanish and German troops of Charles V had humiliated Clement VII. His return to Rome in 1528 opened a new chapter of political rapprochement with Charles, and the fight against the Lutheran heresy offered one of the best arguments for the necessity of an understanding. In this situation a new diet of the Empire was called to Speyer, and it was opened by Archduke Ferdinand in the presence of an unusually large representation of princes and cities.

✍ *The Speyer Protestation of 1529*

FERDINAND PRESENTED AN IMPERIAL MESSAGE, which actually was his own. It announced the imminent appearance of the emperor in Germany and categorically demanded the nullification of the resolutions of the Speyer Diet of 1526, which, it stated, had been grossly abused. Furthermore, in view of the fact that an understanding between the emperor and pope would make the early convention of a Christian council possible, all religious innovations were to be stopped and the jurisdiction of the bishops was to be restored. With the support of an overwhelming majority of Catholic electors, princes, and bishops, the imperial proposition, in slightly modified form, was promulgated as law on April 19, 1529. The handful of Lutherans thereupon presented their official "protestation," from which the name "Protestant" was originally derived. In it they argued that under the laws of the Empire a unanimously passed law could not be abrogated by a majority. They declared themselves, therefore, bound by the Speyer resolution of 1526 and added that they would not conform to the resolutions of the current diet, "since in matters concerning God's honor and our soul's salvation everyone must stand before God and answer by himself, nobody can excuse himself in that place by the actions or decisions of others, whether they be a minority or majority." Thus exactly eight years after a lonely monk had challenged hierarchical authority before the Diet of Worms, a group of political governors rejected both the hierarchical and the majority principle in religious affairs. It should not be overlooked, however, that these princes and city governments asserted in the same breath their personal right to determine the religious faith and the devotional practices of their own subjects. Religious liberty of the individual was claimed only for the leaders of communities, not for their members.

The protestation was signed by a small group of princes and by fourteen cities. The Saxon elector, Landgrave Philip, Margrave George of Ansbach, Prince Wolfgang of Anhalt, and the envoy from Brunswick were the princely signatories. Among the cities, Strasbourg, Nürnberg,

Ulm, Constance, Nördlingen, and Heilbronn stood out as the most important. All who signed performed a courageous act by joining in protest, since the imperial proposition threatened violators with the ban. But the cities, all of them located in Catholic territories, ran the greatest risk, particularly Strasbourg in its peripheral geographical position. Three days after the signing Electoral Saxony, Hesse, Strasbourg, Ulm, and Nürnberg concluded a defensive alliance in case they should be attacked "on account of God's word," but little was gained as these diplomatic understandings were not implemented by real power. They were not even backed by a common spirit. For some time splits over doctrines had sapped the unity of the Protestant movement. For this reason its opponents had been hopeful that it could be defeated piecemeal.

✍ Division Among the Protestants

THE ISSUES THAT TENDED TO SEPARATE the Protestants are already known to us. They centered around the contrast between Luther and Zwingli, and after 1525 found their theological expression in sharp controversial writings on the doctrine of sacraments. With some modifications Zwingli's teachings were adopted beyond Switzerland in the cities of southern Swabia as well as along the Rhine from Strasbourg to as far down as the Netherlands and East Friesland. The north German principalities and Nürnberg as well as the Franconian and north Swabian cities clung to Luther. Apart from some geographical factors, deeper political motives appeared in this division.

In Zurich, a politically active republican community, every move of religious reformation had to be examined from the beginning also with reference to its potential impact on the politics of the city as well as of the Helvetian Confederation with its world-wide relations. Here political implications could not be divorced from religion and left to princes as in Germany. The upper German cities were in this respect more similar to Zurich than to the German principalities. After the second Diet of Speyer, it was also important that the Swiss reformer Zwingli felt no moral scruples about opposition to the Habsburgs, against whom the Swiss had won their independence. The Roman Empire seemed to him almost as bad as the Roman papacy, while Luther and Melanchthon retained their respect for the venerable empire and even for the person of the emperor. For Luther, nothing but passive obedience to the emperor seemed permissible, and he defined the relationship of the princes of the Empire to the emperor in these days as comparable to that of town mayors to the territorial prince. In 1529 Luther also revised his opinion with regard to resistance to the Turks. While he had fiercely preached that the inroads of the Turks had to be suffered as God's punishment on a debased Christendom, the approaching Turkish attack against the southeastern provinces of the Empire induced him to call upon the Germans to resist the infidels under the banner of the emperor.

Questions of religious faith were thus closely interwoven with political attitudes, as one might expect in an age that had to justify and rationalize all political decisions in terms of a divine justice or commandment. Philip of Hesse, who took an intermediary position between Wittenberg and Zurich not only in dogmatic matters but also with regard to the permissibility of opposition to the emperor, became suspect in the eyes of the Wittenbergers. A common alliance appeared possible only with people of a common faith, and a serious effort had been made to unite the northeastern group in a common creed. But Philip wished to gain the initiative against the Habsburgs and the Catholic princes. So did Zwingli, whose attempt to carry the Reformation to all of Switzerland was meeting the stubborn opposition of the old, so-called "forest" cantons, behind which Habsburg influence lurked. Philip and Zwingli dreamed of an alliance that would unite all Protestants from the Lake of Zurich to the Danish Belt, tying in France and Venice, and that could cripple any designs of the Habsburgs. To this end, Philip persuaded Luther and Zwingli as well as the theologians of Strasbourg, Swabia, and Franconia to meet together in an effort to resolve their religious differences.

The theological conference took place in Marburg in the first days of October, 1529. Although the debates and conversations were conducted in friendliness, and agreement was reached on fourteen out of fifteen articles that contained the fundamentals of faith, the union broke down on the interpretation of the Lord's Supper. Luther's Biblicism stood against the philosophical rationalism of Zwingli, and Luther, sensing in Zwingli a likeness to Erasmus and the sectarians, stubbornly refused a compromise. "They have another spirit than we," was Luther's conclusion, and he was not willing to love the Swiss as brothers, only to grant them the love that a Christian owes his enemies. In spite of the genuine concern felt on both sides regarding the religious issues, unity might still have been achieved if a common political will had existed. But the Wittenbergers had a passive mind with regard to all political planning.

✍ *The Alliance Between Charles V and Clement VII, 1529*

IT WAS A TRAGIC HOUR in the history of German Protestantism, which as a result moved toward a narrow orthodoxy and political isolationism. At this moment it could already be seen that German Lutheranism was not likely to become the power that would represent the Protestant princi- ple in the great European struggle. It is true that the fall of 1529 was an unpropitious time for the political schemes of Philip and Zwingli. On June 29 Charles V and Clement VII signed an "eternal" alliance, which was to seal the Spanish domination of Italy and prepare for the imperial coronation. On August 3 the Peace of Cambrai ended the war between Charles V and Francis I. Charles V spent the months that followed in Bologna in intimate conversation with the pope. Here he received the good news that Sultan Suleiman, who had appeared before Vienna in September, had been forced by the brave defenders, the cold weather, and an approaching army of the Empire to lift the siege of the Austrian capital. On his thirtieth birthday, in the presence of Italian and Spanish princes, grandees and generals, Charles was crowned Roman Emperor by Clement VII in the cathedral of Bologna. Almost no prince of the German Empire was present at this last imperial coronation by a pope.

Charles did not succeed during his Italian stay in persuading Clem- ent VII to call a council, of which the pope had an ineradicable fear. Clement VII recommended the use of naked force against the heretics, and, if the worst came to the worst, was inclined to make concessions like those that the Church had made to the Hussites rather than expose the papal power and practices to the scrutiny of a Christian council. This narrowed the emperor's political possibilities in his dealings with the religious situation in Germany. Charles' attitude toward the Lu- theran heresy had not changed since the days of Worms, but what had then been the errors of a single friar had grown into an institutionalized religion backed by large groups of people and firmly entrenched politi- cal authorities. There was no need for threats; the aura of the emperor's power was visible for everyone. Conscious of his strength, Charles showed willingness to listen to the parties and to negotiate. He wanted, too, certain political concessions from the German princes. In the first place, the position of his brother Ferdinand in Germany was to be made secure by his election to the Roman kingship, which would proclaim him to be the successor of his brother as ruler of Germany.[1] In addition,

[1] See pages 156–7.

Germany was to contribute men and monies for the reconquest of Hungary and the defense of the eastern marches against the Turks.

✍ The Diet of Augsburg of 1530

THE DIET OF AUGSBURG, which was officially opened on June 20, 1530, became almost a national council in which the emperor, though accompanied by Lorenzo Campeggio, the papal nuncio, seemed to sit in judgment over the religious parties. The representatives of the old faith presented a document, prepared by Dr. Eck, which incorporated 404 errors from the writings of the Lutherans, Zwinglians, and Anabaptists. Melanchthon, who had brought with him a brief written defense of the Wittenberg Church, in which he declared the religious differences as variations of practices rather than of faith, was now driven to expound both faith and practices at greater length. Thus, the *Augustana*, the Augsburg Confession, with its twenty-one articles of faith and seven on rites, came into being. It was to be the foremost religious symbol of the Lutheran churches in subsequent centuries, but it was also the most decisive step in the development of these churches as mere fortresses of orthodox doctrine. Some of the fundamental tenets of Lutheran faith were stated in the Confession with the lucidity that Melanchthon commanded, but for diplomatic reasons other essential elements were left out or toned down. Universal priesthood was not mentioned, nor were papal supremacy, indulgences, purgatory, and the existence of seven sacraments challenged. On the other hand, the sacrament of the Lord's Supper was treated in a way that left a Catholic interpretation open, while excluding any Zwinglian or sectarian position.

Melanchthon wanted to separate the Wittenberg group radically from Swiss and sectarian Protestantism. One of his main objectives was to make the Saxons and their friends appear as loyal members of the old Church and not as basically different in faith, though they had discontinued certain abuses and medieval interpolations. The representation of the Evangelical cause proved a crushing burden for Melanchthon. As the banned Luther could not be brought into the presence of the emperor, he had to stay during these days at the Coburg castle, from which he sent letters full of abiding courage and faith. Melanchthon, fearful of a civil war and appalled by the decline in public morals and education, saw in a compromise the only means for preserving the unity of the Church and, thereby, of orderly authority. The Augsburg Confession was signed by the princes who had made the Speyer Protestation and by two cities, Nürnberg and Reutlingen. The Protestant estates succeeded in having the document read in Latin and German before Charles V. The Catholic princes refused steadfastly to present a similar statement of faith. They said that theirs was the well-known creed of the universal Church, but they were willing to criticize the Confession.

While the Catholic theologians worked with grim determination on their critique and the emperor remained silent, Melanchthon, in his sorrowful panic, made contact with the emperor's confessor and even with the papal nuncio in order to find out what concessions the Lutherans might receive if they returned to the jurisdiction of the Roman Church. He insisted eventually only on communion in both kinds, marriage of priests, and a few changes in the mass ritual. He chanced to remark that the Jews had also lived under Pharao and Caiphas. But Melanchthon's cringing made the Curia less inclined to make concessions, and particularly less amenable to the emperor's entreaties for the convocation of a Christian council. Charles V took care to suppress some of the violent acrimony with which the Catholic theologians, with Eck leading again, had written their *Confutation* of the Augsburg Confession. Yet when presenting it to the estates, he announced the rejection of the Confession. He invited the Protestants to return to the Roman Church and threatened to act under his obligation as the supreme protector of the Church if they refused to do so.

The Protestant princes showed greater firmness than their theologians. Philip of Hesse rode off without taking leave of the emperor, the others waited a month in order not to give offense. But working in a committee, busily trying, with the participation of Charles, to patch up new compromises, the princes did not yield ground on any fundamental questions. They declared their faith identical with the Gospel and not disproved by the *Confutation*. Melanchthon, who found it easier to debate with colleagues than to address majesties and highnesses, wrote his *Apologia*, which dropped political considerations and supplemented his *Confession* in a forthright fashion. Still, Charles marked time, until the Catholic estates finally urged him on. Then when he inquired what help they would lend him, he found them unprepared to assist him with force. After the departure of the Protestant princes great pressure was brought on the cities. Their plight was grave, since they were not only geographically separated but also, in some cases, in conflict with the Wittenberg theology. Four of them, Strasbourg, Constance, Lindau, and Memmingen, unable to accede to Melanchthon's *Augustana*, had presented their own confession, the *Tetrapolitana*, about which, however, nobody at the diet cared very much. But with the exception of two small cities, Nördlingen and Esslingen, which returned to the fold, all the cities that had reformed their churches remained steadfast. It made a deep impression that even Augsburg, with the emperor within its walls and Catholic Bavaria before its gates, did not yield.

The final recess of the Diet of Augsburg, passed by the Roman Catholics in the absence of the Protestant estates, returned completely to the Edict of Worms of 1521 and canceled all decisions of intermediary diets. All heretical innovations, whether Lutheran, Zwinglian, or Anabaptist, were forbidden; ecclesiastical properties and revenues were to be restored; married ministers were to be punished; and a strict censorship over preaching, printing, and bookselling was to be established. The Protestants were to conform to these rulings by April 15, 1531. Thereafter any violation could be prosecuted through the Imperial Cameral Tribunal.

✍ *Habsburg Policy in 1530–31*

THE PROVISION FOR DELAY in enforcement announced in the final resolution, and perhaps even more the stipulation that the Protestant estates would have to grant Catholics the right of unhindered emigration of person and property, indicated that restoration of the old politico-ecclesiastical order was not expected in a matter of days. It has been pointed out with some right that with the setting of a late deadline Charles V wished to protect himself rather than the Protestants. For he had no troops at his disposal to execute the law that had been passed on his prompting. He himself seemed to question whether a restoration could be brought about by force alone, since he promised to have a Christian council convened. But the pope proved intractable with regard to this project, and when the emperor scanned the horizon, he could see many warnings against a war with the Protestants. The pope was not a reliable ally; Francis I of France was always ready to exploit any embarrassment of Charles; and Henry VIII of England, through his divorce an enemy of the pope and emperor, could possibly be driven to the side of Francis. Finally, the Turks remained unconquered.

With swelling pride Charles had coins stamped bearing the inscription that as Sol ruled heaven, so the emperor was the lord of the earth, but he could not remove the clouds that impeded the free exercise of his authority. The strengthening of the government of the Habsburg lands seemed most urgent. His aunt Margaret, the prudent regent of the

Netherlands, died in November, 1530, and Charles had to go to the Netherlands to reorganize the government and install his sister Mary, the widow of King Ludwig of Hungary, as the new regent. On January 5, 1531, the election of Ferdinand as king took place in Aachen. The Saxon elector declared such an election unconstitutional, but the other five electors, extracting a financial price as in 1519,[2] gave their vote to Ferdinand, in whom Germany again gained a ruler of her own, though, according to a secret understanding between the Habsburg brothers, Ferdinand was only to have the authority that Mary held in the Netherlands.

The election was not only opposed by the Protestant princes but also brought discord to the Catholic camp. There were precedents for the election of a Roman king by the electors in the case of an ailing or absent emperor. The elevation of Ferdinand to this rank, however, seemed to establish the Habsburgs on a hereditary throne. If the Catholic princes had been so brave in urging Charles to fight the Protestants, but so chary in offering active support, it had been for fear that their political liberties, their so-called *Libertät*, would be placed in jeopardy by the subjugation of their Protestant confreres. How could the Catholic princes hope to maintain their relative independence against a victorious monarch? In no territory was jealousy more alive than in Bavaria, where friction with neighboring Austria was old and had recently increased with the acquisition of Württemberg by the Habsburgs. Moreover, the Bavarian dukes had been scheming for some time to gain the royal dignity for a member of the Wittelsbach dynasty. Fear and ambition led the most Catholic land in the Empire into co-operation with the Protestants. The event was more than an episode. The antagonism between Bavaria and Austria, though apparently at times merely smoldering and at times buried in a common effort for the common religious cause, revived again and again, and had an important impact on the course of German history.

∽ *The League of Schmalkalden, 1531*

DISRUPTIVE AS THIS AUSTRO-BAVARIAN CONFLICT WAS, it also showed that, in spite of the religious division, there remained certain common concerns that operated, if not for unity, at least for peace among the German estates. But at the close of the Diet of Augsburg, the impression of a complete collapse of the few national institutions of the Holy Empire

[2] See pages 74–5.

prevailed. Once the negative result of the diet had become imminent, the Protestant princes acted with unusual speed. Suddenly the moral scruples about resistance to the imperial majesty were dispelled. As early as September, Martin Luther said, "Thus one of two things must happen, war or revolt; maybe both together." In this mood he was persuaded by the Saxon councilors to modify his opinion about the authority of the emperor and to admit the independent rights of the princes, particularly in religious affairs. Martin Bucer had called on Luther at Coburg and had succeeded in dispersing his animosity against the reformed cities of southern Germany.

The way was open then for a coalition of the Protestant estates, and on February 27, 1531, the charter of the League of Schmalkalden was signed by six princes and ten cities. Among the latter were the north German cities of Magdeburg and Bremen. A few months later the cities of Brunswick, Göttingen, Einbeck, and Goslar joined the League. Within the next fifteen years it was to bring together most of the Protestant estates of the Empire in an alliance for the defense of the Evangelical faith and doctrine. This implied not only common resistance to mandates of the Imperial Cameral Tribunal but also the planning of armed defense. In the spring of 1532, at a meeting in Schweinfurt, the League gave itself a constitution. In 1536–37 the constitution was further strengthened and adjusted to the growing membership. Not all the internal tensions were overcome by the League. The differences in doctrine and Church organization between the Wittenberg group and the upper German cities were still causing some mutual distrust. The relations between princes and cities suffered, as they had on the diets of the Empire, from the attempts of the princes to saddle the cities with most of the expenditures. For the general policy of the League, the divergence in views between the timorous Saxon electors and the bold Landgrave Philip was troublesome. Yet the Schmalkaldic League consolidated the position of German Protestantism within the Empire and without. In fact, for a while it established Protestantism as the superior political power in Germany.

The Swiss cantons were not accepted into the federation, although some political ties existed between certain south German cities and Hesse on the one side and Zurich on the other. The isolation of the Swiss was, however, not exclusively caused by the orthodox squeamishness of Wittenberg but also by the unwillingness of the Swiss to be drawn too much into Empire politics after they had fought the Empire so hard. In 1531 five Catholic cantons defeated Zurich. Zwingli lost his life on the battlefield. Zurich's position of leadership in Switzerland was ruined, and Protestantism was put on the defensive for some time to come. Zurich's influence on Germany was, of course, very weak after this time, and the south German cities that had been oriented toward Zurich were compelled to look for support in the north. Zwingli's death contributed to a strengthening of the Schmalkaldic League and, within it, of strict Lutheranism.

↝ The "Nürnberg Standstill" of 1532

EMPEROR CHARLES AND KING FERDINAND had subventioned the war of the five cantons, but they were unable to exploit the defeat of the Swiss Protestants. The Habsburg brothers had to get ready to meet the approaching Turkish invasion, for which they had to gain the support of the German estates. The diet that opened in Regensburg in April, 1532, was completely overshadowed by the Turkish problem. Separate negotiations were conducted with the Protestants in Schweinfurt and Nürnberg. If marriage of priests and the Lord's Supper in both kinds had constituted the essence of the religious controversy, the Protestants could have gained these concessions at this moment. But they aimed at an assurance against the threats to their religion contained in the recess of Augsburg of 1530, and they wished to have such protection extended to those who might join Protestantism in the future and those living in Catholic territories. This time the Catholic estates protested against any change in the constitutional order. The emperor, however, finally granted the concession that all litigation in matters of religion at the Imperial Cameral Tribunal was to rest till a council convened or, if this was not to happen, till the next diet. Moreover, during this period the estates were not to make war on one another for reasons of religion and faith. The present members of the Schmalkaldic League, as well as Ansbach and Nürnberg, were protected by this "Nürnberg Standstill" of 1532. The limitation of the Standstill to specific Protestant estates as well as the uncertainty about the definition of matters of religion and faith caused endless altercations in the subsequent period, when the Imperial Cameral Tribunal continued to prosecute cases concerning Church properties.

But the Nürnberg Standstill brought help from all the estates against the Turks. The Protestants were particularly eager to prove their patriotism. Nürnberg, for example, sent twice as many soldiers as it was required to send. A total of 80,000 men, including the troops of Ferdinand and Charles, were under the command of the emperor. The fighting along the Hungarian frontier did not lead to major battles, and Suleiman II withdrew in the face of this powerful enemy. But the Empire forces could not be persuaded to conduct a sustained pursuit of the Turks into Hungary. After holding victory parades in Vienna, Charles V had to dismiss the German troops.

The Nürnberg Standstill was the first of a long series of temporary armistices that Charles V had to grant the Protestants, as the international situation required all his strength. He never achieved a reliable relationship with the Curia, even after the fickle Clement VII had been succeeded by Alessandro Farnese as Paul III (1534–49). The Turkish danger continued basically undiminished. In 1535 Charles V went to Tunisia to coerce Khair ed-Din Barbarossa, the reckless vassal of the Sultan, whose naval enterprise threatened southern Italy and, equally serious, constituted a direct military link between the French and the Turks. The political ties between France and Turkey were formalized in 1536 on the eve of a new war between Spain and France which was ended by a truce in 1538, but the years from 1542 to 1544 saw a renewal of the conflict. The policies of Henry VIII, through most of these years, added further to the difficulties of the emperor.

The preoccupation of Charles with his Sisyphean task allowed German Protestantism to grow and spread. The Schmalkaldic League itself was a political power with which all the chancelleries had to reckon. There were many moments when even Rome was pleased that the League had weakened the emperor's political position. The League was in continuous contact with France, England, and Denmark. Yet these relations with non-German powers were not built up into a lasting alliance that might have enabled the Protestants in those years to gain full recognition. Distrust of the French king, hostility toward the Turks, and a lingering respect for the emperor kept the leading Protestant princes from a determined participation in power politics.

Philip of Hesse demonstrated what could be gained from European alliances when, in 1534, he helped the exiled Duke Ulrich of Württemberg recover his duchy, which, after 1519, had been in the hands of the Habsburgs. France provided the money for Philip's armaments. After a brief campaign the land was occupied and Ulrich reinstalled. In order to avoid an attack of Philip's troops on Austria, Ferdinand had to accept the loss. Ulrich received the duchy, though as a fief from Austria, which it remained officially until 1599. But Ulrich could appear at diets as a member of the imperial estates. These stipulations were not in harmony with German constitutional law. The Protestant princes for their part accepted the election of Ferdinand as Roman King as valid; this showed again that they were in general acting as if feeling the pangs of an uneasy conscience.

ᖇ Consolidation of Protestantism

THE CAPTURE OF WÜRTTEMBERG by the Protestants was a tremendous gain for their cause, and greatly reduced Habsburg influence in southern Germany. The event brought the final demise of the Swabian League, the mightiest of all the many regional German unions and the one on which Habsburg policy in the Empire had most heavily relied. The League had been tottering before, owing to the desertion of many cities that had embraced religious reform. Now it was dissolved entirely. The reformation of the duchy of Württemberg gave German Protestantism a firm political and intellectual center in the southwest of the Empire, which was to become even more important when the imperial cities of Swabia grew weak. When Duke Ulrich returned, his personal inclinations pointed in the direction of the Swiss Reformation, which was the dominant Protestant creed in the southern part of the territory. But after Zwingli's death the connection between the southern and the northern Protestants had to be strengthened, and the duke chose forms of church organization from both Lutheran and Zwinglian models. In subsequent years, however, Württemberg, except for some superficial modalities, became a thoroughly Lutheran country.

The reformation of Württemberg led to the full reformation of both Augsburg and Frankfurt. But Lutheranism made its greatest gains in the north. The cities along the Baltic coast—Lübeck, Wismar, Rostock, and Greifswald—had come over as early as 1530–31, and Pomerania followed in 1534. To what extent many of these reformations were dominated by political motives or sheer cupidity in regard to the acquisition of church goods, was demonstrated in Pomerania, where the dukes had to overcome the opposition of a section of the Protestant *Junkers* who did not wish to divide the spoils of Reformation with the princes. Mecklenburg reformed its church more gradually between 1533 and 1540. Simultaneously, the movement engulfed Brandenburg and Saxony-Dresden, the two northern lands on which the emperor had been able to depend in the earlier period of his reign. After the death of his father in 1535 Elector Joachim II (1535–71) of Brandenburg first began to allow the preaching of Evangelical doctrine, while trying to steer a middle course between Catholic and Protestant Church administration. But cities and estates urged more drastic action, and between 1539 and 1542 the Lutheran Reformation was fully realized in his territory.

In April, 1539, Luther's old enemy, Duke George of the Albertine line of the Wettin dynasty, died and was succeeded by his senile brother Henry II, who, largely under the influence of his wife, favored the Protestant cause. Henry II gave the signal for a general reformation after the Wittenberg model. But he was too weak to overcome all the opposition that was led by substantial groups among the territorial estates. In particular, they wanted to withhold from him the use of the sequestrated Church properties. His son Maurice, who succeeded him in 1541, pushed the reform with greater energy. Part of the Church goods were to serve educational purposes, the endowment of Leipzig University and the founding of the three "princely" schools in Schulpforta, Merseburg, and Meissen.

In Brunswick-Grubenhagen and Brunswick-Kalenberg the Lutheran Reformation was officially introduced in the years after 1538. The ambitious Duke Henry of Brunswick-Wolfenbüttel, a noisy opponent of the Reformation, was finally chased from his territory by Elector John Frederick of Saxony and Landgrave Philip of Hesse, after Henry had threatened the freedom of the cities of Goslar and Brunswick. The adjacent bishoprics of Magdeburg and Halberstadt were not officially reformed for another twenty years, but Archbishop Albert of Mainz had to give up his residence in these territories and to tolerate the spread of Lutheranism under the protection of the estates. The government of the archbishopric of Magdeburg came into the hands of a Brandenburg prince as coadjutor.

Schleswig-Holstein followed the course set by its Danish rulers, and this led, between 1533 and 1542, to the establishment of a Lutheran Church according to the Danish organization, which had been drafted, like so many others, by the Pomeranian Johann Bugenhagen, Luther's Wittenberg colleague. With the reformation of Schleswig-Holstein the whole southern coast of the Baltic as far as Prussia and Livonia was in Protestant hands. The German shore of the North Sea from Schleswig to Oldenburg and East Friesland, too, was practically dominated by Protestantism around 1540. All the territories along the sea and, except for a few enclaves, the inlands from the Vistula to the Weser were swayed by the new faith. Its position was not fully consolidated in Silesia. In 1534 the principalities of Liegnitz and Brieg were reformed, and Sagan followed in 1540. In other parts of Silesia, Protestantism was progressing in the 1540's at a rapid pace, in spite of the attempts of King Ferdinand to stop its development among the estates, both cities and nobility. Bishop Balthasar of Breslau, a former student of Luther and Melanchthon, did not even try to block the expansion of the revolt against the old Church. In Lusatia, then belonging to the Bohemian crown, the estates virtually removed Catholicism.

Thus by 1545 all of northeastern and northwestern Germany had become Protestant, as well as large parts of southern Germany. In 1544 even the Palatinate territories changed sides by giving up opposition to Protestant preaching. Officially, only Bavaria, Austria, and the bishoprics along the Main—Bamberg, Würzburg, Mainz, and the imperial abbey of Fulda—remained Catholic, but with the exception of Bavaria, the Protestant movement was active in all of these territories in varying degrees. The situation was the same in western Germany. The Protestant movement spread from Hesse to Nassau and farther north. It also spread from the east into Westphalia and the lower Rhineland. A number of Westphalian cities, such as Soest and Herford, as well as a number of countships, such as Lippe and Waldeck, accepted the Reformation. The victory of the Reformation in the city of Münster in 1533 was the greatest single gain, but it led, as we have seen [3] to the Anabaptist upheaval of 1534 to 1535. Catholic and Protestant princes and imperial cities co-operated in the siege, which, in July, 1535, ended in the fall of the city and the annihilation of the Münster Anabaptists. But along with this the Protestant character of the city was lost forever. It was the first serious loss that German Protestantism suffered through the force of its opponents.

✍ Reforms in the Prince Bishoprics

NOT EVERYWHERE did the disaster of Münster help a Catholic reaction. Some princes and bishops felt that such popular outbreaks were largely the result of the existing ecclesiastical system, which the pope, by his stubborn refusal to hold a council, tried to keep in its unreformed state. In these circumstances, it could seem wise to introduce reforms on a local level, possibly adopting an intermediary position, which many hoped would contribute to a final reunion of the warring religious factions. The prince-bishoprics were beset with additional problems. For a long time the secular rulers had looked at the secular government of bishops with misgivings sharpened by dynastic greed. Charles V,

[3] See page 180.

anxious to strengthen the Netherlands, had annexed the bishopric of Utrecht in 1536, and there could be no question but that a prince was in a stronger position to defend the Church than a prince-bishop. The Protestants had shown another method of meeting this new problem. The secularization of the state of the Teutonic Order by its Grandmaster Albert von Hohenzollern and its transformation into the duchy of Prussia saved the territory from being absorbed by neighboring political powers.[4] The bishoprics of Schleswig, Lübeck, Schwerin, and Brandenburg followed a similar course. Others—such as Ratzeburg in Mecklenburg; Lebus and Havelberg in Brandenburg; Naumburg, Merseburg, and Meissen in Saxony—had practically ceased to participate in the affairs of the Empire and had become territorial estates.

Count Hermann von Wied, elector and archbishop of Cologne, belonged to the groups of princes stirred up by the Münster events. Through Johann Gropper, an Erasmian theologian, he attempted to introduce reforms in his diocese after 1536. The results were disappointing. Six years later he moved closer to Protestantism, but the clergy opposed him and he found support only among the nobility and the cities. In 1543 he took communion in Protestant form, and Protestant preachers began their work in the archbishopric, which included the duchy of Westphalia. While Archbishop Hermann's attitude was dictated by an earnest desire to live up to Christian principles, his suffragan, Franz von Waldeck, bishop of Münster, Paderborn, and Osnabrück, was a reckless politician and profligate sensualist. In Münster, which the latter had reconquered in 1535, he found too much resistance to introduce reforms, but he opened Osnabrück to Lutheran preachers in 1543.

✧ Policies of Jülich, Hesse, Brandenburg

STILL GREATER SUPPORT of the reformatory endeavors of the archbishop of Cologne and of the whole cause of Protestantism in this corner of the Empire appeared in the new policy of the most powerful secular ruler of this region, William V of Jülich-Cleves (1539–92), who also inherited Mark, Berg, and Ravensberg. Potentially at least, his was one of the most powerful princely realms in Germany, and for a short time it seemed on its way to equaling Saxony or Hesse as the political center of German Protestantism. Duke William had already antagonized Charles by inheriting, in 1538, the last autonomous duchy of the Netherlands,

[4] See page 204.

Geldern-Zütphen. This land connected Cleves with the Zuider Zee, thus cutting the southern from the northern dominions of the Habsburg Netherlands. One of William's sisters was the wife of the elector of Saxony; another became the wife of Henry VIII of England in 1539. The latter marriage did not last long, but the duke, turning his attention from England to France, was betrothed to a niece of King Francis. The announcement of William in 1543 that he would follow the religious reform policy of Archbishop Hermann, and his application for membership in the Schmalkaldic League, seemed to make Jülich-Cleves the hub of a great anti-Habsburg alliance. But this time Charles V was prepared. He succeeded in isolating the duke and defeated him in a short campaign during August and September, 1543. Duke William had to cede Geldern-Zütphen to the emperor, dissolve all his European alliances, and give up the reformation of his German territories. With this imperial victory the expansion of Protestantism in the lands along the lower Rhine received its second setback after Münster. Although Charles V avoided intervention in Cologne at this moment, the opposition to the elector in the archbishopric felt greatly encouraged by the event and was soon to take the offensive.

Special circumstances had allowed the emperor to strike this time. From 1540 on, the Schmalkaldic League showed signs of breaking up. Its most gifted political head, Landgrave Philip, through his personal passions, became a virtual captive of the emperor. His bigamous marriage with a court lady brought him in conflict with the criminal law of the Empire. It was a moral blot on the Reformation that he had prevailed on Luther, Melanchthon, and Bucer to exculpate him for this step. Thereafter he was dependent on the clemency of Charles V, which he received at the Diet of Regensburg in 1541. The emperor promised not to make war on him because of religion "unless he made war on all the Protestant princes." In exchange, Philip had to vow that he would not conclude any alliances with foreign powers and would keep Jülich-Cleves out of the Schmalkaldic League.

Elector Joachim of Brandenburg was still hopeful that his half-Evangelical Church organization would serve as a model for future religious reunification. He was glad to see his ecclesiastical policies tolerated by Charles V, and did not join the League or assist Charles against Jülich-Cleves. Although the introduction of Lutheranism in the duchy of Saxony should have brought the two Saxonies closer together, animosity between the Albertine line in Dresden and the Ernestine line in Wittenberg continued. Discord centered around the future of the neighboring Saxon bishoprics. The old controversy concerning the doctrine of sacraments flared up again between the Wittenberg theologians and the southern Germans. In 1536 Bucer had succeeded in working out with Luther the Wittenberg Concord, which had enabled the various Protestant groups to forget the conflict and co-operate in politics. The forms of the Reformation in Cologne, inspired by Martin Bucer, aroused Luther's ire anew. The years from 1540 to 1546 could have been used by the Protestants to gain full recognition of their religious independence if they had been capable of initiative and joint political action. But preoccupation with local dynastic feuds and low moral and intellectual stature made it impossible for the German princes to take an effective lead in important political and religious enterprises. Charles V felt deep contempt for them in his heart. Something like Coriolanus' "go get you home, you fragments" must often have come into his mind, and it is certain that recognition of the depravity of the German princes strengthened his confidence in his own ultimate victory.

✧ *Religious Conferences*

CHARLES V SHOWED HEROIC PATIENCE in waiting for the hour of victory. King Francis I and Suleiman II kept him under severe pressure over the years, and his relations with the other head of Christendom, the pope, also were a continuous source of apprehension. In the history of the Roman papacy, the reign of Alessandro Farnese as Pope Paul III (1534–49) represents a period in which many of the motives and ideas of the Italian Renaissance lived on in undiminished strength, while new ideas and forces were budding. Paul III acted like a secular ruler, and his politics were much affected by his desire to establish members of his family on princely thrones. But at the same time he brought into the College of Cardinals men of learning and serious moral purpose, such as Gasparo Contarini, Jacopo Sadoleto, Jeronimo Aleander, Pietro Caraffa (subsequently Pope Paul IV), Giammaria del Monte (Pope Julius III), and Reginald Pole. Under the influence of the new dignitaries the character of the Curia began to change, and the ecclesiastical policies of the Farnese pope reflected this change to some extent. In contrast to his predecessor, Paul III was not entirely opposed to the calling of a council, but, understandably, he did not wish for a council that, abetted by kings, would assume an authority above the papacy, as the Councils of Constance and Basel had done. Nor did he want to cast doubts on the main body of Church doctrines and traditions through the convocation of a council.

A papal nuncio, Paul Vergerio, was dispatched to Germany in 1535 to explore the attitude of the Protestants toward a council. Vergerio, who was destined to end his life as a Protestant minister in Württemberg, even saw Luther in Wittenberg and brought back the report that the German Protestants were under certain conditions willing to attend a council. Actually, Pope Paul III, urged by the emperor, called a council that was to convene in Mantua in 1537. But although he requested a safe-conduct for the Protestants, he described the ending of the "recent heresies" as the real task of the assembly. This gave the Protestants an opportunity for denouncing the project as a parody of a free general Christian council. The pope in turn was afraid that in the absence of France and England the convention might largely come under imperial direction. Thus the council was suspended without ever meeting.

Whether an early meeting of a general council could have restored the unity of the Church is highly doubtful. As early as 1520 Luther had declared that councils could err. And in 1536 he wrote the Schmalkaldic Articles, next to the Augsburg Confession the most important symbol of Lutheran faith, as a creed to be professed before a council and before God's judgment. No doubt Luther would not have bowed to a majority decision, even if it had been made not by bishops, but by scholars and teachers, as the Protestants demanded. But Luther no longer represented all of Protestantism. There were those who, like Melanchthon, could not long resist a compromise or who, like the elector of Cologne and Brandenburg, searched for one. The prestige of a council was still very great, and even in the England of Henry VIII statesmen saw in it a threat to the independence of the English Church. In Germany the religiously indifferent and the half-hearted could still have been stopped from full separation, and the loyally faithful encouraged. The application of force would have received strong moral support.

All the concessions that the emperor had made after the Nürnberg Standstill of 1532 had been made on a temporary basis till a general council or a national synod could be held. But such a synod would not have been held without great danger, considering the popular opinion in Germany, and would have deepened the emperor's conflicts with the pope. Depending upon the help of the Protestant estates in the struggle with Turkey and France, Charles finally attempted to employ his authority as imperial protector of the Church by calling religious conferences. The first were held in Hagenau and Worms in 1540–41, but they were moved to Regensburg in April, 1541, when Charles held his first diet in nine years. The Catholic side was represented by two Erasmian theologians, Gropper and Pflug, and also by Dr. Eck, who was held in check by the wise and noble papal nuncio Contarini, who dominated the conference. The Protestant speakers were, Melanchthon, Bucer, and Pistorius from Hesse. This time Melanchthon proved rather uncompromising, and his attitude has often been explained by the influence of the young John Calvin, who had come to Hagenau and Regensburg as a member of the Strasbourg delegation. Martin Bucer was willing to make doctrinal concessions in the belief that the chief objective was the destruction of the papal hierarchy and that Protestantism had enough momentum for permeating the Empire once it could wedge its way into the few remaining Catholic territories. He may have been right in this assumption, but it was a false hope to expect Charles V to champion the national cause against the pope.

It was startling that the Regensburg conference agreed on a formula on the doctrine of faith and justification, but on sacraments, confession, absolution, and the whole definition of the Church no harmony was achieved. Even the agreement on justification was disavowed by all authorities. Contarini, who died a year later, got the reputation of being a pro-Lutheran, while Luther and most of his friends rejected the compromise on justification as unsatisfactory. Nothing was really achieved in these circumstances, except that the emperor appeared to be disinclined to use force in religious matters. This helped him to gain the assistance of the Protestants against the Turks and also, in 1544, for his last war against Francis I. But the Regensburg conference convinced Charles V that nothing could be gained from debates, and the idea of solving the religious division by violent means, first conceived in 1530–31, began to occupy his mind. In 1541–42 operations against the Turks failed to keep the sultan from turning Hungary into a Turkish province, but his further progress in the next years was checked by payments. Greater military successes were reaped in the French campaign of 1544, which brought the emperor close to the gates of Paris. A conciliatory peace opened the way for an active anti-Protestant policy. In the Treaty of Crépy, Francis promised to co-operate with Charles in the convocation of a council with or against the pope. He also undertook to abstain from alliances with German Protestants. The latter, who had given the emperor ample help in his recent foreign ventures, found themselves suddenly isolated. Still, Charles V hesitated.

On the day of the signing of the Peace of Crépy in September, 1544, Pope Paul III called a council that was to meet in Trent the following year. The Curia was determined to avoid a council dominated by princes. It was also prepared to direct the council toward the consolidation of the Roman Catholic faith and not toward diplomatic compromise. Soon the pope offered funds and men for a war against the Protestants. But Charles needed time to prepare against the risks of such an undertaking. He was warned against acting, in the first place by his shrewd sister Mary, regent of the Netherlands, and by his leading minister, Cardinal Granvelle. The German situation was, indeed, most threatening. In 1544 Frederick II, the elector of the Palatinate, had opened the pulpits in his dominions to Protestant preachers. With all the secular electors favoring Protestantism and with the elector-archbishop of Cologne leaning in the same direction, a Protestant majority existed in the College of Electors, and with it the possibility of the future election of a Protestant emperor. These very dangers made action urgent. Thus Charles V cautiously began the preparation of the most personal undertaking of his career.

∾ *The Schmalkaldic War, 1546–47*

IN 1545, AT THE DIET OF WORMS, Charles seemed to radiate peace, and though he pressed the Protestants to attend the Council of Trent, a new bipartisan theological discussion was arranged for the Diet of Regensburg in 1546. But in Regensburg, Charles V finally decided on war. A compromise was made in the recurring smoldering feud between the Houses of Habsburg and Wittelsbach. Duke William of Bavaria was given some hope that the electoral dignity would be transferred from the Palatinate to Bavaria. The understanding was sealed by the marriage of Albert, William's eldest son, to Anna, the eldest daughter of King Ferdinand. In these same days Ferdinand's second daughter married the duke of Jülich-Cleves. Even more important, however, were the agreements Charles reached with a number of Protestant German princes. Foremost among these was young Duke Maurice of Saxony. Twenty-one years of age, he had taken over the rule of the duchy of Saxony-Dresden in 1541. To him, Protestantism was already an established fact, and as a member of the new generation he followed his personal dynastic interests rather than religious considerations. With regard to the tension between Dresden and Wittenberg, the young prince felt his ambitions best served on the side of the emperor. Expectations for the bishoprics of Halberstadt and Magdeburg, to which some vague promises for the Saxon electorate were added, made him promise neutrality in the approaching showdown. Brandenburg had been committed to a neutral attitude for some years. Some disgruntled Protestant princes were won over by the offer of commissions in the imperial army, while others were sidetracked by the emperor's assurances that no war for religious causes was being considered. In all his public announcements Charles V maintained that the disobedience of the elector of Saxony and the landgrave of Hesse to the laws of the Empire and their use of religion for illegal conquest was the reason for his policy. But Pope Paul III frankly announced the impending war to the world as a crusade against heresy, in which he supported the emperor with troops and generous financial contributions.

The Protestants were slow in gauging the intentions of Charles V, but when the break occurred after the middle of June, 1546, they were still able to mobilize their forces faster than he. For a good many weeks Charles had been sitting in Regensburg with little military protection awaiting the arrival of his own Spanish-Italian forces and the papal troops from Italy, as well as the army of the Netherlands. The opportunities for a quick and decisive victory of the Schmalkaldic League were ample. Its powerful army could easily have captured the emperor or have forced him to flee over the Alps. The army of the League could also have defeated the two armies of the emperor separately. Instead, Charles V was allowed to unite his forces on the Danube in September. Even then the army of the League was a match for that of the emperor, though the morale of the soldiers suffered from poor leadership and almost from the outset from shortages of supplies and pay. If the southern German cities had forwarded to the League only a part of the money that the emperor was to find in their coffers a little later, the campaign might not have petered out so miserably.

At the beginning of the war, which killed his hopes for a peaceful restoration of Christian unity, Melanchthon said that in view of the relative strength of the two armies, the Protestants were likely to win, but that the stars predicted the opposite. Actually, the future was determined by men who proved unequal to the historic task. The mobilization of the League's army was well done, yet leaders for both its military and political conduct were missing. No single command existed. The ideas of the flabby and indolent Elector John Frederick and of the active Landgrave Philip clashed continuously, while the timidity of the city governments added still more confusion to the direction of military operations. In the political field the same incapacity was shown. For the first time in twenty years something like a widespread popular sentiment within the nation manifested itself. Particularly during the few preceding years the emperor had shown himself in favor of a peaceful solution of the religious conflict. Now keen disappointment was felt at seeing him suddenly appear in alliance with Rome as the bellicose suppressor of the new faith. Equally repulsive seemed his intention to bring foreign troops into the German Empire. Even Luther, to his last days, had spoken of Charles as "our dear emperor"; now he was spoken of as "the Spaniard," who was set on imposing the "cattlelike servitude of Spain" on the free German nation. But the leaders of the League failed to give the popular enthusiasm a clear political program. They might have declared themselves the diet of the Empire and this diet the true national government, at the same time denouncing the emperor as a breaker of his oaths. But the cities distrusted the princes, and the princes as a group were not united with regard to their ultimate objectives. Nor were they able to link political and military warfare in a constructive fashion. Operations against Tyrol, which was honeycombed with Protestants, could have produced popular revolution against the Habsburg, while Bohemia offered a similar opportunity.

A tiresome campaign of maneuver took place in southern Germany, until in November, Duke Maurice of Saxony invaded the Wittenberg lands of his cousin John Frederick. John Frederick, elector of Saxony, marched hurriedly with his troops from the Danube northward. Soon the other contingents, from Württemberg and the Palatinate, from the cities, and finally from Hesse, gave up and went home. Thus Charles V was master of southern Germany and the Rhineland. Everyone remembered that the emperor was not fighting religious but civic disobedience, and tried to make peace. Charles made no major political changes in southern Germany. Württemberg and the Palatinate were left under their old princes. The cities had to make heavy payments; these enabled the emperor to continue the war in Saxony. As long as it lasted, Charles V did not interfere in religious affairs. Only in Cologne was the elector-archbishop deposed and the Protestant reform abolished.

Duke Maurice had decided to throw in his lot with the emperor, as he wanted to be sure to receive the electoral crown of Saxony. He had easily occupied most of Electoral Saxony but found himself in a precarious military situation after Elector John Frederick had returned, the more so since King Ferdinand's support was limited by unrest in Bohemia. Only then did the north German Protestant estates enter the contest in force. From Hamburg and Bremen to Silesia and Prussia, cities and principalities placed themselves on a war footing. If these great energies had been concentrated and properly marshaled, the cause of the Habsburgs might still have been completely ruined. But John Frederick frittered away his opportunities until the emperor appeared in Saxony with his Spanish troops. On April 24, 1547, Charles V surprised and routed the Saxon army after crossing the Elbe river at Mühlberg. The elector was captured. (Four centuries later, in April, 1945, American and Russian armies met only a few miles north of this fateful spot.) In order to avoid further military operations, the emperor used terror against John Frederick. On May 10 he had him sentenced to death by a court; this was without any justification in the law of the Empire. In adversity the elector acquired both firmness and dignity. He firmly rejected every pressure to make him accept the decisions of the Council of Trent, and he declared that he was willing to lose his lands rather than his faith. In the so-called Wittenberg Capitulation of May 19, 1547, John Frederick gave up the territory around Wittenberg on which the electoral title rested. Only some Thuringian territories—Weimar, Gotha, Eisenach, and Coburg—were left to the Ernestine line of the Wettin dynasty, whose members were allowed to call themselves Dukes of Saxony. John Frederick's death sentence was commuted into imprisonment.

Maurice of Saxony received Electoral Saxony and the electoral dignity. But the political survival of the Ernestine line and the fact that the emperor claimed other Wettin territories as fiefs of the Bohemian crown indicated that Charles did not wish to give Albertine Saxony too much power. For similar reasons he had not given the Palatinate to Bavaria. He wanted to keep the German princes under control, and after years of toil he seemed to have achieved his aim completely when, in June, Philip of Hesse surrendered. Philip believed, and was made to believe by his son-in-law Maurice of Saxony and the imperial councilors, that Charles V would treat him lightly. Instead, he was made a prisoner. Parading the captured Protestant princes, the emperor appeared at the Diet of Augsburg in the fall of 1547. In German history this convention has been called the "iron-clad" diet, and actually the victory by arms allowed the emperor to lay down the law. The international situation had momentarily eased, too. The Turk was quiet. In January, 1547, Henry VIII had died; Francis I, in March. Moreover, France and

England were neutral for the time being due to internal tension and mutual conflict.

✍ The Council of Trent, 1545–47

ONE BLACK CLOUD DARKENED the political horizon. The pope, afraid of the growing might of the emperor, had recalled his troops from Germany. Moreover, the council that was opened in Trent in December, 1545, under his influence, had taken a direction that offered little support for the emperor's policy. Only thirty-four bishops had been present at the opening in this city that officially belonged to the Holy Empire but, in geography and culture, was an Italian place. Most of the attending bishops were Italians who were willing to follow the leadership provided by the able Roman legates. Thus from the outset the ecumenic character of the council as well as its independent authority were questionable, particularly in the eyes of dissidents. There was another, even more serious factor. The actual work of the council was not directed toward a solution arrived at with the Protestants, rather, it aimed immediately at a clarifying restatement of the Roman Catholic tradition in contrast to Protestant heresies. Decrees were promulgated on such fundamental doctrines as the authority of Scripture and tradition, original sin, and even, on March 13, 1547, on justification. Thereafter, for no good reason, the pope moved the council to Bologna, in the Church states. The Spanish bishops protested, as did also the emperor, who, deeply wounded by the papal action, was unable to hold back passionate expressions of anger.

✍ The Augsburg Interim, 1548

CHARLES V was compelled to settle the religious question in Germany by himself. He had some Protestant theologians co-operate in the drafting of a religious compromise and had Protestant princes make the motion in its favor at the assembly of the Diet of Augsburg. But with the exception of the concessions of clerical marriage and communion under two kinds, the Augsburg *Interim* was a thinly veiled reformulation of the old faith. It is true that the *Interim* allowed a half-Protestant interpretation of justification in the sense of the Regensburg conference of 1541, and that indulgences and the restoration of Church properties were not mentioned, but not even with regard to rites did it leave much leeway. The *Interim* was promulgated as law on May 30, 1548, but it was binding only on Protestants, who had to petition for papal dispensations if they wanted to take advantage of permissible exceptions, such as clerical marriages. A month later a *formula reformationis* was issued, which the emperor had negotiated with the ecclesiastical princes. It envisaged the abolition of the worst grievances, such as cumulation of benefices and annates, and a reform of the Catholic clergy under the direction of provincial synods. Altogether it was a rather weak beginning of a Catholic reform, and certainly out of balance with the far-reaching counter reformation that the *Interim* tried to impose upon the Protestants. In addition, the *Interim* offered only a temporary solution, ultimately to be superseded by the decisions of a universal council.

The *interreligio imperialis*, as the provisions of the *Interim* were often called, in which the emperor's consciousness of the spiritual authority inherent in his office expressed itself, was disliked by practically everybody. The Curia saw in it an illegal assumption of its supreme religious prerogative. Grave political conflicts exacerbated the relations of Charles V and Paul III. The papacy delayed and upset the execution of the *Interim* by refusing its recognition for over a year, thereby strengthening the opposition of the Catholic princes to the emperor in Germany. But the greatest weakness of the *Interim* was its transparent character as a mere diplomatic instrument. No one arose to praise it as the highest form of Christian faith. It could only be recommended in comparative terms as being more or less acceptable for a Catholic or more or less tolerable for a Protestant. It had no religious basis of its own that could have given it true life. Since the Catholics were exempted, the *Interim* could not even be considered as a national concord. Quite the contrary, to the Protestants it looked like a device for reestablishment of the old, and that meant foreign papal, Church.

Charles V never came to grips with the power of popular sentiment. On his political chessboard emotional forces did not find a place. The German princes filled him with contempt, and after Mühlberg he made no effort to hide his feelings. He had too often seen the Protestant theologians shuddering in fear to believe that they could not be coerced into submission by political power. He had, however, no idea of the attitude of the people, many of whom had been brought up in the Lutheran faith.

The incredible Luther was dead; his political protector, the Saxon Elector, was a captive of the emperor. Luther had died on February 18, 1546, on the eve of the outbreak of war that ended in the military catastrophe of German Protestantism. The religious reformer had felt ill at ease in the period after 1530, when political considerations dominated more and more the life of Protestantism. The man who had said, "God, I am in secular affairs too childish," had in his last fifteen years concentrated on the purity of Christian doctrine. That this theological work had political effects as well, was not quite clear to him. Luther, however, occasionally expressed himself on public affairs in these years, railing against both the sectarians and the sins of the papacy. His last polemic pamphlet, *Against the Papacy in Rome* (1545), written in a most un-Christian and obscene language, attempted again to deepen the antipapalist sentiment of the Germans. Although his angry stubbornness had made his theological colleagues and pupils tremble, people at large obviously enjoyed his outbursts. Perhaps, at the time of his death, he was to the majority of the people the liberator of Germany rather than the religious reformer. But his religious thought had taken root in the hearts of many. In the course of the years, it had become widely known through his oral and published sermons, his German Bible, his great religious hymns, and his academic lectures. It had not only reached individuals, but had also created new forms of community life. Luther, as we have seen, had been reluctant to part with most of the old ceremonies of the Catholic Church, although he considered them as the lesser part of religion. Melanchthon remembered this when he described the ritualistic demands of the *Interim* as indifferent matters of faith. But to the mass of the members of the new churches the former rituals had become hated symbols of a dead past. They were decried as "ceremonies of Mamelukes."

✧ Protestant Opposition to the Interim

THE EMPEROR HAD NOT FORESEEN this popular reaction to the *Interim*. It was welling up all over Germany, although the opposition could not show itself openly in many places. In southern Germany the presence of Charles V with his Spanish troops compelled all the Protestant estates to lie low. The main pressure was used against the cities. The emperor did his best to humiliate the civic pride of the burghers. In many places the government of the guilds was replaced by the rule of patrician families of the old faith, and recalcitrant burghers were often silenced by dragonnades. The city of Constance lost its freedom after a heroic fight and was annexed to Anterior Austria. In general, little fortitude was shown by the leading groups of southern Germany in these hard days. Willing co-operation came particularly from the capitalistic merchants. Their dependence on Spain made them vulnerable, and the emperor could also cripple their economic activities by his control of the Netherlands. The great merchants were berated by the Protestant people as traitors, but the city councils could not deny that the trade of southern Germany was at the mercy of the emperor and they accepted the *Interim*. A good many of the leading Protestant ministers had to leave not only their pulpits but also the country. Among them was Martin Bucer, who was received with great honors in Cambridge and in the two years before his death, in 1552, left his mark both on the English and Scottish Reformations.

Still, there were too few able Catholic priests left to perform the functions that the *Interim* had envisaged to be assumed by orthodox priests. Very often they celebrated mass, and former Protestant predicants were brought back as preachers. The multitude of the people ran to them and eschewed mass, while fomenting a campaign of slander against the priests. Some monasteries were reopened and some parishes fully reconstituted, chiefly in former bishops' cities, with the result that these cities, for example Augsburg, remained bi-confessional after 1555. But while the policy of the *Interim* produced some, if small, results in the south, it made little headway in northern Germany. Not even the Brandenburg elector Joachim II—who had always steered a middle course and whose court chaplain, Agricola, was one of the authors of the *Interim*—or the new Saxon elector Maurice dared introduce the law without curtailment of its rules. Philip Melanchthon, who behaved in these sad days like a denying Peter, co-operated in the drafting of a document known as the *Leipzig Interim*, into which a more Lutheran interpretation of doctrines could be read with great effort. But he did not defend a large group of practices which he called "indifferent," or, in theological Greek, *adiaphora*, in the basic Christian sense. This Philipistic version of the imperial "interreligion" was introduced in Saxony and Brandenburg.

But the other Protestant princes in the north refused outright to recognize the *Interim*. The stalwart Margrave John of Küstrin, who had fought on the side of the emperor in the belief that the religious issue would not be raised, became a staunch opponent. The princes of Mecklenburg and Anhalt, as well as the territorial estates of the bishopric of Magdeburg and Halberstadt, rejected the *Interim*. So did a group of northwestern cities from Bremen, Hamburg, and Lübeck down to

Göttingen. But the real center of resistance was the city of Magdeburg. Here, in "the chancellery of God and Christ," as it was called in these years, the orthodox Lutherans had come together. From Wittenberg, which had fallen to Maurice of Saxony, had come Nicolaus von Amsdorf (1483-1565), Luther's loyal friend and colleague who had accompanied him to Worms in 1521, and young Matthias Flacius Illyricus (1520-75), recently appointed professor of Hebrew. The fierce and fearless Flacius, a Slovene from Istria by birth, became the heart and brains of the fight against the *Interim*. A torrent of pamphlets, songs, political ditties, and satirical posters poured from the presses to arouse all classes. But serious scholarly work also continued. Surrounded by a group of assistants, Flacius started the work that became known as the *Magdeburg Centuriones*, a history of the Christian Church purporting to show how from century to century the original Christian truth had been corrupted by ulterior forces, chiefly the papacy, but had also found its witnesses, until Luther had restored the Gospel. The new concept of history, presented with great learning and novel methodology, was to have an important influence on historical study in the next century.

The labors of the "genuine" Lutherans (*Gnesio-Lutheraner*) were directed not only against the pope, the emperor, and the Catholics but also, with equal fury, against the "Philipists" or "Adiaphorists" and all those ready to emasculate the Lutheran faith in deference to the political powers of the day. While this struggle foreshadowed the acrimonious internal discords of German Lutheranism in the subsequent period, it immediately gave strength to the popular resistance and revolt against the *Interim* and led many political authorities to stand pat or sabotage to the best of their ability the execution of the *Interim*. The emperor's strong hand did not reach far into central and northwestern Germany, and some signs, which he himself refused to read, indicated that his power was not unlimited elsewhere either. Violations of the *Interim* were violations of the law of the Empire and as such justiciable before the Imperial Cameral Tribunal, but to execute judgments against princes or, even better, to keep them from breaking the law, a reliable system of enforcement was needed. In addition, a military organization had to be created in order to withstand the ever-repeated threat of France and Turkey, which was also a source of much internal trouble. Not even the "iron-clad" Diet of 1547-48 solved these problems. Charles V achieved a better control of the Cameral Tribunal. The estates also granted him a war chest, but it was only a small purse of a single Roman Month.

✍ *Opposition of the Princes to a Strong Monarchical Power*

THE EMPEROR'S MAIN PROJECT, the establishment of a league of German estates, was not adopted. He wanted the new league to differ from that earlier instrument of Habsburg power, the Swabian League, which had dissolved after 1530, chiefly in that it would extend to the whole Empire and that it would be placed more directly under his control. Charles V wanted to keep his Netherland dominions in a separate position. The "Burgundian circle" was to be exempt from the legislation of the diet of the Empire and the jurisdiction of the Cameral Tribunal, but the Empire was supposed to come to its defense, while the Netherlands would contribute to the defense of the Empire. The plan was brought to naught by the princes, particularly the Bavarian duke. In their eyes, the idea of an Imperial League was a revolutionization of the old constitution of the Empire in favor of a strong imperial monarchy. Irrespective of religion, the princes were determined to preserve their free position.

That Charles intended to wreck the position of the princes seemed to be proven by another plan, which at the same time diminished the support of his staunchest ally, King Ferdinand. Charles V conceived of the imperial office as one designed not only to give the Christian world political leadership but also to assure religious unity. He thought of it, too, as a dynastic possession without considering that dynastic feeling might also be the mainspring of action in his closest relatives. His brother Ferdinand, through almost thirty years, had been his loyal lieutenant, subordinating his personal judgment to Charles' predilections and whims. In these years Ferdinand had become a German prince, both in personal manners and political interests. It was clear that the defense of the southeastern frontier against the Turks depended largely on the support he could receive from the Empire. Naturally he considered himself and his family as the successor to his brother in the German realm. It was a painful shock to Ferdinand when Charles V proposed that his own son Philip, to whom he had transferred his deep love for his deceased wife, should become Roman King when Ferdinand became emperor, and that thereafter the imperial dignity should alternate between the Spanish and Austrian branches of the Habsburg house.

This project entirely disregarded Ferdinand's sentiments and those of Ferdinand's son Maximilian, who felt himself to be a German and was popular with the Germans.

The announcement of these intentions of the emperor caused a rift between the brothers which not even their sister, Queen Mary, could bridge, though Ferdinand, most reluctantly, agreed to Charles' ideas. But the plan proved most unpopular among the German princes. The affable and generous Maximilian was much better liked than the stiff and pale Philip. Moreover, Charles' proposal challenged directly the constitutional rights of the German princes, particularly of the electors. It raised the specter of a hereditary monarchy, in which the German princes would be merely grandees, like the Spanish noblemen of Charles' entourage. Charles' treatment of the question of succession seemed to make the Holy Roman Empire of the German Nation a mere appendage of the Spanish crown. The German princes felt that they represented the German nation, which in that century meant only that they considered their corporative rights jeopardized by the emperor. The arrest of Elector John Frederick and the humiliating imprisonment of Landgrave Philip placed dire prospects before their eyes. It was of the greatest consequence that Maurice of Saxony began to dread the power and intentions of the emperor. What Charles had granted him, he might withdraw just as quickly. As a matter of fact, even in 1547 he had not made good his earlier promises, and he could still use the captive John Frederick against this Dresden upstart.

Maurice had not received the bishoprics of Halberstadt and Magdeburg; he was now anxious to gain at least the city of Magdeburg. But while he had himself commissioned as imperial executor of the ban pronounced on the brave city, he was already conspiring against Charles V. This generation of German princes emulated Machiavellian tactics easily, and Maurice was the most gifted pupil of the school. The nucleus of an armed opposition to the emperor had originally been formed by Margrave John of Küstrin, John Albert of Mecklenburg, and Albert of Prussia. But theirs had been a defensive alliance only. When Maurice changed sides, he gave the alliance an offensive purpose by drawing in, together with Landgrave William of Hesse, the Franconian Margrave Albert Alcibiades of Kulmbach-Bayreuth. Still, the emperor, as Maurice put it, was too big a bird to be conquered lightly. Much money was required, and since the southern German cities were downhearted and exhausted, it could come only from foreign sources.

Actually the pendulum of European politics had already swung in the other direction, threatening the emperor. England and France had made peace in 1550; the French king, Henry II, had sided with the pope against Charles in Italian affairs; and a new war was brewing. Although Henry II suppressed ruthlessly any Protestant heresy in France, an alliance with the German princes seemed desirable to him. But he wanted their co-operation not merely to strengthen the front against Charles V, but to insure palpable French gains. In entering into the alliance the German princes had to declare that Cambrai, Toul, Verdun, and Metz, cities that had belonged to the Empire since earliest times, but were not German-speaking, should be occupied by Henry II. They were careful to reserve the rights of the Empire and recognized the king as "vicar of the Empire" in these cities. On the other hand, Henry II was in addition called a protector of German liberties, and the princes promised to work for him at a future election of an emperor.

The treaty between Henry II and the German princes, which was signed at Château Chambord on January 15, 1552, was immediately directed against Charles V as ruler of the Burgundian Empire. With Toul, Verdun, and Metz in French hands, the Franche-Comté was cut off from the Netherlands. It was also true that Metz would be a strong position from which, in the future, the German Rhineland could be profoundly influenced, though only if Germany remained divided. The very division of Germany made the treaty a serious threat to her future. The emperor had never been motivated by national sentiment. He always wanted to separate the Burgundian lands from the German Empire, and he had not felt any compunction in leading foreign troops into the heart of Germany. Now, in revolt, the German princes, with even lesser justification, drew France into the internal conflicts of the Empire.

The death of Pope Paul III, late in 1549, and his successor's willingness to reconvene the council in Trent in 1551 seemed to relieve the emperor for a while. In 1551 he even had the satisfaction of seeing Protestant representatives appear at the council. But the Protestants were only allowed to present statements of faith and were not admitted to any discussion. Their protest against the early decrees of the council constituted the last formal breach between old and new Christian faith. The Council of Trent continued to work in this period to evolve a restatement of the doctrine of sacraments, until the approach of the army of Maurice of Saxony caused its dispersal.

↶ *The Revolt of the Princes*

IN MARCH, 1552, the storm broke. King Henry II advanced in Lorraine and took possession of the cities promised to him illegally by the German princes. Maurice of Saxony had taken Magdeburg in November, but not without giving assurances about the preservation of its religion in exchange for the city's acceptance of his overlordship. Keeping his army together, Maurice marched to Franconia at the time of the French seizure of Metz. The southern German estates remained neutral. The cities had been profoundly discouraged by the events after 1546 and believed that they would fare no better at the hands of the princes than under the emperor. The Catholic states, such as Bavaria, refrained from any action; the fight for princely "liberty," which the princes had proclaimed as their chief aim, struck a sympathetic chord. King Ferdinand, preoccupied with the defense of Hungary against the Turks, but also impressed by the opposition to Charles' personal regime, which had wounded him too, confined his succor mostly to diplomatic mediation. A strange inertia befell the emperor in these months. He refused to believe that these miserable German princes would have the fortitude to attack him. But on May 18 Maurice occupied the pass that opened the way to Tyrol. If the mutiny of one of his regiments had not delayed him, he would have captured Charles V in Innsbruck. As it was, Charles fled south over the Brenner Pass. These events were a shock from which he did not recover, though even then he showed unbroken pride and hard determination. He needed time, however, to mobilize his forces in Spain, Italy, and the Netherlands, and in the meantime the political initiative was in other hands.

While Maurice and his conspirators had scored a complete surprise, they could not make their initial success pay off fully. Their resources were limited and likely to dry up with time. Maurice was concerned about the opposition of the Saxon nobility to his ambitious foreign policy and afraid that Elector John Frederick, who had been freed by Charles V, might cause him trouble at home. He began to negotiate with King Ferdinand in Passau, where south and west German princes or their representatives also appeared. Maurice demanded the liberation of the captured princes, particularly of his father-in-law Philip of Hesse, who was held on orders of the emperor in a vexatious imprisonment. Maurice also insisted upon the restoration of a "free Empire of the German nation," which meant the free operation of the diet, the exclusion of foreign troops and foreign councilors of the emperor.

At the same time Maurice proposed not only the renunciation of the Augsburg *Interim* and the recognition of all former secularizations but also a permanent religious peace. There was general agreement with regard to the political and constitutional demands, and the idea of a religious peace also met with approval. The next diet of the Empire was to decide once more whether the religious division was to be settled by a universal or national council, by a theological conference, or by the estates themselves. But even if this attempt should fail, the peace was to last just the same.

Ferdinand accepted the Passau understanding. He wished to gain the support of the German princes against the Turks, which Maurice promised. But his imperial brother rejected the agreement and offered only a temporary standstill of religious policy and a suspension of the *Interim* until the next diet. Charles' hope was to achieve religious unification and a monarchical reform of the German constitution. Maurice and his Protestant allies, among them young Landgrave William of Hesse, had to accept the Passau treaty in August, 1552. While Maurice went to war supporting King Ferdinand in Hungary, the emperor arrived in southern Germany and seemed set both on the establishment of an imperial league and on the succession of his unpopular son Philip in the Empire, plans that were bound to be fought by the German princes and even by his brother. Feeling driven to extremes, he took another false step that undermined the respect he enjoyed in Germany.

Margrave Albert Alcibiades of Bayreuth had refused to accede to the Passau treaty. This Hohenzollern prince possessed one of the meanest characters ever produced by the high nobility. "An enormous, insane, wild beast," one of Ferdinand's councilors called him. A cynical criminal, he burned and pillaged the land, extracting huge sums for the payment of his soldiers from the frightened governments. Albert Alcibiades denounced Maurice of Saxony as traitor to the French alliance and the cause of Protestantism, and declared he would carry on the war against all Roman priests and the treacherous merchants of the cities. He left hundreds of villages, monasteries, and castles in ashes in city territories, such as that of Nürnberg, and in the bishoprics of Bamberg and Würzburg. The prince-bishop of Bamberg was also forced to cede to Albert a third of his territory. The margrave thereafter moved to the upper Rhine, hoping to continue the war with France's support. But King Henry II hesitated to pay the price. At this moment Charles V, bent on the reconquest of Metz, took Albert Alcibiades in his service.

This action of Charles V, which implied the grant of indemnity for the crimes committed by Albert against other estates of the Empire, caused deep moral indignation in Germany. It also proved a useless act, since the emperor, during the winter of 1552–53, failed to capture Metz, which was ably defended by the Duke de Guise. In January, 1553, Charles V went to the Netherlands, never to re-enter the Empire. Albert Alcibiades was on the loose again, repeating his outrages. Finally he turned to northern Germany, where he expected the Protestants to rise to his support. But beside the threat of lawlessness and chaos, to which the emperor seemed impervious, religious conflicts paled. Irrespective of religion, princes began to associate. In southern Germany the Heidelberg Union was formed, led by the Catholic Duke Albert of Bavaria and the Lutheran Duke Christoph of Württemberg, with the electors of the Palatinate, Mainz, Trier, and the duke of Jülich as members. More important became the league of northern princes, concluded by Maurice of Saxony, King Ferdinand, the Franconian bishops, and the old Duke Henry of Brunswick-Wolfenbüttel. In July, 1553, its army defeated Albert Alcibiades in a long bloody battle at Sievershausen. But Elector Maurice was fatally wounded. The war was carried to Franconia, and Albert Alcibiades, deprived of his possessions and men, had to take refuge in France.

By their own strength and association the German princes had restored a lawful order in the Empire. The question was whether they would be able to make it a lasting order, which, of course, could not be done if the subordination of religious to political issues could not be preserved. They worried about the future plans of the emperor and suspected him of hatching new schemes for the resumption of his older policies. But with the accession of Mary Tudor to the throne of England in July, 1553, the brooding mind of Charles V was engaged in new directions. The union of the crown of Spain and England would still allow him to realize the dream of world empire. In these circumstances the succession of Philip of Spain in Germany appeared unnecessary. The expectations of the emperor connected with the marriage of Philip and Mary, which took place in July, 1554, proved to be short-lived. But the impact of the emperor's thought on the course of German affairs was important. From 1554 on, Charles V earnestly planned to divest himself of his dignities as ruler. In July he informed his brother that he would not come to the diet and intimated that his conscience did not permit him to make concessions in religious matters. King Ferdinand received full authority "to act and settle."

✍ *The Strengthening of Regional Powers*

IN THE ABSENCE OF THE EMPEROR Ferdinand opened the Diet of Augsburg on February 5, 1555. The papal influence was weak, too. Pope Julius III died in early March and his successor, Marcellus II, on May 1, 1555. Pope Paul IV Caraffa (1555–59) had little time to devote himself to the problems of the diet. Only a few German princes attended in person. The negotiations were mostly carried on by diplomatic representatives. In fact, a larger assembly of princes, all of them Protestants, convened in March in Naumburg and decided to adhere to the Augsburg Confession and to oppose any majority decision of the diet in religious matters. It was high time for such a resolution, as political considerations were about to swallow up all other convictions. Elector Joachim II of Brandenburg went so far as to propose the *Interim* as a suitable basis of reunification. He made every effort to appear as an orthodox Christian in the eyes of the papacy in order to gain the confirmation of one of his sons to the see of Halberstadt. At the same time the Brandenburgers promised the estates of the bishopric their support of the Lutheran religion. Political morals in Germany had reached a low point, but the effort to preserve Protestantism and restore law and order constituted beacons in the general chaos.

King Ferdinand insisted on early discussion of internal security. The result was the Order of Imperial Circles and the Order of Execution,[5] which made the major prince responsible for the maintenance of peace in his region. In other words, the attempts of Charles V to build a strong monarchical power in the Empire were finally abandoned in favor of the particularist regional powers. But most disturbances of public peace in the last decades had originated from religious causes or at least causes that appeared under the guise of religion, and the establishment of public peace depended on the arrangement of a religious peace. Everyone believed that he held the eternal truth and that the chief function of government was the protection and furtherance of true Christianity. The "members of the old faith" and the "members of the Augsburg Confession," as the two groups were officially called, trusted that in the future Christian unity would be restored. If the Catholics admitted the Lutherans, they did so because they felt that for the time being they could not subjugate them even at the greatest sacrifice. The Protestants were still convinced that their faith was spreading and that once it was freed of persecution it would become universal. Both parties were far removed from toleration based on mutual respect.

[5] See pages 44–9.

✍ *The Religious Peace of Augsburg of 1555*

THE NEGOTIATIONS IN AUGSBURG took more than half a year. The Passau understanding served as the basis for the deliberations, much though King Ferdinand would have wished to get away from it. From the beginning only a peace between two parties was contemplated. Only members of the Augsburg Confession were to enjoy the privileges that the new law provided. "Sacramentarians," i.e., Zwinglians and Calvinists, and "Sectarians," i.e., Anabaptists, were not included in the peace. Moreover, freedom to embrace one or the other religion was granted only to the individual estates of the Empire and not to every German, as the electors of the Palatinate and of Brandenburg had once proposed. However, the individual subjects were given the right to emigrate with wife and children after selling their property at a reasonable price, as well as paying a tax for release from existing personal servitudes. No doubt this provision saved many Lutherans from the inquisition of the Church and many Catholics from Protestant jails. But in an age of feudal and agrarian economy the number who could freely migrate was limited. The right of the territorial princes to determine and change the religion of their dominions was bound to lead to disregard and corruption of the consciences of their subjects. The prince had the exclusive *jus reformandi*, the right to order the religious affairs of a territory, but promised to confine the exercise of his rights in religious affairs to his own territories and to abstain from the protection of correligionists in other territories and from any missionary activity. Jurists of the next generation defined these rights and obligations in the formula *Cuius regio, eius religio* (He who owns the land determines the religion).

While the ecclesiastical rights of the princes were extended to the imperial nobility, special provisions were made for the free cities. We have seen that, as a consequence of the *Interim*, some Catholic churches and monasteries had been reopened in a number of cities. In order to preserve these minorities, the cities were placed under the obligation of maintaining parity among the confessions. This rule has often been described as the only article expressing the principle of true toleration. Granted that after another century it contributed to the growth of a more tolerant spirit, its origins were exclusively political. It was the first important gain that the Catholics achieved at the Diet of Augsburg. In addition, it was a clear sign of the loss of influence that the cities had suffered after 1546 as a result of their vacillating policies, and meant the final emergence of the princes as the lords of the Empire. But the

Catholics fought with great stubbornness about the future status of the ecclesiastical principalities. On this issue the whole settlement threatened to break down. King Ferdinand for a while thought of adjourning the diet. Already at that time the secular electors in the college of electors were Protestants, while the college of princes still had a strong Catholic majority, owing to the large groups of ecclesiastical rulers. Here lay the key to a Protestant control of the Empire. In many of the ecclesiastical dominions the territorial estates, nobility and towns, had already been won for the Protestant cause. It could be expected that, armed with the *jus reformandi,* many an ecclesiastical dominion would be changed into a secular principality or joined to an existing one.

The history of the German ecclesiastical principalities in the age of the Reformation was rather deplorable. Leaving aside the question of the extent to which the alienation of the German bishops from their spiritual duties contributed to the outbreak of the Protestant movement, the bishops and abbots had shown themselves utterly incompetent in fighting Protestantism with either moral or political weapons. The reports of the papal legates were full of disgust about these weak-kneed gentlemen. But while Ferdinand readily suspended the jurisdiction of the bishops over Protestant territories and handed such territories to the princes, it seemed highly objectionable to interfere with the jurisdiction of the bishops in Catholic lands and quite impossible to abolish the princely power of the bishops in their own territories. The bishops stood out as the symbols of the union of imperial and hierarchical authority, which had characterized the Holy Roman Empire from time immemorial. On their continued existence hinged the defense of Catholicism. Here King Ferdinand took his stand and demanded that archbishops, bishops, and abbots turning Protestant lose their dignity, benefices, rights, and privileges, and that the chapters have the right to elect an orthodox successor. The Protestants fought against this "ecclesiastical reservation," but although they refused their free assent, they tolerated its inclusion in the final Augsburg law, where it appeared not as a part of the compact between emperor and estates but as an announcement based on imperial authority.

An even greater departure from customary constitutional practice, and, we may add, from the intended spirit of a permanent religious compromise, was the concession made to the Protestants by Ferdinand in return for their acquiescence in the *reservatio ecclesiastica.* In a secret document, which did not become part of the Augsburg recess, King Ferdinand declared that the estates of the ecclesiastical dominions—

nobility, towns, and communities—which had introduced the Protestant religion, should remain unmolested. In other words, while the *reservatio ecclesiastica* limited the *jus reformandi* of the ecclesiastical princes in favor of Catholic rulers, this so-called *declaratio Ferdinandea* protected their Protestant subjects. But while the *reservatio* was inserted in an oblique fashion in the text of the Augsburg recess, the *declaratio*, though given with the passive approval of the ecclesiastical princes, was given secretly to the Protestants. It did not become part of the law of the Empire, nor was the Imperial Cameral Tribunal informed of its existence.

As it turned out, the ecclesiastical principalities were saved by the "ecclesiastical reservation" for another 250 years. It is also true that this "reservation" helped the eventual survival of German Catholicism more than any other legal act. But the form in which the compromise was achieved, with each party looking the other way and unwilling to commit itself, was telling proof that in this crucial question only a temporary truce had been achieved. Both groups were convinced that any advantages that might be gained by the resumption of open hostilities would not be worth the sufferings that would be entailed, but they were not without hope that future developments would work in their favor. All were eager, therefore, to keep the problem of ecclesiastical dominions in a fluid and uncertain state. The Religious Peace of Augsburg, embodied in the recess of the diet of September 25, 1555, contained other controversial articles. It was understood, for example, that princes could secularize bishoprics and monasteries within their own territories, but possessions of prince-bishops and prince-abbots were to be respected. These were rather nice distinctions, open to much legal argument.

The Religious Peace of Augsburg, intended "to protect the German nation, our beloved fatherland, against ultimate division and collapse," contained much tinder that could set off new flames of discord. But with all its shortcomings it was of the greatest significance. The medieval unity of Christendom was broken, and for the first time heretics received a civil and political status equal to that of members of the old Church. Under the conditions of the age such an event could take place only in a state that had as little unity as the German Empire. In a strict sense the Empire was no state at all, nor were the territories states as yet. The emperors had failed to regain the monarchical power lost in the thirteenth century, while the territorial authorities had not only kept their hold on the Empire but also advanced their own monarchical position against the local forces. This development was not caused by the Protestant Reformation. A look at Bavaria shows that Charles V could have broken the opposition of Catholic princes as little as that of Protestant princes. But the rise of Protestantism deepened the division among the territorial rulers. The reform movement of Berthold of Mainz had already shown how weak the chances were for giving the Empire more unity through a federation of the estates of the Empire. The religious split dimmed hopes much further.

The Peace of Augsburg would not have been possible, however, if there had not remained among Germans a feeling of common interest and even common obligation. Emperor Charles' attempt to subordinate Germany to his universal schemes had awakened it. Nevertheless, events from 1546 to 1555 had demonstrated that the German princes did not have the resources for making themselves complete masters of the Empire. As a consequence they were satisfied to find in King Ferdinand a ruler who was willing to reach a settlement on a German basis, in full recognition of the place of the princes in the Empire. But there was no guarantee that the princes would not split among themselves in the future over the questions left undecided in the Augsburg Peace. If this happened, internal German conflicts might again become European wars.

At the same time the Peace of Augsburg culminated the transformation of the religious into a largely political struggle. The Protestant Reformation had begun with the assertion of the freedom of the individual conscience. It ended with the grant to the territorial lords of the absolute right to determine the faith of all their subjects. The authoritarian territorial churches were recognized by the law of the Empire, and the Protestant territorial prince was not only allowed to impose the Augsburg Confession, but was also obliged to suppress differing creeds. Sweeping spiritual powers were given to secular rulers, who, irrespective of their moral character and the strength of their religious convictions, were tempted and compelled to judge religious issues within the framework of their general political interests. The Peace of Augsburg paid little attention to the life of genuine religion. It was inevitable that in the period that followed politics claiming to be motivated by religion would exploit the power of religion in human hearts even more recklessly.

The Catholic Reformation and the Great War

CHAPTER 10

The Confessional Age, 1555–1618

THE PERIOD FROM 1555 to the outbreak of the Thirty Years'
War in 1618 was one of the longest periods of peace in
German history. While western and northern Europe went
through wars and revolutions, Germany was at rest. The
division of the Habsburg dynasty helped to remove the German Empire from the scene of universal conflict. Charles V had handed over
Spain, Italy, Burgundy, and the Netherlands to his son Philip. The
universal character of the imperial crown was further minimized by
the futile protest of the pope against the unanimous election of Ferdinand as German Emperor, in which three Protestant electors participated. It was decided that confirmation and coronation by the pope
was unnecessary for the creation of an emperor. Beginning with Ferdinand I (1555–64), no German emperor was crowned by the pope.

Interconfessional and Federative Policy of the Emperors, 1555–1612

WHILE CHARLES V, who had grown up in the Netherlands, became during the course of his life a Spaniard, his brother Ferdinand had been
educated in Spain but later became a German. Charles V always appeared to the Germans as alien in manner and attitude. Ferdinand, in
contrast, seemed to them affable and easy. Over the years Ferdinand
had been a loyal deputy of his older brother, whose iron determination
and glowing, if veiled, political passion he could not match. In the
1520's Ferdinand had been the champion of unconditional suppression
of the Protestants. In his religious faith he wavered as little as Charles V,
but political considerations induced him to adopt an accommodating
course. Charles' plan for the succession had made Ferdinand a secret
ally of the German princes, and with the negotiation of the Peace of
Augsburg Ferdinand inaugurated a new system of rule in the Empire.
Monarchical aspirations were toned down, and the emperor came to

be thought of as the chief member of an alliance formed by the major German princes of both confessions. Among the Catholic princes were Duke Albert V of Bavaria and William V of Jülich-Cleves, sons-in-law of the emperor. On the Protestant side Ferdinand found in the electors August of Saxony and Joachim II of Brandenburg, as well as in Duke Christoph of Württemberg, supporters of those federative policies that for their ultimate success depended on the emperor's capacity for stabilizing the peace between the confessions. Ferdinand I was undoubtedly not motivated in his actions by the wish to cut the Empire away from its religious roots but by considerations of national policy. The confessional struggle might have lost some of its acrimoniousness, as it had to some extent in the southern German cities, if the Empire had launched great enterprises of common interest to all, which could have captured the popular imagination. One such project, both Christian and German in nature, was obvious; the removal of the Turkish threat, which would have been quite possible if emperor and princes had shown a modicum of co-operation. Such common projects were favored by Lazarus von Schwendi, one of the foremost councilors and generals of Ferdinand I and his son Maximilian II.

Emperor Maxmilian II (1564–76) seemed destined to bring such a policy of reconciliation to full fruition. He was happily married to the daughter of Charles V, who bore him fifteen children. But he felt cold resentment against Spain and all things Spanish. In his youth he had become interested in Lutheran ideas. His sympathies were with the Protestants, and he had alarmed his father by his open statements against Catholicism. Threatened with exclusion from the succession, he found little encouragement from the Protestant electors and decided to sacrifice his religious inclinations to his political future. In 1561 he promised his father to stay in the Church, and soon thereafter to send his two eldest sons for six years to the Spanish court to be educated. The highly talented and diligent Maximilian originally maintained during his reign an attitude of studied neutrality toward both confessions, though telling his Protestant friends that his heart was still on their side, as was probably the case. But his will power was not equal to his intellect, and this made him a poor military commander. In 1566 the diet gave him a large army, the like of which had not been seen for a long time in Germany. But by his hesitant and overcautious conduct of the Hungarian campaign, Maximilian frittered away the opportunities that were greater than the imperial side realized. Unknown to them, the death of the aged Suleiman II had deprived the Turks of their ruler and military leader. Maximilian had to accept a humiliating peace and to continue the payment of tributes to the infidels. In the later years of his reign Maximilian's policy, in all its outward manifestations, clearly tended to favor Catholic interests. The illness of Don Carlos, son of Philip of Spain, opened the prospect of a future reunion of the Austrian and Spanish lines of the House of Habsburg.

With the death of Maximilian and the accession of his son, Rudolf II (1576–1612), hopes for a strengthening of the Empire through an inter-confessional and federative policy began to look illusory, although in spite of Rudolf's orthodoxy his practical policy in German affairs fol-lowed the provisions of the Peace of Augsburg. Leopold von Ranke has judged that the Empire could have recovered a central place in Ger-man public life even after 1555. The opinion of a great master ought not to be regarded lightly, but it is difficult to see how the anemia of all the institutions of the Empire could have been cured by a generation of Germans who were prepossessed with their own particular interest and advantage and incapable of great political conceptions. The mass of the people was politically silent. To the extent that scholars gave their attention to political questions at all, they were absorbed in attempts merely to harmonize the chaotic laws of the Empire, while among the unlearned some vague dreams about a coming utopia or a return of former great days lingered on. Both the idea and the reality of the Em-pire had grown dim in the popular consciousness and were completely overshadowed by a concern for the smaller community in which the individual lived, and beyond this with the soul's salvation.

The Empire could have been saved if there had arisen something com-parable to the so-called *parti des politiques* in France, i.e., a group of statesmen bent on subordinating religious conflicts to the national inter-est and to a *raison d'état*. Even in France this happened only after the turn of the century, after a long internecine struggle, and the mon-archy of Louis XIV was still largely founded on religion. In the Ger-many of the late sixteenth century *politiques* did not emerge, nor could they have found a response in a country in which the belief in govern-ment as the instrument for establishment of a Christian order was un-shaken. If there had still been a chance to unite Catholics and Protes-tants in a single creed, it might have been possible to give the Empire new life. The Peace of Augsburg expressed the hope that the "split re-ligion" would be joined together again, and this hope died only slowly. But the practices of theological conferences under imperial auspices, of which the last one was held in Worms in 1557, proved of no avail.

Actually, the Council of Trent had already gone too far in committing the Church to an uncompromising course. Protestantism, for its part, had become so strongly identified with the importance of true doctrine that it was equally intractable. The emphasis on doctrine, however, not only set Protestantism against the old Church but also led to division within its own camp, and this was a major reason for its failure to win the whole nation.

✧ *The Continued Expansion of Protestantism*

THE EXPANSION OF PROTESTANTISM continued after the Peace of Augsburg. The most important single addition was the reformation of the Palatinate lands: the Electoral and Upper Palatinate under Elector Otto-Henry in 1556, and Palatinate-Simmern in the years following. Many imperial countships, among them most of the Nassau territories and smaller ones in Swabia, Hesse, and the Rhineland, were officially reformed. By 1560 all of northern Germany east of the Weser had turned Protestant. Only the Eichsfeld, southwest of the Harz mountains and belonging to Mainz, and parts of the bishopric of Hildesheim continued as Catholic enclaves. Essentially, all these countries were reformed from Saxony. Geographically, this north German territory became the most integrated Protestant block. Another group of Protestant territories developed from Hesse, reaching north from the Main along the Rhine down to the Sieg river and along the Weser to the North Sea. Although Protestantism affected some of the Westphalian bishoprics, such as Osnabrück, barriers were set by Münster and Paderborn, and also by Cologne and the lands of the duke of Jülich-Cleves, against its further extension toward the northwest. In southeastern Germany, Protestantism won half of Franconia. Here the center was Nürnberg and the neighboring Hohenzollern principalities, Ansbach, Bayreuth, and Kulmbach. This Protestant region reached southward to the Danube, and, at Regensburg, even beyond the Danube. Another cluster, predominantly Swabian, had its fountainhead in Strasbourg and the southern German cities north of the Lake of Constance. The accession of Württemberg gave this group coherence, though it had outlying enclaves, particularly in Alsace. With the reformation of the Palatinate, there was a closer linking of the Swabian, Franconian, and Hessian groups in a half circle from the Main to the Moselle. The Protestant territories finally formed contiguous entities.

The largest central region left in Catholic hands consisted of the

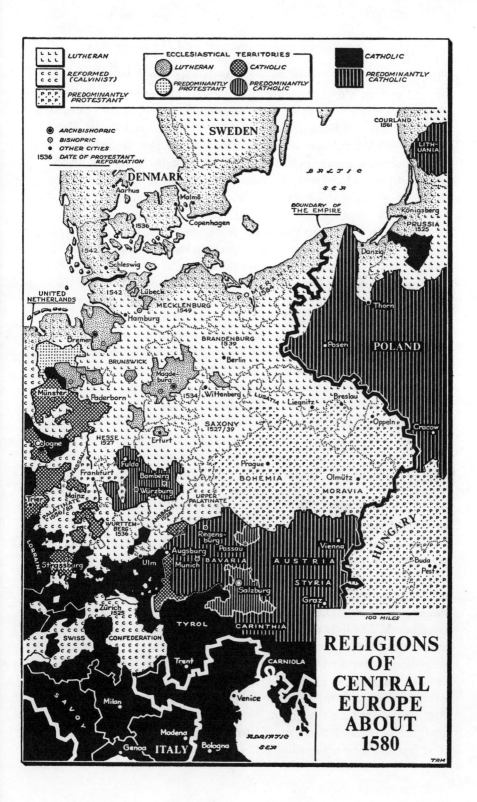

LUTHERAN

REFORMED (CALVINIST)

PREDOMINANTLY PROTESTANT

ECCLESIASTICAL TERRITORIES
- LUTHERAN
- CATHOLIC
- PREDOMINANTLY PROTESTANT
- PREDOMINANTLY CATHOLIC

CATHOLIC

PREDOMINANTLY CATHOLIC

⊚ ARCHBISHOPRIC
◉ BISHOPRIC
● OTHER CITIES
1536 DATE OF PROTESTANT REFORMATION

SWEDEN

COURLAND 1561

LITH-UANIA

DENMARK

Aarhus

Malmö

Copenhagen

BALTIC SEA

BOUNDARY OF THE EMPIRE

Königsberg

PRUSSIA 1525

1536

1542

Schleswig

Danzig

Thorn

UNITED NETHERLANDS

1542

Lübeck

MECKLENBURG 1549

POMERANIA 1534

Hamburg

BRANDENBURG 1539

Posen

POLAND

Bremen

BRUNSWICK

Berlin

Münster

Magde-burg

1534

Wittenberg

LUSATIA

Liegnitz

Breslau

Paderborn

Cologne

HESSE 1527

Erfurt

SAXONY 1527/39

Oppeln

Cracow

Frankfurt

NASSAU

Fulda

Bamberg

Würzburg

Prague

BOHEMIA

Olmütz

MORAVIA

Trier

Mainz

PALATINATE 1556/63

UPPER PALATINATE

ANSBACH 1525

WÜRTTEM-BERG 1536

Regens-burg

Passau

Vienna

HUNGARY

LORRAINE

Strassburg

Ulm

Augsburg

Munich

BAVARIA

AUSTRIA

Buda

Pest

Zürich 1525

SWISS CONFEDERATION

TYROL

Salzburg

STYRIA

Graz

CARINTHIA

100 MILES

SAVOY

Milan

Trent

CARNIOLA

Venice

RELIGIONS OF CENTRAL EUROPE ABOUT 1580

Modena

Genoa

ITALY

Bologna

ADRIATIC SEA

TRM

three Franconian bishoprics along the Main—Bamberg, Würzburg and Mainz—and the old imperial abbey of Fulda. Other important areas of Catholic resistance lay in the northwestern and southeastern corners of the Empire—in Bavaria and Austria on one side, and in the lower Rhenish and Westphalian territories on the other. But the situation of Catholicism was highly precarious even in these three regions. In the northwest, as we have seen, the forceful intervention of Charles V had kept Catholic authorities in the saddle, and the closeness of the Spanish Netherlands remained as a warning. This foreign threat created a temptation for the active Protestant movement to look for foreign assistance, and once the Netherlands were divided in revolt, it was almost inevitable that such support would be sought. In the ecclesiastical principalities of the Main valley, towns and the nobility of the bishoprics had turned Protestant, and thereby the Catholic character of the chapter organization and the election of bishops was endangered. Even in Bavaria and Austria and in the bishoprics that adjoined them— Salzburg, Augsburg, Eichstätt, and Passau—the municipal communities and the aristocracy were widely on the Protestant side. In Austria the nobility was overwhelmingly Protestant, and in 1571 Maximilian granted the nobility of Upper and Lower Austria free exercise of the Lutheran religion in their castles and urban houses. In Styria and Carinthia even more far-reaching concessions had to be made by 1578. In the lands of the Bohemian crown Protestantism could build on what was left of the Hussite antecedents. In Moravia the old Church was stronger than in Bohemia, but here Anabaptism had its stronghold under the protection of the nobility. Silesia, however, was even more permeated by Lutheranism than Bohemia.

A Venetian diplomat reported in 1557 that nine-tenths of Germany was already Protestant, and this does not have to be taken as statistically accurate. However, the Catholic Church had disappeared from most of Germany, and even in areas that still had Catholic rulers it was in desperate condition. On all levels, moral strength seemed to have left the Church. The lives of the prince-bishops and chapter members were scandalous. These scions of the German high nobility, with hardly an exception, knew no ambition other than to lead profligate lives like their secular cousins. The state of the low clergy was equally deplorable. Most of the parish priests lived in open concubinage; moreover, they had not received the training necessary for the proper performance of their ecclesiastical duties. Few of them had had a theological education. The few Catholic universities still in existence had only a small number of students and not a single outstanding teacher. Small wonder then that even devout Catholics had lost respect for hierarchy and clergy. Protestantism, in contrast, had by 1560 produced a generation of ministers who were not distinguished, but who were earnest and reasonably well equipped to fulfill the functions that Luther had assigned to servants of the Word. A large number of universities had become Protestant. Wittenberg was followed by Tübingen, Leipzig, Frankfurt on the Oder, Greifswald, Rostock, and Heidelberg. A new Protestant university was founded in Marburg in 1527, and in Königsberg in 1544. Elector John Frederick founded Jena in 1548 (opened in 1558) after the loss of Wittenberg to Albertine Saxony. Nürnberg established the beginnings of a university in Altdorf in 1573, while Brunswick developed Helmstädt beginning in 1574. In the twenty-five years after the Augsburg Peace, Protestantism commanded greater moral and intellectual resources within Germany than did the Roman Catholic Church.

✍ *Factionalism Within Protestantism*

YET IT WAS ONLY A RELATIVE SUPERIORITY. The bitter internal feuds that broke out over theological questions weakened, and even broke, the unity of German Protestantism, and in political action Lutheranism revealed itself as unwilling to conquer. In Chapter 8 we tried to show how the religious and theological divisions originated in the years around and after 1525. The crises of the Schmalkaldic War, the *Interim*, and the final establishment of "territorial churches" after the Passau treaty brought many of them into the open, and the Protestant theologians made war on one another with unbridled passion. Their profane language and reckless name-calling were an unhappy heritage from Luther. It was to the credit of the belligerent ministers of this period that many of them had the courage of their convictions and were prepared to give up their homes and positions for an uncertain future in another territory. Moreover, it would be unfair to challenge their intellectual honesty and assert that the problems they fought about were meaningless, because the modern world has moved far away from the theological distinctions in which they expressed their ideas. The angry condemnation of all opponents as heretics showed, however, that these Protestant ministers had no feeling for national and ecumenic responsibilities. Their rabid factionalism mirrored the narrow reality of the petty states of Germany.

In the center of most conflicts stood the figure of Philip Melanchthon.

His conduct at the time of the *Interim* had shaken the confidence of many of his students and colleagues. He himself admitted his errors, but he remained under suspicion, since, after the Wittenberg capitulation, he stayed on at Wittenberg University. The latter, incidentally, prospered through his presence, while the new university at Jena, which was supposed to take its place, had hard beginnings. From Jena Matthias Flacius and others began their fight against Melanchthon's deviations from true Lutheranism. They were not aware to what large extent they themselves were Melanchthon's pupils. Luther's most fundamental belief, that Christian religion could only be derived from the Bible through personal experience and could not be imposed by doctrine and authority, had already lapsed. But the new Lutheran orthodoxy saved Lutheranism from dissolution in a rationalistic humanism, which, in the late sixteenth century, would not have been very likely to survive against a renewed Catholicism.

In the foreground of the long series of theological feuds, and greatest in influence upon the layman, was the controversy over sacraments. We have seen what this issue had meant to Luther, and that ever since the Marburg Colloquy of 1529 it had endangered Protestant unity. Melanchthon, who in Marburg had rather held forth against compromise with Zwingli and Bucer, had changed his attitude in the endeavor to find a broader basis for Protestant unity. In the various editions of the Augsburg Confession he had presented new doctrines of the Lord's Supper, particularly in the edition of 1540, which became known as the *Confessio Augustana Variata*. In the *Variata*, Melanchthon moved toward a symbolic and mystical interpretation of the sacraments, which Bucer could accept. But the *Interim* removed Bucer from Germany, and Strasbourg never recovered its great position in the Protestant world. Instead, John Calvin (1509–64) asserted his leadership in the southwest, and, opposed as his theology was to Melanchthonian humanism, in the doctrine of sacraments the views of the two men coincided. This soon became an argument for accusing Melanchthon and his school, the "Philipists" of being secret Calvinists (Crypto-Calvinists). But Calvin and his impact on German history must be seen in a wider perspective.

✎ The Tenets of Calvinism

CALVIN OWED HIS FAITH, as he always stressed, to Luther, and no one ever understood this German reformer's religion better than the young French lawyer who was to become the real savior of Protestantism and the one to give Protestantism its world-wide influence in the modern age. He was briefly in Germany after his flight from France in 1534, then again in 1538, after his expulsion from Geneva. He spent the three years following his second visit to Germany in Strasbourg as minister of the small congregation of French refugees. Here he was in close contact with Bucer, from whom he learned the fields of both theology and church administration. He was also present at the theological conferences of Hagenau, Worms, and Regensburg, gaining insight into the problems of the interconfessional struggle. In 1541 he returned to Geneva to establish what John Knox called the most perfect school of Christ that existed on earth since the days of the apostles. The city was not completely controlled by Calvin before 1555, but his theological as well as political influence was soon felt beyond the canton and beyond Switzerland. With his *Institutes of the Christian Religion*, first published in 1536, Calvin created the greatest systematic work of Protestantism, which in its later editions became a competitor of Melanchthon's *Loci* in Germany. Through the *Consensus Tigurinus*, Calvin reached, in 1549, an agreement with Zurich on the definition of the Protestant faith, which brought the various branches of Swiss Protestantism closer together. The statement of the *Consensus* on sacraments aroused considerable attention in Germany.

In contrast to Melanchthon's teachings, and also to Lutheran orthodoxy, Calvin restored the original motives and forms of Luther's religious thinking. The "otherness" of religion as against human reason and opinion was the core of Calvin's thought. Faith was an absolute miracle produced by God, and as such was totally beyond human understanding. As a consequence, it was illogical to expect that man could exercise influence upon divine action in any way, by good works or human conduct. This was good Lutheran thought, which Luther himself, in some of his writings, e.g., in his *On the Serfdom of the Human Will* against Erasmus, had carried to great length. Still, Luther had shown a respectful shyness in describing the intentions of a "hidden" God. It had seemed to him enough to derive from the "revealed" God an enlivened trust in divine love. Calvin insisted on full clarity about the plans of God, who elected one individual and condemned another. The doctrine of predestination became the heart of Calvin's religion and the most pointed theological expression of the supremacy of God's will, in the face of which man could not raise any demand and had to feel only gratitude for the place that this majestic God had given him in His creation.

The experience of the omnipotence of the creator led to conclusions very different from those of Luther. In Lutheranism the individual derived from his justification a bliss that lifted him beyond the sinful world. The faithful had to obey the will of God by accepting the orders of the world. By fulfilling the tasks of his worldly calling in the right spirit, the individual did his duty as a Christian, though he could not change the world. What personal good works he might perform were left to his spontaneity, or, as Luther put it, he could do "what happened to come to hand." To Luther, religion was chiefly faith, and he and his Church did not stress "Ye shall be holy; for I am holy." But Calvin deduced from the recognition of the sovereign majesty of the Lord the absolute obligation to honor and serve Him with untiring zeal. In Calvin's view, faith was one criterion of Christianity; action was the other. Consequently, ethics had to be made specific with regard both to the individual and to the community. This conception of religion was clearly reflected in Calvin's church program. The Church was not only an institution for the dissemination of the Word but also for the sanctification of the individual and the community. In contrast to Luther, Calvin was intensely concerned about the correct organization of the Church, but he, too, insisted on keeping it as an entity separate from the state. The four Church offices—ministers, teachers, deacons, and elders—indicate the wide scope of ecclesiastical activities, which were at the same time designed to reform the secular community. It is not correct to call this Church organization theocratic, since Calvin always acknowledged independent functions of the secular government, but no doubt the government was to become imbued with a Christian spirit and use its power for the furtherance of God's cause.

From similar premises Calvin drew conclusions that led in new directions; we will examine these chiefly with regard to their impact on German history. In this connection, it seems noteworthy that original Calvinism did not get lost in minor theological controversies as easily as did Lutheranism. To be sure, Calvinism developed very elaborate theological speculations, as one could expect from a religious attitude based so strongly on logical clarity and rational discipline. But Calvinist theology elevated the doctrine of God far above all other subjects and could, therefore, be more liberal with regard to other dogmas. The emphasis on action made the Calvinists conscious of the necessity for unity. Whereas orthodox Lutherans soon came to consider Calvinism as outright heresy and declared that they would "rather turn popish than Calvinist," the Calvinists considered Lutherans as brethren who had not quite overcome certain medieval superstitions. They called themselves "the more reformed" or simply "the reformed," a label that finally became the official designation of Calvinism in Germany.

Another main characteristic of Calvinism was the mobilization of laymen for participation and action in the Church. Original Calvinism was by no means democratic; the mass of the people was supposed to obey, and had no direct role in the government, which inclined toward the oligarchic, whether it was patrician as in Geneva and the Dutch cities, or even baronial as in the Huguenot movement. But Calvinism took root most easily in countries in which corporate ideas were represented by politically conscious classes who were willing to fight for their way of life. Here were the origins of the subsequent development of human rights which made Calvinism one of the most important builders of the modern world. Growing in a city civilization and led by a man who, as a trained lawyer, possessed practical understanding of worldly affairs, Calvinism was not disposed to consider manufacture, commerce, and banking as anomalous phenomena of economic life, though Calvin tried through strict regulations to bring them into conformity with Christian ethics. Only at a much later date did Calvinist groups in England and America embrace modern business philosophies. But even original Calvinism showed a strong inclination to understand the underlying rationality of practical life, and this applied not only to economics but also to politics. The chief motive of Calvinist politics was religious, the duty to serve the honor of divine majesty and to gather God's children in a world-wide community devoted to such service. For this ultimate objective, however, unflagging action had to be tempered by an appreciation of existing legal and political conditions. Calvinists demonstrated not only an activist political attitude but also an early affinity to the *raison d'état*.

✍ The Influence of Calvinism in Germany

CALVINISM WAS TO UNFOLD its great potentialities in the western European world, and it was characteristic of the differences between Germany and the West which already existed in the late sixteenth century that Lutheranism proved able to exclude Calvinism as a dominating influence in Germany and, where Calvinism did gain a foothold, to transform it to its own image. A genuine Calvinism came to life only in the northwestern Rhineland and Westphalia, where the model of the Netherlands and the actual settlement of Calvinist refugees created congregations in which the full Church organization of Calvin was realized. On the whole Germany did not adopt Calvin's Church ideal but only his theology, and even this in a modified version. The first prince of the Empire who accepted Calvinism was Elector Frederick III of the Palatinate (1559–76), and under him Heidelberg became the foremost center of German Calvinism. The theologians of the university wrote the Heidelberg Catechism of 1563, which became the chief creed of the Reformed churches in Germany. A second focus of German Calvinism developed after 1574 in Nassau and adjacent territories, which, through the Orange dynasty, were closely connected with the Netherlands. In the north, Bremen and Anhalt became Calvinist.

But nowhere in these territories were the Calvinist Church constitution and discipline accepted, and the Heidelberg Catechism did not contain the doctrine of predestination. The reformed churches were authoritarian territorial units, very much like the Lutheran churches, of which the Hessian church also had some weak synodal and presbyterian elements. A corporate system did not seem to grow on German soil. It was a straw in the wind that a native of Switzerland, Thomas Erastus, as professor in Heidelberg, developed a theory of state domination of the Church, which, as "Erastianism," was a source of dissension in English Calvinism. For its part, German Calvinism produced Johannes Althusius (1557–1638). He was an Erastian with regard to Church government. But in his *Politica* of 1603 he presented a system of politics based on the social contract, sovereignty of the people, and the right of opposition to illegal acts of government. This great political thinker, who was one of the most important forerunners of Rousseau, expressed clearly the democratic trends hidden in Calvinism at a time when its scholars turned from a theological to a more rationalistic world view. But Althusius had the revolutionary Netherlands before his eyes, and he himself was the syndic of the city of Emden, which had just then reached the highest state of civic pride and commercial prosperity in its history as a consequence of the Spanish-Dutch wars. The average thought of German Calvinism was not reflected by Althusius. Most of the German Calvinists followed the Lutheran pattern with a modified Lutheran or Philipist creed, in which the doctrine of sacraments was the most divisive, although the two groups elaborated other differences in theology and rites as the feud between Lutherans and Calvinists grew ever more bitter.

The full influence of original Calvinism was experienced only by a few individual German princes. The acceptance of Calvinism always meant the adoption of an activist foreign policy, based on the consciousness of a common danger from Rome and Spain and a common obligation to the Protestant cause. The dynasty of the small Nassau, the House of Orange, lived in these ideals and was to translate them into great actions on the stage of European history. Not all the Palatinate electors showed an equal zeal. For seven years, under Elector Ludwig VI (1576–83), the Palatinate saw a Lutheran reaction. But the invigorating influence of Calvinism could still be seen when, in 1613, Elector John Sigismund of Brandenburg turned Calvinist and his grandson Frederick William, the "Great Elector," opened a new chapter in Brandenburg's history. In contrast, Lutheranism displayed a merely defensive or even passive political attitude. One cannot help being impressed with how neatly Lutheran social ethics, with its hankering for a static medieval society, without capitalistic enterprises and expansionist power politics, corresponded to the general needs, particularly of central and northeastern Germany. This predominantly agrarian society, not capable of mobilizing large internal resources for external efforts—a measure which would in any case have threatened the precarious balance of internal forces—found in the Lutheran religion and ethics a natural expression of its aspirations. The theological and dogmatic squabbles within Lutheranism, though taken with deadly seriousness by the intellectual groups, were, in this light, ripples on the surface of a deep, unmoved sea, and much of the excitement that accompanied them was aroused not by religious but by political concerns.

The region in which Philipism was strongest was Electoral Saxony, even after Melanchthon's death in April, 1560. The head of the Ernestine branch of the Wettin family, Duke John Frederick II of Gotha (1554–67), had been led by the Franconian knight Wilhelm von Grumbach, a former member of Albert Alcibiades' gang, into adventures that were designed to regain for him the electoral dignity, which had been taken away from his father by Charles V.[1] Grumbach was finally captured and executed. John Frederick lost his throne; he was taken prisoner and held in Vienna until his death in 1595. Thus Elector August of Saxony, as guardian of the Ernestine princes, was able to introduce Philipism in Thuringia. August's policy was entirely directed toward the internal growth of his dominions. He had taken the Saxon bishoprics by circumventing the rules of the Augsburg Peace, but he

[1] See page 230.

was eager not to come into conflict with his Bohemian neighbor, the emperor. In Empire affairs he remained a supporter of Maximilian without pressing for concessions to the Protestants. When Frederick III of the Palatinate, at the Diet of Augsburg of 1566, proposed to make contributions to a Turkish war dependent on the nullification of the "ecclesiastical reservation," August rejected such a policy. But he refused to co-operate with Maximilian in declaring Elector Frederick a violator of the Peace of Augsburg, which, as will be remembered, had excluded Calvinists. Many Lutheran princes were inclined to follow Maximilian in this respect. A cautious middle course between the emperor, the Lutheran princes, and Calvinism was August's ideal.

∾ *The* Book of Concord *of 1580*

IN 1574 AUGUST WAS PERSUADED that his Philipist theologians were secretly working toward bringing Saxony over into the Calvinist camp. This Crypto-Calvinist crisis brought Saxony over to Lutheranism entirely. As a result, the attempts to unify Lutheranism with regard to all of its basic doctrines, which had been carried on from Württemberg and Brunswick for a good many years, gained fresh strength. They led, in 1580, a half century after the Augsburg Confession, to an agreement, called the *Book of Concord*. It was signed by the three electors—the Palatinate was in these years Lutheran—20 princes, 24 counts, and 38 cities. It excluded Philipism and Calvinism, as well as radical Flacian doctrines. Some important territories, among them Pomerania, Holstein, Hesse-Cassel, and a number of cities, did not accept the Concord of 1580. The reasons varied. Some Lutherans wanted modifications of the provisions; others felt it unwise at that moment to take a strong stand against Calvinism. As a matter of fact, in 1577, Queen Elizabeth of England had urged the princes to conclude a universal Protestant alliance. But while the *Book of Concord* terminated the cleavages within Lutheranism, it deepened the gulf between Lutherans and Calvinists in Germany, and in doing so it cut Lutheranism off from contact with western European Protestantism.

∾ *The Lutheran Territorial State in Germany*

BY 1580 PROTESTANTISM HAD FAILED to advance its political and constitutional position in the Empire except for some small gains. It achieved important results only in the realization of its religious and political ideals in the territorial states. Nowhere in the Lutheran parts of Germany was the dualistic state of the late Middle Ages [2] substantially changed. The prestige and authority of the prince was enhanced by his position as head of the Church. The secularization of Church goods increased the princely property and gave the princes the possibility of extending their governmental activities into the field of education and social welfare. But it should not be assumed that the princes were absolute rulers of the new churches. The ministers of the countryside usually depended on the noble landlords who were the patrons of the local churches. This merely reflected the general influence of the estates on public life. The clergy disappeared from the territorial diets, but the nobility and representatives of the town governments maintained their positions, the more so since the resources of the prince did not prove entirely adequate to cover his expenditures. Public and private expenditures were hardly distinguished even in theory, and although the princes of the sixteenth century spent less than those of the eighteenth, often enough they ran into debt because of personal luxuries. None of them, however, could afford to equip armed forces even of the size of a single regiment, and the hiring of troops in war depended on contributions from the estates.

All these princes were essentially agrarian landowners, and they derived the major part of their revenues from the management of their demesne (*domanium*). In this respect the princes were not different from landed noblemen. In addition, however, they derived income from their regal rights (*regalia*), for example, minting money, collecting customs revenue, and controlling mining, as well as from certain small taxes of long standing such as the so-called *Bede*, a land tax, and the Jewish head tax. The estates were willing to give money only on special occasions, for example, for a dowry for a princess, as a contribution for the emperor's war against the Turks, or for the defense of their territories in an emergency. But as a rule the estates undertook the administration of these taxes through agencies of their own, and they did so particularly when they were asked to pay debts of the rulers. The princes were everywhere closely related to the estates, which not only developed financial administrations in addition to those of the princes but often even conducted foreign negotiations. Elector Joachim II of Brandenburg (1535–71), who was a poor manager, was not the only prince in his generation to feel the power of the estates, and his conflicts with them led repeatedly to the breakdown of all legislation and orderly administration.

[2] See pages 25–36.

None of the Lutheran princes of the sixteenth century felt capable of changing this precarious balance of power within their dominions. They could solidify their own positions only by a better administration of their *domanium* and *regalia* as well as by the avoidance of military expenditure. William IV of Hesse-Cassel said, "There is no more terrible thing on earth than a war, and one must expect from it no profit but extreme peril, disobedience, opposition, contempt, and other misfortune." He was the son of Landgrave Philip and, from 1567 to 1592, the ruler of one of the four lands into which Hesse was divided after his father's death. William IV was one of the foremost representatives of those Lutheran princes who devoted themselves with prudence and diligence to the internal administration of their patrimonies. He applied his personal interests in mathematics and astronomy to the planned development of his "economic state," using statistics and accounting as the chief instruments. Of greater immediate consequence was the domestic administration of his cousin, Elector August I of Saxony. We have discussed the weakness of August's foreign policy. His placement of younger members of the dynasty in neighboring sees and matchmaking with other houses in the hope of future peaceful aggrandisement of the family fortunes were the only signs of an active interest in foreign affairs. Aside from this, the preservation and betterment of the existing state was his main preoccupation.

August I (1553–86) and his wife Anna—to the people affectionately known as "father August" and "mother Anna"—were prototypes of the patriarchal regimes of this period. Their care extended from the court, where Anna, mother of fifteen children, managed the kitchen and did the laundry for her husband, to agriculture, handicraft, mining, and commerce. Strictest economy was enforced on the court and on governmental officers. Insofar as it was possible, payments that they received in kind were converted into money, and in this way the foundation for regular budgets was laid. August, in his early years, was saddled with a debt of 2 million fl. He left his successor a treasury filled with 1,825 million fl., half of them in gold, half in silver coins. But the accumulation of bullion was not the only aim of his economic policy. August extended his care to the stimulation of all the productive forces of the land by turning his domains into model estates, by starting a rational management of forests, and by improving mining and metal manufacture, transportation, and commerce. His administration of princely property and rights came to include concern for the economy and welfare of the land.

The most comprehensive and systematic activity was shown by Duke Christoph of Württemberg (1550–68). In the years of his reign he issued thirty-one organization statutes (*Ordnungen*). These covered every imaginable aspect of life: the relations between duke and estates, justice, church and education, marriage, guild production, weights and measures, sheep raising, as well as drinking bouts of journeymen—in short, nothing was left unregulated. Duke Christoph demonstrated even more clearly than August of Saxony the close connection between religious convictions and political practices. Government meant to these Lutheran princes a conscientious interest in the earthly and eternal welfare of their subjects. The cultivation of the true doctrine in church and school was the fundamental ideal justification of all authority, and the prince had to conceive of his office as a duty toward God and his God-serving people. The administration of justice was the highest function of government; next to it came the preservation of the divinely ordained structure of society, and this included care for the material welfare of the various classes. The ideal of an even distribution of social burdens, however, was entirely absent. The monarchs were much too weak to challenge the power of the estates. If the nobility gained by the impositions of new burdens on the peasants or if the guilds exploited their monopoly in trade or in the employment of labor, the princes could not intervene, nor would they have wished to do so. Religion told them that people should obey and toil. It was not the well-being of the individual that mattered, but that of the community, which was no longer Christendom or even the nation but merely a small political entity, half-church, half-state, struggling for unity in life and faith.

Respect for law was not confined to internal government but was supposed to enter into the relations among the states as well. Figures like Maurice of Saxony and Albert Alcibiades were exceptions among the German princes of the sixteenth century. Indulgence in power politics in the Italian style was beyond the means of these princes, and it was not according to their inclination. As they enforced peace in their territories, they avoided the feuds in which their ancestors had found great satisfaction and avoided also the costly and bloody wars that the new age had brought. Luther had not been a pacifist but he had allowed war only in defense. Offensive wars, whether fought for materialistic or religious aims, he had denounced as absolutely un-Christian. Occasionally he had gone so far as to say that a prince should at times suffer an injustice passively, though he admitted that this was more than could normally be expected of a prince. War was consequently considered by German Lutherans of the sixteenth and seventeenth centuries as the great source of evil, a destroyer of life and property as well as of religion and morals. The desire to win glory through military deeds was pagan, as the Saxon councilor Melchior von Osse wrote in his famous *Political Testament* of 1556.

We should not assume that all Lutheran princes lived up to the standards achieved by August I and Duke Christoph. However, there were also others who were outstanding, among them Duke Julius of Brunswick-Wolfenbüttel, who was not only a good economic administrator but also a gifted businessman, and John George (1571-98), with his twenty-three children, who was Brandenburg's first Lutheran patriarch. But the average German prince of this period—and this applied equally to the Catholics—was given to little more than gluttony, drinking, wenching, and hunting. Considering the unholy conduct of these princes, one hesitates to call their often pronounced interest in theological questions particularly saintly. The coarseness of the German courts of the century was appalling, and in many territories the welfare of the people was shamefully neglected. Nevertheless, in some lands the basis for a tradition of decent administration and common life was laid, which not even the Thirty Years' War ruined completely. It was true, however, that not even the best Lutheran princes did anything to stave off the coming national disaster.

Up to the 1570's, perhaps to the early 1580's, Protestantism continued to advance in Germany. If the Protestant estates of the Empire had acted in concert, it is difficult to see how they could have been prevented from dominating the Empire altogether. It would presumably have required foreign alliances, but western Europe, involved in terrible wars, could not have become at this time the master of German politics as it did 50 years later. However, German Protestantism missed its political opportunities, as it also weakened its religious heritage. In the twenty-five years after the Peace of Augsburg, Roman Catholicism, slowly gathering momentum, gained fresh moral power, which was to win political expression.

✎ The Catholic Church at the Beginning of the Counter Reformation

BY 1555 THE OLD CHURCH IN GERMANY had reached a new low with respect not only to the size of the geographical areas over which it still ruled, if only in name, but also to its internal life and institutions. The decay and corruption that had existed at the time of Luther's appearance had not been removed; on the contrary, things had outwardly gone from bad to worse and continued to do so after 1555. The most loyal sons of the Church were filled with dismay, often bordering on despair, when they saw the Church continually losing ground and its professed servants besmirching its ideals.

The members of the high nobility, from whom the high clergy were almost exclusively drawn, vied with the princes and knights in secular pursuits and sins. Many bishops, abbots, and canons were not priests, and few had had a theological education, if they had had any education at all. There were some exceptions, but the few earnest bishops were powerless, since the lower clergy and monks were in an equally bad state. The Catholic schools and universities soon suffered from a lack of students and teachers. Already by the end of the 1530's, many hundreds of parishes had no priests, and most of the existing priests were either married or living in concubinage. Poor and untrained, they were often incapable of performing the simplest functions of their office. They could not claim to be moral, intellectual, and religious leaders of their congregations. Many monasteries were empty, and others were centers of the worst depravity, though some maintained respectable standards. From the beginning of the Protestant revolt the Catholic Church in Germany suffered from a scarcity of eminent theologians who could have conducted the fight against Wittenberg on a high level.

The most eminent German Catholic theologian was Johann Eck (1486–1543), who in the course of his life moderated the violent tone of his early attacks on Luther. The determination and untiring labor that he put into all his efforts without receiving much help from Rome showed character, and he was a knowledgeable scholar. But he was rigid and obstinate and unable to meet Luther with new ideas. His polemic against Wittenberg remained entirely defensive. This was true of another active writer, Johannes Cochlaeus, who had once been the companion of Ulrich von Hutten, but from 1520 on dedicated his life to the defense of the Church. It is not necessary to mention the few other Catholic writers and theologians, none of whom had religious depth or was master of words that would call forth a response from the layman. Moreover, the Catholic theologians were too isolated to reply to the flood of publications from the Protestant presses, and they had difficulty in finding printers and booksellers. Eventually academic audiences dwindled. The study of theology declined and was almost discontinued. After Eck's death the University of Ingolstadt had only one professor of theology, in the later 1540's none. In the same years Cologne repeatedly had no theological course to offer. When Ferdinand I wanted to send German Catholic theologians to Trent in 1551, he could not find any.

All pulsating life seemed to have ceased in the Catholic Church of Germany, and that it did not break down entirely was largely due to the protection it received from a small group of secular rulers. Perhaps there was more fire in the ashes than was apparent at this moment even to the faithful. But it was clear that any effective leadership would have to come from outside the country, where in the past so much of the deterioration in the German situation had originated. Through the centuries the German Church had been bound to Rome with innumerable bonds of the most intimate nature. The worldly character of the Renaissance papacy, its lack of religious purpose, and its domination by stark political motives whereby it exploited its universal position for Italian ends was even more detrimental to the Church in Germany than in Italy. Although the Curia had at all times had men able to recognize the grave dangers of the German developments, papal policies were not centered around the German problems. A major responsibility for the ultimate failure of Charles V's political hopes and labors lay with Leo X, Clement VII, and Paul III. But equally serious was the incapacity of the Curia to direct the resistance of its members against Lutheranism. It was even unwilling to support its brave defenders, such as Eck and Cochlaeus, with the simple aid of a printing press and similar propaganda necessities, and it was firmly opposed to general reforms in the Church. With his admission, in 1523, of the corruption in the Church, Pope Hadrian VI had given the isolated friends of reform a first program, but for decades thereafter the Church lapsed into its old state.

Hadrian VI represented the earnest religion of the Netherlands and also was well acquainted with the condition of the Church in Spain. In Spain the long struggle against the infidels had kept a crusading spirit alive, and the leadership of the kings in religious wars had given them control over the Church. After the reconquest of the peninsula, the Church had displayed a rich life of devout piety and higher learning. German and Dutch mysticism had a strong influence on Spanish religion in the sixteenth century, although it assumed in Spain an enthusiastic and visionary character. Erasmus, too, had a great effect on the formation of the new Spanish civilization, although his ideas became suspect after the middle of the century. His example encouraged the development of a new literary style and a fresh study of the classic schoolmen and Church Fathers. There was a revival of Thomistic theology which was more than an artificial restoration, since it was born of genuine religious experiences.

Catholic Spain was the reservoir from which flowed the religious and political forces that reawakened the old faith on the Continent. Its impact on Italy was most immediate, particularly after 1527. But Italy's own contribution to the Catholic reformation of the Church could only become world-wide after the papacy had opened itself to the new ideas. It would be a serious mistake to call the civilization of the Renaissance, as described by Jacob Burckhardt, a mere façade. Burckhardt was quite right in emphasizing its roots in the aspirations of the Italian people. But he neglected, in his work, the spiritual qualities of Renaissance thought. The Italian Renaissance contained spiritual motives of great depth, which were expressed not only in aesthetic but also in religious and ethical values. But Renaissance civilization did not comprise the totality of Italian life. Much of the customary medieval thought lived on. According to Machiavelli, the belief that providence ruled human history not only continued to be held by most people but also won new converts under the impact of the misfortunes that befell Italy as a consequence of the foreign invasions after 1494. The sack of Rome in 1527 and the subsequent domination by foreigners became an irrefutable proof of the divine judgment on the wickedness of the nation. Even the advanced intellectual and artistic groups of Italian society began to pay serious attention to religion. In the decade after 1530 Luther was much studied in Italy, although few Italians turned Lutheran and not many embraced the sectarian forms of Protestantism. The search for a restoration of Christian truth and action generally kept closer to the Church.

In the early 1520's a number of new or reformed monastic orders came into being, and after 1527 they began to win members from all classes. At a later date some of these orders gained great significance in Germany. Among them were the Theatine order of 1524, members of which dedicated themselves to pastoral work among the higher classes; the Franciscan Capuchins (1528), who carried their message to the people at large; and the Ursulines (1537), who concentrated on nursing and the education of girls. It has been mentioned that in the pontificate of Paul III (1534–49) friends of an ecclesiastical reform entered the college of cardinals. For a while it seemed that a somewhat more conciliatory humanistic course might prevail among them, although it should not be forgotten that Gasparo Contarini was not only the nuncio who, at

Regensburg in 1541, agreed with the German Protestants on a formula of justification but also the man who introduced the unknown Spaniard, Ignatius of Loyola, to the pope. But at the time of Contarini's death, in 1542, the policy of Pietro Caraffa was already in the ascendant. Caraffa (Paul IV) aimed at the complete suppression of new ideas, the full restoration of traditional theology, and the supremacy of papal power. The organization of the Italian inquisition was the first step in this direction, but even more important was the course imposed on the Council of Trent, which determined the character of modern Catholicism.

✒ *The Council of Trent, 1545–63*

THE COUNCIL OF TRENT MET in three different periods. It was first convened in December, 1545, and lasted until March, 1547, when it was transferred to Bologna. It will be remembered that this was a move against the emperor which failed, since few bishops followed the call and nothing was accomplished in Bologna. The Council was reconvened in May, 1551, under Julius III, on the insistence of Charles V, and it continued until April, 1552, when the approach of Maurice of Saxony dispersed the convention. During this session Protestant delegates presented statements of faith but gained no direct or indirect influence on the deliberations. For ten years thereafter the Council rested, because Pietro Caraffa, as Pope Paul IV, resumed the struggle against the Habsburgs. His strong anti-Spanish sentiment and his nepotism made this chief exponent of a Catholic reform the last belligerent secular ruler on the papal throne. His successor, though endowed with a more worldly mind, brought the reform of the Church to a first conclusion. Under Pius IV (1560–65) the Council was assembled from January, 1562, to December, 1563. By this time the idea of using the Council for a reconciliation with the Protestants had completely waned, and suggestions of Emperor Ferdinand aiming at such a reconciliation were easily pushed aside. Differences in the Council with regard to religious dogmas were small, and consequently more attention could be given to practical reforms than at the earlier meetings. The chief conflict in this period, however, centered around the authority of the papacy over the Church. For the last time the theory of the full independence of the episcopal office, which implied the superiority of the Council over the pope, was asserted, particularly by the Spanish bishops. The great issue was not really settled at Trent; rather it was carried on between the courts by political negotiations. Without the support of the kings, a conciliar movement was helpless, and papal diplomacy succeeded in convincing Ferdinand I and Philip II that a monarchical papal regime of the Church would be preferable not only for the Church but also for the states.

The Council of Trent reconstituted the Church on a threefold level, that of Church government, Church practices, and dogma. The papacy emerged again as the dominant authority in the Church. From the beginnings of the Council the Curia had directed its organization and deliberations through able papal representatives, and the Council acted more like an advisory assembly than as the highest representation of the Church. It was in fact denied the official title "representative body of the universal Church." The supremacy of the pope was not officially proclaimed, in view of the strong opposition of the Spanish and French bishops. But in the end the Council presented all its decrees and resolutions to the pope for confirmation, after having given him in these decrees authority to dispense with the recommended ecclesiastical reforms at his discretion. Thus the Council acknowledged the superiority of the pope. The papacy assumed the interpretation of the decrees and canons of Trent and implemented the reforms, thereby advancing its position further in many directions.

With the practical establishment of papal absolutism, it became possible to give back to the bishops many functions within their own dioceses which they had lost in the course of the previous centuries. Much of the jurisdictional power had fallen into the hands of the archdeacons, whose office was now strictly subordinated to the bishop. Although monasteries retained most of their exemptions, priests were placed under the supervision of the bishops in all their activities outside the monasteries. In general, the clergy again came under the control of the bishops, and the diocese became a living unit. The restoration of the dioceses as centers of ecclesiastical life and action was an important aspect of the Catholic reformation. But while the bishoprics were reorganized, old ecclesiastical provinces under the archbishops were neglected. Confirmation and consecration of bishops became a papal privilege, and the archbishops retained merely certain jurisdictional rights of appeal. The papacy was always fearful of placing too much power in the hands of a few metropolitan bishops. In Germany this decision has contributed toward frustrating any movement in the direction of a national Church.

The reform of the organization of the Church led directly to the reform of the clergy on all levels. The accumulation of benefices was forbidden, residence was obligatory, and appointed bishops were compelled to become ordained priests within a period of three months. The Council of Trent resisted the wishes of the emperor to abolish celibacy and merely admonished the clergy to lead a life befitting its vocation. A comprehensive system of education for the clergy was envisaged by the Council fathers. During the Middle Ages only the monastic orders had had systematic provisions for the training of their members. Few members of the secular clergy in Germany had had more schooling than the elementary city schools provided. Only a small number attended the universities, which were given to the general teaching and not to the personal education of young men. Apparently under Cardinal Reginald Pole's influence, the idea of boarding schools, which he called seminaries, was adopted. In each diocese a seminary was to be established and maintained through a tax on benefices. From the age of 12, a group of prospective priests were to be educated in the arts, theology, and the practice of the clerical vocation.

Through the Council's initiative and subsequent papal execution the clergy received a new breviary, missal, and catechism. At the same time a general Index of Prohibited Books was created as a chief weapon against heresy. Lists of forbidden books had been used before on a local or national level, but from 1564 censorship became a centralized institution of the Church. Little was achieved in financial administration. Not even indulgences were abolished, although the trading of indulgences by special salesmen was discontinued. The creation of a new marriage law that stamped out some medieval abuses was a beneficial act. But important as the formulation of a program of Church reformation was, it remained to be seen how soon and how completely it could be carried into practice.

The Council had fortified papal absolutism, but while the papacy had defeated the conciliar movement within the Church, it was now in a position where it had to rely on the secular arm even more than before for the advancement of its cause in the world. The Trent decrees on doctrine were readily accepted by all Catholic countries, but the reform decrees met considerable opposition and were not readily translated into action everywhere. Italy, Savoy, Portugal, and Poland approved them immediately, but in the Empire only Austria and Bavaria took initial steps for their realization. At the request of Emperor Ferdinand and Duke Albert V of Bavaria, the pope conceded communion in both forms to the churches of their lands. It was thought that this concession would weaken the Protestant movement, but it was soon learned that it had the opposite effect and was then revoked. For a long time clerics in the Church in Germany did not meet the standards laid down by the Council of Trent. The development of educational institutions saw many reverses. As late as the eighteenth century few Catholic seminaries existed in Germany. But for the two centuries after the Council German Catholicism had a concrete and enlivening task in carrying out the reform program of Trent.

The suppression of abuses and the reform of the Church through certain practical measures was only one aspect of the work of the Council. The basic definition of the Catholic faith was, in the main, and particularly in the early sessions, its chief concern. Throughout the history of the Christian Church clarifications and subsequent proclamations of dogmas had been answers to heretical movements, and the Church had usually adopted some of the ideas of the opposition. But the decrees of the Council of Trent did not show any positive influence of Protestantism. Although the Council promulgated more dogmas than any council before it, none of them made any concessions to Protestant doctrine. The shadow of Protestantism was present at the deliberations of Trent, and the Confession of Augsburg affected the formulation of the Council's decrees in many respects. But the decreees rejected every major tenet of the Protestant faith and pronounced a thunderous anathema on them. The division of Western Christianity was declared in an uncompromising fashion.

The Council of Trent reasserted the existence of the Church as a hierarchical and sacramental body. The Church was the Church militant and triumphant, the visible representation of the kingdom of God on earth and at the same time the divine institution that prepared the souls of men for eternal life. So far as the Council of Trent modified medieval faith, it did so chiefly by establishing Thomism as the right arbiter. Post-Tridentine Catholicism was more Thomistic than that of the Middle Ages. The dogmatic structure erected by the Council was, however, open to changes and adjustments by the pope; he was given the exclusive right to expound the Council's decrees and thereby could make them relative in character to the needs of the Church. The modern Catholic Church thereafter did not have as firm a theological position as the pronouncements of the Council of Trent might indicate, since they were chiefly intended to express unalterable opposition to Protestantism. But in the polemics against the Protestants the Council also excluded the chief principles of humanism. The declaration that both "Scripture and tradition" were the common sources and authorities of

Christian truth was directed chiefly against Protestantism, but the proclamation of the apocrypha of the Old Testament as canonic writings and of the Latin Vulgate as authentic text also made the critical historical study of the Bible, as begun by the humanists, meaningless.

✍ The Society of Jesus

THE CHURCH WITHDREW in order to be able to attack again with its forces reorganized and united. In the new advance its chief leaders came from the new Society of Jesus, which Ignatius of Loyola (1491–1556) had founded with six companions on the Montmartre of Paris in 1534. In September, 1540, Pope Paul III officially constituted the Society as an order of the Church. At the time of the death of Ignatius the order had about one thousand members; in 1624, sixteen thousand. The real name of the society was *Compañia de Jesus*—*compañia* meaning a military troop. Ignatius had originally conceived of his order as consisting of fighting units to be employed by the Church wherever the need was greatest, but although neither the fighting spirit nor the objective or strengthening the primacy of the pope were lost, the Jesuit order found its main field of activity in missionary, pastoral, and educational work. This formed the broad foundation of its influence on the religious and political life of the coming age.

Ignatius was a true son of Spain, where the ideals of Christian chivalry and deep piety were still alive. These qualities reached a new stage in Ignatius. It has often been pointed out that Ignatius had a military mind. But the armies of his time knew only the medieval knight and the undisciplined mass soldier. The discipline that Ignatius conceived of, and that in the period after him was to change even armies, was the discipline of the officer who finds his honor in strict obedience to his superiors and who leads his soldiers through his example. Ignatius, though naturally adhering to many medieval ideals, such as the unity of the Church under its pontiff and the incessant struggle against the infidels, represented a new spirit, which characterized also his religious feelings. Mysticism was the life blood of his genuine religion, but was a very different form of mysticism from that of Germany and the Netherlands. The mortification of the flesh and of the ego was, of course, nothing new, and the imitation of Christ had already in older mysticism served to bring before the eyes of the mystic events that prepared him for the ultimate vision of God. This, however, was carried to much greater lengths in the *Spiritual Exercises* of Ignatius. The detailed and exact visual realization of Christ's passion was the means for the elevation of the individual beyond this world. But ecstatic experiences were directed to the real presence of the supernatural in the mass, and thereby to the Church.

But this side of Loyola's religious exercises was complemented by an equally detailed analysis of the individual's life and thinking. Ignatius demanded from his disciples what amounted to a psychological auto-biography. Self-examination, together with contemplation of the divine, was to lead to a spiritual rebirth, in which the individual mortified his own will and intellect and became capable of absolute obedience in the service of God. Through the *Spiritual Exercises,* an active human being was to be trained, a man aware of God's supreme power and of the passing nature of the world, which had been created by God for the single purpose of saving the souls of men. Indifference to all personal pleasures of life was, therefore, the proper attitude of Christians, but they were also required to mold the conditions of this world to the ends that God had set for His creation. Ignatius frowned on escape from the world, but expected the faithful to organize society according to God's plan, which had its embodiment in the Church. Asceticism appeared in a new form, its essential virtues being obedience and readiness for action. Ignatius recognized that in the mere performance of ascetic practices much of the strength that he wished to preserve for Christian action could be lost. He did not intend to crush the individual but wanted him to experience in his religious life the highest fulfillment of his personality. The capacity for self-abnegation was considered the highest self-perfection.

Active rather than contemplative perfection was the goal of Ignatius' mysticism, and the asceticism that he taught was designed to make man indifferent to the world, but at the same time its conqueror. This attitude showed certain parallels between Ignatius and Calvin. But although the two religious reformers were children of the same historical age, they differed completely in their concrete objectives and concepts. For Ignatius, the hierarchical Church represented the reality of the supranatural on earth, and the priest could demand absolute submission to the Church and destroy the recalcitrant disbeliever. The *Spiritual Exercises* were meant to serve as a manual for the guidance of souls, and they actually extended the role of the priest as the tutor of his charges to deeper layers of human life. In the regimentation of souls, however, Ignatius' belief in the presence of the supranatural in the physical world led to the widest use of sensual tokens, such as amulets or relics, for the

enticement of religious feelings; and the intermediary heavenly order
of the holy virgin, saints, and angels was brought into view with glowing colors. In general, Ignatius urged the use of all the arts for the symbolic presentation of the full range of religious realities. The religious
life of the people was thereby greatly stimulated, but undoubtedly also
circumscribed. Martin Luther, whose creative power of symbolic thinking was far superior to that of Ignatius, always remained conscious of
the word of the prophet: "Eye hath not seen, nor ear heard, neither have
entered into the heart of man, the things which God hath prepared for
them that love him."

Still, its capacity for the visual demonstration of the contents of religious faith explained much of the strong appeal that the Roman Catholic Church regained by the new spirit, which originated chiefly with
the Jesuits. The new Italian baroque style became its artistic expression.
Its first great model, the church *Il Gesù* in Rome, was erected by the
Jesuits in 1568. In Germany the first important baroque church, St. Mi-
chael's in Munich, was begun in 1583. The new baroque churches mirrored correctly the religious sentiment of reformed Catholicism. Their
rich façades and lavish use of color and other devices for captivating
the senses in the interior of the buildings seemed intended to embellish
and glorify this world. At the same time, however, through sculptures
and paintings as well as the treatment of the rooms themselves, which
appeared to overcome finiteness, the mind was directed toward a
higher dimension of reality. The roots of baroque art lay in the new
religious experiences, although its strong worldly elements made its
early and successful adaptation to secular artistic tasks possible.

In this influence of revived Catholicism in all fields of private and
public life one may find a great gain for Christian religion, but undoubtedly religion was identified by Ignatius and his pupils almost completely with the absolute authority of the Church represented by the
unchallengeable authority of the papacy. This passion for the enhancement of papal power soon made the Jesuits opportunistic politicians. At
the Council of Trent it was already noticeable that the two most active
Jesuit theologians, Diego Laynez and Alfonso Salmeròn, in contrast to
the two most influential Dominican divines, Melchior Cano and Domini-
cus a Soto, both masters of the new Spanish Thomism, were inclined
to settle dogmatic issues according to the political convenience of
Rome. The tendency of the Jesuits toward the political manipulation of
dogmatic questions increased as time went on and deprived the Church
of the loyalty of many thoughtful laymen, and in the end not even cen-

sorship and thought-control could halt their defection. A similar development took place in the pastoral activities of the Jesuit order. The desire to bring and hold everyone within the fold and to advance the influence of the Church on the secular rulers led to compromising practices in the guidance of Church members, which the Jesuits had originally taken up with force and talent. Casuistry, as adopted by the Jesuits, weakened the Christian character of confession and absolution and offended the most conscientious among Church members.

The genius of Ignatius showed most clearly in his ability to build a disciplined corps of Christian soldiers ready to carry out their mission with enthusiasm, prudence, and disregard of danger. The selection of members was made with greater care than in the older orders. After a two-year noviciate prospective members became "approved scholastics"; this required the taking only of simple vows. They could be dismissed from the order and absolved from their vows during the eight to fifteen years that they devoted to the study of arts and theology—they might teach during the last four years. After this stage they would be ordained as priests and become either spiritual coadjutors or professed fathers. As spiritual coadjutors they would serve the order as scholars and teachers or in other superior positions. Even the spiritual coadjutors could be relieved of their obedience to the order and dismissed from the order under certain conditions. Only the small and select group of the professed fathers took the indissoluble vows, which included absolute obedience to the pope. They lived in separate Jesuit houses, dedicated to a spiritual life as long as they did not serve the papacy in special assignments. The professed fathers were under the rules of the mendicant orders. This meant that, in contrast to the colleges and houses of probation, their houses could not acquire possessions, but the fathers received a generous living. No special habits were introduced; choir services and other monastic duties were held to a modest level. Dismissal from the order was the only sanction employed in discipline. Ignatius believed that penalties could not produce a genuine will, which alone could sustain good actions.

For the manual and purely administrative work in the Jesuit houses "secular coadjutors" were employed in order to set all highly trained members free for the missionary, educational, and political activities of the Society. The Jesuits entered into these activities not as individuals but as representatives of the order. They were not allowed to accept Church offices and benefices or personal honors. Their lives were absorbed in the advancement of the supreme objectives of the order. The centralization of government which had already characterized the mendicant and knights' orders was carried by the Society to an absolute limit. The national provinces were practically insignificant administrative subdivisions, while the general chapter elected the general of the Jesuit order but had no real supervisory powers. In a way the Jesuit order foreshadowed the coming of the absolute monarchy in Europe.

✍ *The Catholic Revival*

THE REVIVAL OF THE RELIGIOUS FORCES of Catholicism after the middle of the sixteenth century had its origin in Spain and Italy. With the reorientation of the papacy, the program that the Council of Trent had devised, and the new militant servants, a new spirit slowly reawakened life in the universal Church, particularly in Germany. Nowhere had the Catholic religion fallen as low as in Germany, and had it not received foreign support, it would have vanished from the country. Even with foreign support only a small part of Germany was regained by the Catholic Church. Protestant German historians have often asserted that modern German Catholicism must be judged a foreign importation, the more so since the revival of the Catholic Church in Germany depended to a large extent on the use of political weapons. But the spread of Protestantism in its peculiarly German forms was not an exclusively religious event either. Without the ecclesiastical government of the princes, sectarian Protestantism would still have flowered, and more Catholics would probably have survived in the Protestant parts of Germany. Political power injected itself into all the religious decisions of the age. It is also untenable to label Catholicism as unGerman or less German than Protestantism. If we do so, what should we think of the German Middle Ages, which were preparatory not only to the history of modern Catholicism but also to that of Protestantism? If the latter soon ceased to have any universal connections, this was not from intention but rather as a result of external historical circumstances. No Lutheran of the sixteenth or seventeenth centuries fought Calvin because he was a Frenchman, nor did German Protestants who embraced Calvinism feel that in doing so they gave up their German character. Christian ideas were still considered common to all the people of the West. Therefore it was natural that German Catholics, who believed in the visible unity of the Church, would readily accept the assistance that came to them, after such a long wait, from the centers of their own Church.

Admittedly, the most active persons in the German Catholic Church of the second half of the sixteenth century were foreigners. Characteristically, the Germans of the period frequently called the Jesuits the "Spanish monks." But the new religious leaders could not have gained influence if they had not been invited and had not worked together with indigenous groups. Our knowledge of the state of Catholic piety in this period is rather incomplete. Much of popular religion was hidden behind anonymity and was often enough the expression of an unreflective and almost atavistic attitude. But centers of a conscious will for Catholic reform and mission did exist, and some of them, such as the Carthusian monastery in Cologne, showed great strength. The ideas of German and Netherlandish mysticism, to which Ignatius owed much, were the invigorating force in the religious activities of these German Carthusians. When they seized the first opportunity that offered itself to establish contacts with the Jesuits and drew them to Cologne, not only was practical co-operation established but also a deeper community of faith. How many such cells of unspoiled Catholic piety had survived in Germany by the middle of the century, we do not know. We can, however, observe that even where the Jesuits could count on some help and protection from native sources, their activities often bore little or no fruit among the people at large in the years before 1560. Their great success began only when their colleges had trained an entirely new generation of theologians and priests and their schools had turned out a new, disciplined type of layman. As these entered public life as princes, noblemen, officials, or soldiers, the Jesuits themselves extended their influence more directly into German politics.

The first Jesuits visited Germany shortly after the formal papal confirmation of the order in 1540. They were present at the theological conferences of Worms and Regensburg, but these early visits served chiefly for the study of German conditions. The first permanent settlements of Jesuits were founded at Cologne in 1544. This Rhenish city became their most important German center, although neither archbishops nor city authorities favored them. The opposition that they had to meet probably steeled their energies. In 1577 they were placed in charge of teaching at the arts faculty, and in the next year, at the theological faculty. The University of Vienna was opened to the Jesuits by Ferdinand I in 1551, the Bavarian Ingolstadt first from 1549 to 1552, and again in 1556. From these three places settlements spread to Prague (1556), Munich (1559), Mainz and Trier (1560), Innsbruck (1561), Braunsberg and Dillingen (1564), Speyer and Würzburg (1567). By their lives and actions the Jesuits demonstrated the strength of Christian asceticism. Luther had declared the monastic ideal unnatural and un-Christian, and the average German priest or monk seemed a telling proof of such a judgment. But the Jesuits, by their irreproachable personal conduct, refuted all such doubts and accusations. They were not rich worldly prelates or wayward clerics, and could be found where Christian charity struggled with human needs and misery. If the Protestants asserted that the Holy Scriptures were the only authority of faith and that it proved the falsity of most of the tenets or practices of the Roman Church, the Jesuits pointed to the division among the Protestants. The Scriptures were a source of true faith only if interpreted by the Church on the basis of the latter's unbroken tradition. Bishop Hosius, in his conversations with Emperor Maximilian II, went further by stating that the Nicene Creed did not say: *Credo in bibliam* but *Credo in unam sanctam ecclesiam.*

The unity of the Church over the ages and nations was still a tremendously powerful ideal, and, similarly, the ethics of good works had a great appeal. When at this time Flacius Illyricus went so far as to propose that good works were detrimental to salvation, he underrated the popular sentiment that any ideal is worth as much as the sacrifices people are ready to make for it. In general, the Jesuits in this period avoided as much as possible entering upon protracted controversial discussions with Protestants. They endeavored to restate the eternal truth and beauty of the promises of the Catholic faith, as well as the dire threats of hell likely to descend upon the disobedient.

The most representative and influential Jesuit of the first generation was Peter Canisius of Nijmegen (Peter de Hondt, 1521–97). First active among the Cologne Carthusians, this young Dutchman joined the Society of Jesus in 1543, and as a preacher, missionary, professor, and advisor he went from Cologne to Ingolstadt and Vienna. From 1556 to 1569 he was the director of the upper German province of the Jesuit order. There was little that was original or intellectually brilliant about him. His strength was chiefly in his character and his ability to bring the traditional faith to the people. In 1555 and thereafter he issued a number of catechisms of the Catholic religion, which, through their classic simplicity of thought and expression, could match Luther's practical writings. These *Canisi* went through hundreds of editions.

But in the early years the seeds seemed to fall largely among thistles, and not even the founding of schools in Rome seemed to improve matters. In 1552 Ignatius established in the Christian capital the Collegium Germanicum for the education of young Germans for service in the

Church in Germany. But the young Teutons sent there proved so ob-streperous that most of them had to be sent home in 1554. Only in 1573 did the Collegium, reorganized and amply endowed by Pope Greg-ory XIII, attain its full objectives. By that time the Catholic revival in Germany had also reached a strong momentum. After the conclusion of the Council of Trent the papacy adopted a consistent policy of pro-moting the acceptance and execution of the decrees of Trent. Standing nunciatures were created not only to urge the princes into action but also to advise bishops and clergy on reforms in the dioceses. Vienna and Munich—later, in 1584, also Cologne—became the permanent seats of Roman nuncios in Germany. It was a sign that the strengthening of the Catholic Church depended largely on the policies of the princely au-thorities. Bavaria took the lead in an active policy of Catholic restora-tion.

✎ *Bavaria's Active Policy of Catholic Restoration*

THROUGHOUT THE AGE of the Reformation, Bavaria had shown the great-est resistance to Lutheranism. But finally even the seemingly monolithic structure of this relatively compact German territory seemed to crack. Neighboring Württemberg and the Upper Palatinate, together with the Protestant cities and imperial countships, affected Bavaria, and un-der the conditions of the dualistic state the estates found in Protestant-ism the means for advancing their independence from the princely rulers. From 1550 on, Albert V reigned in Bavaria. He was a man given to elegant living and artistic interests. The foundations for the art col-lections of Munich were laid by him. His fast accumulating debts gave the territorial estates a lever for concessions in religious affairs. Albert made these concessions, though he kept all Protestant influences away from his court. But finally the religious issue provided the excuse for suppression of the opposition of the nobility. In 1563, he began an open fight against the Lutheran nobility, which he accused, with doubtful reasons, of conspiracy. At the same time he aimed at bringing under Bavarian rule some knights and counts who claimed independence within the Empire. With papal permission, communion in both forms was permitted for a while, but on ducal initiative this concession was soon withdrawn, and Protestants unwilling to submit were forced to leave the country. In these ecclesiastical measures the state took the leadership. In 1557 Albert V had entrusted the "religious council," a committee of his privy council composed of laymen, with the supervision of all religious affairs. In 1570 the agency was reorganized as the Spiritual Council, still under the predominant influence of secular councilors. It held annual visitations of all Bavarian churches and acted as the chief educational office.

In practice, the Spiritual Council was not very different from the consistories that administered ecclesiastical affairs in the Protestant territories. The general religious policies, however, were formulated by the Church and only their local execution was supervised by the state. Bavaria accepted the Trent decrees and in 1569 created a strict system of censorship. It proved difficult to reform the clergy, but the support given by the Jesuits and Capuchins slowly improved conditions. Although the dukes did not hesitate to demand from the Church considerable contributions to the state finances, the old Church retained its vast possessions in Bavaria. The protection extended to it was the means for the establishment of absolutistic rule in the country. The exclusion of the Protestant noblemen and town representatives from the diet broke the power of the estates. The debates became perfunctory. Soon the government called only a committee of the estates to have its financial requests approved. Thus Bavaria became the first German territory in which the dualistic division of government between prince and estates was resolved in favor of the absolutistic authority of the duke. This development explained the great position that Bavaria assumed in Germany at the turn of the sixteenth to the seventeenth century. Albert V continued spending money in great style, as did his bigoted successor William V (1579–97). Maximilian I, who became coregent in 1591 and reigned for sixty years, brought order into the Bavarian finances, and this made it possible for Bavaria to enter the Thirty Years' War with great strength. Under Maximilian, Bavaria became a state in which the orthodox faith was enforced in public and private life without reservations. The last Protestants were driven out, usually losing their possessions. Attendance at church as well as use of the sacraments and the confessional became obligatory, while thought and morals were strictly controlled. The length neither of girls' skirts nor of the leather pants of the boys were exempted from governmental regulation.

Under Albert V the new course of Bavarian affairs led to an active foreign policy. The most immediate objective was the absorption of small dominions, such as imperial countships or cities, within or in the neighborhood of Bavaria. The next step was to gain influence over the adjacent bishoprics. Augsburg, under its bishop, Cardinal Otto Truchsess von Waldburg (1543–73), was securely in the Church, but this was not true of the other bishoprics. In 1566, the elevation of twelve-year-old Prince Ernest to the see of Freising, and in 1579, of three-year-old Prince Philip to that of Regensburg, extended Bavarian power along with restoring religion. Passau, Eichstädt, and Salzburg were also permeated by the new spirit radiating from Munich, and in 1583 Bavarian policy reached far beyond its own region by intervening in the conflict that developed in Cologne.

CHAPTER 11

Prelude to War, 1582–1618

THE STRUGGLE OVER THE ARCHBISHOPRIC and electorate of Cologne became the turning point in the relationship between
Protestantism and Catholicism in Germany. A shift of political climate had already occurred with the accession of
Rudolf II to the imperial throne in 1576. This gifted son of Maximilian
II had received his education under Jesuit tutelage. For six years he
had been at the court of Philip II of Spain. Rudolf never wavered in
his devotion to the Catholic Church, but the weakness of his character
made his reign one of the least effective in the history of Austria as
well as of the Empire. He was not lacking in political acumen or in
the consciousness of the significance of his high office, but it was
almost impossible for him to reach decisions or to adhere to those he
made. His mind and personality deteriorated as the years went on.
Melancholy turned into deep suspicion of his entourage and distrust
of the world. His interests in science, which had induced him to draw
first Tycho Brahe (1546–1601) and then Johannes Kepler (1571–
1630) to his court in Prague, were largely a means of forgetting the
obstinacies of the world. Rudolf II amassed rich collections of curios
and art, which formed the beginnings of the modern Austrian galleries.
In spite of his piety, Rudolf's taste and personal conduct ran somewhat
toward the sensuous. After the turn of the century the morbidity of
his mind led to open fits of insanity. The emperor, who secluded
himself in the Hradschin castle in Prague and ultimately was surrounded by inferior creatures, was incapable of exercising the leadership that the Catholics expected, but Maximilian's attempts to maintain
the unity of Germany through the promotion of co-operation between the two religious parties came to an end under Rudolf.

✍ Difficulties Arising from the Peace of Augsburg

THE MAIN DIFFICULTIES ARISING from the Peace of Augsburg hinged on
the "ecclesiastical reservation" and the "declaration" of Ferdinand.[1]

[1] See pages 244–5.

Both stipulations, formally as well as materially, were open to many interpretations. The *reservatio ecclesiastica* stated specifically that any prince-bishop or abbot who turned Protestant would lose his princely dignity, which rested legally on his enfeoffment by the emperor. But Protestant princes after 1555 had argued that the "reservation" did not preclude the election of a Protestant to an episcopal see. In view of the strength of Protestantism the emperor had acquiesced in this interpretation, by granting so-called feudal indults to enfeoffed Protestants elected in the bishoprics east of the Weser. It remained doubtful, however, whether these "administrators" could claim to be princes of the Empire and demand a vote at the diet. The extent to which the territorial estates of the ecclesiastical principalities should enjoy freedom of religion raised many similar controversies.

The Protestant princes had failed to bring about a binding legal settlement of these issues in the two decades after 1555, when their own position had been strongest.[2] Elector August of Saxony was chiefly responsible for this omission. The last opportunity for a revision of the Peace of Augsburg was afforded by the negotiations over the succession of Maximilian II. If the three secular electors, as the Count Palatine proposed, had demanded political concessions as the price for voting for the Habsburg heir, they would presumably have gained their points. At the first diet of the Empire under Rudolf II, in 1582, the Turkish problem still provided a lever, but the political atmosphere had already changed very noticeably. This Diet of Augsburg showed the secular and ecclesiastical Catholic princes in a bellicose mood; and that the diet did not collapse was due to the timid policy of the Protestant princes.

The problem of ecclesiastical principalities was debated in connection with the demand of Prince Joachim Frederick of Brandenburg, administrator of the archbishopric of Magdeburg, that he be permitted to take his seat at the diet. He had been elected in 1566 by a Lutheran chapter. When it had become apparent that he might before long inherit the electoral throne of Brandenburg, he had married, with the approval of the Magdeburg estates. But Emperor Maximilian had procrastinated about granting the indult, and his son Rudolf refused to give indults. The appearance of Joachim Frederick in Augsburg was met with the threat of the Catholic princes to shun all meetings. Elector August of Saxony was afraid of a real test of strength, and Joachim Frederick was left without support and had to withdraw. The attempt of the Protestants to have their gains in the ecclesiastical realm recognized in the

[2] See page 266.

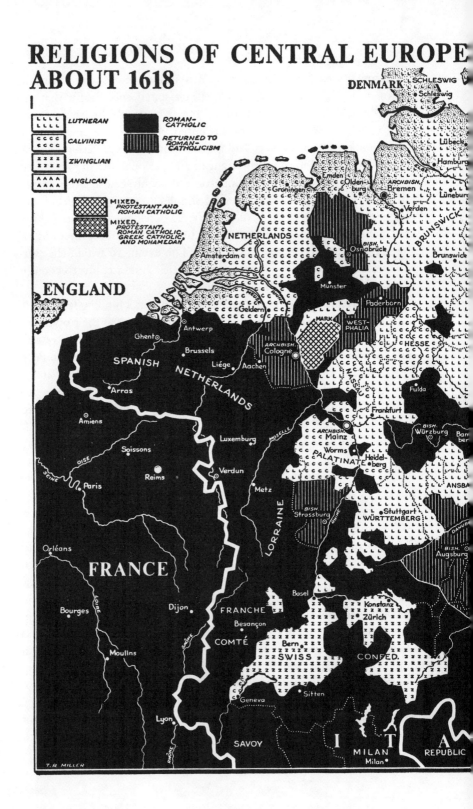

RELIGIONS OF CENTRAL EUROPE ABOUT 1618

Legend:
- LUTHERAN
- CALVINIST
- ZWINGLIAN
- ANGLICAN
- ROMAN-CATHOLIC
- RETURNED TO ROMAN-CATHOLICISM
- MIXED, PROTESTANT AND ROMAN CATHOLIC
- MIXED, PROTESTANT, ROMAN CATHOLIC, GREEK CATHOLIC, AND MOHAMEDAN

DENMARK
SCHLESWIG
Schleswig
Lübeck
Hamburg
Emden
Olden-burg
ARCHBISH. Bremen
Lüneburg
Groningen
Verden
BRUNSWICK
NETHERLANDS
BISH. Osnabrück
Brunswick
Amsterdam
Münster
Paderborn
Geldern
WEST-PHALIA
HESSE
ENGLAND
MARK
Ghent
Antwerp
ARCHBISH. Cologne
Brussels
NASSAU
SPANISH
Liége
Aachen
Fulda
NETHERLANDS
Arras
Frankfurt
BISH. Würzburg
Bam-berg
Amiens
ARCHBISH. Mainz
Luxemburg
Worms
PALATINATE
Heidel-berg
Soissons
Verdun
Reims
Paris
Metz
ANSBA
LORRAINE
BISH. Strassburg
Stuttgart
WÜRTTEMBERG
Orléans
BISH. Augsburg
FRANCE
Basel
DANUBE
Konstanz
Bourges
Dijon
FRANCHE
Zürich
Besançon
COMTÉ
Bern
SWISS
CONFED.
Moulins
Geneva
Sitten
Lyon
SAVOY
I   T   A
MILAN
REPUBLIC
Milan

T. R. MILLER

councils of the Empire was thereby defeated, and all future attempts failed, too. At the same time the college of princes in the diet of the Empire retained its preponderantly Catholic majority.

Another issue proved even more explosive but was also left undecided. The Peace of Augsburg had stated that in imperial cities that were religiously divided both Churches were to continue. But this referred to the situation as it existed at the time of the Peace. No provision was made for such a situation developing after 1555, nor was it clear whether the cities, like the princes, had the right of reformation and if they did, whether this right was vested in the city council. The most serious conflict arose in the corner of the Empire which bordered on the political storm center of Europe in this period, the Spanish and Protestant Netherlands. Largely through the immigration of Protestant refugees from the Netherlands, Aachen had become a religiously divided city. The emperor had attempted to exclude Protestants from all city offices in 1581, while Spanish troops invaded the Aachen territory. At the diet the city received the support of all the imperial cities, and these refused to grant any contribution to the Turkish war unless their right of reformation was officially recognized. The final recess of the Diet of 1582 was passed without the consent of the city bench, a significant breakdown of the legislative machinery of the Empire. The problems of Aachen itself were turned over to a committee of mediation, and dragged on for many years.

✍ *The Defeat of Protestantism in Cologne*

SHORTLY AFTER THE CLOSE OF THE DIET a new and decisive conflict broke out over the archbishopric of Cologne. For a long time its archbishops, though nominally adhering to the Catholic Church, had shown little interest in the ecclesiastical duties of their office. In the fashion of the high German nobility they treated their positions as princely sinecures. Often enough they refused ordination and exercised their authority as archbishops-elect. Count Salentin von Isenburg was merely the last in a series of unordained archbishop-electors. In 1577 he decided to retire from Cologne, to become again an imperial count, and to get married. His successor, Gebhard Truchsess von Waldburg, the nephew of a cardinal, agreed to be ordained and in general seemed more inclined to devote himself to the government of the diocese. But he was not priestly in character either, and a love affair led him to follow the example of his predecessor and marry his mistress. However, he was persuaded by the Protestant members of the Cologne chapter and by one of the counts of Nassau, who represented a link with the Netherlands, to retain his position as archbishop and become a Protestant. At Christmas, 1582, Archbishop Gebhard announced publicly his change of religion and a little later he granted freedom to the practice of Protestant worship.

The majority of the chapter turned against Gebhard. The pope declared him deposed and gave a dispensation, which made possible the election of Ernest of Bavaria. This prince was already bishop of Freising, Hildesheim, and Liége, and later became also bishop of Münster. He was a profligate person, whom the papal nuncio called a "great sinner," but the political aim of committing the power of Catholic Bavaria to the defense of the lower Rhine in co-operation with Spain's fight for the Netherlands was more important than the personality of the new archbishop. Whereas his brother, William of Bavaria, was willing to give him every help in establishing himself in Cologne, Elector Ludwig of the Palatinate did not succeed in persuading the electors of Saxony and Brandenburg to defend with him the electoral rights of Gebhard. "One had to leave it to God the Almighty how he wished to preserve his wholesome Word against the onslaught of the Pope and the devil," said the Lutheran August of Saxony. Little money was forthcoming, and Count Palatine John Casimir, who assumed command of the troops fighting for Gebhard, saw his forces dwindle fast. The death of his brother, Elector Ludwig VI, in October, 1583, gave him the chance to withdraw from the campaign and go to Heidelberg.

Gebhard's cause was quickly lost and he himself forced to take refuge in the Netherlands. In January, 1585, the electors formally accepted Ernest as his successor in the electoral college. Far into the eighteenth century, Cologne remained in the hands of the Bavarian Wittelsbach family. At the time, however, it was more important that all attempts of German Protestants to add the prince bishoprics that had survived after 1555 to their domains and to break the deadlock in the Empire had failed. The unhappy lands along the lower Rhine experienced the devastating fury of war. Cologne's position as a great commercial center had already been gravely lessened by revolution and wars in the Netherlands, which had cut it off from the sea. The invasions of foreign troops crippled its strength at the source.

✂ *General Advance of Roman Catholicism After 1586*

THE DEFEAT OF PROTESTANTISM in Cologne became the signal for a general advance of Roman Catholicism in Germany. The Westphalian bishoprics—Münster, Paderborn and Osnabrück—felt the revived Catholic power most immediately and were safely brought back into the fold during the next generation. But the successful counter reformation in the northwest and in the Bavarian southeast affected the center of Germany as well. A strong beginning had already been made before the Cologne feud in the territories of the imperial abbot of Fulda. There, in the venerable foundation of St. Boniface in the heart of the Empire, the young abbot Balthasar von Dernbach (1570–1606), a convert from Protestantism, reintroduced the Catholic faith in the years after 1570. His complete disregard of the rights of the estates, which were predominantly Protestant and claimed the protection of the "declaration" of Emperor Ferdinand, led to a bitter struggle with the indigenous nobility, who forced Balthasar to resign in 1576. But the emperor had the territory taken over by his own commissaries, and they continued the abbot's work. Although a majority of the noble families and a few villages maintained their Protestant allegiance, the territory as a whole was restored, with the help of the Jesuits, to ecclesiastical government and orthodox religion. After twenty-five years of litigation Abbot Balthasar was restored to his office, and brought his efforts to final fruition.

The bishop of Würzburg, Julius Echter von Mespelbrunn (1573–1619), as young as his neighbor at Fulda and himself a canon of Fulda, had joined forces with the Protestant estates of Fulda in the hope of joining the abbey to his bishopric. But the weakness of the Protestants, as shown in Fulda and in the Empire in general, together with a serious conception of his episcopal office, turned him into the most outstanding princely representative of the Counter Reformation in Germany. Hundreds of Protestant preachers were driven out of the bishopric, many dozens of village churches were built or restored to Catholic worship, and the capital of Würzburg was made into a show place of renewed religion. In 1582 the Jesuit college became a full university. Bishop Julius was ruthless in imposing uniformity of faith but at the same time he was an unusually effective secular administrator of his territories. After the expulsion of many Protestants, Würzburg, beautified by Bishop Julius' interest in artistic display, became the model of a reformed spiritual principality. Bamberg, which adjoined it, followed the same course more slowly, though in the end with equal thoroughness.

During this whole period the religious state of the Habsburg territories remained in doubt. Emperor Ferdinand I had divided his realms. Maximilian II had received Austria, Bohemia, and Hungary; Archduke Ferdinand (1564–95), who had married the beautiful Philipine Welser of Augsburg, inherited Tyrol and Anterior Austria; and Archduke Charles (1564–90) had received so-called Inner Austria, i.e., Styria, Carinthia, Carniola, and Goricia. In Tyrol, where Anabaptism had been uprooted by 1530, the old Church was maintained without great difficulty, but in Inner Austria, Archduke Charles had to make far-reaching concessions in order to gain the co-operation of the estates for the payment of tributes to the Turks. In the "pacifications" of Graz (1572) and Bruck (1578) the nobility received freedom of Lutheran worship and education, in which the towns were allowed to participate. But Archduke Charles endeavored to strengthen the Catholic Church to the best of his ability. No Protestants were tolerated at the court or as archducal officials, and after 1582 the townspeople and peasants were deprived, step by step, of the benefits of the pacification of Bruck. In 1586 a university was founded in Graz and placed under the direction of the Jesuit order. Ferdinand, son of Charles, after coming of age in 1595, continued the extermination of Protestantism with even more determination. Lutheran churches and cemeteries were destroyed; schools maintained by the Protestant nobility were closed; and Protestants in the towns were made to accept the Catholic faith under duress or deprived of their rights as citizens. The emigration from Inner Austria between 1598 and 1605 was reported to have reached as high as 10,000. But large numbers of Lutherans held out during the first half of the seventeenth century. As long as the nobility retained freedom of conscience, Protestantism could not be fully uprooted.

In Upper and Lower Austria the concessions of Emperor Maximilian II in 1568 and 1571 gave the Lutheran nobility practical freedom of religion. The legal situation of the townspeople was not clearly defined, but the nobility let them participate in Protestant services held not only on their landed estates but also in their city residences. The "land house" in Vienna, i.e., the house of the Austrian estates, served as a center of worship for all Protestants, and schools financed by the estates in the cities were turned into theological schools. But with the accession of Rudolf II the government began to interpret the law strictly. In Vienna, Protestant worship was forbidden, and between 1578 and 1580 Protestant preachers were expelled. This still left Protestant burghers the opportunity of going to the suburbs and to attend services on the noble estates, but eventually such traffic was placed under penalties. Melchior Khlesl, a converted burgher's son from Vienna, led the movement of Catholic reform after 1579. In 1598 he became Bishop of Vienna. In 1595 a revolt of serious proportions broke out among the Austrian peasants, caused by economic suffering and the expulsion of Protestant preachers. The noblemen sided with the government in the suppression of these revolts, only to find themselves thereafter more isolated in their resistance against new religious impositions of the government. At the diets the estate of the prelates was closely allied with the government, and, with the towns intimidated, the nobility was in a weak position.

In Bohemia the Roman Catholic Church had shrunk to a small minority, and Lutheranism had found it easy to spread within the Hussite Church, called the "Utraquist" Church, since it was granted communion in both forms. But some of the traditionalist elements of utraquism moved closer to the Roman Catholic Church, which at Trent had declared utraquism permissible under certain conditions. Thus a concentration of Catholic forces became noticeable and was further developed by the Jesuits. But to the end of the century, all actions of religious persecution by Catholic noblemen were directed against the Bohemian Brethren, and in 1602 Emperor Rudolf renewed the edict of King Vladislav of 1508, which had recognized only the Utraquist and Roman Catholic Churches and had banned the Bohemian Brethren. A general suppression of Protestantism by the government seemed imminent. In Moravia, where both the Protestants and Brethren were outwardly less powerful than in Bohemia, the nobility had practiced great toleration just the same. Even Anabaptists found refuge there. But conditions began to change during the last two decades of the century. Only in Silesia and Lusatia did the counter reformation fail to make any progress. The independent principalities had Protestant dukes, and Protestantism was strong also in the ecclesiastical territory of the bishop of Breslau, where it proved unshakable for the present. Only Bohemian borderlands, such as Glatz and Troppau, fell victims to the Catholic revival. The attempts of the Habsburgs to preserve or renew the Catholic Church in Lusatia, the northernmost land of the Bohemian crown, failed altogether.

Except for Bohemia, Silesia, and Lusatia, the lands of the Habsburgs were slowly brought back to the old Church. Particularly in the years around the turn of the century, the tide seemed irresistible. But Emperor Rudolf's illness gave the Protestant estates a new chance to press for recognition of their rights. Rudolf's brother, Archduke Matthias, won over the estates of Austria, Moravia, and Hungary for the support of Rudolf's resignation in his favor, while the Bohemian estates backed Rudolf, who wished to retain his throne. A war between the brothers was avoided by a compromise in June, 1608, which gave Matthias Hungary, Moravia, and Austria, leaving the royal Wenceslas crown of Bohemia in Rudolf's possession. But in all the Habsburg dominions the territorial estates extracted very considerable rights, particularly in the religious sphere. In March, 1609, Archduke Ferdinand had to grant the estates of Upper and Lower Austria free practice of religion in town and country and admit Protestants to governmental positions. Of even greater consequence was the Letter of Majesty of July 9, 1609, through which Rudolf gave all Bohemians, including burghers and peasants, protection against a forceful imposition of religion. Moreover, the members of the estates received full power over their own churches and the right of ecclesiastical organization under the general supervision of the diet. The Silesian estates, a month later, won a Letter of Majesty which in certain respects went even further.

✍ *Trend Toward Open Hostility*

THE RELIGIOUS STRUGGLE was inseparably linked with the conflict between prince and nobility. The Protestant estates of the Habsburg territories had seemingly gained a powerful position. The division of the lands among the various lines of the dynasty, the illness of Emperor Rudolf, the feud between Matthias and Rudolf, together with the unabated threat from the Turks, all contributed to the rise of the Protestant nobility. But the Austrian Protestants knew that since the days of Maximilian II every Habsburg prince had his mind set on the restoration of the old Church. They knew, too, that even in their own ranks the Catholic minority had grown, and if they searched their conscience, their own Lutheran faith could not give them moral justification for carrying their opposition against legitimate authority too far. Some of them embraced Calvinism, among them Georg Erasmus von Tschernembl, the leader of the Austrian nobility in these years. But while some could put aside personal scruples regarding the duty of passive obedience as taught by Lutheranism, many of their fellow noblemen were unwilling to do so.

As long as the internal situation of the Austrian territories remained unsettled, Habsburg policy vis-à-vis the Empire was handicapped. Without the strength of Bavaria, the forces of the Catholic Reformation could not have continued their political progress. The relationship with Spain, the greatest European power of this age, even after the failure of the conquest of England, increased Austrian prestige and also paid immediate dividends, as in the repeated interventions of Spanish troops in the Rhineland. But Austrian policy, rather than leading, was largely led by events. This, however, appeared to be in keeping with the general character of the period: no one was able to rise above his party or change the trend toward ever-increasing hostility and open clashes. In all groups there was a feeling that beyond the conflicts of religion and politics a bond of unity existed among Germans. A general civil war in Germany was dreaded by all. It is only by assuming the existence of German patriotism that the policy of Saxony in these years can be fully understood. In his later years Cardinal Khlesl was affected by patriotic sentiments, and such sentiments reasserted themselves, as will be seen later, in the middle of the Thirty Years' War. Yet this German patriotism was too vague and impotent to stave off the virtual collapse of the few remaining common institutions of the nation.

The "ecclesiastical reservation" of the Religious Peace of Augsburg and the provisions for the status of the churches in the free cities were the red thread that ran through most of the fights and squabbles that poisoned the relationship between the religious parties and tended to make any settlement by adjudication or arbitration impossible. Brute force determined the course of events, and such force came to be provided increasingly by foreign powers. After the Cologne war, and with the formal recognition of the rule of Joachim Frederick of Brandenburg in Magdeburg still in abeyance, the struggle over the prince-bishoprics shifted to the upper Rhine. In Strasbourg, the zealous bishop had excluded the evangelical members of the chapter in 1583, but after his death, nine years later, the evangelical groups boldly elected young John George of Brandenburg bishop, whereas the Catholic chapter chose Prince Charles of Lorraine. The Protestants succeeded in occupying the strong places. They had the support of the city and of Henry of Navarre. Bishop Charles could rely on neighboring Lorraine and was seeking the help of the French League. But Henry's adoption of Catholicism, in July, 1593, changed his active interest in the Strasbourg case and thwarted the extension of the French civil war into Germany and its coalescense with the growing feud of the German parties. A compromise was arranged that temporarily divided the bishopric. But by 1604 the Protestants had to give up their position at the upper Rhine.

ↄ Collapse of the Cameral Tribunal and the Diet of the
Empire

A SIMILAR DEFEAT was inflicted upon them in Aachen. In 1598, when
Spanish troops from the Netherlands were swarming into the Rhineland, Emperor Rudolf deposed the Protestant mayor and councilors of
the city. Catholicism was restored and the Protestants were forced to
leave Aachen. This established an important precedent whereby cities
were forbidden to turn Protestant. The execution against Aachen was
based on a judgment issued by the Imperial Aulic Council (*Reichshofrat*), the emperor's high court in Vienna. This legal procedure by itself
was an attempt to extend the power of the emperor, since the matter
belonged undoubtedly under the jurisdiction of the Cameral Tribunal
of the Empire. But the Cameral Tribunal had lost all authority in such
controversial cases. Judgments of the Tribunal could be appealed and
then came before a committee of visiting princes. In stated order the
German princes took part in this committee. When, however, in 1588
it was Magdeburg's turn to serve, the seating of Joachim Frederick,
administrator of the archbishopric, was protested, and the committee of
visitors became defunct. In 1598 the diet of the Empire appointed a dep-
utation of princes in its place, but when the majority was about to pass
sentences detrimental to the Protestant cause, a number of Protestant
princes sabotaged its operations by their withdrawal. A highly controversial matter was at stake in this so-called case of the four monasteries,
namely, the right of Protestant princes to secularize monasteries that
had not been secularized by 1552, the time of the Treaty of Passau.
Since the Protestants had proceeded to dissolve monasteries and appropriate Church goods in their territories without regard to the Passau
Treaty, an adverse judgment would have placed them in great jeopardy.

The Cameral Tribunal of the Empire thus lost its effectiveness
through the withdrawal of the Protestant princes. But even worse, the
existence of the diet of the Empire was imperiled. In the little imperial
city of Donauwörth, where a Catholic monastery had survived the Protestant reformation of the city, fracasses broke out between monks and
burghers. Without much delay, the emperor placed the city under the
imperial ban and entrusted the duke of Bavaria with its execution. Duke
Maximilian subdued the city, demanding at the same time an extrava-
gantly high indemnity which allowed him to remain in possession of
Donauwörth. With the help of the Jesuits, the city was soon brought
back to the Catholic Church.

The Protestant estates were outraged by this aggressive act on the part of the emperor and duke. At the diet of the Empire which convened in Regensburg, in February, 1608, under the immediate impression of the violation of the Religious Peace of Augsburg, they demanded a reaffirmation of the law of 1555 before they would discuss any other business matters—the representatives of the emperor had, as usual, placed the question of assistance against the Turks among the first to be discussed. But the Catholics countered this demand by insisting upon the restitution of ecclesiastical properties secularized after 1552, since in their opinion a simple restatement of the Religious Peace would merely have given the Protestants a potent legal weapon. They offered instead postponement of all debate and decision till a future diet. The Saxon elector, following the traditional conciliatory line of his house, was willing to accept some such compromise. But the representatives of the Palatinate, joined by Brandenburg and the majority of the Protestant estates, were not willing to do so and left Regensburg in protest. As a result the Saxons ceased to be willing to co-operate with the Catholics in actual legislation, and the Catholics were hesitant to set themselves up as a Catholic rump diet. Accordingly, the diet of 1608 dispersed without granting taxes for the Turkish war or declaring a regular recess. The chief organ of the Empire had collapsed.

✍ Formation of the Union and of the League

MOREOVER, the parties now began to organize and arm. A beginning was made by the Palatinate, whose policy in these years was directed not so much by its ruler, Elector Frederick IV, as by Christian I of Anhalt, prince of one of the small north German territories, who served the elector in various capacities. At a conference at Anhausen in Ansbach during May, 1609, a "Union" was formed by the elector of the Palatinate, the duke of Württemberg, the duke of Neuburg, the margraves of Baden and Ansbach, the prince of Anhalt, and the cities of Strasbourg, Ulm, and Nürnberg. Within the next few years the elector of Brandenburg, the landgrave of Hesse-Cassel, and a number of south German cities became members of the Union, and it elected Frederick IV as its director and Christian of Anhalt as its lieutenant-general. The members of the Union agreed to relatively high financial contributions. But the membership was small; Saxony and the whole northwest kept aloof. The ugly rift between the Lutherans and Calvinists weakened the Union from the beginning. The Lutherans were not prepared to recognize the claims of the Calvinists for equal protection of their faith, which the Peace of Augsburg had not granted. The religious aim of the Union was, therefore, not even stated. Its members called themselves the "peace-loving estates." Its exclusively defensive purpose was exaggerated, because the cities were suspicious that some of the princes might draw the Union into European power politics, and it opposed any ties with foreign powers. Consequently, the relations between the Union and the Netherlands or France remained superficial. The actual strength of the Union and its ability to conduct an active policy were limited, and when Neuburg, in 1615, and Brandenburg, in 1617, seceded, its weakness was fully demonstrated.

The Catholic estates had discussed associations for many years. But only in the summer of 1609, in conferences in Munich, was a Catholic "League" constituted. It included Bavaria; the prince-bishops of Bavaria, Franconia, and Swabia; and the three Rhenish archbishop-electors. Duke Maximilian of Bavaria was chosen as its political and military director. The League frankly stated as its objective the protection of Catholicism and announced its opposition to the secularization of ecclesiastical dominions and property in contravention of the Passau Treaty of 1552. Nor did Maximilian hesitate to enter into intimate political negotiations with Spain. However, the League was not a strong political grouping. Rulers of the ecclesiastical principalities had no military power and dreaded warlike complications. Among them were princes who hoped that conflict with the Protestants could be avoided, even if considerable concessions were required. In addition, the Rhineland had to cope with political problems quite different from those of southern Germany. The conflict of interests raised criticism of Bavarian leadership. As a consequence, the League proved to be a rather ineffective alliance. Duke Maximilian decided, in 1617, to reorganize the League by confining it to southern Germany.

Conflict over the Succession in Jülich-Cleves

THE FORMATION OF THE UNION and League in the wake of the collapse of the diet showed that mutual distrust had reached a new stage. Minor incidents could easily set fire to the tinderbox, as occurred after the death of the last ruler of Jülich-Cleves—or, more precisely, of that agglomeration of territories in the lower Rhineland which consisted of Jülich, Cleves, Berg, Mark, and Ravensberg. This dynastic state was potentially the strongest political power in the northwest of the Empire, but the incapacity of the mentally deranged Duke William made it the battleground of the political and religious forces of the age. The emperor backed the Catholic councilors against the estates of Cleves and Mark, which remonstrated against their pro-Catholic church policies. These estates had the support of the Baden princess Jacobe, wife of John William, the son and successor of the duke. The estates of Jülich and Berg, however, championed the Catholic cause. The confusion increased when, in 1590, John William became mentally deranged. He succeeded his father in 1592, and five years later Jacobe died childless, probably the victim of a murder plot on the part of the councilors. John William was induced to marry Antoine of Lorraine, and for the next few years she and the Catholic councilors ruled the territories. When Duke John William died in March, 1609, without leaving an heir, formidable problems were raised concerning the future government of his lands.

The legal issues involved in the succession were sufficiently intricate to allow clever lawyers and politicians to fight over them indefinitely. The Brandenburg elector, John Sigismund, had the best claim, but Wolfgang William of Neuburg also had a case, whereas the Saxon elector, Christian II, could raise only dubious demands. But politics played an important part from the beginning. To the emperor, indeed to all Catholics, it seemed dangerous to have these principalities pass into the possession of Protestant princes, as this would place in jeopardy all the gains made in the struggle for Cologne and the Westphalian bishoprics. As the succession was so controversial, the emperor was tempted to sequestrate the territories of Jülich-Cleves in the hope of eventually granting them to a Catholic ruler.

In view of the threat to the peace of the Empire arising from the presence of a number of pretenders, the emperor at first attempted to use his right to administer the Rhenish territories himself. He left Antoine of Lorraine as regent and appointed imperial commissars. But before these arrived at the lower Rhine, both John Sigismund and Wolfgang William had formally taken possession of the territories. The Neuburg prince had come in person, and though he had few soldiers, he had more money than was at the disposal of the Brandenburg representatives. Elector John Sigismund did not appear on the Rhine, as he was preoccupied with gaining the recognition of his succession in Prussia. His brother, Margrave Ernest, led the case of Brandenburg. It was clear that neither of the contenders could by himself win the estates over to his side against the emperor's announced policy. With Landgrave Maurice of Hesse-Cassel acting as mediator, the Brandenburg and Neuburg princes, in June, 1609, signed the Treaty of Dortmund, whereby they agreed to hold all the territories in common possession until their conflicting claims would be settled by friendly negotiation or by arbitration through a committee of Protestant princes.

The emperor then sent Archduke Leopold, bishop of Passau and Strasbourg, as imperial administrator. He occupied the fortress town of Jülich with small forces, at the same time mobilizing troops in Strasbourg. But Leopold could not hope to dislodge the so-called "possessor princes" without the help of greater powers. The "possessor princes," for their part, hesitated to attack the emperor's deputy without the backing of strong allies. In 1609 a twelve-year armistice had been concluded between Spain and the Netherlands. Both in Brussels and Madrid the governments were disinclined to make a move that might rekindle the flames of a European war, and the archduke received only limited financial support. But the Union slowly decided to give some assistance to the "possessor princes." Its means, however, were highly inadequate. The elector of the Palatinate, the margrave of Baden, and the duke of Württemberg mobilized troops to counter the assembling of soldiers in the bishopric of Strasbourg, and in March, 1610, they invaded Strasbourg. This led to the organization of a League army under Count Tilly.

Foreign Intervention in the Jülich-Cleves Dispute

THE UNION DID NOT FEEL STRONG ENOUGH to intervene in Jülich without the co-operation of France, so Henry IV was approached through Prince Christian of Anhalt. The French king had never been reconciled to Jülich's being in Habsburg hands. But during the year 1609 his plans took on ever greater dimensions. In alliance with Savoy and other Italian states, France made plans to launch war against Spanish Milan, while at the same time the Spanish bastion on the Maas was to be attacked in alliance with the Netherlands and the Union. But Henry's death at the hands of a Catholic fanatic ended these designs, which undoubtedly would have led to a general European war. Under the vacillating regency of Henry's widow, Marie de Médicis, French policy changed its course, going so far as to seek a full compromise with Spain.

But even the new French government was not prepared to leave Jülich to the emperor. In August, 1610, an Anglo-Dutch army under the command of Prince Maurice of Orange, Union troops, and a French force converged on Jülich, from which Archduke Leopold had fled. One month later the fortress surrendered. All of the territories of Jülich-Cleves came under the administration of the "possessor princes." The attempt of the emperor to cause conflict in the Protestant camp by recognizing the claims of the Saxon elector to Jülich-Cleves was of no avail. For a moment it seemed as if the Protestants had gained a great victory, which, even after the withdrawal of the foreign troops, no one seriously dared contest. The Catholic League mobilized an army, but Duke Maximilian of Bavaria was too prudent to court renewed foreign intervention by putting up a fight for Jülich. He wished only to see the bishopric of Strasbourg liberated from the troops of the Union which had invaded Alsace. But neither the League nor the Union were in a mood to fight. In October, 1610, an agreement was reached. The troops were withdrawn and both coalitions disarmed.

The danger of a general war appeared to be over, and it even seemed that Germany was a step closer to internal peace. However, as the years before had shown, the German princes were no longer masters of war or of peace. Foreign intervention had settled the Jülich issue in 1610 through arms, and foreign diplomacy maintained the peace in the years when the "possessor princes" began to quarrel among themselves. The condominium gave neither prince a real control over the Jülich-Cleves territories. The actual administration rested in the hands of the indigenous councilors who represented the estates, and who argued that the princes, as long as they had not become the final rulers, could not assume full powers. In the relations of princes with councilors and estates the religious problem gained crucial significance. Both princes had assured the estates, in the Treaty of Dortmund, of freedom of religion not only for Catholics and Lutherans but also for Calvinists. Friction soon developed between the two princes, as Wolfgang William was a strict Lutheran, while Elector John Sigismund and his brother Margrave Ernest began to look with favor upon the expansion of Calvinism in the Rhenish territories. Margrave Ernest, who represented Brandenburg till 1612, openly joined the Reformed faith in 1610, as did George William, his successor in Jülich, the heir to the electoral dignity. While collisions became more frequent, the two "possessor princes" jockeyed for position. John Sigismund for a time tried to come to an understanding with the elector of Saxony; this drove Wolfgang William to explore the possibilities of winning the support of Duke Maximilian of Bavaria, leader of the Catholic party in the Empire. The latter was successful not only in persuading Wolfgang William of the usefulness of League support in this world but also of that of the Catholic religion in the world hereafter. Wolfgang William became a Catholic, secretly in July, 1613, then openly in May, 1614, and married the sister of Maximilian of Bavaria.

Developments in Brandenburg came to a head at this same time. John Sigismund had already been deeply impressed by Calvinism when as a young prince he had visited at the court of Heidelberg. The Lutheran complexion of the Brandenburg estates and even more of Prussia, which he was to inherit shortly, kept him for a time from announcing his preference. Moreover, his wife Anna, daughter of the last duke of Prussia and granddaughter of the last ruler of Jülich-Cleves, was a staunch Lutheran, and since she held the actual hereditary claims to both of these lands, her attitude could not be disregarded. But at Christmas, 1613, John Sigismund professed his Calvinist faith. The expression of his personal convictions had direct political implications. The cooperation with the Netherlands, so necessary in the Rhineland, was thereby further facilitated. On the other hand, John Sigismund's relations with the Brandenburg, and even more with the Prussian, estates were aggravated. He gave the assurance that he would not use his *jus reformandi*—that is, impose his personal faith upon his territories. Thus he was the first prince to forego the principle of *cuius regio, eius religio*. It was a step toward limited religious toleration in that the prince placed himself outside the special forms of religious practice without, however, giving up the control of ecclesiastical life.

The conflict between the two "possessor princes" in Jülich-Cleves soon led to open strife, for which neither had the means. The war was fought for them by foreign powers. Under the command of Marquis Spinola, a Spanish army marched to the lower Rhine, conquering Wesel, the strongest fortress of Cleves. Quickly a strong army under Maurice of Orange approached to meet the challenge. But neither Spain nor the Netherlands were prepared to give up the dearly bought armistice of 1609. With the assistance of England, France, and the Union, negotiations were conducted in Xanten, and resulted in what amounted to a division of the territories. According to the provision of the Treaty of Xanten of November 12, 1614, Wolfgang William received Jülich and Berg; John Sigismund, Cleves, Mark, and Ravensberg. In theory, they were still to be considered common rulers of all the territories, but separate administrations led necessarily to the division of the old lands.

Thus a European conflagration was avoided by the Treaty of Xanten, just as a fratricidal war in Germany had been averted by the disarmament of the Union and the League four years earlier. The two hostile German coalitions were actually losing strength during this whole period. Neither at any time comprised either all the Catholics or all the Protestants in the Empire. Austria was never a member of the League nor was Saxony of the Union. Brandenburg, disappointed by the refusal of the Union to give full support to its policy in the Rhineland, stood aside when it was renewed in 1617. By that time the League was limited to Bavaria and its neighboring bishoprics. In Saxony there was still hope that a lasting understanding between Lutherans and Catholics would eventually be found, and Archbishop-Elector Schweikhart of Mainz was not entirely unrealistic when he advocated the admission of Saxony to the League, which would have neutralized it in the confessional field.

Election of Matthias as Emperor, 1612

THE GHASTLY CONSEQUENCES OF A WAR between the factions were dreaded by many princes, and this fear of war accounted for the unanimous election of Archduke Matthias as emperor in 1612. None of the electors were prepared to face the chaos that might follow an attempt to deprive the Habsburgs of the imperial dignity. Matthias himself tended toward a compromise with the Protestant estates. The aging emperor, however, preoccupied with the enjoyment of a comfortable and pleasurable court life, was not able to assume active leadership in the government. This task fell to Cardinal Melchior Khlesl, who had risen to his position as staunch leader of the Catholic cause in the Habsburg lands, but whose influence now extended to the affairs of the Empire. Khlesl was not lacking in patriotic German sentiment, but he felt that the fight against Protestantism and the estates in the Habsburg realm could only be won if peace prevailed in the Empire. He aimed at what was called the "composition" of the controversies that had arisen from the interpretation of the Religious Peace of Augsburg. Khlesl proposed to seek a compromise through conferences at which the two parties would be represented equally. This seemed to him to be the only way to restore the authority of the Tribunal of the Empire, the diet, and the emperor.

The cardinal believed that the dynastic position of the Habsburgs could be made secure only through such a pacification. Therefore he insisted that the problem of imperial succession be solved in conjunction with the other questions and by the same methods of reasonable negotiation. The composition of the religious controversies would have called for concessions on the part of the Catholic princes. The minimum would have been recognition of the secularization of bishoprics and monasteries which the Protestants had brought into their possession after 1552. Khlesl was actually far from granting this much. But the discussion of some such concessions aroused the opposition of Maximilian of Bavaria, while Khlesl's policy in the question of succession was fiercely opposed by members of the Habsburg family. Considering the circumstances of the election of 1612, it could perhaps be argued that Khlesl exaggerated the difficulties of the succession. On the other hand, the wish of the archdukes to have the next emperor elected exclusively by the Catholic electors if the Protestant princes made their vote dependent upon special concessions, was a rather irresponsible policy.

ᔥ Matthias Displaced by Archduke Ferdinand

EMPEROR MATTHIAS and his two brothers were all childless. His brothers, Maximilian, grandmaster of the Teutonic Order, and Albert, regent of the Spanish Netherlands, were willing to drop their own hereditary claims and see their young cousin Archduke Ferdinand, who had two sons, become Roman King. Ferdinand was the ruler of Inner Austria (Styria, Carinthia). Through the influence of his Bavarian mother, his studies at the Jesuit College of Ingolstadt, and his elder cousin Duke Maximilian of Bavaria he had become a convinced and inflexible Catholic. Although he was friendly, amiable, and somewhat aimless in other matters, Ferdinand tolerated no dissension in religious matters. He had restored the predominance of the Catholic Church in Styria and Carinthia with forceful determination, once he had become ruler there. Small wonder that the Protestants everywhere feared him.

The Austrian government had planned to make Ferdinand King of Bohemia and Hungary before having him elected Roman King. But action was delayed, as King Philip III of Spain claimed to have a better title to the kingdom of Bohemia and Hungary as a grandson of Emperor Maximilian II. Under German law the Spanish claims were untenable, but the Austrian line of the Habsburgs depended too much on Madrid to disregard them altogether. What Spain actually wanted was support for her great European scheme: the further strengthening of her position in upper Italy as well as the building of a land bridge over the Spanish Franche-Comté and the upper Rhine to the Netherlands. In the summer of 1617 Philip III recognized the rights of succession of

Archduke Ferdinand and his male descendants in Hungary and Bohemia. At the same time the Spanish ambassador Oñate negotiated a secret agreement with Ferdinand, by which Ferdinand promised upon his accession to the imperial throne to see that King Philip received not only the principalities of Piombino and Finale but also the imperial possessions and rights in Alsace and the countship of Ortenau on the eastern bank of the Rhine. The Oñate agreement demonstrated Spain's utter disregard of the common interests of the German people. Germany had become merely a geographical name, and its different parts could be used by this or that foreign power as building stones for strategic bastions of their own. In the event of grave conflicts among the German princes, the big European powers were likely to use Germany ruthlessly as a battlefield.

The Oñate agreement opened the way for Ferdinand's coronation in Bohemia and Hungary. The Habsburg officials, by the clever use of haste and pressure, succeeded in keeping the Bohemian estates from asserting their electoral rights without, however, gaining outright recognition of the hereditary monarchical principle. Habsburg diplomacy had stolen a march on the opposition of the estates when Ferdinand was crowned Bohemian King and "accepted" by the estates in June, 1617. Under similar conditions he was proclaimed King of Hungary, but before he was crowned in Pressburg, on July 1, 1618, revolt had broken out in Bohemia. The news of events in Bohemia fanned the dissatisfaction with Khlesl's policies which prevailed in the minds of the radical Catholics. Archduke Maximilian, brother of Emperor Matthias, who had been working strenuously for several years to bring about Ferdinand's election as Roman King, made the most of the situation. He arrested Khlesl in the Hofburg, the imperial palace of Vienna, on July 20, and imprisoned him in Innsbruck. Only in 1622, through the pope's intercession, was Khlesl allowed to go to Rome. The ailing Emperor Matthias was angry but helpless in face of the coup that made Ferdinand the actual ruler of Austria before the emperor's death on March 20, 1619.

Thus the Bohemian revolt led to the concentration of the power of the German house of Habsburg in a single person who was conscious of his imperial dignity and profoundly convinced that it rested on unity of faith. A new epoch dawned for Germany. No one in 1618 or in the years immediately following realized that the apocalyptic horsemen had begun to ride.

CHAPTER 12

The Thirty Years' War: I. 1618–30

IT WAS NOT A CONFLICT among European powers, not even an
acute controversy between the emperor and the princes of the
Empire or among these princes themselves that led to the outbreak of the long war that lived on in the memory of the German
people as the "Great War" and in the books of the historians as the
Thirty Years' War. Rather, it was a struggle between the estates and
the monarchy in the territories of the Habsburg dynasty which set
fire to all of Germany and to the European continent. Without the
grave crisis in the constitutional life of the Empire, the weakness of
the German states, and the ambitions of the great powers of Europe,
the events that occurred in Bohemia could not have developed into
a disaster from which Germany was to emerge crippled and mutilated.

It is difficult to determine to what extent differences in the interpretation of Christian faith were a direct cause of the catastrophe. There is
no doubt but that religious motivation was strong in the lives of individuals and societies, and even in the relations among states and nations,
in this age. But the confessional war started at a time when enthusiasm
for the religious revivals, both Protestant and Catholic, had lost much
of its original force and religious ideas had again become conventional-
ized. Frank skepticism was rare in Germany, but ever larger groups of
people had ceased to find in religious ideals the full satisfaction of their
human aspirations. Nevertheless, the reality of heaven and hell was nowhere questioned, nor was the necessity of basing the political and social order on principles that would keep Satan from undoing the work
of God. Religious zeal found expression not only in the ghastly fury of
witch trials, which reached its climax during these years, but also in
the care with which all governments attended to the direction of church
life in their dominions. Yet while on the one hand religion deteriorated
into superstition, on the other it tended to become formalized and to

lose genuineness. Every political action was publicly cloaked in religious terms, but religion seemed to be used more and more to rationalize actions motivated by secular interests. Under the general cover of Christian orthodoxy there came to be a separation of religion and politics. It is usually assumed that the failure of the religious reunification of Germany during the Thirty Years' War led to toleration and to the secularization of politics. But the process was more complex. In countries such as France, where the religious division was overcome at an early date, the secularization of politics went forward at a much faster pace than in Germany. It began in Germany before the Thirty Years' War, and although in the end it limited the influence of religion on politics very considerably, the survival of denominational churches contributed in some measure to the strong position of religion in the intellectual life of Germany well into the eighteenth century.

The Revolt in Bohemia

ALREADY UNDER EMPEROR MATTHIAS the Austrian government had made strenuous efforts to strengthen the position of the Catholic Church in Bohemia and to counteract the Protestant movement, which had won great liberties with Emperor Rudolf's Letter of Majesty of 1609 granting all Bohemians protection against a forceful imposition of religion. Much power still rested with the crown and the old Church. Particularly in the royal and ecclesiastical lands, much activity on behalf of the old faith was possible, and both crown and Church had the support of a strong group of the Bohemian nobility as well as of such cities as Pilsen and Budweis. After the accession of Ferdinand II to the throne action favorable to Catholic institutions was intensified and carried on openly. The Protestant opposition among the nobility was incensed by a number of incidents, and it pressed for strict adherence to the Letter of Majesty. On May 23, 1618, a large group of noblemen appeared at the castle of Prague to protest to the royal governors, Martinitz and Slavata. The meeting was a stormy one. A minority in the group managed to turn a verbal exchange into a physical scuffle. The governors and one of their secretaries were thrown out of the window in deliberate imitation of the defenestration that had started the Hussite revolution two centuries before. Only one of the governors suffered bodily harm, but the incident had a symbolic quality that made any compromise in the future practically impossible.

A radical group of Bohemian magnates and squires was in the saddle.

With the approval of the majority of the estates, they succeeded in setting up a directorate of thirty men, which was to organize the defense of the rights of the country. Wenzel von Ruppa was made president of the government formed by the estates; Count Matthias Thurn, commander of the army that was to be mobilized. The revolt was declared directed, not against King Ferdinand, but against his governors and the bad priests, the Jesuits. It was almost inevitable, however, that such distinctions would be dropped once the movement gathered sufficient strength. From the outset, hopes were entertained of forming a union with the Protestant estates of the other Habsburg lands, particularly with those of the Wenceslas crown—Bohemia, Silesia, Lusatia, and Moravia—but also those of Lower and Upper Austria. The revolt of the Protestant Netherlands against Spain could not fail to throw a shadow over the Danube. But with the exception of Silesia, the estates of the other Habsburg territories were slow in joining Bohemia.

It was apparent that the attitude of the German and European states was of paramount importance for the ultimate outcome of the Bohemian revolution. The Union of the Protestant German princes had become a rather small and pronouncedly defensive association, slow to reach decisions. In the fall of 1618, however, it did announce that it considered the violations of the Letter of Majesty as endangering the evangelical faith and German liberty, and that its members were expected not to tolerate the recruitment of soldiers for war against the Bohemian estates or the passage of troops through their territories. But some members of the Union such as the margrave of Ansbach were already convinced that the Bohemian events were the last warning to Protestants that they must fight if they did not wish eventually to be submerged by the Catholic reaction. This was also the opinion of Prince Christian of Anhalt, who was still virtually in control of the policy of the Palatinate.

Christian of Anhalt was a man of large conceptions and an untiring inventor and promoter of political projects, though of projects that were not always founded upon a realistic appraisal of persons and conditions. His greatest diplomatic success had been the marriage between the young Elector Palatine, Frederick V, and Princess Elizabeth, the cultured, beautiful, and vivacious daughter of King James I of England. Planned as an ordinary political marriage with a view to strengthening the ties between England and the Union, it did not in the end achieve this aim. At the time of the Bohemian crisis, King James was pursuing the dream of a conciliation between England and Spain, an occupation that made him neglect his role as the self-styled leader of European Protestantism.

The marriage of the young couple—both were only sixteen at the time of their wedding in 1613—was an unusually happy one. They shared an interest in the arts and fine aesthetic judgment. The last addition to the Heidelberg castle, as well as its magnificent terrace and garden, is a lasting monument to their happy days in the Palatinate. But Frederick had little political acumen and even less energy. On the whole, he depended on his councilors. His wife was often suspected of having persuaded him to accept the Bohemian crown. This accusation is unjust. But the Stuart princess, who showed much greater fortitude and pride than her husband during the long years of exile in the Hague, which followed the Bohemian adventure, had no knowledge of the intricacies of German politics.

Only one European prince was willing immediately to assist the Bohemian estates. Charles Emanuel, the ambitious duke of Savoy, saw in the Bohemian revolt an opportunity to wreck the position of the house of Habsburg. Together with Venice, he hoped to break the Spanish domination of Italy. At the same time he wished to thwart the election of Ferdinand in Germany and win both the Bohemian and German crown for Savoy. He offered the leaders of the Union an army of 2,000 men to be employed at their discretion. They accepted the offer and placed the troops, which were under the command of Ernst von Mansfeld, at the disposal of the directorate in Prague.

Mansfeld was the first of a number of adventurous military captains to enter the stage. For the next decades these captains were to play roles out of all proportion to their station and character, even for so martial an age. Nothing showed so clearly the breakdown of the traditional political order and the complete failure of the German princes to set a model of leadership as the rise of these "soldiers of fortune," as they called themselves. Religion and fatherland meant nothing to them. They talked boisterously about their honor, but it actually consisted only of physical courage; their actions revealed the most unscrupulous pursuit of personal advantage and the most flagrant disregard of all commitments and common decency. Ernst von Mansfeld was an illegitimate scion of the Belgian, Catholic line of the Counts Mansfeld. He had served in the Spanish army in the wars against the Netherlands. In the Jülich war he had commanded troops of Archduke Leopold. But the unwillingness of the Spanish government to recognize him as a count drove him to embrace Calvinism and serve the Union. Simultaneously, he took service under the duke of Savoy. While in Bohemia, he negotiated with every faction, always eagerly looking for the turn of fortune that would serve his own interests best. His gift for tactics was only moderate, but he had a talent that every military entrepreneur of the age needed, a knack for recruiting soldiers and keeping them even without regular pay. Lack of funds made the quartering of troops among the civilian population inevitable. Foraging developed quickly into plundering, regardless of whether the soldiers were in the country of friends or foes. The conduct of campaigns was greatly affected by these conditions. Valuable strategic positions often had to be given up because an army had eaten everything that could be wrung from a region. Like a swarm of locusts it would then descend upon greener fields and continue its destructive work. Economic conditions go far to explain the rise of the cold-blooded managers and profiteers of war. But the appearance of these self-serving men was a reply to the political and moral failings of the German princes as well.

✆ *The Outbreak of Hostilities*

FLEMISH TROOPS hired with Spanish money came to the help of Emperor Matthias, or rather Archduke Ferdinand. The Bohemian troops were poorly organized, but with the arrival of Mansfeld they could engage in offensive maneuvers. They conquered Pilsen, the chief place held by the Catholic loyalists, in November, 1618. In the spring Moravia was occupied, and her estates joined the Bohemian cause, as did those of Lusatia. The death of Emperor Matthias on March 20, 1619, opened up new possibilities. It enabled the estates of Upper Austria and the Protestant section of the estates of Lower Austria to make their recognition of Ferdinand contingent on a guarantee of religious and political liberties, and it enabled the rebellious Bohemian estates to take over the full government of the kingdom. The Hungarian estates seemed prepared to assert their rights as well. The moment seemed favorable for creating a union of the estates of the Habsburg lands and laying down the law to Ferdinand. A bold military offensive by the main body of Bohemian troops under Count Matthias Thurn was meant to clinch this objective. Early in June, 1619, they entered the eastern suburbs of Vienna, but although the city was only lightly defended, Count Thurn was not able to conquer the Austrian capital and had to retreat to Bohemia, where a few days earlier Ernst von Mansfeld had suffered a serious reverse. While Ferdinand brought up Walloon regiments hired with Spanish money, as well as Hungarian horsemen, the Bohemian directorate fell more and more into arrears in paying its ill-disciplined troops.

Ferdinand traveled to Frankfurt in June, 1619, to attend to his election as emperor. As the Bohemian elector, he was to vote for himself. The Bohemian rebels wished to see the imperial election postponed, so as to give them time to elect a new king of Bohemia. In July, 1619, delegates from the estates of all the territories over which Emperor Matthias had formerly ruled assembled in Prague to draft the terms of a confederation. The estates of the lands of the Wenceslas crown—Bohemia, Moravia, Silesia, the Lusatias—joined together for the defense of their political and religious rights against king, Catholic loyalists, and foreign states. A second agreement between these estates and the Protestant estates of Upper and Lower Austria was concluded in August. It provided for mutual support in the fight for the maintenance and acquisition of religious and political liberties.

It is noteworthy that national differences were not an obstacle to formation of this federation. Bohemia and Moravia were largely Slavic; Silesia and Lusatia, predominantly German; Austria, exclusively German. Particularly, the old German-Czech conflict of Hussite days was buried for the sake of the "evangelical" cause, as the united front of the Utraquists, Moravian Brethren, adherents of the Bohemian confession, Lutherans, and Calvinists was called. It is true, however, that the estates of the individual lands under the Bohemian crown insisted not only on equal participation in the election of kings but also on their local privileges and their own administration. Still, this was probably little affected by feelings of national sentiment; rather it reflected the political outlook of the landed class, which wanted to make its own customary independence unassailable through the achievement of religious liberties.

✑ Elector Palatine Frederick V Elected King of Bohemia

ON AUGUST 26, 1619, the estates in Prague elected the Elector Palatine, Frederick V, King of Bohemia. A strong movement in favor of Elector John George of Saxony had existed. The majority of the Protestants in the Bohemian crown lands were Lutherans and looked to neighboring Saxony as their natural friend and leader. But John George had rejected all entreaties. He was a prince of small stature, both as a human being and as a public figure. A devoted family man and honest politician, a man of simple character and plain tastes, he made even his virtues seem drab. His generous consumption of native beer may not have been the cause of his dullness, but it did not make his mind any brighter. In politics he continued the traditional Saxon policy of defending the constitution of the Empire, which meant in Dresden friendly devotion to the emperor and simultaneous insistence on the role of the princes, particularly those "chief pillars of the Empire," the electors. It also signified full protection of the Lutheran faith. But Calvinism appeared in Saxon eyes as a perversion of Christianity. The slogan "rather Popish than Calvinist" was heard all over Saxony, and John George's court chaplain, the pompous and conceited Hoë von Hohenegg did his best to stir up animosity against the Calvinists. John George abhorred the political activism of the Calvinist princes. He stayed out of the Union, and although he could not deny that as emperor Archduke Ferdinand was not likely to respect Protestant rights, and that the suppression of Protestantism in Bohemia would create great dangers for Saxony, he refused to do more than offer to serve as mediator in Bohemia. He did not move closer to the Union than before. He was even prepared to give his electoral vote to Ferdinand. Actually, the latter's election proved much easier than Khlesl had thought it would. On August 28, 1619, Ferdinand was elected and proclaimed emperor. In addition to the three ecclesiastical electors, Bohemia and Saxony could be counted on to support Ferdinand, and Brandenburg was inclined to follow the example of Saxony. The Palatinate made a clumsy attempt to nominate Maximilian of Bavaria, in order to split the Catholic group. But Elector Ferdinand of Cologne replied to the Palatine councilors that his brother Maximilian did not wish to become a candidate, and the councilors accepted the majority vote two days after the election of their own prince as Bohemian King in Prague.

Frederick took the fateful step of accepting the Bohemian crown late in September. On October 31, 1619, he arrived in Prague with a large entourage and great display. It would have been well if he and his advisers had at least scanned the European horizon. Yet not even his father-in-law James I was properly consulted. Still preoccupied with the project of an Anglo-Spanish alliance, he was shocked by Frederick's acceptance of a crown from rebel hands. Young Louis XIII was at the time struggling to install himself as ruler of France and so was eager to have friendly relations with Ferdinand, and was not in sympathy with the Bohemian "Huguenots." A deep internal crisis, the struggle between the orthodox Calvinists and the liberalizing Arminians, divided the people of the Netherlands. This religious conflict was intertwined with the grave issues of centralism and regionalism: the latter was championed by the aristocratic elements and the former by the stadholders, the Oranges, who advocated at the same time the renewal of the war against Spain. The Orange party emerged victorious after a sequence of events which began with the trial and execution of John Oldenbarneveldt in May, 1619, and kept the country in convulsion for some time to come. The contribution of the Netherlands to the Bohemian war was therefore nominal.

Yet fortune seemed to smile on the new Bohemian king, who began his residence in Prague with the establishment of a luxurious court and lavish festivities. Bethlen Gabor, the half-independent ruler of Transylvania, had decided that the time had come to try to become independent of both the emperor and the sultan by making himself master of that part of Hungary which was still under Habsburg rule. By posing as the protector of the evangelical groups, he was able to rally sufficient support in Hungary to gain his objective. He concluded a defensive and offensive alliance with the Bohemian confederation and captured most of Upper Hungary in the last days of August, 1620. The imperial army under Count Buquoi, which had operated deep in Bohemia, was forced to fall back to the Danube to protect Vienna. But after the Bohemians and Hungarians had joined forces, Buquoi could not stop their progress to the environs of the city. In the last days of November it seemed likely that Vienna would be occupied by enemies who, in their march through Lower Austria, had proved themselves ruthlessly cruel. But, as in the previous year, the Austrian capital was saved at the last moment. Spanish troops dispatched from Milan reached Innsbruck. Still more alarming was the news that Bethlen Gabor received from Hungary. One of the Magyar loyalists had broken into Upper Hungary with 5,000 Cossacks, whom he had collected in Poland. Gabor hurried back to Hungary, while the Bohemians, strengthened by troops of the Upper and Lower Austrian estates, were able to maintain themselves for a while in Lower Austria.

Thereafter the political and military situation deteriorated rapidly. The Bohemians were unable to gain foreign support, except that in the summer of 1620 arrangements were made with Bethlen Gabor for some Magyar troops. In the decisive battle, however, these proved of the most doubtful value. Little power was left in the hands of the Protestant Union, and its leaders would not do more than assist in the defense of Frederick's electoral lands in Germany. Meanwhile, Frederick's government did not succeed in mobilizing Bohemia for the grave tasks ahead. Frederick was king in name only, since the estates, through their old leaders, continued to run the administration. Sensing a lukewarm attitude among the common people, they hesitated to impose the taxes that would have been needed to build up the army and keep it a disciplined force. In these circumstances the appointment of Prince Christian of Anhalt as commander-in-chief was of limited usefulness. Ernst of Mansfeld, an obstreperous lieutenant in any case, could refuse to co-operate as long as his army was not paid by Prague.

At the same time the morale of the country was ebbing. When Frederick permitted his zealous Calvinist ministers to remove precious works of art from the Prague cathedral, the Bohemian Utraquists and Lutherans were antagonized, nor were fresh sympathies gained in Lutheran Germany. Frederick's carefree, and in many respects alien, manners cooled the enthusiasm of the people. Even his Protestant friends felt disappointed that this prince from abroad could not deliver the alliance with foreign powers for the sake of which his electors had chosen him. Already during the winter of 1619–20 his Catholic enemies whispered that Frederick was only a "winter king," who would be doomed with the arrival of a new season.

✑ Maximilian of Bavaria and the Bohemian War

INDEED, the political climate had begun to change. The election of Ferdinand as emperor, on August 28, 1619, indicated that the house of Austria still commanded respect in the Empire, and in long negotiations with the Catholic princes, during and after the Frankfurt convention, the Austrian government initiated plans for the active support of Ferdinand. Simultaneously, discussions were started with Philip III, through the Spanish ambassador, aiming at the direct intervention of Spain in the German fighting. This was the hour of Maximilian of Bavaria. He was superior to most of the German princes of his age, not only morally but also as a statesman and administrator. He had shown that he would not risk lightly the peace of the Empire. Nor was he unaware of the fact that strengthening imperial power in Austria was not improving Bavaria's independence. But Frederick V's actions had jeopardized the last semblance of constitutional order and peace in Germany, and if Bohemia were to become a bulwark of Protestantism, the future of the Catholic Church in Germany would be uncertain.

Then, too, if Maximilian intervened on behalf of Ferdinand, he would secure the gratitude of the restored Catholic emperor, who would not easily wish to undermine the position of such a loyal and strong neighbor. Moreover, intervention could itself be used to make Bavaria stronger. It was this reasoning that led to the agreement of Munich of October 8, 1619, between Ferdinand and Maximilian. According to this agreement Maximilian, as leader of the Catholic League, was to be given "absolute command" of an army of 24,000 men which was to be organized and financed by the League. He was to be reimbursed by Ferdinand for all his own expenses, and as a guarantee of payment he was to hold all the lands of Ferdinand which he freed. Furthermore, Ferdinand offered his cousin Maximilian the transfer of the electoral dignity from the Heidelberg house of Wittelsbach to the Munich house. For this, the transfer of the electoral dignity of Saxony from the Ernestine to the Albertine line in 1547 served as a precedent.[1] The Elector Palatine and his allies were to be placed under the ban of the Empire, and Maximilian was to keep the territories that he might conquer while carrying out the ban. With these assurances from the emperor, Maximilian undertook the organization of the League and its army, and by July he had brought together an army of 30,000 and raised money for its maintenance.

In the eight months following the Munich agreement Austrian diplomats sought to gain further help. The Spanish government hesitated for a while to promise direct participation in the war. It was afraid that this might precipitate new hostilities with the United Netherlands or possibly war with England. However, Spain was eager to protect the Austrian Habsburgs and to use the occasion to gain a strong foothold along the Rhine for her operations against the Netherlands. Thus a strong army was eventually made ready under the command of Ambrosio Spinola, to move against the Rhenish Palatinate.

It remained to keep the Protestant princes of Germany from lending assistance to Frederick of Bohemia. In this respect it was decisive that John George of Saxony was won over. Hostility to Calvinism and his conservative, quietistic attitude toward the constitution of the Empire predisposed John George in the direction of neutrality, but he was apprehensive that a victory of the emperor and of the Catholic reformation in the Bohemian countries, which included not only Bohemia south of the Saxon mountains but also Lusatia to the northeast of Saxony, would place his electorate in an insecure position, particularly with regard to the bishoprics that the electors had annexed after 1552. He felt that lasting assurances from the emperor could not be bought

[1] See page 230.

with neutrality. Only a definite stand against Frederick could win him gratitude from Ferdinand, who might even go so far as to give some protection to the Lutherans in Bohemia. Thus John George entered into agreements with the emperor and the League. He was to restore order in Lusatia and Silesia, in return for which he was to be allowed to keep Lusatia as a pledge of reimbursement for his expenses. He also received certain vague promises about the state of secularized bishoprics and the rights of Lutherans. The agreements were a shameful reflection on the complete inadequacy of Saxon policy. Even its underlying religious principle, blind hatred of Calvinism, was made illusory by the naked desire for aggrandizement through the annexation of Lusatia.

Additional assistance for the Habsburg cause came from Poland. With a considerable Protestant minority at home and with the dangerous hostility of Sweden, King Sigismund III did not dare take sides openly with his brother-in-law Ferdinand. But he allowed the recruitment of troops in the Polish kingdom. Thus the anti-Bohemian coalition reached from Spain to the northeast of Europe. Behind it stood the papacy giving financial and moral support. For Pope Paul V, the brewing struggle was a crusade for the true Church and the right faith. As had been done in centuries gone by, he imposed a tax on ecclesiastical income and placed the funds thus raised at Ferdinand's disposal.

It was ironical that French diplomacy made a most important contribution to the anti-Bohemian coalition. The small group of Protestant estates which made up the Union had brought together an army that could have forced Maximilian to leave considerable forces behind when he marched into Austria and Bohemia. The Union had intended to defend the integrity of Protestant territories in Germany, including the Palatinate. But its leaders lost heart over the Bohemian issue, for which they were unwilling to fight. Under the influence of French diplomats they concluded an understanding with Maximilian at Ulm, in early July, 1619, by which the League and the Union promised to abstain from attacks upon each other's territories. The emperor and Bohemia were members of neither alliance, however. Therefore, Maximilian could move his troops against Bohemia without fear of a Protestant offensive against Bavaria. Under the terms of the Ulm agreement, it could not be called a violation even if Duke Maximilian occupied Palatinate territory, provided he acted as commissioner of the emperor in execution of the ban of the Empire. The grave threat against the Rhenish Palatinate that was posed by the military preparations in the Spanish Netherlands was met by an ostrichlike attitude on the part of the Protestant princes. That this attitude was fostered by French diplomacy proves that political shortsightedness was not an attribute of German princes alone.

The stage was set for Maximilian; even then it was no longer German but European. Late in July, 1620, he invaded Upper Austria and compelled the estates to pay temporary homage to the emperor but to turn over to him the actual powers of government. Leaving some occupation forces behind, Maximilian went north against Bohemia, accompanied by the imperial army under Count Buquoy, who did not consider himself under the command of Maximilian. Maximilian was not a professional soldier, though his good political sense made him an able judge of the strategic fundamentals of the campaign. The military chief of the League army was Count Johann Tserclaes Tilly. Tilly was the scion of a Liége family and a noble representative of the Catholic Reformation. A pupil of the Jesuits, he had originally wished to enter the order himself but then decided to serve its ideals as a Christian knight. He fought with the Spanish army against the Dutch, under Henry Guise against the Huguenots, and in the emperor's service in Hungary from 1600 to 1612, when Maximilian put him in charge of the Bavarian troops. This ascetic "monk in armor," who despised the low pleasures of the contemporary officer, was no politician. He wanted to advance his faith by an unswerving devotion to the art of war. Although he considered terror a permissible weapon of warfare, he endeavored to keep the cruelty of war within bounds. Tilly and Maximilian were deeply shocked by the ferocity that the undisciplined imperial troops displayed in Upper Austria, and they lodged heated complaints with the emperor. Maximilian's full treasury made it easier for him to maintain discipline in the League army.

Entering Bohemia, Tilly negotiated an armistice with the self-seeking Ernst von Mansfeld which opened the road to Prague. The main Bohemian army was forced to evacuate Moravia, and took a strong position at the White Mountain just west of Prague. Though the two generals, Tilly and Buquoi, were cautious tacticians, Maximilian prevailed on them to engage the Bohemian army in a decisive battle. In combat that lasted less than two hours, the Bohemians, under Christian of Anhalt and Count Thurn, were thoroughly beaten. Some of the Bohemian troops showed such a lack of military discipline that even great feats of bravery performed by individual officers and units could not stop the rout of the army. As the disorganized and dispirited Bohemian troops floated back to Prague, they found the capital unprepared for any kind of defense. Frederick V, taken by surprise, made a swift escape with his pretty wife and his chief advisers. He tried in vain to rally support in Silesia. Lusatia had already been occupied by Elector John George of Saxony, almost without opposition, and the estates of Silesia, impressed by the disasters in Bohemia and Lusatia, were crestfallen and anxious for peace.

✍ Aftermath of the War in Bohemia and Moravia

THE VICTORS' REVENGE WAS TERRIBLE. But this did not spur the vanquished to new efforts. Whereas, in the revolt of the Netherlands, loss in the early phase of the rebellion and the execution of the leading noblemen, Count Egmont and Hoorne, had been a signal for the outbreak of a full revolution carried on by the majority of the Dutch people, the mass of the Bohemians did not rise. The Hussite spirit, which a century before had made Bohemia the first nation to stand up against the uniformity of faith in the medieval world, had evaporated. Already in the development of the Bohemian Brethren, and in the history of the German Anabaptists after the suppression of the Münster revolt, the trend toward a quietistic attitude in politics was visible; the Lutheran creed did not engender a revolutionary spirit either, and the divisions among Protestants in matters of creed and custom dampened their common effort even more. People were willing to follow the leadership of the nobility and town patricians as long as these were in the saddle, but they were far from identifying themselves with their cause, which, after all, was concerned with the liberty of a small social minority. The Bohemian noblemen wanted to become little archdukes on their own domains, invested with the rights and privileges of independent rulers. Tschernembl had said at the time of the confederations that a truly dynamic force could be unleashed if the Austrian and Bohemian noblemen would liberate their peasants. But although the nobles were bent upon enhancing their own freedom from the crown, they did not think of depriving themselves of any of the economic advantages that their class possessed. With the defeat of the nobility, no organized popular group was left to carry on the struggle, and the people suffered the vengeance of the old rulers in silence.

Frightful punishment was meted out to the leaders of the Bohemian risings. On June 21, 1621, twenty-six noblemen were publicly executed in Prague, and heavy penalties were inflicted on eighteen others. But the most widespread punishment of the rebellious nobles was the confiscation of their property, carried out under the governor, Prince Karl von Liechtenstein. About half of the land of Bohemia was taken from its former owners and given away or sold. Land was freely given to Bohemian and Moravian noblemen who had demonstrated their loyalty to emperor and Church, and to officers, Austrian or foreign, who had served the good cause with merit. There were many others, including generals and colonels, who presented bills, with interest, for personal expenses incurred in the imperial service and never-ending claims for the pay of their soldiers. These demands for money induced the confiscation commissions to go even further than a stern punitive policy might have demanded.

Yet the money collected in this way slipped quickly through the emperor's fingers. Religious orthodoxy did not improve the honesty in financial affairs of those to whom Ferdinand II had to leave the administration of these transactions. The economy of Bohemia was already badly shaken by the war. It was further disorganized by emigration and the continued violence of the soldiers. Prices rose, though little money was in open circulation. On the other hand, the sudden sale of an enormous number of estates brought on a terrific slump in land prices, and confiscated properties were sold at less than bargain prices. To increase the circulation of money, the imperial government launched currency operations that allowed a group of manipulators, including some of the imperial councilors, to act practically as counterfeiters. The emperor's financial gains from the confiscations were consequently limited, and the Bohemian economy was thrown into a state of weakness from which recovery would have been difficult even if the country had not suffered additional destruction through religious oppression and war.

A new Bohemian nobility was thus founded. It included many owners of latifundia as well as a number of foreigners, for example, Belgian and Italian officers. The greatest profiteers were the governor, Prince Liechtenstein, and Ferdinand's closest councilor and adviser, Ulrich von Eggenberg. Next was a young adventurer, Albrecht von Wallenstein. Born in 1583 of a noble, though poor, family, Wallenstein became a Catholic at the age of twenty and married an aged widow, who after her death a few years later left him estates that made him quite a rich man. He administered his properties unusually well, with a talent that grew with his fortunes. He had served as an officer in the Turkish wars, before receiving his first small commands from the Moravian estates. Soon he had begun to employ his wealth to recruit troops for Archduke Ferdinand and Emperor Matthias on a loan basis. When the Moravians joined the Bohemian rebellion, Wallenstein went to Austria. By 1621 he had organized three regiments of his own. In 1622 he was made the commandant of Prague; this gave him the authority to distribute and billet troops all over the country. As these were the chief methods of coercion through which confiscation and religious conversion were carried out, his opportunities for further enrichment multiplied, the more so since he placed Ferdinand II under growing obligation by large advances. Wallenstein, or Count Friedland, as he was now called, expanded his fortunes with incredible recklessness and shrewdness. But he also showed great talent for the economic administration and development of his properties. He was an early example of the mercantilistic managers of territories. It was asserted that he came to own a quarter of all Bohemian land, and it can at least be said that by 1625 he had at his disposal larger resources than the revolutionary estates of Bohemia had been able to mobilize in 1619.

In social outlook the new Bohemian nobility was not different from the old. Since many people had been killed in the war, the new magnates forced the remaining peasants to work even harder than before. But the new nobility was politically bound to the Habsburg dynasty, to which it owed its rise. For this reason it did not oppose the radical constitutional changes that the Vienna government imposed, flouting old customs and legal traditions. According to the provisions of the "renewed land order," which was finally issued in 1627 for Bohemia, and in the following year for Moravia, the two countries became hereditary Habsburg territories like the Austrian archduchies. The king assumed the rights of legislation, appointment of officials, and command of military forces, as well as the right to convene the estates and to propose an agenda for them. He also arrogated to himself the power to revise the judgments of the Bohemian courts. A "Bohemian Court Chancellery" was established in Vienna as the agency for the preparation of policies and administrative measures. In time it became the highest judicial organ of the government, as well as the supreme source of legislation.

The "renewed land order" also made the Catholic Church the only church and declared the clergy the first estate of the kingdom. This was merely the crowning event in the restoration of the old Church, a process that had started soon after the battle of the White Mountain. In 1621 not only Calvinist and Baptist ministers, but all Protestant ministers compromised by open participation in the rebellion had been expelled from Bohemia at short notice. A little time later all distinctions were dropped, and, in spite of earlier assurances given to Saxony, even Lutheran ministers were driven out. During the next years the people were dragooned into returning to the Catholic Church. Emigration was made difficult by a declaration that the right to emigrate could not be granted to dependent peasants and by confiscatory taxes against townspeople attempting to leave the country. Nevertheless, about 150,000 persons are supposed to have left Bohemia in the years after 1621, most of them going to Saxony. Many Moravians went to Hungary.

The policies of the imperial government revealed no specific anti-Czech aims. They were concerned exclusively with constitutional or religious matters. Many German noblemen had played leading parts in the rebellion, and the divisions between the denominations did not follow national lines. No attempt was made to suppress the Czech language, although German was given equality with it. However, the destruction of all Protestant books did great damage to Czech literature, as it consisted largely of nonconformist religious writings.

∽ Effect of the Conquest of Bohemia and Moravia on Other Habsburg Lands

THE CONQUEST OF BOHEMIA AND MORAVIA spelled victory for the monarchical principle and for the Catholic counter reformation in all the other Habsburg lands. An exception was Lusatia, which was occupied, and later annexed, by Saxony. In Silesia, Habsburg supremacy was restored, but very substantial Protestant groups survived the Thirty Years' War. In Lower and Upper Austria, Styria, and Carinthia, between 1622 and 1628, Protestants lost all their rights, and those who persevered in their faith were finally forced to emigrate. In 1628 eight hundred members of eighty-five noble families in Styria and a hundred Carinthian noblemen left the country, and thousands of Austrians went northward during these years, particularly to Franconia. The political power of the estates was broken. The establishment of religious uniformity made monarchical sovereignty unchallengeable.

∽ The Palatinate War

THE BATTLE OF WHITE MOUNTAIN was a decisive turning point in the history of Bohemia and Austria. It opened the age of absolutism in the Habsburg realm. Unfortunately, the Bohemian war was only a prelude to the war in the Palatinate, which then spread to the north, to lower

Saxony and Denmark. The Bohemian war, as we have seen, was from the beginning linked with problems of German and European politics. Lutheran princes, such as the elector of Saxony, had chosen to disregard this connection, but in doing so they had only betrayed their unwillingness to face facts. Immediately after the conclusion of military operations in Bohemia, the emperor's allies—King Philip of Spain and Duke Maximilian of Bavaria—urged a campaign against the Rhenish Palatinate. Spanish policy with regard to the acquisition of Palatinate territory was not pushed too far, and the problems of the upper Rhine were judged in Madrid chiefly with a view to the reconquest of the Netherlands. Spain's twelve-year truce with the Netherlands was to run out with the year 1621, and already King Philip III had decided to resume hostilities, a decision carried out after his death, in March, 1621, by his son Philip IV. The strategic position on the Rhine remained an important consideration for Spain merely because of the northern objectives. In September, 1620, Spain's great military commander, Marchese Ambrogio di Spinola, occupied the Palatinate territories on the left bank of the Rhine, and he turned over his command to Gonzales de Córdoba when he was called to Brussels to prepare for the campaign in the Netherlands. That such a military investment on the part of Spain posed a serious threat was seen belatedly not only by the Protestant princes of Germany, but also by the Netherlands and England.

None of these, however, were willing to take decisive steps to dislodge the Spaniards from the upper Rhine, or to see the "Winter King" restored to his patrimony. Emperor Ferdinand II placed Frederick V under the ban of the Empire in January, 1621. The legality of this action was not beyond doubt, since it was taken without consultation with the electors and in disregard of other procedural formalities. Be that as it may, depriving not only Frederick himself, but also his legitimate heirs, of their rights and possessions was unquestionably a grave breach of the constitution. It should have been the function of the Protestant Union to resist such arbitrariness, but the Union felt unable to act. In May, 1621, it decided to dissolve. King James sent two English regiments to the Palatinate under Sir Horace Vere and paid some subsidies, and larger payments were made by the Dutch, but the forces with which the fight for the Palatinate was to be conducted were altogether inadequate.

Ernst von Mansfeld and his army had watched from Pilsen the catastrophe that overtook Bohemia He now became Frederick's captain and withdrew to the Upper Palatinate; this gave Maximilian an excuse to march into this German land. Cornered by Maximilian and Tilly, Mansfeld promised to quit if paid a high sum. But after receiving the money, he led his army to the Rhenish Palatinate, and subsequently crossed the Rhine and broke into Alsace in search of quarters, provisions, and funds.

The operations in Austria and Bohemia had already unveiled the barbarity of seventeenth-century warfare, but a new stage of atrocity was reached in the Palatinate war. It had become customary to demand for soldiers, in addition to quarters, certain services and provisions from the population. Duke Alba, Spanish commander in the early years of the revolt of the Netherlands, had been the first to request such tribute in addition to the full pay of the army, and Spinola carried this system over into Germany. These contributions opened resources for warfare, which the governments had previously lacked. How large and essential they were showed the example of Bavaria. It has been estimated that the cost of the Bavarian League troops amounted to 54 million gulden during thirty years of war, while the total annual revenue of Bavaria was between one and one-and-a-half million. Bavaria was one of the best administered states, and particularly in the first few years of the war she was able to expand her credit. With the system of contributions even poor princes could maintain armies, provided they had some military reputation. War was an attractive business so long as cash or property could be forced from the populace.

This method had its shortcomings even from a strictly military point of view. It was necessary to spread terror in order to intimidate the people; accordingly, violence by soldiers against civilians had to be tolerated, and this inevitably had the most deleterious consequences for military discipline. Furthermore, contributions did not always come in on time, nor were the additional services and provisions easily available, and this led to insurrection within the armies and crimes against civilians. The armies were accompanied by large trains of women and children, stable boys and other camp followers, whose irregular upkeep was an unending source of friction and struggle. Small wonder that the tormented civilians, particularly the hapless peasants, often banded together to avenge their misery; but such action only gave the soldiers a new excuse for lawlessness. Lawlessness was particularly great in armies, such as those of Mansfeld, that were not backed by state authority and finances. But also state finances were weak and usually soon exhausted. The Bavarian troops showed much better discipline in 1619–20 than the poorly paid regiments of the emperor. But by the time they appeared in the Palatinate in 1621–22 under Tilly, they showed no better order than the hordes of the reckless Mansfeld. The intention of punishing members of an unholy, alien faith was often given as an excuse for bestiality, and governments often used this excuse to instigate it. While religion thus helped to unlock the forces of hell, passions could not be held in bounds. Already Frederick V, who joined Mansfeld in the Palatinate in 1621, complained bitterly: "There ought to be some difference made between friend and enemy, but these people ruin both alike . . . these are men possessed of the devil and who take pleasure in setting fire to everything." What had originally applied to Mansfeld and people like him became in the end the common characteristic.

After 1625 Wallenstein sometimes kept his armies in check. With his sense of economy, he realized that the untrammeled waste of assets and supplies would eventually make the pursuit of warfare impossible. The highest standards of conduct for a seventeenth-century army were set by the Swedish army, which Gustavus Adolphus brought to Germany in 1630. It was composed chiefly of Swedish and Finnish peasant boys, though it included some German and Scottish troops, and under Gustavus Adolphus it showed an unusually high degree of discipline. After his death the Swedish element in the army was soon completely diluted and discipline fell to the customary low level. Most of the Swedish army after 1632 consisted of German mercenaries. From the beginning, a large variety of nationalities were represented in the army of the emperor, and later of Wallenstein, and the Bavarian army, whose foreign element had at first consisted chiefly of Walloon cavalry, became less homogeneous as the war dragged on. Lines of nationality came to be relatively meaningless, and even those of religion were blurred. A military society grew up outside the civilian society which it was supposed to defend or even to purify. It lived on its disregard of the traditional value of human life and made its perverse concept of honor the supreme rule. The soldier mob could feel superior to the helpless civilian and enjoy its plunder, which was usually lost even sooner than the soldier's life.

In contrast to the rank and file, the officers could hope to make fortunes. Many of them were foreigners. On the Catholic side Italians, such as the imperial generals Prince Octavio Piccolomini (1599–1656) and Count Matthias Gallas (1584–1647), and Belgians, such as Tilly and Buquoi, were most conspicuous, while on the Protestant side there were many Scotchmen, Englishmen, and Irish. However, the majority of officers came from the German nobility, and in the higher ranks, among those who served not only as tactical commanders but also as entrepreneurs on contract, the small princes and their numerous offspring were strongly represented. Among these were a few highly idealistic figures, and probably a good many who had entered upon a military career determined to serve a good political and religious cause. Yet in a world of utter moral depravity they conformed to the common pattern of acquisitiveness, which occasionally took the form even of hoping to found a principality. War for its own sake, irrespective of the objectives of the commander-in-chief, was declared to be the true ideal of nobility.

Relatively few soldiers were killed in battle—many more civilians were the victims of military violence. But large numbers of soldiers perished as a result of illness. The largest armies were decimated in a few months by epidemics, and, worse still, armies served as the carriers of the plague and other contagious diseases as they burned and robbed the land, depriving the people of shelter and bread. Ever since Mansfeld's army had marched from the Upper to the Rhenish Palatinate, a heavy cloud of annihilation hovered over the unhappy lands through which it had passed.

In addition to Ernst von Mansfeld, two other fighters rose in support of a Protestant Palatinate—Margrave George Frederick of Baden-Durlach and "Bishop" Christian of Halberstadt. George Frederick was an earnest man of fifty, a devout Calvinist and as much a student of the Bible as of military textbooks; he assembled an army of his own in the fall and winter of 1621–22. Against him and Mansfeld, Tilly had to operate cautiously, the more so since Córdoba failed to co-operate with him. Tilly actually suffered a costly reverse from Mansfeld south of Wiesloch in April, 1622. But the separation of George Frederick from Mansfeld and the arrival of Spanish aid enabled Tilly to defeat the margrave in a bold battle at Wimpfen on the Neckar on May 5, 1622. Shortly afterward George Frederick dismissed the remnant of his forces, which he did not have the funds to pay over a long period of time. Help for the Protestant side seemed to be on its way from the north, however, and both Tilly and Mansfeld marched toward the Main to meet the army that Christian of Halberstadt had recruited on his own in lower Saxony.

Christian, the younger brother of the ruling duke of Brunswick, was the Protestant administrator of the bishopric of Halberstadt, but his heart was in war and adventure. Though not uneducated, he was completely uninhibited in actions and words; the "mad" Halberstadt, he was commonly called, and "God's friend, the priest's foe" was the title he adopted. This master of plebeian profanity shocked a generation that was used to coarse German language. In contrast, he gave his venture a romantic color by pronouncing it a chivalrous fight undertaken on behalf of the beautiful queen of Bohemia. During the winter of 1621–22 Christian had plundered the rich Westphalian bishoprics of Münster and Paderborn. Finally, he turned south to join Mansfeld in the Palatinate. Tilly succeeded in preventing Mansfeld from meeting Christian at the Main, and he inflicted heavy losses on Christian when he crossed the Main at Höchst on June 20. But it was not really a decisive victory, because Christian effected his meeting with Mansfeld at Mannheim. But Christian and Mansfeld felt unable to defend the Palatinate against Tilly, Córdoba, and a third army that Archduke Leopold was gathering in the south, so they headed for Alsace and further robbery and extortion.

Meanwhile Mansfeld had been looking for a new employer, and when the Dutch offered him a contract, he dissolved his relations with Frederick V. He moved through the bishoprics of Metz and Verdun and through the Spanish Netherlands, broke through the lines of Spanish forces which Córdoba had sent against him, and made his way to Maurice of Orange. It was no longer a great force that Mansfeld and the wounded Duke Christian delivered to the United Provinces, but they arrived at the right moment. Events had not gone well for the Dutch since hostilities with Spain had been reopened. Spinola had occupied Jülich and laid siege to Bergen op Zoom. The United Provinces were short of allies and troops, and Maurice of Orange did not feel that he had sufficient strength to lift the Spanish siege. With the reinforcements from Germany he was able to do so on October 4, 1622.

The fate of the Palatinate drew to its inevitable conclusion. After a siege of eleven weeks Heidelberg was stormed by Tilly's troops on September 16, 1622. Three days later the brave German-Dutch garrison, which had retreated to the castle, was allowed to march out. On November 5, Sir Horace Vere and his English troops surrendered Mannheim under the same conditions. Tilly had his troops ransack Heidelberg. The Calvinist Church of the Palatinate was declared dissolved. Heidelberg's Church of the Holy Spirit was turned over to the Jesuits.

The Palatina, the finest and largest German library of the time, which was kept in the choir of this church, was sent over the Alps as a gift from Maximilian to Pope Gregory XV.

∽ Maximilian of Bavaria Made an Elector, 1623

WITH THE CONCLUSION of the Palatinate war, Emperor Ferdinand II could act in Germany. In January, 1623, a meeting of German princes was convened in Regensburg. It was designed to give him some semblance of constitutional support. The meeting was not well attended. Even Elector John George of Saxony, who was shocked at the persecution of the Lutherans in Bohemia, was only represented by diplomatic agents. Papal policy had been active, however, not only in urging Ferdinand to use the opportunity to establish a Catholic majority in the Electoral College but also to gain foreign assent to such a step. Such help was needed, since with the exception of Elector Ferdinand of Cologne, Maximilian's brother, even the Catholic princes were not eager to see Maximilian made an elector, for they were afraid that this would cause endless conflict. A concession to the traditional theory of the German constitution was made by Ferdinand when he granted the electoral dignity to Duke Maximilian on February 25, 1623, with the academic reservation that the electoral rank might revert after Maximilian's death to recognized heirs of Frederick V.

The counter reformation in Bohemia and the Regensburg decisions brought Ferdinand into conflict with the pacific group of Lutheran princes. But he could stand their distrust. John George of Saxony could only revert to complete neutrality, after his own betrayal of principle through his co-operation with the emperor against Frederick V, and after his acceptance of Lusatia. On the other hand, the Catholic League remained an active force. Maximilian, the new elector, received the Upper Palatinate. The Rhenish Palatinate remained under occupation, with the left bank territory in Spanish hands, the right bank under Bavarian administration.

Austria and Spain achieved an important success in gaining control of the strategic passes that connected Spanish Lombardy with Tyrol. The Swiss Grisons had extended their control over the Engadine and Valtellina. By using the spirit of factionalism and religious division in these remote valleys, the Spaniards occupied the Catholic Valtellina from January, 1622. In this way a strong link was created between the Mediterranean possessions of the Habsburgs and their northern territories. This was especially important for Spain, since in wartime the Dutch could cut the maritime connection between Spain and the Netherlands.

✍ *Preparation for Conflict in the North*

THE OCCUPATION OF THE VALTELLINA aroused great misgivings in Venice, which saw herself now fully surrounded by Habsburg territories. It also caused some alarm in France, which was practically encircled by Spanish positions in the Franche-Comté, at the upper Rhine, and in the Netherlands. But neither France nor England was ready to give up the appeasement of Spain. The United Provinces, however, were again in the war, and it was Spanish strategy to conquer them by encircling them from the east. Spinola's earlier occupation of Jülich was only the first move in a north-eastward envelopment that was bound to affect the whole of northwestern Germany profoundly. The Dutch were, therefore, anxious to see the German northwest armed against the Spaniards. They allowed both Mansfeld and Christian of Halberstadt to collect new forces in neighboring German territories. Mansfeld built up an army in East Friesland, leaving the area badly devastated, but the *condottiere* failed to intervene in the events of the next period. In contrast, Christian used his position as administrator of Halberstadt and brother of the ruling duke of Brunswick to advance deep into the Lower Saxon "circle" (*Kreis*). Elector Maximilian and Emperor Ferdinand were afraid, and not without reason, that the "mad man of Halberstadt" would break through the Main bishoprics to Bohemia and unite with Bethlen Gabor, who was on the rampage again. Accordingly, Tilly was dispatched to northern Hesse and finally moved into the Lower Saxon circle at Göttingen.

The imperial estates of the Lower Saxon circle had been frightened by the progress of Catholic arms, but had decided on a policy of caution. In a rather timid mood they had resolved to maintain an armed neutrality. Since no defenses had been built, Christian marched in and declared himself their protector. It was true that on the Catholic side plans for intervention in the northwest were being debated. A great number of prince-bishoprics were located in this region. Under the terms of the Religious Peace of Augsburg they were to have remained in the hands of the Catholic Church, but with the exception of Hildesheim they had all come under the administration of Protestant princes, among whom descendants of the Danish, Brunswick, Saxon, and Brandenburg houses were most prominent. Osnabrück, Minden, Verden, Halberstadt, and Magdeburg formed the inner ring of bishoprics; Bremen, Lübeck, and Schwerin dotted the seashores. An excuse for interfering in the northwest was not unwelcome in Vienna. There was, moreover, good cause for concern that King Christian IV of Denmark, who as duke of Holstein was also a prince of the Empire and member of the Lower Saxon circle, might throw his full weight into the military defense of the northwest. One of his sons had recently become bishop of Verden, and Danish policy aimed at the acquisition of Osnabrück as well.

But King Christian was not ready to come to the support of Christian of Halberstadt, and the Lower Saxon estates were restless. The mercurial Christian of Halberstadt did not feel capable of defeating Tilly single-handed. He proposed that he join Maurice of Orange and, with him, overwhelm Spinola. Hurriedly he went west with his army, but not hurriedly enough. He lost precious time in Westphalia, where he hoped Mansfeld would join him. This gave Tilly time to catch up with him, and at Stadtlohn, ten miles from the Dutch frontier, he practically annihilated Christian's army on August 6, 1623. Tilly would have liked to invade the Netherlands, and such an operation might well have meant the end of Dutch freedom. But Elector Maximilian was unwilling to take a step that might bring the European powers into action. He was relieved when imperial troops succeeded in defeating Bethlen Gabor during the winter of 1623–24, but he was still apprehensive of the intentions of other states, above all France and England.

There was good reason to worry about the attitude of the European powers. In spite of the great popularity of the cause of the Elector Palatine in England, King James I had been lukewarm in his support of his children Frederick and Elizabeth. But his attempts at establishing peace between England and Spain through a Spanish marriage of his son came to an end in the spring of 1624. England moved closer to France, where at this time Richelieu was beginning to gain a hold on the direction of French policy. Years of grave struggle still lay ahead for this builder of the modern absolute monarchy in France and French supremacy on the Continent. Though he was determined to wreck the European position of the house of Habsburg, irrespective of the effect this would have on the universal dominance of the Catholic Church, he had to heed the feelings of French Catholics, particularly so long as he had not suppressed the Huguenots. Nor could he disregard the bonds that united French, English, and Dutch Protestants. For a long time to come Richelieu had to move with extreme caution. Often he had to conceal, and change, his course.

In 1624 Richelieu's immediate intention was to employ French arms only in Italy, in co-operation with Venice and Savoy. France's rapprochement with England, which took the form of a proposed marriage between Henrietta Marie, Louis XIII's sister, and Prince Charles, the heir to the British throne, was designed to build up an anti-Habsburg coalition in the north. In June, 1624, an alliance was concluded between France and the United Provinces, and in the same month England joined the combination. King James I had already equipped Mansfeld with the beginings of an army that was to operate in Holland and north Germany. But additional strength was to be won in the north. Sweden and Denmark were also eager to intervene in northern Germany. Gustavus Adolphus of Sweden had been warring with Poland, which in religion and through dynastic ties was closely connected with Austria, and Christian IV of Denmark had his eyes on expansion in northwestern Germany. Both Scandinavian kings wanted to gain control of the Baltic Sea and northern trade. But though they agreed that the Catholic powers, notably Austria and Poland, should be excluded from control of the Baltic and its approaches, they were not willing to co-operate in any large enterprise. Actually, Sweden was already stronger than Denmark, but this was not clearly perceived in western Europe. The military scheme that Gustavus Adolphus proposed, a well-conceived operation along the Oder toward Silesia, Bohemia, and Moravia, seemed to the English like a mere extension of the anti-Polish objectives of Sweden. Christian IV's plan to fight in northwestern Germany and gain for his son the bishoprics of Osnabrück and Halberstadt, from which Christian of Halberstadt had resigned when retreating to the Netherlands, had greater appeal to the English government.

Before King Christian moved, the French acted to close the Valtellina to the Spaniards, while the duke of Savoy blockaded Genoa from the north. The threat to the Habsburgs was serious, and Elector Maximilian was also alarmed. His was the only big army in Germany, but he feared that it might be incapable of defending the Catholic gains of the last five years against a combination of European powers. He urged the emperor to find additional military forces. It was in this situation that Ferdinand II accepted Wallenstein's offer to bring together an army of 20,000 men at his own expense. It was clear from the outset that such an army could only be maintained by living off the land, as the imperial coffers were empty. When Ferdinand, appointing the new duke "*capo*" (captain) of all his forces, authorized him to enforce "tolerable" contributions in "conquered" places, he in effect consented to ruthless exactions for the support of the army. A new force of destruction was thus created, a force, too, that was not fully under the control of the emperor. Wallenstein tried to win the personal loyalty of his officers by having colonels and captains contribute to the funds for raising the army, thus making them, along with him, creditors of the emperor.

The confusion, division, and panic that existed among the princes of the Lower Saxon circle defies description. Understandably, they were afraid that, after his victory at Stadtlohn, Tilly would extend his operations to lower Saxony. They wished to close the land to invasion, but the method they chose, the election of King Christian of Denmark to captaincy of the circle, did not help the cause of their neutrality. He moved his army to the Weser valley. Mansfeld moved his troops from the Netherlands to the lower Rhine, while Christian of Halberstadt came to Brunswick, where his brother ceded to him the government of the duchy. In July, 1625, Tilly crossed the southern boundaries of the circle. Soon the sufferings of the population cried to heaven, yet neither side was strong enough to risk battle. In October, Wallenstein arrived in Lower Saxony. But he did not feel ready to go into action with his untried troops. Tilly made his winter quarters in the bishopric of Hildesheim west of the Harz Mountains; Wallenstein, in Halberstadt and Magdeburg farther to the east.

The year 1626 brought changes in the general political situation. In Upper Austria, where Ferdinand II had carried out the counter reformation with seeming success, a violent revolt of the peasants broke out, bringing with it a repetition of the horrors of the Peasants' War of the sixteenth century. However, the government suppressed the movement with relatively small forces, under Count Gottfried Heinrich Pappenheim. It was also fortunate for the Habsburgs that a Huguenot uprising in France forced Richelieu to withdraw the French troops from the Valtellina, and that the sympathies entertained by the Dutch and English for the Huguenots disturbed the co-operation between these nations and France. Prince Charles, who in May, 1625, succeeded James I as king of England, had married Henrietta Marie, but England planned to launch a direct naval attack on Spain rather than take an active part in fighting on the Continent. The Protestants in Germany were therefore left without much support. Soon England, as a result of internal conflicts, was to cease to exercise any influence upon European politics. In the United Provinces the war was going badly for the Protestants. The death of Maurice of Orange in April, 1625, had not brought a change in policy, but Frederick Henry, his successor, had not been able to avert the fall of Breda to Spinola in June, 1625. On the other hand, Bethlen Gabor was again willing to attack Austria.

∽ The Lower Saxon War, 1626

IN THIS STATE of general uncertainty the Lower Saxon war opened in 1626. Mansfeld, trying to dislodge Wallenstein from his position on the Elbe river, lost a third of his army at the Dessau bridgehead on April 25, 1626. Mansfeld managed, however, to reorganize his forces and break through Silesia in July, aiming at a meeting with Bethlen Gabor. In the end Gabor failed to keep his part of the bargain. Wallenstein was nevertheless forced to follow Mansfeld with most of his army and leave operations in lower Saxony in Tilly's hands. Tilly had already overcome Christian of Halberstadt's bold attempt to cut his southern lines of communications in Hesse. In June, 1626, death ended Christian's short, adventurous life. On August 27 Tilly's masterful leadership crushed the army of King Christian IV south of Brunswick, at Lutter near the Barenberg. The princes of the Lower Saxon circle sued for peace, and only the dukes of Mecklenburg stayed with Christian IV, who retreated to the lower Elbe. As a result of Tilly's victory Saxony and Brandenburg were practically immobilized. The Altmark of Brandenburg, on the left bank of the Elbe, served as a base of operations for the imperial forces. At the same time Gustavus Adolphus, who had resumed his war against Poland, used East Prussia as his base.

The power of the Protestant estates in northern Germany had been destroyed, and in the southeast the Habsburg position had been made secure. The peasants' revolt in Upper Austria had been quelled. Bethlen Gabor made his peace with the emperor in December, 1626, forswearing all co-operation with Mansfeld, who died a short time later. Bethlen himself was ailing. He did not take up arms again, and in 1629 he died. Even more important, Austria succeeded in concluding a twenty-five-year peace with the sultan. The internal conflicts of the Ottoman Empire relieved the Austrians on their southern flank and gave them a chance to concentrate on Germany.

Were Wallenstein and his army really needed in Germany? His contribution to the remarkable enhancement of Habsburg power appeared negligible compared to Tilly's great services. Wallenstein's system of contributions had antagonized both enemies and friends. His dismissal was urged by many. However, the emperor was not willing to throw away the power, unwieldy though it might be, that Wallenstein's army gave him. Wallenstein, who cleverly offered to resign, was retained and given broader authority. He was allowed to quarter his troops in the imperial territories and in future was not to be interfered with when he raised the number of his soldiers to any level that his extortionist financial practices might permit. At the same time agreement was reached among the emperor and the princes of the League on a war plan for the year 1627. This plan envisaged the removal of all opposition from northern Germany, including the Swedes, who were advancing against Poland from Prussia.

During 1627 Wallenstein mopped up the remnants of Mansfeld's army in Silesia, and then headed north down the Oder, Havel, and Elbe rivers, securing all the bases of Brandenburg and Mecklenburg. Meanwhile, Tilly, too, had reached the estuaries of the lower Elbe and Weser. Wallenstein pushed into Holstein and soon reached the northern tip of Jutland. In the winter of 1627–28 he quartered his army not only in the conquered territories of the north but also in Franconia and Swabia. Practically the whole Empire came under the shadow of imperial troops. The handwriting on the wall became quite clear to the German princes when Ferdinand II declared the rights of the Mecklenburg dynasty forfeited and gave the duchy of Mecklenburg to Wallenstein. It had shocked the princes of the Empire to see the ruling dynasty removed from the Palatinate and its possessions and title transferred to Maximilian. But Maximilian was a member of one of the oldest princely families, and the transaction had had the approval of the spiritual electors. The elevation of Wallenstein, a Bohemian parvenu, by mere fiat to the rank of a prince of the Empire was a grave warning that the Empire, as the learned councilors expressed it, was changing from a *regimen aristocraticum* into a *regimen monarchicum.* Under Maximilian's leadership the German princes complained about the oppression that Wallenstein brought to friend and foe with his system of recruitment, enforced contributions, and quartering. They demanded a reduction of his army and a change in his methods, and they wished to have the imperial army placed under the command of a German prince. They rebuffed Ferdinand II, who was anxious to settle the problem of the Habsburg succession by the election of his son, Archduke Ferdinand, as Roman King.

✍ Ferdinand's Attempted Conquest of the Baltic

FERDINAND II was committed to carrying through the conquest of the Baltic. Since the days of the Hohenstaufen no German emperor had held so much power along the shores of Germany's "East and West Seas." Spain in particular urged him to make this power secure against Denmark and Sweden, for she saw in it the means of defeating the Netherlands by throttling Dutch trade in the Baltic. On April 21, 1628, Wallenstein was appointed "general of the oceanic and Baltic sea," but it remained to be seen whether he could create a navy overnight, as, three years earlier, he had raised an army. Neither Spain nor Poland could give him ships. Only the Hanseatic cities could have helped in this, but they denied the imperial troops entrance within their walls and even refused to lend the emperor ships. They were afraid that naval supremacy on the emperor's part would mean the destruction of their political and religious liberties. In these circumstances the creation of a reasonably good naval base in Wismar in Mecklenburg was useless. "The eagle cannot swim," gibed the pamphleteers. Wallenstein could still prevent the Swedes from landing, and he sent Hans Georg von Arnim into Pomerania to do so. But he found the city of Stralsund practically an island city facing the shores of West Pomerania, and it was unwilling to grant him admission.

Stralsund, a Hanseatic town, was, next to Stettin, the most important port of Pomerania. A decade earlier the townspeople had fought successfully for a more democratic town government, and they had watched over the city's privileges against the dukes of Pomerania. The resistance to Wallenstein also started with the people rather than with the city council. The siege of Stralsund occurred at the same time as the siege of La Rochelle, the stronghold of French Protestantism. But while La Rochelle ultimately succumbed to Richelieu, the intrepid burghers of Stralsund were more successful. They received some assistance from Denmark, and shortly after Wallenstein arrived at the city gates Gustavus Adolphus sent help, though on condition that the city enter a treaty of alliance with Sweden giving her the use of the port in case of war for a twenty-year period. Wallenstein could not hope to subdue the city from the land and broke off the siege in the last days of July, 1628. A few weeks later he had the satisfaction of completely defeating a landing attempt by King Christian on the Pomeranian coast. This success did not change the general military situation, but it did make Christian eager for peace. Wallenstein had the good sense to disregard the exaggerated aims of Emperor Ferdinand. In the Treaty of Lübeck of May 22, 1629, King Christian kept all his Danish possessions and Holstein, but he withdrew from the captaincy of the Lower Saxon circle and renounced all Danish claims to north German bishoprics. Arnim was dispatched to Poland with his corps to help King Sigismund against Gustavus Adolphus. If it was hoped to keep the Swedish king out of Germany, this hope was short-lived. Gustavus threw himself into a new campaign against Poland, which was already too weak and demoralized to be saved by Arnim. Pressed by the Polish magnates, Sigismund was forced to make his peace with Gustavus in September, 1629, leaving control over the coast of Poland and Prussia to Sweden. Gustavus Adolphus now had his forces free to intervene in Germany, so on June 6, 1630, he landed with an army on the Pomeranian island of Usedom.

Other imperial military operations in 1629 led to similar failure, even where they brought military gains. Relations with Spain in these years became a liability rather than an asset for Emperor Ferdinand. No doubt the magnificent restoration of the imperial position in Germany could not have been achieved without the co-operation of Spain. But it was not a sense of gratitude alone that moved the emperor to return the support he had received. The concept of the pre-eminence of the house of Habsburg in Europe was alive in him. Just then the ties between the lines had been reaffirmed by the marriage of Archduke Ferdinand to his cousin Infanta Maria of Spain. The emperor was not exclusively motivated by cool appreciation of his political interests but also by religious devotion and strong dynastic sentiments. At a moment when circumstances demanded that he give undivided attention to the consolidation of his victories in the Empire, Ferdinand was involved in Spanish affairs. This involvement caused opposition within Germany. Elector Maximilian saw in the emperor's efforts outside of Germany only a trumped-up excuse for the maintenance of an army that threatened the vitality of Germany as well as the liberties of the German princes.

The war between the Dutch and the Spaniards had brought serious reverses to Spain. Prince Frederick Henry, in his calm and efficient manner, had been able not only to stabilize the Dutch position after the fall of Breda, but also to win the initiative by laying siege to Hertogenbosch. In 1628 the Dutch navy captured the whole Spanish treasure fleet off Cuba; it carried money and goods valued at 11.5 million gulden, and its loss jeopardized the maintenance of the Spanish army in the

Netherlands. Emperor Ferdinand, under heavy Spanish pressure, could not persuade the estates of the Empire to declare the war against the United Provinces a concern of the Empire. He could only detail some of Wallenstein's troops, and under John of Nassau these invaded Holland from the lower Rhine. But the capture of Wesel by the Dutch forced them to retreat, which, incidentally, caused the surrender of Hertogenbosch in September, 1629. With the Dutch occupation of Wesel—which had earlier been taken by Spinola—the Spanish lost easy access to the lands north of the Rhine and Meuse, and the Dutch gained a controlling influence over the territories along the lower Rhine, thus denying the emperor the chance to undo the result of the Jülich-Cleves war, as he had desired.

∽ *The Problem of Mantua*

THE PROBLEM OF MANTUA, though less directly connected with Germany than the fighting in the north, proved of even greater consequences for German history. At the end of the year 1627 the Gonzaga duke of Mantua and Montferrat, territories adjacent to Milan to the east and west respectively, died. A French ruler was to follow him. Spanish prodding made Ferdinand sequester the duchy, which was technically a fief of the Empire, and a corps of Wallenstein's army was sent to Italy to co-operate with the Spaniards in the occupation of the Gonzaga territories. The war, which started auspiciously for the Habsburgs only to run into difficulties later, is of no particular interest to German history except that it brought on the immediate intervention of France in upper Italy as well as the most determined efforts by Richelieu to wreck the position of the emperor in Germany. As a result of these efforts France entered into an alliance with the United Provinces and negotiations with Gustavus Adolphus favoring Swedish intervention in Germany as well as direct contacts with the German princes. French policy was tremendously helped by the policy of Pope Urban VIII, in whom the old papal policy, centering around the secular interests of the Church state, revived. In the Mantua affair he came out openly against the emperor.

Personally, Pope Urban was no doubt chiefly motivated by his concern over Italian politics and by his predilection for France, but his attitude brought other forces within the Church to clear expression. For two generations at least, the Church had been under the prevailing influence of the Jesuits. It could not be denied that they had been the

leaders of a profound regeneration of religious life as well as of the
political restoration of the Church. Still, it was inevitable that once
Catholicism had regained some strength and confidence, it would also
examine its losses. At that point the exclusive reliance on the house of
Habsburg appeared to be detrimental to the role of the Church as the
mother of nations, and the imposed centralism of the Jesuit order as depriving the Church of its roots in the local and national societies of
Europe. Opposition against the Jesuit order found active expression particularly in the Capuchin order, whose members were indefatigable in
weaving political schemes for the defeat of the militant universalism of
the Jesuits. And behind the Capuchins the older orders, such as the
Benedictines, pressed their claims for recognition as the traditional
representatives of indigenous religious life.

It is astounding, though on close examination it will not appear acci-
dental, that these conflicting trends came to the surface just at the moment when the emperor was attempting to restore Catholicism to its
old position. Ferdinand II was no tyrant, coldly plotting the advance of
his personal power. He was not a clever man, and his good nature was
genuine. Although he was naïvely convinced that orthodoxy would reward his "apostolic" dynasty, he was always animated by devotion to
his faith, which was explained to him in its personal and political implications by his confessor Wilhelm Lamormaini (1570–1648). But
raison d'état appeared more and more unashamedly in European politics.

✍ The Edict of Restitution, 1629

WE HAVE ALREADY SEEN how Ferdinand II carried on the counter reformation in his own lands during the 1620's. Naturally, the intensity of
this endeavor reached its climax after the great victories of 1626, which
seemed to make it possible to abandon caution and regard for the
Protestant estates of the Empire. Moreover, the conquest of north Germany in 1627–28 seemed to open the divinely willed opportunity for
restoring the old Church all over Germany. On March 6, 1629, the emperor promulgated the Edict of Restitution. To him it was the most
coveted result of a decade of war and painful toil. With a stroke of the
pen it stipulated that all the Church goods appropriated by German
princes after the Passau agreement of 1552, as well as all the imperial
bishoprics and convents that had become Protestant after 1555, were to
be restored to the old Church. Expressed in the technical, legal language
of the age, this meant the literal enforcement of the "ecclesiastical reser-

vation" and annulment of the "declaration" of Emperor Ferdinand I which had been given at the time of the Religious Peace of Augsburg. The Peace itself was now definitely understood to apply only to the followers of the original Augsburg Confession. In other words, the Calvinists were to be excluded from its benefits.

The Edict of Restitution would have "counter reformed" two archbishoprics and twelve bishoprics as well as more than fifty major convents. At short notice Habsburgs and Wittelsbachs were appointed to the bishoprics of Bremen, Magdeburg, Osnabrück, Verden, Minden, Hildesheim, and Halberstadt. For the time being, no attempt was made to restore the bishoprics absorbed by Brandenburg, Pomerania, and Saxony, but the restoration of convents and church lands taken by secular principalities that did take place was carried on by imperial commissions backed by the armies of Wallenstein. Württemberg and Brunswick were the immediate victims of the Edict. Its early enforcement created strong bases of Catholic power in regions of Germany which were overwhelmingly Protestant, and the ax was held ready for the ruin of the large Protestant states as well. The status of the religiously mixed cities was not treated in the Edict of Restitution, as it seemed more practical to deal with them individually. An example was set by the imperial intervention in Augsburg. Though only one-tenth of the Augsburg citizens were Catholic and their rights had been carefully respected, it was argued that the bishop could resume his spiritual jurisdiction over the free city. With the help of a Catholic majority in the city council, the exercise of Protestant religion was forbidden. Eight thousand Augsburg citizens, among them the famous Elias Holl, who had just built Augsburg's city hall, went into exile.

Similar judgments were issued against Strasbourg, Magdeburg, and Bremen, but for the time being these were not carried out. It was, however, only a question of time before the counter reformation and the suppression of political independence would be extended to all sections of the Empire. On the whole, little resistance was shown where the Edict of Restitution was actively enforced. Hope had fallen low in Protestant Germany. Only in the Netherlands was some organized power of resistance left; this the emperor had successfully neutralized but not yet subdued. When issuing the Edict, Ferdinand had assured the elector of Saxony that it was not directed against him. But he had not promised him that the case of the annexed Saxon bishoprics would not be litigated in the future. For the time being John George of Saxony only protested weakly. As will be remembered, Saxony was well administered and had preserved its wealth, for the war had not really touched it yet. Still, Saxony by itself could not fight the emperor, and it was separated from the majority of the estates of the Empire, since they favored the counterreformatory objectives of the Edict of Restitution, although they might dislike the unconstitutional manner of its promulgation without the approval of the diet, and might fear its political result, the predominance of the emperor in Germany.

In 1628 Maximilian had received the Palatinate territories on the right bank of the Rhine in exchange for the evacuation of Upper Austria. The Wittelsbach dynasty had also been rewarded with some of the bishoprics in north Germany. Whereas Ferdinand's son, Archduke Leopold William, had received Magdeburg, Hildesheim, and Halberstadt, a Wittelsbach had received Osnabrück and Verden. But lands meant little as long as the emperor, with Wallenstein's army, could impose his will on all. In the fall of 1630 a meeting of the electors with the emperor was held at Regensburg—Saxony and Brandenburg were not represented. At that time Maximilian demanded the dismissal of Wallenstein and the reduction of the imperial army. He also urged the restoration of the duchy of Mecklenburg to the Mecklenburg dukes as a step toward achieving peace with Sweden, and he opposed German participation in the Habsburg war against the United Provinces. Meanwhile, he was busily negotiating with France, whose representative, Père Josèphe, was fanning the spirit of opposition to the emperor. Ferdinand was anxious to gain acceptance of the election of his son Ferdinand as Roman King and of the entrance of the Empire into the Dutch war, but he was unconcerned about the landing and progress of Gustavus Adolphus in Germany. After the easy defeat of the Danish king, he thought of Gustavus as just another "snow king."

Emperor Ferdinand might have got the full support of the Catholic princes and even of the Protestant electors, and thereby have gained the strength to fend off both French and Swedish intervention if he had dismissed Wallenstein and modified the execution of the Edict of Restitution. But he did only the first. On August 13, 1630, he announced his willingness to depose his military commander and reduce the imperial forces. By this step Bavaria was kept from fully joining the French camp. But this was all that Ferdinand gained. He continued to be in a seriously weakened position, which was not improved when he placed a greatly diminished imperial army under Tilly's command. The Catholic princes continued to be suspicious, while the Protestant electors were hostile and inclined to look for foreign help. The German stage was set for Gustavus Adolphus.

CHAPTER 13

The Thirty Years' War:
II. 1630–48

❦

✍ Gustavus Adolphus

WHEN GUSTAVUS ADOLPHUS LANDED at Peenemünde in Pomerania in July, 1630, his army was small and he still had to arm politically before he could hope to take the offensive. He was 36 years of age, and he had been the ruler of Sweden for 19 years. Since his early youth he had lived in the midst of political and military enterprises. With his administrative genius he had developed Sweden into the strongest Baltic power and had given its one and a half million Swedes and Finns an orderly regime such as no other contemporary country enjoyed. In his wars with Poland he had won Livonia and thus brought Sweden's control of the entire Baltic nearer to realization. The progress of imperial arms posed a clear threat to Sweden. Politics and religion were inseparably connected. Gustavus Adolphus was a sincere Protestant, holding a warm faith that was little concerned with doctrine and was not hostile to Calvinism. In his aversion to Catholicism he did not forget that an enforced religion was meaningless. Gustavus Adolphus was an unusual soldier; strong and sturdy, he bore all the hardships of actual fighting easily. He was also a great commander and organizer. A close student of the tactics and military administration of Maurice of Orange, he introduced the Dutch battle order into Sweden and explored new ways of using artillery and firearms. His courage and self-confidence were combined with great subtlety in planning. He radiated not only strength but also trustworthiness. Gustavus Adolphus had at his side the scholarly chancellor, Axel Oxenstierna, a master of sober political analysis and an unfailing judge of men and affairs, a man cool and silent in outward appearance but warmhearted and humane. Unfortunately, for many years this most civilized statesman was to serve only a martial cause.

Gustavus Adolphus forced Duke Bogislav of Pomerania into an alliance, which, like most of the subsequent alliances with German princes, meant actual subordination to the Swedes. It was also evident that Sweden intended to hold on to Pomerania after the present emergency. Although the Protestant people showed great enthusiasm and the recruitment of troops was quite successful, the German princes were not eager to fight on Gustavus Adolphus' side. Apart from the exiled dukes of Mecklenburg, he won as allies, before the end of 1630, only Landgrave William V of Hesse-Cassel and Christian William of Brandenburg, the deposed administrator of the archbishopric of Magdeburg. Arousing support among the burghers of Magdeburg, the arch-Lutheran city, Christian William returned, and he concluded an alliance with Sweden in August, 1630. Magdeburg, with its 30,000 inhabitants, was one of the big cities of Germany. Its dominant position on the middle Elbe made it a pivotal point for the military control of north-central Germany, and its past role in the history of Lutheranism gave it a prominent place in the hearts of German Protestants. But Gustavus needed more troops and funds for his operations.

Sweden's Alliance with France, 1631

IN JANUARY, 1631, at Bärwalde in the Neumark, where Gustavus Adolphus had his headquarters, the alliance of Sweden with France was finally signed. The "liberation of the East and North Seas" and "the restitution of the suppressed estates of the Empire" were set out as the aims of the compact. The second objective was couched in general language in order to leave the question of the Palatinate open and thus not exclude a further rapprochement between France and Bavaria. Gustavus Adolphus had to agree to protect the practice of the Catholic religion where it was found to exist in conquered territories. He undertook to maintain a 30,000 man infantry and 6,000 man cavalry for the next five years and was to receive a million pounds in annual subsidies. This was an impressive sum, and it was further augmented by Dutch subsidies. But it soon proved inadequate, because large forces were called for, and the Swedes had to fall back on "contributions" from the land.

Activities of the Protestant Princes

AT LAST the Protestant German princes began to bestir themselves. In February and March, 1631, they met in Leipzig in large numbers, and a strong protest was lodged against the Edict of Restitution, imperial war contributions, and the disregard of the constitution of the Empire. The general intention of the Protestant princes to make preparations for arming, however, was not tackled with great zeal except in Saxony, where John George devoted himself with energy to the building of an army. Hans Georg von Arnim, a Brandenburg *Junker* who had left the imperial army after the promulgation of the Edict of Restitution in 1629 and had probably been Wallenstein's best general officer, was made a Saxon field marshal. Originally, Arnim had thought of the war exclusively as a political and constitutional conflict. It will be remembered that Saxony was a relatively wealthy and well-governed state. It had not suffered any serious ravages of war so far, and consequently it had the resources for the formation of an army.

Few Protestant princes in Germany, with the exception of those who, like the dukes of Weimar, had set their sights on high appointment in the Swedish army, contemplated active co-operation with the Swedes. John George and Arnim rather intended the creation of a third force between Sweden and the Habsburgs, which was to induce the emperor to abandon the Edict of Restitution, but which would also stand ready to expel all foreigners from German soil in co-operation with the emperor. The Lutheran oracle, the Saxon court chaplain Hoë von Hohenegg, presently found justification for co-operation with the Calvinists and also for armed resistance against the imperial Edict of Restitution, but it was always possible that Saxony would return into its former policy of nonintervention, once the emperor made a conciliatory gesture.

These developments left Gustavus Adolphus in a precarious position, the more so since Tilly's forces were constantly being reinforced, chiefly by imperial troops brought back from Italy. Gustavus could not even hope to reach Magdeburg without gaining the support of Brandenburg. Only after protracted fencing between Gustavus Adolphus and Tilly in Brandenburg and Mecklenburg was Gustavus Adolphus successful in dragooning his brother-in-law, Elector George William of Brandenburg, into an agreement, in June, that gave the Swedes virtual domination of the electorate. But meanwhile Magdeburg had been conquered by Tilly. On May 20, 1631, imperial troops had broken into the city and dealt with its citizens in the most savage fashion, till fire destroyed the whole city with the exception of its old cathedral. Two thirds of the inhabitants, together with many of the plundering soldiers, were caught in the holocaust. The behavior of the soldiers in the early Swedish war had already been incredibly cruel on both sides, but the destruction of Magdeburg brought the hatred of the two parties to fever pitch.

✍ The Battle of Breitenfeld

THE MAGDEBURG FIRE and the destruction of its fortifications and provisions made the city useless as a military base. However, to maintain his large army and also to keep the Saxons from further arming and possible co-operation with the Swedes, Tilly broke into the electorate in the first days of September, reaching the rich city of Leipzig at the middle of the month. A few days earlier John George and Gustavus Adolphus had concluded an alliance, on the basis of equality. The Saxon troops gave Gustavus a very slight numerical superiority over Tilly. This advantage encouraged him to look for a decision in battle at once. On September 17, 1631, battle was joined just north of Leipzig at the village of Breitenfeld. The Saxon army, one of the best-trained forces of the seventeenth century, proved inexperienced in combat and John George would have been too timid to avert defeat, but the leadership, morale, and superior organization and tactics of the Swedes turned the battle into a decisive victory. More than half of the imperial and League army was annihilated, and all their artillery lost, as was the war chest of the League. This great victory encouraged active resistance and co-operation among the Protestants everywhere, even if co-operation meant subordination to the Swedes. John George would have liked to see the Swedes operate against the lands of the emperor so that he might pose as the liberator of the Empire and gather a party of his own. The poor showing of the Saxons at Breitenfeld enabled Gustavus to dictate the war plan. The Saxon army was to take the offensive through Silesia, while the Swedes were to enter southern Germany.

In spite of this plan, however, Bohemian noblemen, exiles since 1619, persuaded Arnim to march directly into Bohemia. On November 15 he took Prague. Gustavus Adolphus turned south by way of Erfurt to take the bishoprics along the Main. In the middle of October he occupied Würzburg and marched down the German "priest-lane," reaching Frankfurt on November 27 and Mainz on December 23. Young Duke Bernhard of Weimar, whom the king had made colonel of his own horse-guard regiment, was dispatched to the Palatinate. He conquered Mannheim on January 8, 1632, when the main Swedish army was already in winter quarters. With these results, there was great rejoicing among the Protestant people, but the military issues were not settled as yet, and the political problems assumed a new, possibly more perilous, complexion.

✂ *The Development of Opposition to Gustavus Adolphus*

NORTHERN GERMANY was not entirely conquered. Imperial and League forces under the bold Pappenheim still shielded Westphalia and the lower Rhine. Behind them lay the Spanish Netherlands. Tilly had succeeded in leading some of his troops to the Danube, where Maximilian was active to reinforce them. The political situation was fraught with still more serious dangers. As Gustavus Adolphus approached the Rhine, French policy became more restless. French diplomacy had tried from an early date to exploit the conflict between Maximilian of Bavaria and the emperor.[1] Ferdinand's decision to dismiss Wallenstein delayed a close understanding between Maximilian and Richelieu, but in May, 1630, Maximilian agreed to sign an alliance with France. The agreement excluded the emperor as a possible enemy. Though puzzling even in the involved and ambiguous diplomatic practices of the age, it was chiefly directed against Spain and in any event did not dampen the efforts of Maximilian and Tilly against the king of Sweden. It helps explain, however, the expectations that Richelieu harbored when he brought Gustavus Adolphus into the Empire through the alliance of Bärwalde of January, 1631. The cardinal had thought that Sweden's influence would not extend beyond northern Germany and that he could use Gustavus Adolphus to curtail the emperor's power in Germany, but would still be able to play off the Catholic League under Maximilian against a revived union of Protestant princes under Swedish leadership.

Obviously, Richelieu was surprised when he suddenly saw Gustavus Adolphus well on his way to defeating both emperor and League and making himself complete master of Germany without regard for the political wishes of France. He hurried to safeguard at least the French interests along the Rhine. French government over the three bishoprics of Metz, Toul, and Verdun, which had become French protectorates in 1552, was strengthened; the duke of Lorraine brought to heel; and the archbishop of Trier induced to turn over the strong bridgeheads over the Rhine—the Ehrenbreitstein at Coblenz and Philippsburg—to French garrisons. Franco-Swedish relations showed signs of strain,

[1] See page 338.

as did the alliance of Sweden with Saxony. For John George the moment seemed ripe for making peace. This would also have brought liberation from the liberator, whose plans for the Empire seemed to run as strongly in a monarchical direction as the defeated policy of Ferdinand II. What Gustavus Adolphus' ultimate aims actually were, has been the subject of much study and speculation. It is doubtful whether he himself had made up his mind in every respect. A certain trend can be noticed. Whereas in the beginning the confederate element in his German policy was much emphasized—he called himself the "director of the evangelical defense organization"—he imposed greater obligations on his German allies after Breitenfeld. The restored princes received their territories as Swedish fiefs. Moreover, direct Swedish annexations took place, both along the Baltic coast and, by grants of principalities and estates to Swedish generals, in southern Germany. Clearly, Gustavus Adolphus had set his eyes on the imperial crown in a reorganized Empire. But he was sufficiently realistic to know that prior to any definitive political settlement he had to win an unassailable position by arms.

∽ Recall of Wallenstein

THE GOVERNMENT IN VIENNA soon recovered from the shock that the disaster of Breitenfeld had at first produced. It was a bitter experience for the emperor that not even at that time of gravest peril was Pope Urban VIII willing to support Austria. The relations between Vienna and Madrid were tightened, but help could not be expected from Madrid in view of the serious situation in the Netherlands. Maximilian, who in the preceding year had been the one most responsible for Wallenstein's deposition, now, in his fear, suggested to Ferdinand his recall. Prince Eggenberg, the emperor's chief chancellor, urged the same course. Ferdinand agreed to bring Wallenstein back, but now the general could lay down his conditions. After much begging Wallenstein undertook to organize an army for a period of three months only. After that time, in March, 1632, he had to be implored to become its commander-in-chief (*Generaloberstfeldhauptmann*). He was not bound by special instructions; rather, as he had demanded, everything was committed to his "great dexterity, loyalty, and diligence." The selection of officers was also his prerogative. Large financial guarantees were given, and, naturally, premiums for the commander as well. But even more significant, he was granted authority for political negotiations with Saxony.

Wallenstein had spent the two years after his dismissal on his princely Bohemian estates. He was in a revengeful mood against the German princes as well as against the emperor. He had bluntly refused to send provisions from his well-stocked duchy to Tilly's army when it suffered near-starvation in the summer of 1631; he had remained in intimate contact with his former lieutenant, Hans Georg von Arnim, now the Saxon commander, and through old Count Thurn he had offered his assistance to Gustavus Adolphus for a revolt in Bohemia. Wallenstein dropped communications with the Swedes for the time being, but he assumed his new command determined to make himself the arbiter of policy as well as military leader. Pride and passion for personal power were the mainsprings of his thought and action. Religion was alien to him; he trusted astrology and his own capacity for unraveling the laws and forces of politics. The dynamic strength that derives from a deep commitment to ideals or persons was missing in his saturnine personality. He always kept aloof from others, including his closest officers, and was a poor judge of people. In 1632 Wallenstein was an ailing and senescent man. His strategy had always been slow, and, conscious of the cost of war, he had taken to heart the advice against unnecessary battles which was common in contemporary military writing. Said Count John of Nassau: "One should not easily and without great advantage accept battle, even if the enemy presents himself, unless one is compelled to do so by the lack of supplies and money for the continuation of the war; for not to be beaten is also a big victory."

Wallenstein's prestige was great enough to attract soldiers to his regiments. He devised the organizational structure for a powerful army of more than 40,000 men, and his own north Bohemian duchy provided arms and supplies. But he did not move his army before May, and meanwhile Gustavus Adolphus had been able to extend his operations to southern Germany. Nürnberg welcomed him with jubilation. On April 7, 1632, he crossed the Danube at Donauwörth. On April 14–15, Tilly, now 73 years of age, but still brave and bold, tried to block the Swedish advance into Bavaria at Rain, but in vain. Tilly was seriously wounded and died two weeks later. At this moment Maximilian rose above dynastic policy. He might have led the League troops south to defend the Bavarian capital, in which case the Swedish army could have placed itself along the Danube between the armies of the League and of Wallenstein. It was an act of great self-abnegation when Maximilian decided to sacrifice his own country. By retiring to Regensburg and Ingolstadt he made a future union with Wallenstein possible and also discouraged Swedish operations against Austria.

Gustavus Adolphus deliberately destroyed the countryside of Bavaria. On their way to Augsburg and Munich, his soldiers cut a great swath of ruin through the land. Only the towns, including Munich, which was reached on May 17, could buy off destruction. Meanwhile, Wallenstein pushed the Saxons out of Bohemia and then crossed the western Bohemian mountains to unite his army with the troops of Maximilian, thereby forcing Gustavus Adolphus to march north. In the neighborhood of Nürnberg, Gustavus Adolphus, faced with a vastly superior enemy, was put on the strategic defensive. After strengthening his army by calling troops from northern Germany, he attacked Wallenstein—who had refused to employ his superiority in the weeks before—in his fortified encampment at Zirndorf (close to Fürth) on September 3, 1632. Although the army of Wallenstein and the League had been enormously weakened by epidemics, ten hours of bitter fighting did not dislodge them. The Swedes suffered terrible losses.

✍ *The Death of Gustavus Adolphus at Lützen, 1632*

WALLENSTEIN NOW HOPED to achieve by arms what he had been unable to accomplish through negotiations, namely to induce Saxony to break its alliance with Sweden. With his plundering soldiers he marched north into Saxony. On November 2, Leipzig surrendered to him. Gustavus Adolphus had originally felt that Arnim would be able to hold his own against Wallenstein. The Saxons had made surprising gains in an invasion of Silesia and news of the fighting at the upper Rhine and in the northwestern German and Dutch war theater was also good, so Gustavus Adolphus felt free to turn against Bavaria and possibly Austria. But in sudden concern over the military and political situation in Saxony, and probably in the hope that once he had overwhelmed Wallenstein he would have no further worries about either enemies or allies, he marched hurriedly into Thuringia and Saxony. After engaging for some time in a maneuvering campaign, a strategy which persuaded Wallenstein that Gustavus Adolphus wanted to postpone a military decision till the next year, the latter fell upon Wallenstein 15 miles southwest of Leipzig on November 16, 1632, a damp and foggy winter day. The battle of Lützen was a furious struggle, lasting from the time in the morning when the fog lifted somewhat till darkness fell. In the early afternoon Gustavus Adolphus led one of his cavalry regiments into the fray to confound Wallenstein's right wing. He ventured too far into the enemy's ranks and was killed. Maddened with grief, the Swedes fought on with unflagging determination under Bernhard of Weimar's command. They held their ground, and then broke the strength of both wings of Wallenstein's army. Wallenstein decided to retreat, even though he had to leave his cannons to the Swedes, as all his trace horses had been lost. In this same battle the idolized Field Marshal Pappenheim was mortally wounded. Wallenstein did not even feel that he could quarter his army in Germany, as he had intended. This burden fell again to the Emperor's Bohemia.

The death of Gustavus Adolphus, causing deep sorrow among the Protestant people all over Germany, changed the course of history more than the loss of the battle of Lützen alone might have done. No one can say with certainty that his survival and ultimate victory would have resulted in a major unification of Germany. It is certain that his intervention defeated the attempt of Ferdinand II to impose a monarchical regime on the Empire and also saved Protestantism in Germany from annihilation. But Gustavus Adolphus could not have disentangled Germany from involvement in European politics and the pressures of foreign powers. Yet it is true that the death of "the lion from the north" increased the impact of the foreign world on Germany many times. An early peace between the embittered German factions might have prevented this impact or at least mitigated it. Voices counseling such a course were heard in Vienna but not listened to. It was pointed out that any successes of imperial arms would call forth the full entrance of France into the war against the house of Habsburg, whereas French policy would be satisfied with the present exhausted state of all German parties. On the other hand, it was argued, this was the time when the Protestant estates might free themselves with little risk that a foreign power would win a permanent foothold in Germany. Wallenstein must have known these arguments and sympathized with them, though his personal ambitions beclouded his thinking.

✍ The Heilbronn Confederation, 1633

SAXONY, AS ONE MIGHT HAVE EXPECTED, was inclined toward peace. John George was even willing to make a separate peace, while Arnim aimed at a general peace. After the death of the Swedish king Saxony seemed to have a chance to assume the leadership of the Protestant estates. But Axel Oxenstierna, Gustavus Adolphus' successor as director of Swedish foreign policy in Germany, blocked this. The Swedish Reichsrat, which conducted the government during the minority of Christina, the six-year-old daughter of Gustavus Adolphus, had given him unlimited authority in all German affairs. His first efforts were directed toward organizing the allies and subordinates which Sweden had gained through the conquests of the late king. In the Heilbronn Confederation of April 23, 1633, he brought the Protestant members of the four southern German circles together under a Swedish directorate. The German estates formed only an advisory council and assumed the obligation to provide for the maintenance of the armies. The Confederation proved capable of isolating Saxony and also of checking the overbearing trend of French policy, which was viewed with grave suspicion in Saxony and upper Germany. The Heilbronn confederates were also annoyed by French attempts to protect German Catholicism. It caused satisfaction among them when Sweden acted as a protagonist of the Protestant cause by restoring an indigenous Palatinate government. The insipid Frederick V, who had not grown wiser through misfortune, had been with Gustavus Adolphus in the last months of the latter's life, expecting that his lands would be restored to him. He died of the plague two weeks after the death of the Swedish king. Oxenstierna invited Frederick's brother, Philip Ludwig, as guardian of Frederick's children, to join the Confederation and to establish himself in Heidelberg. Richelieu had no choice but to renew the Bärwalde alliance with Sweden.

But there were already signs that Sweden could not hope to maintain the full initiative it had acquired under Gustavus Adolphus. In the future the Swedish army had to live almost exclusively on German resources and foreign subsidies, and without its interest in gaining repayment for its early war expenditure and in getting control of the German coast, Sweden might have chosen a much smaller part in the war. Oxenstierna found it difficult to solve the succession in the military command of the Swedish forces. The young Duke Bernhard of Weimar demanded the chief command. He had entered military life as a youth of 17, and in twelve years had risen to the highest military rank. He was a man of deep political and religious ideals, which were reflected in his impeccable personal life. Yet he also had the exaggerated pride of a German prince and the personal ambitions of the warriors of the age. Oxenstierna granted Duke Bernhard a title and the rule of a duchy of Franconia, which was formed out of the bishoprics of Würzburg and Bamberg. In this way he avoided making him the sole commander of the Swedish armies, but the rivalry between Bernhard and the Swedish generals, among whom Count Gustav Horn was the most eminent, weakened the army thereafter.

✍ *The Treachery of Wallenstein*

IN THE MEANTIME Wallenstein had made his army ready for further action. One might have expected that he would lead it against the main forces of the enemy, the armies of Duke Bernhard and of Horn. The Swedes looked for a military decision in southern Germany; here, in the territories of the Heilbronn allies, they had their chief German support. While along the Rhine a number of places, such as Constance, Breisach, and Philippsburg, were still defended by Catholic garrisons, the Protestant domination of the middle Danube and Bavaria deprived Maximilian of his power and threatened Austria. But Wallenstein left Bavaria to the misery of spoliation, and kept the emperor in anguish and the Spanish government in fear of losing its last secure stations on the road to the Netherlands. He turned against the relatively weak Saxon army of Arnim, which was supported by a Swedish contingent under Count Thurn. Instead of conquering them, however, Wallenstein concluded a series of armistices with them and opened negotiations for a separate peace with Saxony and Brandenburg. In this he went far beyond the instructions that had defined his authority as commander-in-chief. He had never hidden his aversion to the Edict of Restitution, which Vienna was still unwilling to give up. Wallenstein proposed that he and Arnim, by a *fait accompli*, compel their rulers to accept a peace. But Arnim took his loyalty more seriously, and Elector John George distrusted offers that did not have the backing of the emperor.

Soon Wallenstein began to open conversations with Thurn, in which he raised hopes that he might avenge the Bohemian nobility and lead a revolt against the Habsburgs. For such an undertaking, however, he wanted help from Sweden and France, the very powers that, in his talks with the Saxons, he had promised to chase from Germany. Oxenstierna expressed disbelief in Wallenstein's words and demanded irrefutable proof by action before he would collaborate with him. In October, 1633, Wallenstein gave evidence of an opposite inclination. It had become high time for him to bolster his sinking prestige as a military commander and restore his political reputation with the government in Vienna. He probably also wanted to demonstrate the actual weakness of Saxony. He opened hostilities and succeeded in capturing Thurn and his forces. Then he had one of his corps move down the Oder as far as Frankfurt and Landsberg. By directing his troops into Pomerania, he could have destroyed the communications and coastal bases of the Swedes. But he broke off these operations and retired to Bohemia. Negotiations with the enemies were resumed, and Thurn was not handed over to imperial justice but set free, since he declared himself ready to deliver the Silesian fortresses to his captor. In spite of all Emperor Ferdinand's entreaties to Wallenstein that he detail forces to southern Germany, the latter had looked on coldly while the Swedes gained superiority and ruined the country. When he finally made a gesture of help, it was too late to stave off the crowning triumph of Duke Bernhard, the conquest of Regensburg on November 14, 1633. Moreover, Wallenstein's troops were again in winter quarters in Bohemia, ravishing Habsburg lands still further.

On the last day of December, 1633, the emperor, urged on by Elector Maximilian and the Spanish government, decided to depose the unsuccessful and refractory commander-in-chief. But at once the question arose whether Wallenstein would not be backed up by his army in resisting such a move. Therefore the imperial government tried to win over the officer corps of his army. With the connivance of his immediate lieutenants, Octavio Piccolomini, Count Gallas, and Johann von Aldringen, it proved surprisingly easy to undermine the officers' loyalty. Wallenstein realized that Vienna was planning his deposition; this drove him to speed up his negotiations with Saxony, France, and Sweden and to assure himself of the loyalty of his army. He thought he could exploit the colonels' dependence on the return of their personal capital investment from the common enterprise. Wallenstein induced 49 of them to sign a document by which they promised to hold to him. In this Pilsen declaration of January 12, 1634, the imperial government saw, not incorrectly, a conspiracy, and they accordingly deprived Wallenstein of his command. Piccolomini was entrusted with the task of winning over the colonels for the emperor and of arresting Wallenstein or, in case of resistance, killing him as a notorious rebel.

Wallenstein's counteractions were weak and hesitant. He tried to win his officers to his cause by denying any plans against the emperor or any indifference to religion. He failed to realize that these men, like himself, were anxious to safeguard their personal and mercenary interests, and that they saw a higher authority of law in the emperor than in their captain. While Wallenstein corresponded with Vienna about an honorable retirement, he invited both Arnim and Bernhard of Weimar to send troops for a rendezvous with his own forces. But his enemies moved faster than he could plot or make up his mind. On February 20, 1634, the garrison of Prague was taken over by a devoted imperial officer, and when the imperial letter pronouncing Wallenstein's removal was made public, the defection of his army manifested itself at once. With a few troops Wallenstein moved to Eger to await the Saxons and Swedes. It is hard to see what the Protestants could have gained from the desertion of the imperial commander-in-chief who had already lost his army.

Even the forces with which Wallenstein arrived in Eger were no longer reliable. A group of officers, eager not to be drawn into treasonable activities against the emperor and alarmed at the impending approach of Arnim, decided to kill Wallenstein. Butler, an ardent Irish Catholic, and two Scotch Calvinists, Gordon and Lesley, who felt duty-bound to the emperor, collaborated in the murder of Wallenstein's confidants, Ilow, Trčka, Kinsky, and Niemann, at a dinner at the castle during the night of February 25. It would not have been difficult to capture the general thereafter, but blood-stained hands could not rest too quickly. Before midnight the halberd of an English Captain Deveroux had ended the life of Wallenstein.

✍ *Reviving Strength of Habsburg Power*

EXCEPT FOR A FEW MINOR REVOLTS, no protest was raised following Wallenstein's death, nor was there a serious outcry against the method chosen by the imperial government for disposing of him. It had not acted without collecting ample evidence of his treacherous activities. This evidence was now published. That in these circumstances the government had acted as it had, appeared unobjectionable to contemporaries. With the removal of Wallenstein the army became in the full sense an imperial army. The young heir to the throne, Ferdinand III, king of Hungary, was made its official commander and Count Matthias Gallas placed at his side. The Bavarian and League forces were now overshadowed by the military power of Austria. Maximilian, in despair about the misfortunes that had befallen Bavaria, ceased to oppose active cooperation with Spain on German soil, to which Wallenstein, too, had strenuously objected.

The reverses suffered by Spain in the Dutch war had driven the government of King Philip IV to new and strenuous efforts. His brother, Infante Ferdinand, who had once been destined for Church office and had received a cardinalate, but whose heart was in military affairs, was appointed governor of the Netherlands. He was to proceed to Brussels from Milan with a large army, which, on its way, was to make the Rhine secure for Spain. With King Ferdinand III as chief of the imperial army, co-operation between the imperial and Spanish troops was assured. The imperial and Bavarian armies joined forces at the Danube and reconquered Regensburg in July, 1634. But in the meantime the armies of Arnim and the Swedish general Johan Banér occupied Silesia and Bohemia. If they had continued their offensive operations in the direction of the Danube, they, together with Duke Bernhard and Horn, might have gained superiority over King Ferdinand and the "Cardinal-Infante." Saxony, however, wanted to negotiate with the emperor, and Bohemia was evacuated. Thus Bernhard and Horn were left to deal with a considerably stronger enemy. Relying on the better tactics of the Swedish army, Bernhard and Horn rather reluctantly decided to attack the Habsburg forces besieging the town of Nördlingen, which protected the approach to Swabia. The battle of Nördlingen, on September 6, 1634, ended in catastrophe for the Swedes: many thousands were killed; others, including Field Marshal Horn, were taken prisoner; and all their artillery was lost. It was a blow that shattered any future chance of Swedish control of Germany. Most immediately, it put German Protestantism in frightful danger again. By spring, 1635, all of southern Germany east of the Rhine had fallen into the hands of the imperialists, and all that Gustavus Adolphus had done for the restoration of Protestantism was lost.

Duke Bernhard, with whatever troops he could scrape together, tried for a while to defend the region between the Rhine, Main, and Neckar, but eventually he had to retreat to Alsace. Oxenstierna could give him a high command but could not provide him with much support. Thus Bernhard lost his newly constituted "duchy of Franconia," and was largely left to fight his own war. This naturally strengthened the self-centeredness of his mind, but it also gave him greater opportunities for standing up for his evangelical convictions and German patriotism.

✎ *The Peace of Prague, 1635*

THE LOSS OF FRANCONIA AND SWABIA ruined the Heilbronn Confederation. At this same time support for Sweden in northern Germany collapsed. In November, 1634, Saxon and Austrian diplomats reached agreement on the preliminaries of a treaty, out of which the Peace of Prague of May 30, 1635, was molded. In the Peace of Prague the Edict of Restitution was superseded by the provision that ecclesiastical dominions be returned to, or remain in the hands of, the princes who had been in actual possession of them on November 12, 1627. This stipulation, however, was meant to be valid only for a period of forty years, when litigation before the courts of the Empire or emperor might be resumed. Aside from this provision, the treaty did not challenge the secularization of ecclesiastical properties in Saxony and all territories east of the Elbe, but it left the bishoprics between the Elbe and the Weser—the archbishopric of Bremen, the bishoprics of Osnabrück, Minden, Verden, Hildesheim, and Halberstadt—in Catholic hands. All Protestant administrators were denied representation on the diet; and imperial knights and imperial cities, with the exception of Ulm, Strasbourg, Frankfurt, and Nürnberg, were refused the benefits of the status of 1627. In general, the benefits, insofar as they helped Protestants, were confined to the Lutherans. This was in accord with Saxon policy, but the attempts of the Saxons to gain some protection for the Lutherans in Bohemia were in vain. Only in Silesia was Ferdinand inclined to make some concessions. Saxony received further palpable gains by the full cession of Lusatia and the appointment of Prince August of Saxony as administrator of Magdeburg. Maximilian of Bavaria, for his part, was to retain the Palatinate on the right bank of the Rhine and his electoral dignity.

In addition to the purpose of concluding peace between Saxony and the emperor, the Peace of Prague had national German aims. It was significant that the treaty was made at the time when Spanish co-operation had reached fruition at Nördlingen, for in the eyes of the Viennese government a common Habsburg policy in Europe and the national aims advanced by the treaty were intended to support each other. To the Saxons and German princes, including Elector Maximilian, the welfare of Germany was the predominant aim. The treaty was accordingly negotiated with the intention of restoring peace in the Empire and removing foreigners from German soil. Every member of the Empire was invited to join, as well as Sweden and France, but the latter only on condition that they would evacuate their troops from Germany and restore Lorraine and Pomerania to their rightful German rulers. In order to enforce the provisions of the peace, including the restitution of the rights of the Church against obstruction by any estates of the Empire, the emperor was to mobilize an army to be financed by tax contributions from the estates. The army was to be under oath to the emperor, though the Saxon elector, as well as any other elector later joining the treaty, was to command a special corps. With the exception of some territorial garrisons, no prince was to keep an army of his own, and there were to be no special confederations or alliances among princes. Even the Catholic League became illegal through this provision.

The Peace of Prague was a great victory for the emperor. It increased his monarchical powers considerably and gave German Catholics the dominant position in the Empire. If the Protestants accepted this treaty, it was under the shadow of military defeat. Still, it seemed to the Lutherans that at least the light of true Christian faith had been saved and was not likely to be put out by the imperial government. Confidence in the emperor had not died, and patriotic sentiment made it possible to hope that expulsion of the foreigners and restoration of peace at home would create within the nation a law-abiding spirit. But any expectations that were entertained with regard to the growth of national cohesion could be justified only if the new unity proved capable of actually restoring peace and expelling the Swedes and French. It was at least seventeen years too late for this. Soon it became evident that not even a unified Germany had the strength to defend its borderlands and achieve peace for herself.

Maximilian of Bavaria accepted the Peace of Prague. On the Protestant side, the decision of Brandenburg was most important. The exclusion of Calvinism dismayed Elector George William, as did the acquisition of Magdeburg by Saxony. Against this the Pomeranian question had to be weighed. Brandenburg had hoped to acquire this Baltic duchy on the death of Duke Bogislav XV, who had no children. A valid treaty had been concluded between Brandenburg and Pomerania concerning the inheritance, but the landing of the Swedes and their insistence on a foothold on the Oder stood in the way of consummation of the treaty. George William chose the imperial side, and accepted the Peace of Prague. Count Adam Schwarzenberg, a Catholic nobleman from Cleves, assumed the direction of the political and military affairs of Brandenburg-Prussia, in the course of the next years becoming an almost dictatorial leader. Apart from the banned princes—Margrave George Frederick of Baden and Duke Eberhard of Württemberg—only Duke Bernhard of Weimar, Landgrave William of Hesse-Cassel, and the city of Strasbourg refused to accede to the Peace of Prague.

For a moment it seemed as if even Sweden would sign the peace. She could hardly continue the war by herself, especially as Denmark had assumed a threatening attitude and Sweden's armistice with Poland was running out. However, she bought Denmark off by ceding Bremen to her. In Sweden's negotiations with Poland, France helped greatly in getting a twenty-five-year extension of the armistice. This was only one of the many political moves by which Richelieu organized the French war against the Habsburgs. In May, 1635, three months after she had concluded an alliance with the United Provinces for the subjugation of the Spanish Netherlands, France declared war on Spain. In July she made an alliance with Savoy, Mantua, and Parma for the conquest of Milan. Duke Henri de Rohan was dispatched to occupy the Grisons passes. But Richelieu did not wish to renew the alliance with Sweden on the old basis. He had disliked seeing Gustavus Adolphus win a strong position on the Rhine in 1631, and had at that time brought Lorraine and Trier within the grip of France. The adversities in which the imperialists found themselves before Nördlingen and the collapse of Swedish military power enabled the French to collect strongholds along the upper Rhine like fallen apples. They occupied most of Alsace. Richelieu managed to draw Duke Bernhard and his army to the French side. The duke was paid French subsidies for an army of 18,000, and he was promised the "landgravate" of Alsace. The landgrave of Hesse-Cassel was also taken into French pay. Relations between France and Sweden remained muddled for a few years. France's payment of subsidies to Sweden was not resumed until 1638. But Sweden's armistice with Poland made it possible for Oxenstierna to transfer Swedish troops from Livonia and build up an effective Swedish army in northeastern Germany under Banér. The fact that all the Germans had become allies of the emperor removed the last vestiges of decent restraint in plundering the area.

✍ The Thirteen Last Years of Destruction

THUS THE WAR CONTINUED for thirteen long years. What had started as an internal revolt in the Habsburg territories was carried into the heart of the Empire by the conflict of the religious parties after the battle of White Mountain. Increasingly, the war had merged with the struggle of the European powers for predominance. With the Peace of Prague the Germans had tried to end the war within their borders, but France and Sweden were unwilling to terminate the fighting and give up the opportunity for making their power in Europe secure. After 1635 Germany was almost exclusively the battlefield and prize of war of outside powers, although the Peace of Prague had not succeeded in putting out the sparks of discord among Germans, themselves, and these were fanned into flames again.

French intervention did not at once change the tide of the war. In the Grisons, in Milan, and in the Netherlands, the French were unsuccessful, and simultaneously they suffered reverses on the Rhine; Trier was taken by the Spaniards and the elector of Trier brought as prisoner to Vienna. Even Lorraine was invaded. Emperor Ferdinand II had his last triumph: he assembled the electors in Regensburg in the fall of 1636 and had his son elected King of the Romans on December 22. Seven weeks later Ferdinand II died, and his son became Emperor Ferdinand III (1637–57). It was a warning of future trouble, however, that Banér with his restored army had won a brilliant victory over an imperial and Saxon army at Wittstock in September, 1636, and had advanced to Erfurt. That city again became a chief base of Swedish operations, as it had been under Gustavus Adolphus. In the following year Banér retreated to Pomerania under heavy pressure from his opponents. The death of Duke Bogislav of Pomerania stirred Brandenburg into raising an army. Although French subsidies to Sweden began to flow anew in 1638, Banér could do no more then than free Mecklenburg and West Pomerania of imperialist troops.

The same year, however, brought a decisive change on the upper Rhine. On March 3, 1638, Duke Bernhard of Weimar gained a masterly and crushing victory at the Rhine bridge of Rheinfelden. He followed it up with the conquest of Freiburg and, most important, of the fortress town of Breisach. On July 18, 1639, Bernhard, then thirty-four years of age, died of a fever. His brother could not inherit his Alsatian principality, as Duke Bernhard had conquered it for France. His army, the "Weymariens" or "Bernardines," also came under French command. It was in the spring and summer of 1639, too, that Banér broke through Brandenburg and Saxony. He ventured as far as the outskirts of Prague, and then accomplished a work of wholesale destruction in northern Bohemia, as he had done in Saxony and Brandenburg in the years before. He repeated his southward thrusts in the following year, this time supported by French forces, but was pushed back as far as the Weser. In the winter of 1640–41 he attempted to take Regensburg, where a diet had assembled, but was likewise unsuccessful. In May, 1641, Banér died. He was followed as Swedish commander by Lennart Torstensson, a general of high military genius and audacity. In 1642 Torstensson advanced through Silesia to Olmütz in Moravia. Although he then had to fall back to Saxony, he inflicted a drastic defeat on the Austrian army under Archduke Leopold William on the battlefield of Breitenfeld on November 2, 1642. Leipzig was occupied by the Swedes and held until the end of the war.

In 1643 Marshal Torstensson fought the Danes, who had entered the war against Sweden. Denmark suffered defeat and had to give up her possession of Bremen and Verden. In the spring of 1645 Torstensson renewed his invasion of Bohemia, beat the imperialists and Bavarians at Jankau (close to Tabor) on March 6, and advanced to the north bank of the Danube in Upper Austria. Since Prince George Racoczy of Transylvania, a recent ally of Sweden and France, was marching against Austria from the south, Vienna was in immediate danger. Through concessions to the sultan, Racoczy could be compelled to end his campaign. French military progress over the years was slower than that of Sweden. It took time for the French to develop troops, particularly infantry, that could match the veterans of other nations. In these years their chief opponents, the Bavarians, had military leaders of high ability in Franz von Mercy, born in Lorraine, and Johann von Werth, a bold cavalryman. This also gave Elector Maximilian a more important position on the imperialist side. In 1643 Mercy crowned a successful campaign against the French under Guébriant with a stunning defeat of the latter's foolhardy successor, Josias von Rantzau, at Tuttlingen. In August, 1644, he beat the French armies under Turenne and the Duc d'Enghien at Freiburg, and in May, 1645, he defeated Turenne at Mergentheim. But in the summer the Duc d'Enghien brought fresh French troops, which were joined by Hessian and Swedish forces, and an advance to the Danube was undertaken. At Allerheim, a few miles southeast of Nördlingen, a battle was fought on August 3, 1645. It has often been compared with the battle of Lützen. Marshal Mercy was killed early in the fighting, which then continued with unusually heavy losses, but the French held the battleground.

At the conclusion of the fighting the French and Swedish side had a definite advantage, although the victors of Allerheim had to leave southern Germany during the winter. But in the following year Turenne and the new Swedish commander, Karl Gustav Wrangel, marched over the Main and Danube against Augsburg, and devastated Bavaria, down to the Isar, and Bregenz in the most atrocious manner. This time they took up winter quarters in Franconia and Swabia. Elector Maximilian lost heart in view of this disastrous situation and on March 14, 1647, concluded the armistice of Ulm, declaring Bavaria and Cologne, the other Wittelsbach dominion, together with the Swabian and Franconian circles, neutral states. However, it was not simple to disentangle the Bavarian troops from the imperial ones, nor was there much of a chance to save the electoral dignity of the Palatinate for Bavaria except by fighting on the side of the emperor. So Maximilian again joined Ferdinand in September, and his country up to the Inn now had to suffer even more cruel destruction during the summer of 1648. The joint imperial and Bavarian armies suffered a serious defeat at the Zusam. Only with difficulty was Marshal Piccolomini able to assemble a weak army to protect Austria. Already in July a Swedish corps under Count Hans Christoph Königsmarck broke into Bohemia and occupied the Kleinseite opposite Prague. The city was easily captured in 1635, but the counter reformation had done its work in the meantime. Now burghers, students, and monks fought with the soldiers in a mood of utter determination for more than three months. No decision had been reached when, on November 2, 1648, word was received that peace had been concluded in Münster nine days before. Thus the war ended in Bohemia, where it had begun thirty years before.

The last thirteen years were the most disastrous period of the Thirty Years' War, which was actually a bundle of wars. The extension of the fighting showed that no power was strong enough to achieve decisive results quickly. From 1635 to 1640 relatively even strength prevailed among the belligerents, and the scales came to favor the French only slowly. In their major war efforts, which were directed against the Spanish monarchy, they achieved greater successes than in Germany. In 1639 the Dutch annihilated a large Spanish fleet, a blow from which Spanish naval power never recovered, and the overwhelming victory of the Duc d'Enghien over the Spanish army at Rocroy in May, 1643, crippled Spanish land forces north of the Pyrenees. Even more serious were the signs of disintegration within the Spanish monarchy. Portugal separated from Spain and Catalonia revolted in 1640. By 1646 the French and Dutch had reduced Spanish control of the Netherlands to such an extent that the Dutch began to wonder whether the replacement of the Spanish by the French on their southern border was in their best interest.

That these results were achieved only after so many years indicates the lack of resources available even to the strongest governments. The primitive financial administration of the European states at that time led to a system of warfare which rested on organized, and for that matter badly organized, robbery. In the later years of the war plundering was done not only to support one's own army, but also to create wastelands where the enemy could not maintain troops. The sufferings of the civilian population multiplied under these conditions. Hunger, homicide, and epidemics took an ever larger toll, while many homeless and starving people served as replacements for the continuously dwindling armies. A barbarism from which death was the only relief had settled over most of Germany.

✍ Arrival at Peace Negotiations

THE LONGING FOR PEACE was general among the populace and even among the rulers (the only people who managed to avoid the terrible trials of these years). But it was not in their hands to make peace. Peace was not possible until the Dutch found it inopportune to continue fighting on the side of the French, until the Swedes were prepared to lower their demands for territorial and financial compensation, and until the emperor was willing to give up the active co-operation with Spain on which his policy had so largely rested since the removal of Wallenstein. Developments in Germany could not but have an influence on such situations in Europe. The growing isolation of the emperor after 1640 was no doubt of great significance in the denouement of the war. The first prince to break away from the alliance with the emperor which was implied in the abortive Peace of Prague was Frederick William, the young elector of Brandenburg, who succeeded his father in December, 1640. He recognized that the army which Count Schwarzenberg had brought together was more of a burden on Brandenburg than a threat to any potential enemy. He reduced it in size so that it could be developed into a disciplined force. At the same time he began negotiations with the Swedes about an armistice, which was informally concluded in 1644. Saxony was forced into the same course of action. On September 6, 1645, it concluded an armistice with the Swedes at Kötschenbroda. Neither Brandenburg nor Saxony, however, was thereby spared the continuing fate of being exploited as a Swedish base of operations.

Of all those who had been active allies of the emperor after 1635, only Maximilian of Bavaria and the ecclesiastical electors remained. But Archbishop Philip the elector of Trier had always been a French collaborator, and he acted as such again when he was released from his imprisonment after the battle of Allerheim to help in peace negotiations with France. Archbishop Anselm Casimir of Mainz was driven out of his territories on the left bank of the Rhine in 1644, and he made an armistice with the French for his right-bank possessions in May, 1647. Maximilian of Bavaria had already made overtures to France in 1645, and two years later, as we have seen, he tried to protect himself and his brother Ferdinand of Cologne by making a truce.

The desire for peace was already dominant at the diet of the Empire which was held in Regensburg in 1640–41. Ferdinand III had to adapt himself to the general sentiment. He wanted to save the Peace of Prague and with it the co-operation of the estates under his leadership, which would have enabled him to negotiate peace with the foreign powers as the representative of the Empire. But while the emperor still hoped for an improvement of the military situation, minor modifications of the religious provisions of the Peace of Prague were declared unsatisfactory by the elector of Brandenburg, who broke away from the common front of the German estates by opening negotiations with the Swedish government. Sweden and France, for their part, insisted that they were not at war with the Empire but only with the emperor and individual German princes. They also indicated that they considered the constitutional and religious affairs of Germany matters of concern to themselves. Thus in the end the estates were all partners to the peace negotiations. The peace conference was to produce a European peace that was to become at the same time a law of the Empire, or, more specifically, the law that would settle the internal conflicts of the Empire.

At Christmas, 1641, the emperor agreed with Sweden and France on peace negotiations to be held with Sweden in Osnabrück and with France in Münster in the following year. But the opening of conferences was delayed till the end of 1644. Hope for favorable turns of events made one side or the other mark time. In addition to the vicissitudes of war events such as the death of Richelieu in 1642, and of Louis XIII in 1643, and Queen Christina's coming of age in 1644 always raised expectations. But in France, where the Queen-Dowager Anne became the regent during Louis XIV's minority, Cardinal Mazarin acquired Richelieu's position. Although Mazarin did not have quite the same sureness of eye and hand as his predecessor, he continued Richelieu's foreign policy. Queen Christina's more conciliatory political attitude did not change Swedish policy, which remained under Oxenstierna's direction. From the fall of 1645 on, practically all the estates that had a vote in the diet of the Empire were represented in the capitals of the two Westphalian bishoprics.

CHAPTER 14

The Peace of Westphalia, 1648

✧ General Nature of Settlement

SELDOM IN HISTORY, at least before the "cold war" in our own days, were important diplomatic negotiations carried on in such an involved manner as at the peace conferences of Westphalia. In contrast to Münster, Osnabrück had come under the control of the Swedish army, and for this reason the Swedes made the town their diplomatic headquarters. Here they were also protected against the appearance of a papal nuncio, whom they wished to exclude from all negotiations. In Münster the Swedes maintained a *chargé d'affaires,* as in turn both the emperor and France were represented in Osnabrück by diplomats of lesser than ambassadorial rank. The physical separation of the delegates in itself made the proceedings very cumbersome, and progress was further impeded by the excessive emphasis on protocol, which was characteristic of the diplomacy of the age. Moreover, the Westphalian conferences served as a congress for the settlement of peace between Spain, France, the United Provinces, and Portugal all at the same time.

The Protestant estates of the Empire flocked to Osnabrück, because they expected to be in a stronger position for peace negotiations with the emperor and the Catholic estates if they gained Swedish support. But this peace had to take the form of agreements on fundamental laws of the Empire, and negotiations between the Catholic and Protestant estates followed the style of the diet of the Empire. Still, the estates of the Empire were at war with each other and could hold only a divided diet. Actually at Osnabrück and Münster the Protestant or Catholic estates debated in the customary three curias—electors, princes, and cities. Thereafter each curia had to reach a compromise with the corresponding curia in the other place, and finally agreement had to be reached among the three full curias. If such agreement received the approval of the emperor, it was considered ready for promulgation as a law of the Empire. Only the ceremonies of signing the instruments of peace on October 24, 1648, brought the hostile members of the Empire together.

A compromise settled the conflicts between Protestantism and Catholicism as well as between the monarchical aims of the Habsburg dynasty and the desire for peace on the part of the princes. It should not be forgotten that these two conflicts, closely related as they were, were not identical. The balance that the peace achieved in the religious and political affairs of Germany was brought about by mediation and dictation of foreign powers, and it was intended to serve as the fulcrum of a balance of European powers. The internal conditions of the Empire were settled in the light of the power interests of the major states of Europe.

Considering the history of Europe as a whole, one might argue that certain losses which Germany suffered, or some limitations which were imposed on her national development, could have been borne more easily if the peace had truly pacified Europe. But on the European level the Peace of Westphalia was not intended to ban future rivalries of powers. On the contrary, it was meant to create positions of strength, from which further expansion by individual states could be launched in the future. For France, the Peace of Westphalia served largely to isolate Spain. The French continued the war against Spain, and when in 1659 they were victorious, they turned again to the extension of their northern and western frontiers. In contrast, Sweden, desirous of maintaining a central role in European politics as well as political and economic domination of the Baltic, was soon to find herself in an overextended position. Thus the Peace of Westphalia was only one in a long series of treaties through which the expansionist powers, at various moments, settled their gains and losses. For a long time these settlements rested not only on the outward weakness of Germany but also on the direct influence of the foreign powers on her internal life.

✑ Western Frontiers of Empire

THROUGH HER ACQUISITIONS on both banks of the upper Rhine, France secured the separation of the two Habsburg powers and at the same time a firm hold on the development of German affairs. The emperor ceded to France his rights and possessions in upper and lower Alsace. Actually, these were not easy to describe, and, unfortunately, they were ill-defined in the treaty. The Habsburg rulers owned the major part of upper Alsace, but most of lower Alsace belonged to the Empire and not to the emperor. The city of Strasbourg, six small free cities, the bishopric of Strasbourg, and many imperial counts and knights were estates of the Empire, over whom the emperor did not exercise any authority. But in the absence of any clear circumscription of the confused rights of ownership, protective rights, and honorary privileges, the general reservation of the rights of the imperial estates which was inserted in the treaty was a rather helpless gesture. France, however, was not satisfied with the possession of Alsace. She demanded and received from the emperor the strong fortress of Breisach on the right bank of the upper Rhine as well as Philippsburg opposite Speyer, two strong bases for possible offensive operations against the Empire. In addition, the French gained recognition of their possession of both the cities and the bishoprics of Toul, Verdun, and Metz. No agreement was reached on the duchy of Lorraine, whose ruler remained at war with France on the side of Spain. The emperor's promise not to intervene in this war was a bad omen for the future.

The cession of Alsace was the most grievous loss, since it meant not only the occupation of key strategic points by the French but also the withdrawal of the Germans from a province that, through the centuries down to this very age, had played a major part in German political and cultural history. Its significance for Germany had already been disregarded by the Oñate Treaty of 1617, which envisaged Spanish control of German territories on the left bank of the upper Rhine. Even in 1648 the main objection of the Austrian government was not to the cession of these German territories to France but to breaking the land bridge with Spain. Elector Maximilian of Bavaria, eager to win French support for his own gains in the war against the Palatinate, could pose as the defender of German national interests when he argued that Spain's war with France was no concern of the German Empire and that the emperor, by his co-operation with Madrid, deprived Germany of the blessings of peace. This attitude on the part of Maximilian was of crucial importance in dissuading the emperor from active collaboration with Spain. But no one, not even Maximilian, wished to see France win a seat in the diet of the Empire. The territories in Lorraine and Alsace were therefore handed over to the French crown.

Another change in the frontiers of the Empire was officially recognized by the Peace of Westphalia. As early as January, 1648, Spain had conceded sovereignty to the United Provinces. The Treaty of Osnabrück mentioned them as a state included in the treaty, without other-

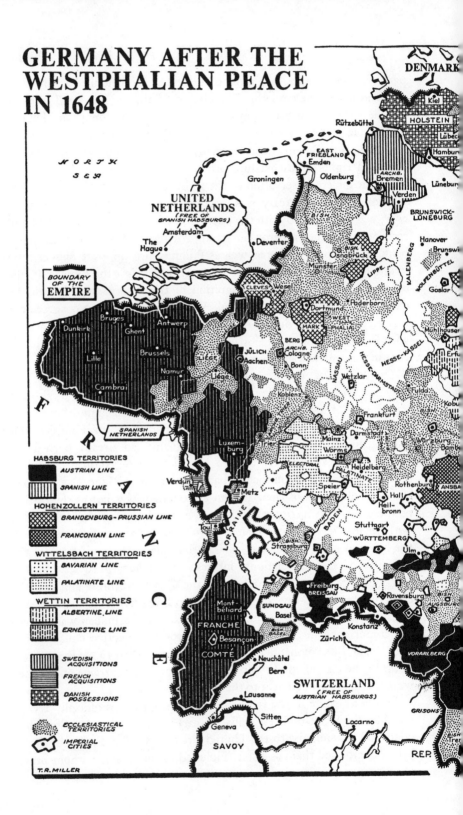

GERMANY AFTER THE WESTPHALIAN PEACE IN 1648

DENMARK

Kiel

HOLSTEIN

Lübec

Rützebüttel

Hamburg

NORTH SEA

EAST FRIESLAND
Emden

Oldenburg

ARCHB.
Bremen

Lüneburg

Groningen

Verden

BRUNSWICK-LÜNEBURG

UNITED NETHERLANDS
(FREE OF SPANISH HABSBURGS)

Amsterdam

Deventer

BISH.

Hanover

Brunswi

The Hague

BISH.
Osnabrück

Münster

LIPPE

KALENBERG

WOLFENBÜTTEL

BOUNDARY
OF THE
EMPIRE

CLEVES Wesel

Dortmund

Paderborn

WEST-PHALIA

Goslar

Mühlhauser

Bruges

Antwerp

Dunkirk

Ghent

MARK

BERG

ARCHB.
Cologne

Bonn

HESSE-KASSEL

Erfu

Lille

Brussels

LIÈGE

JÜLICH
Aachen

NASSAU

HESSE-DARMSTADT

Namur

Liège

Fulda

Cambrai

Koblenz

Wetzlar

Kobu

F

Frankfurt

SPANISH
NETHERLANDS

Luxem-burg

Darmstadt

Mainz

Wor

Würzburg

Bamb

HABSBURG TERRITORIES

▮ AUSTRIAN LINE

▯ SPANISH LINE

Verdun

Metz

ELECTORAL
PALATINATE

Heidelberg

Speier

Rothenburg

ANSBA

HOHENZOLLERN TERRITORIES

▨ BRANDENBURG-PRUSSIAN LINE

▧ FRANCONIAN LINE

Toul

LORRAINE

BISH.
Strassburg

BADEN

RHINE

Hall

Heil-bronn

Stuttgart

WÜRTTEMBERG

Ulm

WITTELSBACH TERRITORIES

▫ BAVARIAN LINE

⣿ PALATINATE LINE

WETTIN TERRITORIES

▤ ALBERTINE LINE

▥ ERNESTINE LINE

Freiburg
BREISGAU

Ravensburg

Mont-béliard

SUNDGAU

Basel

Konstanz

VORARLBERG

FRANCHE
COMTÉ

BISH.
BASEL

Besançon

Zürich

▮ SWEDISH ACQUISITIONS

▤ FRENCH ACQUISITIONS

▨ DANISH POSSESSIONS

Neuchâtel

Bern

SWITZERLAND
(FREE OF AUSTRIAN HABSBURGS)

GRISONS

⣿ ECCLESIASTICAL TERRITORIES

◇ IMPERIAL CITIES

Lausanne

Sitten

Locarno

BISH.
Tre

Geneva

SAVOY

R.EP.

T.R.MILLER

F R A N C E

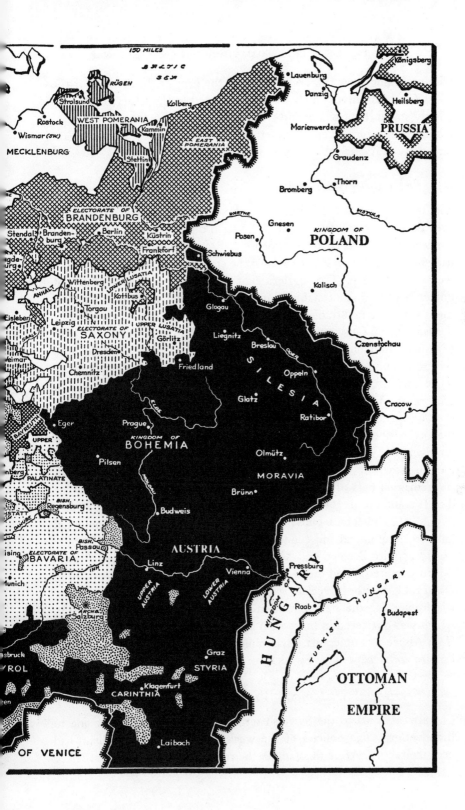

wise recording their full exclusion from the Empire. In the case of the Swiss Confederation, which was also included in the treaty, it was explicitly stated that Switzerland was exempt from all imperial authority. Actually, Switzerland and the Netherlands had separated from the Empire many years earlier.

∽ Peace with Sweden

THE DEMANDS OF SWEDEN WERE SWEEPING, and agreement would have been delayed even beyond 1648 if Austrian diplomacy had not favored concessions to Sweden at the expense of Brandenburg, much as Bavaria had co-operated with France against the emperor on the question of the western boundary. The legal title of Brandenburg to the duchy of Pomerania was incontestable. But Sweden insisted upon possession of the lands at the mouth of the Oder river, which she had occupied since the landing of Gustavus Adolphus in 1630. The emperor's refusal to champion Brandenburg's claim compelled Elector Frederick William to accept a compromise. He received East Pomerania (Hinterpommern) while Sweden retained Stettin, the whole estuary of the Oder, West Pomerania (Vorpommern), and the island of Rügen. Sweden also got the bishoprics of Bremen and Verden, comprising the lands between the lower Elbe and the Weser. Control of the estuaries of the three major rivers of Germany thereby fell into Swedish hands, together with the port town of Wismar in Mecklenburg. However, all these territories remained fiefs of the Empire, with Swedish representatives on the diet. It could not be foreseen in 1648 that Swedish power would decline fast and that Sweden would never be able to exploit fully her potential hold on the political and economic life of Germany. In 1719 Hanover was to acquire Bremen and Verden; a year later Brandenburg-Prussia was to win Stettin and the Oder estuary. Great difficulty was caused in Osnabrück by the Swedish request for payment of twenty million Reichstaler for the demobilization and return of the Swedish army, which was quartered in more than a hundred places all over Germany from Alsace to Pomerania. Five million was eventually offered by the Empire and accepted by Sweden for the *contentement de soldatesque.*

∽ Territorial Settlement Within Germany

CLOSELY RELATED to the Swedish settlement were the grants made to Brandenburg. The policies of the weak Elector George William had been ineffectual. After 1640, under the rule of young Elector Frederick

William, later known as the Great Elector, Brandenburg had given signs of an energetically pursued independence and internal consolidation. Frederick William was quite unable to maintain himself against a Sweden supported by France and eventually by the emperor as well. He had to forego his chief political aim of winning Stettin, the natural Baltic port of Brandenburg, and be satisfied with East Pomerania. His hope that his marriage with Louisa Henrietta, princess of Orange, might induce the Netherlands to intervene with Sweden on his behalf proved in vain. But once Frederick William had accepted a compromise, the Swedish government was eager to please him. He was, after all, the strongest and closest neighbor of Sweden and the most obvious potential ally against Poland. Thus Frederick William was given the bishoprics of Kammin, Halberstadt, and Minden, as well as the archbishopric of Magdeburg, which he was to receive after the death of the present incumbent, Prince August of Saxony (died 1680). Saxony was dismayed at this last provision, but it was compensated by receiving full possession of Upper and Lower Lusatia from the emperor. Mecklenburg, in exchange for the cession of Wismar to Sweden, received confirmation of its possession of the bishoprics of Ratzeburg and Schwerin.

∽ Restitutions

THE YEAR 1618, which marked the outbreak of the Bohemian revolt, was called the "normal year" for all restitutions and amnesties. This meant that all the estates of the Empire, as well as its subjects, who in the course of the war had suffered damages by confiscation of their properties, or penalties for religious or political partisanship, could claim restitution or amnesty. But some of the most important cases could not be treated under this ruling. Maximilian of Bavaria could not be deprived of the electoral dignity or of all the other gains he had made in the war against Frederick V. Backed by French diplomacy, Maximilian retained both the electoral dignity and the Upper Palatinate (north of the Danube), while Karl Ludwig, the eldest son of Elector Frederick V, "the Winter-King," received the Rhenish Palatinate and a new eighth electorate, specially created for himself and his heirs. The margravate of Baden-Durlach was restored to its state of 1622. Landgravine Amalia, widow of William V of Hesse-Cassel, who had continued the war on the side of France with unflinching determination, was substantially rewarded in land and money. Württemberg was virtually restored.

With regard to restitution of the private property of subjects and an amnesty for their political actions, Emperor Ferdinand III would not be bound by any general law. He refused to consider what would have amounted to an undoing of the social and property changes that had transformed the Habsburg territories in the decade after the battle of the White Mountain. He offered restitution and amnesty only to those who had served the Swedes or French after 1630. In these matters the lands of the Habsburgs were placed under a juridical regime distinct from the rest of the Empire. It was of even greater historical significance that with regard to the religious rights established by the Peace of Westphalia the Austrian law was different from the German law.

The Peace of Prague of 1635 already had chosen a "normal year" as criterion for the ownership of church properties and offices. While Prague picked the year 1627, the Protestants in the negotiations demanded the year 1618 and eventually compromised on January 1, 1624. One exception was made in favor of a Protestant dynasty. Whereas Sweden, Brandenburg, Mecklenburg and Hesse-Cassel were to gain ecclesiastical territories, the Brunswick dukes were originally bypassed. But the final peace stipulated that in the bishopric of Osnabrück a Catholic bishop was to alternate with a Protestant administrator, who was to be a Guelf prince. A concession to the Catholics was contained in the agreement that in Augsburg and a few small Swabian imperial cities the distribution of church goods was to be in accordance with the "normal year," but the composition of the councils and all city offices was to be evenly divided between members of the two faiths. The Treaty of Passau and the Peace of Augsburg remained valid, but were modified in important respects. The "ecclesiastical reservation" was extended to the Protestant bishoprics, which meant that in case of a religious conversion a Protestant administrator would have to resign, as a Catholic bishop in the opposite case. Seats in the chapters of all the ecclesiastical foundations were to be distributed strictly according to the religious state of 1624. The long conflict over the representation of the Protestant administrators on the diet of the Empire was settled in their favor.

✍ Decisions Concerning Religion

THE RIGHT OF THE TERRITORIAL PRINCES to determine the religion of their countries, the *jus reformandi exercitium religionis*, was reaffirmed, but in a manner that clarified the meaning of the law. The "right of reformation" was not construed as authority permitting the ruler to impose a religious faith on his subjects but as authority to regulate the manifestations of religion in the life of the community. The law distinguished between the public and private practice of religion. The public practice of religion was defined as the right to build and maintain churches and provide for public worship in them, to acquire property, and possibly to govern and administer churches and schools. Private practice consisted of worship at home, or, in its lesser form, the "domestic devotion" of family prayers and Bible reading, possibly with permission to employ a private tutor for the children and to attend worship and schools abroad. In addition to these forms of religious practice, provision was made for "freedom of conscience," which meant the right to live according to one's faith and not to be compelled to participate in the devotions of another church.

The Peace of Westphalia gave everyone the inalienable right to enjoy such freedom in the practice of religion as he had possessed in 1624, whether warranted by agreement between prince and estates, by princely privilege, or by mere custom. Henceforth not even the change of religion by a territorial ruler was to interfere with this right of his subjects. The Protestants urged in addition abolition of the right of the rulers to expel members of a dissident church who had not had the right to exercise their religion in 1624, but the Catholic estates rejected this idea. The peace recommended toleration in this respect; it prescribed that dissidents of this type could be expelled only within a period of five years, and granted them the right of voluntary emigration. Expellees or emigrants were not to be deprived of their properties; they were to be allowed to appoint managers of their estates, and even to return for short visits to look after their private interests. If the territorial ruler decided on toleration of dissidents, he had to grant them at least the right of "domestic devotion." Dissidents were to enjoy all civil rights, for example, membership in guilds or ownership of land, but not political rights, such as eligibility for councils or state offices. The same legal rules were to apply to persons who would change their religion in the future, except that the ruler could expel them within three years.

The emperor firmly opposed any limitation of his own right of reformation in his hereditary territories. He agreed to tolerate Protestants in some of the Silesian principalities and towns, but they were granted little more than the right of "domestic devotion." The same privileges were given to Protestant members of the noble estates of Lower Austria, but except for these small acts of grace the emperor resolved to maintain, or even complete, the religious uniformity of his own lands. There can be no doubt that religious integrity helped to unify the variegated territorial possessions under Habsburg government. At the same time it placed them in contrast to the rest of Germany. In the "Empire," in contradistinction to "Austria," most of the individual territories became religiously monolithic after 1648, but unity was achieved in the Empire with less suffering than in the Habsburg lands. In western and southern Germany, owing to the small size of the states, Catholics and Protestants were never completely separated. For the future, it was even more important that the settlement of the religious issues in 1648 opened a way to a policy of full toleration to those rulers who wanted it. None adopted such a policy immediately, though Frederick William of Brandenburg and Karl Ludwig of the Palatinate moved in this direction. Nor should it be forgotten that the Peace of Westphalia recognized just Catholics and Protestants. The latter were defined as adherents of the Augsburg Confession, and since no distinction was made between the various editions of the Confession, the German Calvinists were included. The Saxons would have preferred to name Calvinism a third religion, and they were satisfied to the extent that no prince turning from the Lutheran to the Calvinist faith could compel his subjects to follow him. The laws left other forms of Protestantism entirely out of consideration and, as before, without any legal protection. Not much, however, had survived of these "sects," as they have been called somewhat contemptuously in Germany ever since that time. Consequently, German overseas emigration remained very small until the nineteenth century.

The decisions concerning religion were made secure by the agreement that the diet of the Empire was not to pass on religious matters by majority vote. Instead, the Catholic and Protestant groups, the *corpus Catholicorum* and *corpus Evangelicorum*, were to hold separate deliberations (*itio in partes*), and compose their differences by peaceful negotiations. The Imperial Cameral Tribunal was to have an equal number of Protestant and Catholic judges, and Protestant judges were to be brought also into the Imperial Aulic Council (*Reichshofrat*). Thus the Protestation of Speyer of 1529 was finally accepted. In addition to its old territories, German Protestantism, on the whole, kept the ecclesiastical possessions that it had officially won between 1552 and 1560, and suffered serious losses in the Palatinate and Habsburg lands. For two centuries the regulation of religious questions achieved at the Congress of Westphalia determined the ecclesiastical map of Germany. Even the creation of religiously mixed states in the early nineteenth century and the industrialization and urbanization of the last hundred years did not change the general picture to any great extent. Only the great migration after 1945 brought shifts in the distribution of population which have eradicated many of the religious boundary lines of Westphalia.

The religious issues, however, were always involved with constitutional conflicts. The territorial rulers of Germany were the chief winners of the peace negotiations of Osnabrück and Münster. Their power over their own subjects, their *jus territoriale*, or *droit de souveraineté*, as the French draft called it, was recognized without reservations. At the same time, they formally received the right to conclude alliances with foreign states, though such alliances were not to be directed against emperor and Empire. The emperor was forbidden to issue laws, declare war, conclude treaties, levy taxes, or direct military matters without the knowledge and consent of the estates of the Empire. The old controversy as to whether the curia of the imperial cities had a decisive vote in the diet was now settled in their favor, as the Peace gave them the same "right of reformation" as the princes. The cities had become so powerless, however, that they were incapable of playing an important role in the political affairs of the Empire after 1648. The princes made an attempt to increase their weight on the diet, but although the electors had to pay more attention to them than before, the electors maintained their pre-eminence.

✍ Historic Results of the Age

WITH THE PEACE OF WESTPHALIA all attempts to reconstruct a strong central government of the Empire that had broken down in the thirteenth century came to an end. Often the religious division has been held responsible for this outcome, but the problems are actually far more complex than such an explanation would imply. Even if Protestantism had never come into being, Charles V would not have found support for a German monarchy, nor could he have subdued the German princes. The part played by the Catholic princes in depriving Charles V of his victory over the Schmalkaldic princes in the years after 1547 and the dramatic break between Maximilian of Bavaria and Emperor Ferdinand II at the height of their victories over heresy and local autonomy in 1629 are ample proof that a common faith could not have submerged the basic antagonism of German politics.

On the other hand, assuming for a moment that all of Germany had become Protestant by 1580, the Empire would then have become a very loose federation of princes with a merely titular emperor as its head. Maybe this federation might have assumed greater coherence if a defense of its religious faith against strong foreign threats had become necessary. But this is mere speculation, and the actual conduct of the Protestant princes in the gravest political crises of German Protestantism does not lend any substance to such conjectures. It could as well be argued that if Catholicism had vanished from Germany, the Protestant princes might have gone to war among themselves over the booty or the ecclesiastical territories, or fallen apart into various camps of differing Protestant faiths.

The adoption of Lutheranism by the German princes was undoubtedly helped by their feeling that it would strengthen their local and territorial interests. This is not to deny the honest religious motives of a good many of them nor the unholy appetite for possessions of the Church in others. But none of them had national aspirations. It is true that the Lutheran movement started as a popular movement and for a while assumed strong national trends. Yet the territorial authorities remained unmoved and used the social revolutionary outbreaks of the knights' revolt and the peasants' revolution to suppress such unpalatable tendencies. The religious policy of the majority of the German princes choosing Protestantism as the protective shield of traditional local life found its parallels in the nobility of the Austrian territories and in the Huguenot noblemen of France. In England and Scandinavia Protestantism from the beginning was connected with the strong national tendencies that pressed to the surface in that age. No doubt the geographical position of these countries, which had allowed them to weaken the control of Rome long before, was an important element in their particular ecclesiastical history. In the Netherlands Protestantism started as a movement of the estates, but the rise of the Dutch burghers to commercial eminence in Europe made Protestantism here an agent in the birth of a nation. The Dutch revolt contributed to the survival of German Protestantism by keeping a major part of Spain's power occupied. But without the intervention of Sweden which gave the Protestant cause in Germany at a historic juncture an effective European leadership, such as had never been provided by the German princes, German Protestantism would have been doomed.

Yet German Protestantism owed its survival even more to the decline of universalism in the Catholic world. The papacy failed to give Charles V or Ferdinand II unreserved support. On the contrary, both in 1547 and 1629 the policy of the Vatican helped to ruin the triumphs of the emperors. The motives of papal policy were manifold. Leaving aside the considerations stemming from the desire to make the Church states secure, two aims were particularly pressing. The first was the determination not to allow the emperors an overwhelming power that would have made them also the actual rulers of the Catholic Church; the second was the wish to keep the Church above all nations and not to alienate some of them by the exclusive support of the Habsburgs. But such an attitude did not secure the leadership of the Church in European politics any longer. Not even in the face of the rising Protestantism could the solidarity of the Catholic nations be restored. The French monarchy adhered to religious orthodoxy and uniformity but conducted a foreign policy in accordance with national political interests. Richelieu, who ended the Huguenot wars, allied himself with the German Protestant princes and Sweden to defeat the Roman Catholic cause in Germany. The Church of Rome ceased to have a determining influence on international politics. When Pope Innocent X solemnly protested against the Peace of Westphalia, the lack of any response laid bare the impotence of the Church to regulate relations between states.

✆ *The Modern State*

AT THE END OF THE AGE of the Reformation the states emerged as sovereign agencies in foreign affairs. At the same time their internal sovereignty had grown immensely. Nowhere had the popular forces been allowed to organize their own ecclesiastical life by themselves, and under the conditions of the age few groups would have been capable of doing so. The defense of the old Church, reformations, and counter-reformations were always directed by the political governments. The religious struggle permitted the states to extend their control over the Churches far beyond the level that it had reached before the Reformation. The direction of Church affairs by the state never went so far in the Catholic as in the Protestant world. The establishment of a firm canon of faith and discipline by the Council of Trent served as a unifying bond of the Catholic Church beyond political frontiers. Moreover, the personal life of the faithful was enriched by the religious strength dispensed from Rome through the orders, among which the Jesuits were the most prominent. But in the following century the trend was distinctly toward the growth of independent indigenous forces, and religious as well as political causes were eventually to lead to the suspension of the Jesuit order. On the Protestant side, state control usually comprised the whole external administration of the Church, although there was not even a sure protection against interference with matters of doctrine and internal discipline. The territorial Churches of Protestant Germany were, more than any Protestant Church, in the hands of political powers.

As from the beginning political problems largely determined the course of European and German events in the age of the Reformation, it was the state that emerged in the end tremendously strengthened by new powers gained. Yet it was not the pagan state that the Italian Renaissance had seemed to usher in. In spite of all the abuse of religion and of all the violence and crime committed in the name of religion during the Reformation, the political rulers of the age had to admit that the government of men was more than a ruthless technique, and that it had to embody the highest spiritual principles of law and morality. The epoch which followed the Reformation saw absolute rulers almost everywhere on the Continent, but it was not an epoch of unashamed tyranny. Whatever the personal moral capacity of these princes may have been, the existence of laws and customs derived from transcendental absolutes was never questioned in these hereditary monarchies. The secularization of the state which began in the period of enlightened despotism and was completed in the French Revolution had to meet the same standards. We can see today the damage which politics inflicted upon the religious ideas of the age of the Reformation. But by making power *and* law, instead of mere power, the essence of the state, this age regained and preserved one of the mainsprings of Western civilization.

Index

BY ANNEMARIE HOLBORN

(Dates given after the names of persons indicate
the years of the reigns of emperors, kings, princes,
and ecclesiastical dignitaries, and the years of birth
and death for all others.)

A NOTE ON THE TYPE

This book was set on the Linotype in JANSON, *a recutting made direct from the type cast from matrices (now in possession of the Stempel foundry, Frankfurt am Main) made by Anton Janson some time between 1660 and 1687.*

Of Janson's origin nothing is known. He may have been a relative of Justus Janson, a printer of Danish birth who practised in Leipzig from 1614 to 1635. Some time between 1657 and 1668 Anton Janson, a punch-cutter and type-founder, bought from the Leipzig printer Johann Erich Hahn the type-foundry which had formerly been a part of the printing house of M. Friedrich Lankisch. Janson's types were first shown in a specimen sheet issued at Leipzig about 1675. Janson's successor, and perhaps his son-in-law, Johann Karl Edling, issued a specimen sheet of Janson types in 1689. His heirs sold the Janson matrices in Holland to Wolffgang Dietrich Erhardt.